STUDYING SOCIETIES AND CULTURES

Studies in Comparative Social Science

∾ A series edited by Stephen K. Sanderson ∾

Titles Available

Revolutions: A Worldwide Introduction to Political and Social Change,
Stephen K. Sanderson (2005)

Plunging to Leviathan? Exploring the World's Political Future,
Robert Bates Graber (2005)

*The Depth of Shallow Culture: The High Art of
Shoes, Movies, Novels, Monsters, and Toys,*
Albert Bergesen (2006)

*Studying Societies and Cultures: Marvin Harris's
Cultural Materialism and Its Legacy,*
edited by Lawrence A. Kuznar and Stephen K. Sanderson (2007)

STUDYING SOCIETIES AND CULTURES

MARVIN HARRIS'S CULTURAL MATERIALISM AND ITS LEGACY

edited by
Lawrence A. Kuznar
and
Stephen K. Sanderson

Paradigm Publishers
Boulder • London

Copyright © 2007 by Paradigm Publishers

Published in the United States by Paradigm Publishers, 3360 Mitchell Lane Suite E, Boulder, Colorado 80301 USA.

Paradigm Publishers is the trade name of Birkenkamp & Company, LLC, Dean Birkenkamp, President and Publisher.

Library of Congress Cataloging-in-Publication Data

Studying societies and cultures : Marvin Harris's cultural materialism and its legacy / edited by Lawrence A. Kuznar and Stephen K. Sanderson.
    p. cm. —(Studies in comparative social science)
    Includes bibliographical references.
    ISBN-13: 978-1-59451-287-2 (hc)
    ISBN-10: 1-59451-287-6
    1. Harris, Marvin, 1927– 2.   Anthropologists—United States—Biography.
3. Ethnology—Philosophy.   4. Culture.   5. Social evolution.   I. Kuznar, Lawrence A.
II. Sanderson, Stephen K.
    GN21.H37S88 2006
    301.092—dc22
    [B]

2006021982

Printed and bound in the United States of America on acid-free paper that meets the standards of the American National Standard for Permanence of Paper for Printed Library Materials.

Designed and Typeset in Adobe Garamond by Straight Creek Bookmakers.

11 10 09 08 07   2 3 4 5

Contents

Preface

THIS VOLUME BRINGS TOGETHER papers on the scientific research strategy known as *cultural materialism,* which was developed primarily by the anthropologist Marvin Harris (1927–2001) in the 1960s and 1970s. It has been both very influential and highly controversial. Harris taught at Columbia University from 1953 to 1980, when he took a position at the University of Florida, where he remained until his death. Harris's substantive work ranged from exploring the social variability of racial classifications in Brazil and Mozambique, to explaining the origin of the state, warfare, male dominance, food preferences, and cannibalism, to uncovering the causes of culture change in contemporary American society. Harris fought tirelessly against approaches that he thought were theoretically wrong, such as ethnoscience and sociobiology, or scientifically untenable, such as Lévi-Straussian structuralism and interpretivism. He was most alarmed by the rise of postmodernist approaches in anthropology during the 1980s and 1990s, and he combated their influence in numerous publications. Harris was most opposed to their denial of the special epistemological status of science and their moralistic, politicized, and therefore biased nature.

In the wake of Harris's death in October 2001, three symposia were held at national and regional meetings in which the participants provided a retrospective on Harris's influence and the likely future contributions of his ideas. One symposium, "Marvin Harris and the Controversy Surrounding Cultural Materialism: Retrospective and Future Potential," organized by Joyce Lucke and Lawrence A. Kuznar, was held at the 2002 annual meeting of the Central States Anthropological Society in East Lansing, Michigan, and followed up at the 2002 American Anthropological Association annual meeting in New Orleans. The other symposium was also held at the 2002 American Anthropological Association annual meeting and was entitled "Culture, People and Nature: The Role of Marvin Harris in Anthropological Theory and Practice." This session was organized by Maxine Margolis and Conrad Kottak. The presenters at these symposia included former colleagues and students of Harris, as well as other scholars whose work was influenced by cultural materialism. These symposia were very well attended and generated great interest, and as a result we decided that a published collection of many of the papers would be a useful addition to the social science literature. And so, this volume was born. All of the papers were presented at the first two symposia, except for those of Robert Carneiro and David Kennedy. These were invited afterward and prepared only for this volume.

Inasmuch as Harris's work had a broad impact on all subfields of anthropology, we hope this book will be of interest to all anthropologists. Many contemporary anthropologists who embrace a scientific approach generally fall into one of two camps, Harris's own cultural materialism or Darwinian anthropology. Since this book contains a number of proposals for synthesizing the two approaches, both types of scientific anthropologists should find something of value in its pages. Harris's work has in many ways been most influential among archaeologists, many of whom have adopted cultural materialist modes of analysis for explaining such critical issues as the origins of domestication, the origin of the state, and the collapse of civilizations. Some archaeologists have seen value in both cultural materialist and Darwinian perspectives, and we hope that this volume finds an audience among them.

Many individuals contributed to our understanding of cultural materialism and its potential for providing a scientific understanding of the human condition. Either for introducing him to Harris's work, or for providing sounding boards for his thinking about cultural materialism, Lawrence Kuznar acknowledges in particular William Sanders and the late James W. Hatch of Pennsylvania State University, Robert Jeske of the University of Wisconsin at Milwaukee, Lawrence Keeley of the University of Illinois-Chicago, and Bryan Byrne of the University of Chicago Business School. Stephen Sanderson thanks his former anthropology colleagues at Indiana University of Pennsylvania: Anja Olin-Fahle, Tim Murphy, Tom Conelly, Miriam Chaiken, Larry Kruckman, Victor Garcia, Sarah Neusius, and Phil Neusius for opportunities to discuss a wide range of cultural materialist and other anthropological themes over a number of years and for being receptive to Darwinian thinking about society and culture. He is also indebted to Robert Carneiro, a close epistolary colleague for nearly twenty years, for many stimulating anthropological discussions, both face to face and in correspondence. His good friends and close colleagues (also of about twenty years' duration) Chris Chase-Dunn and Tom Hall must also be acknowledged. Chris and Tom are among those relatively rare contemporary sociologists who have paid a great deal of attention to anthropology in general and Harris and other cultural materialists in particular. They are responsible not only for many stimulating anthropological discussions, but also for many great times together at various and sundry conferences. Thanks guys!

Darwinian anthropologists who provided important critiques of cultural materialism that echo throughout this book include William Irons of Northwestern University, Napoleon Chagnon, formerly of the University of California at Santa Barbara, and Lee Cronk of Rutgers University. We also acknowledge the intellectual contributions of the authors in this volume, with whom we have discussed and debated many aspects of cultural materialism over the years. Most of all, we must acknowledge Marvin Harris himself, who always gave generously of his time to discuss and debate his views with anyone who had an interest in improving anthropology and knowledge of the human condition.

Contributors

Robert L. Carneiro is curator of South American Indians at the American Museum of Natural History in New York. A student of Leslie White in the 1950s, Carneiro went on to become one of the leading social evolutionists in anthropology in the second half of the twentieth century. His fieldwork was done primarily among the Kuikuru of South America, a horticultural tribe, but he has also spent time among the Yanomamo with Napoleon Chagnon. Carneiro has written numerous articles on social evolution, the most important of which is "A theory of the origin of the state" (1970). In this article he formulated his famous circumscription theory of state origins. It is probably the best-known theory of the origin of the state ever developed. In recent years Carneiro has written two books that are summaries of his life's work, *The Muse of History and the Science of Culture* (Kluwer Academic/Plenum, 2000) and *Evolutionism in Cultural Anthropology: A Critical History* (Westview, 2003). He is also the author of a novel, *In Solemn Conclave* (AuthorHouse, 2004), whose subject is the political maneuverings of the College of Cardinals in their attempt to elect a new pope.

James W. Dow is professor of anthropology in the Department of Sociology and Anthropology, Oakland University, Rochester Hills, Michigan. A well-known expert on the religion and cultural ecology of the Otomí Indians of Mexico, he has written *The Shaman's Touch: Otomí Indian Symbolic Healing* (University of Utah Press, 1986) and edited (with Alan R. Sandstrom) *Holy Saints and Fiery Preachers: The Anthropology of Protestantism in Mexico and Central America* (Praeger, 2001). His long career and prolific publications involve the application of cultural materialism and Darwinian anthropology spanning three decades.

Melvin and Carol R. Ember are president and executive director, respectively, of the Human Relations Area Files (HRAF) in New Haven, Connecticut. The HRAF Collection of Ethnography is the most extensive database on the human condition in existence. The Embers are true institutions in the discipline of anthropology, each having influential careers spanning forty years and having published in all of the major outlets of the discipline. They have contributed to editing and compiling many HRAF-sponsored publications, including *Cultures of the World* (Macmillan Reference, 1999), *Countries and their Cultures* (Macmillan Reference, 2001), *Encyclopedia of World Cultures*

Supplement (Macmillan Reference, 2002, with Ian Skoggard), *Encyclopedia of Urban Cultures* (Grolier, 2002), *Encyclopedia of Sex and Gender* (Kluwer Academic/Plenum, 2004), *Encyclopedia of Medical Anthropology* (Kluwer Academic/Plenum 2004), and *Encyclopedia of Diasporas* (Kluwer Academic/Plenum, 2004, with Ian Skoggard). Melvin and Carol Ember are also the authors of *Cross-Cultural Research Methods* (AltaMira, 2001) and serve as editor and advisory editor, respectively, of the journal *Cross-Cultural Research*. Their textbooks, *Anthropology* (12th ed., Prentice-Hall, 2007, with Peter N. Peregrine) and *Cultural Anthropology* (12th ed., Prentice-Hall, 2007), are among the most successful textbooks in recent anthropology. They also wrote *Sex, Gender, and Kinship* (Prentice-Hall, 1997, with Burton Pasternak).

William G. Frederick has been a member of the Mathematical Sciences or Computer Science Departments at Indiana University–Purdue University Fort Wayne for 26 years. At present, he is Associate Professor of Mathematics. His current publications and research interests are in the mathematical modeling of human and animal behaviors in decision making under risk.

P. Nick Kardulias is an archaeologist who teaches in the Department of Sociology and Anthropology at Wooster College in Ohio. He is well known as an expert on Greek archaeology, from antiquity through the Byzantine period. He has published numerous articles and edited several books on archaeology, world-systems theory, and the ethnography of pastoralism, including *Beyond the State* (University Press of America, 1994), *Aegean Strategies* (Rowman & Littlefield, 1997), *World-Systems Theory and Archaeology* (Rowman & Littlefield, 1999), and *Written In Stone: The Multiple Dimensions of Lithic Analysis* (Lexington, 2003). He has also published articles on North American prehistory and ethnoarchaeology.

David P. Kennedy is an Associate Behavioral Social Scientist at the RAND Corporation in Santa Monica, California. He specializes in medical anthropology, demographic anthropology, fertility decline, adolescent romantic relationships, qualitative and quantitative methodology, and adherence to antiretroviral medication. His research has been published in the journals *Human Organization, Population and Environment,* and *Field Methods.*

Lawrence A. Kuznar is a professor of anthropology in the Department of Anthropology, and director of the Decision Sciences and Theory Institute, at Indiana University–Purdue University Fort Wayne. His primary research specialty is the ecological and economic analysis of traditional herding societies, and he has conducted research among the Aymara of Andean South America and the Navajo of the North American Southwest. His theoretical interests include risk-sensitive decision making, collective violence, and coevolutionary relationships. His publications on these themes include *Awatimarka: The Ethnoarchaeology of an Andean Herding Community* (Harcourt Brace, 1995), *Ethnoarchaeology in Andean South America* (International Monographs in Prehistory, 2001), and articles in the *Journal of Anthropological Research, Current Anthropology,* and the *American Anthropologist.* Kuznar also has an interest in the philosophy of science and was a strong advocate for a scientific anthropology in his *Reclaiming a Scientific Anthropology* (AltaMira, 1997).

James Lett is an anthropologist who teaches at Indian River Community College in Ft. Pierce, Florida. He is a well-known proponent of scientific methods in anthropology, and has published important articles in the *Journal of Anthropological Research* and other journals. He is also the author of a widely read book, *Science, Reason, and Anthropology* (AltaMira Press, 1997).

James G. Peoples is an anthropologist at Ohio Wesleyan University. Known for his ethnographic research in the South Pacific, he has published numerous articles that apply cultural materialism to understanding both contemporary economies on Pacific atolls and Polynesian cultural evolution. He is the author of *Island In Trust: Culture Change and Dependence in a Micronesian Economy* (Westview, 1985), and the coauthor (with Garrick Bailey) of the popular anthropology text, *Humanity: An Introduction to Cultural Anthropology* (6th ed., Wadsworth, 2002).

Stephen K. Sanderson taught in the Department of Sociology at Indiana University of Pennsylvania for thirty years. A comparative-historical sociologist who has spearheaded the application of materialist and Darwinian approaches in the field of sociology, Sanderson is now an adjunct professor of anthropology at the University of Colorado at Boulder, Colorado. He has published some two dozen articles in scholarly journals and edited collections, and is the author of nine books in fifteen editions. These include *Macrosociology: An Introduction to Human Societies* (4th ed., Addison-Wesley Longman, 1999), *Social Evolutionism: A Critical History* (Blackwell, 1990), *Social Transformations: A General Theory Of Historical Development* (Blackwell, 1995; updated ed. Rowman & Littlefield, 1999), and *The Evolution Of Human Sociality: A Darwinian Conflict Perspective* (Rowman & Littlefield, 2001). His most recent books are (with Arthur S. Alderson) *World Societies: The Evolution of Human Social Life* (Allyn & Bacon, 2005), *Revolutions: A Worldwide Introduction to Political and Social Change* (Paradigm, 2005), and *Evolutionism and Its Critics: Deconstructing and Reconstructing an Evolutionary Interpretation of Human Society* (Paradigm, 2007).

Alan R. Sandstrom is professor of anthropology in the Department of Anthropology at Indiana University–Purdue University Fort Wayne. A recognized authority on the Nahua Indians of Mexico, he has published numerous articles, book chapters, and two major books on these people, including (with Pamela Effrein Sandstrom) *Traditional Papermaking and Paper Cult Figures of Mexico* (1986) and *Corn Is Our Blood: Culture and Ethnic Identity in a Contemporary Aztec Indian Village* (1991), both by the University of Oklahoma Press. He has recently completed three edited volumes: *Native Peoples of the Gulf Coast of Mexico* (University of Arizona Press, 2005, with E. Hugo García Valencia); *Mesoamerican Healers* (University of Texas Press, 2001, with Brad R. Huber); and *Holy Saints and Fiery Preachers: The Anthropology of Protestantism in Mexico and Central America* (Praeger, 2001, with James W. Dow).

Pamela Effrein Sandstrom is head of reference and information services at Walter E. Helmke Library, Indiana University–Purdue University Fort Wayne. She holds an M.L.S. degree (1981) and a Ph.D. (1998) in Library and Information Science from Indiana University Bloomington, and has published in *Library Quarterly, Scientometrics,* and *Bulletin of the American Society for Information Science and Technology.* She has pioneered the application of models from optimal foraging theory to the analysis of scholarly information seeking in the specialty of human behavioral ecology, and is extending the approach to improve opportunities for successful information foraging in the academic library environment. With Alan R. Sandstrom, she has written articles defending scientific anthropology and the value of the emic/etic distinction for library and information science research.

Robert L. Sedlmeyer received his B.S. (1976) and M.S. (1977) degrees from Purdue University. He has been a member of the Indiana University–Purdue University Fort Wayne Department of Computer Science since 1977. His research interests include agent-based modeling, genetic algorithms, and automated tools for software testing and debugging. He has consulted for Raytheon, ITT, Lincoln National, PhD Corporation, and Logikos, and is coprincipal investigator in an entrepreneurial venture developing educational software for the health sciences.

H. Sidky is a member of the Department of Anthropology at Miami University of Ohio. He is an expert on the south central Asian ethnography of agropastoral peoples and has conducted extensive fieldwork in northern Pakistan and Nepal. He has also extended Harris's theories of witchcraft in his *Witchcraft, Lycanthropy, Drugs, and Disease: An Anthropological Study of the European Witch-Hunts* (Lang, 1997). His numerous books on the ethnography of central Asia include *Irrigation And State Formation in Hunza* (University Press of America, 1996), and *Hunza: An Ethnographic Outline* (Illustrated Book Publishers, 1995). His most recent book is *Perspectives on Culture: A Critical Introduction to Theory in Cultural Anthropology* (Prentice-Hall, 2003).

Howard D. White received his Ph.D. degree in Library Science at the University of California at Berkeley in 1974, and then joined Drexel University's College of Information Science and Technology, where he is now an emeritus professor. He is known for author-centered bibliometric techniques, some of them seen in his coauthored chapter in this book. He has also published on social science data archives, reference librarianship, expert systems for reference work, innovative online searching, American attitudes toward library censorship, and library collection analysis. In 1998 he and Katherine McCain won the American Society for Information Science and Technology's best paper award for "Visualizing a discipline: An author-co-citation analysis of information science, 1972–1995." In 2005 the International Society for Scientometrics and Informetrics honored him with the biennial Derek de Solla Price Memorial Medal for contributions to the quantitative study of science.

Introduction

The Potentials and Challenges of Cultural Materialism

Lawrence A. Kuznar and Stephen K. Sanderson

Marvin Harris was the maverick proponent of a materialist view of culture. Although his approach never won acceptance among the majority of anthropologists, his clear expository writing and cogent arguments could not be ignored. Consequently, anthropologists of the last half of the twentieth century had to deal with him. The papers in this volume were written by former students, colleagues, and others influenced by his work. While the authors of these chapters admired Harris professionally, these chapters are not a simple homage (and certainly not hagiography). Instead, the authors aim to extend Harris's cultural materialism beyond its foundations, in some cases even more so than he would have approved. In this introduction, we cannot provide a complete summary of Harris's wide-ranging and influential work, but we will review his most important ideas and draw attention to some of his shortcomings that surface in the papers of this volume. Harris's most important contributions include his commitment to science; his emic/etic distinction; his appreciation of the causal role of environment and demography; his tripartite division of society into infrastructure, structure, and superstructure; and the Principle of Infrastructural Determinism. Harris's rejection of Darwinian models of human behavior and culture was a shortcoming commented upon by many authors in this volume. We review these themes briefly, and then relate them to the volume's chapters.

A Scientific Anthropology

Marvin Harris squarely confronted perhaps the most enduring and troubling issue in anthropology: the ambivalence between humanistic and scientific approaches to

1

understanding the human condition. The tension between the humanities and the sciences has always existed, as evidenced by C. P. Snow's (1959) famous *Two Cultures* book. In many ways, Harris was anthropology's C. P. Snow, advocating science on the one hand, but, as Alan Sandstrom (Chapter 4, this volume) notes, doing so from a humanistic stance. This is nowhere more evident than in Harris's hope that science would save humanity from ideology, fascism, and ignorance (Harris, 1979:28), and in his thoughtful political activities (see Sanjek [1995] for a biography). Despite Harris's own humanistic leanings, he was, however, adamant that at the end of the day scientific objectivity trumps ideological stances and that we should accept scientific findings as the best, even if provisional, understanding of the human world we have (Harris, 1979:27, 1995a, 1995b, 1999a, 1999b:64).

For Harris, science involved a commitment to objective description, methodological transparency, logical coherence, and a willingness to falsify one's theories. Scientific findings are always provisional and probabilistic, but to be scientific they must also be falsifiable so that the theoretical probabilities could be narrowed and the facts made less provisional. Harris sums up his view of science concisely: "The aim of scientific research strategies in general is to account for observable entities and events and their relationships by means of powerful, interrelated parsimonious theories subject to correction and improvement through empirical testing" (Harris, 1979:26). Harris's view of science was clear and straightforward, and served as a guide to many like-minded scientific anthropologists and sociologists (Kuznar, 1997; Lett, 1997; Magnarella, 1993; Sanderson, 2001a; Sidky, 2003, 2004). The authors in this volume share Harris's view of and commitment to science.

Emics and Etics

One of Harris's enduring contributions is his distinction between emic and etic approaches to anthropological knowledge (Lett, 1997; Murphy and Margolis, 1995). Emic approaches "have as their hallmark the elevation of the native informant to the status of ultimate judge of the adequacy of the observer's descriptions and analyses" (Harris, 1979:32). In contrast, etic approaches "have as their hallmark the elevation of observers to the status of ultimate judges of the categories and concepts used in descriptions and analyses. The test of the adequacy of etic accounts is simply their ability to generate scientifically productive theories about the causes of sociocultural differences and similarities" (1979:32). Harris explicitly argued that both emic and etic approaches should be used in anthropology, but in practice he usually privileged etics. In doing so, he recognized that this would often run counter to what insiders thought about their own cultures; for example, this has proven an affront to politically correct trends that privilege "testimonials" and "indigenous perspectives" (Harris, 1999b:48). However, the case of Nobel laureate Rigoberta Menchú Tum, who fabricated Guatemalan military abuses against her family—as though that would have been necessary—demonstrates that even the non-Western "Other" is capable of misperceiving or even lying about reality. One should not construe Harris's position as necessarily pro-Western, despite his assertion that science is a gift of the West to the world (Harris, 1979:27). Harris never shied away from criticizing Western institutions when he thought that necessary (e. g., Harris, 1981). What Harris privileged was objective analysis, despite the difficulty of achieving it (Harris, 1979:75). He recognized that some perspectives were clearly more objective than others, and that the alternative to scientific objectivity was dogmatism, ideology, fanaticism, and a will to annihilate those who disagree (Harris, 1979:28, 1994, 1995b).

Despite controversy surrounding the emic/etic distinction, it has found wide applicability, even among anthropologists who are not cultural materialists. For example, anthropologists concerned with drug abuse epidemics have used the emic/etic distinction to expose how users' views and discussions about drug use influence information flow throughout the community and drug use behavior (Agar, 2005). Darwinian anthropologists likewise have noted how emically stated goals are often subverted by etic reproductively adaptive behaviors (Cronk, 1991b).

Environmental Constraints and Demography

Julian Steward (1955) explicitly added environmental constraints and opportunities to the analysis of culture. Although Steward acknowledged the complex interplay of environment, technology, and demography, Harris emphasized the specifically causal role of demography and population pressure (Harris, 1979:52). Harris's more notable and controversial analyses focused on the recursive influence of sex ratios on tribal warfare and tribal warfare on sex ratios (Divale and Harris, 1976; Harris, 1974a:75), and the role population pressure played in reducing sources of animal protein (Gross, 1975; Harner, 1977; Harris, 1974a:103, 1977: 74; see also Ross, 1978). While demography is indeed fundamental for understanding societies, Harris tended to employ it in a functionalist manner with well-known flaws. He often stressed that culture was somehow designed by people to relieve demographic stresses (Harris, 1974a:65, 1977:51, 1979:51), without specifying the mechanisms by which people decided to limit population, their actual reasons for doing so, or who was empowered in a society to limit population and whether those powerful individuals actually did attempt to limit population (Cowgill, 1975). His emphasis on population regulation was "group selectionist" and, as such, has been challenged by Darwinian social scientists who see people making demographic decisions at the individual or family level rather than the level of entire communities.

Infrastructure, Structure, and Superstructure

Harris was significantly influenced by Marxian historical materialism, and his classic *Rise of Anthropological Theory* (1968b) devoted an entire chapter to "Dialectical Materialism." He restructured the Marxian dichotomous base-superstructure distinction into a tripartite division between infrastructure, structure, and superstructure. The role of Steward is apparent here, and in a sense cultural materialism was a kind of synthesis of historical materialism and Steward's cultural ecology. Harris broadened the Marxian notion of infrastructure so that it included ecological and demographic forces as well as technoeconomic ones. At bottom, a society's infrastructure is its modes of production and reproduction. A mode of production consists of the technology and social practices that people use, within the limits and possibilities afforded by a particular ecological setting, for basic subsistence production, especially the production of food and other vital forms of energy. A mode of reproduction consists of the technology and social practices related to maintaining, limiting, or expanding populations. The structure consists of domestic economy—the organization of production and reproduction within domestic settings—and political economy—the organization of production and reproduction within such forms of political organization as bands, villages, chiefdoms, and states. The superstructure is comprised of art, music, dance, literature, rituals, and sports and games.

Harris then complicated all this by importing into it the emic-etic distinction, as well as the distinction between the mental and the behavioral realms. This produced a final scheme essentially as shown in Table I.1 (Harris, 1979:52–54). Despite Harris's (1968b:660–661) criticism of Julian Steward's cultural ecology, his scheme clearly resembled Steward's with its division of society into environmental influences, exploitative technologies, behavioral patterns, social organizations, and ideologies (Steward 1955:40–42; Wilson, 1999:11–16).

Harris's scheme leaves a lot to be desired, especially in terms of its incorporation of the emic-etic distinction into the infrastructure-structure-superstructure division (see Sanderson, Chapter 10, this volume). However, despite its weaknesses, it does provide a useful framework for comparing societies, and is perhaps even a tacit admission of how anthropologists actually look at cultures (see Wilson [1999] for an application).

The Principle of Infrastructural Determinism

Harris's tripartite scheme also allows for a conception of the causal relationship among the components of a society. For Harris, infrastructure primarily determines structure, which in turn primarily determines superstructure. Or, more precisely, "The etic behavioral modes of production and reproduction probabilistically determine the etic behavioral domestic and political economy, which in turn probabilistically determine the behavioral and mental emic superstructures" (1979:55–56). This is the famous Principle of Infrastructural Determinism, which is generally regarded as Harris's most fundamental, and certainly most controversial, contribution to anthropological theory (Ferguson, 1995; Lett, 1997:109; Magnarella, 1993:5; Murphy and Margolis, 1995). It is important to stress the probabilistic nature of Harris's conception of infrastructural causality. Infrastructural conditions are determinant "most of the time" or "in the long run," not in all instances. This allows for feedback from superstructural and structural phenomena to infrastructural phenomena—for nonlinear, recursive effects that are an important part of the subtleties and complexities of sociocultural systems. Nevertheless, the probabilistic nature of Harris's causal model was often lost on his critics, many of whom continued to see him as a "vulgar materialist" and rigid determinist (e. g., Friedman, 1974).

Table I.1 Harris's Tripartite Scheme

Etic and Behavioral Components	Mental and Emic Components

Infrastructure

Mode of Production	
Technology of subsistence	Ethnobotany
Technoenvironmental relationships	Ethnozoology
Ecosystems	Subsistence lore
Work patterns	Magic
	Religion
	Taboos
Mode of Reproduction	
Demography	
Mating patterns	
Fertility, natality, mortality	
Nurturance of infants	
Medical control of demographic patterns	
Contraception, abortion, infanticide	

Structure

Domestic Economy	
Family structure	Kinship
Domestic division of labor	Political ideology
Domestic socialization, enculturation,	Ethnic and national
education	ideologies
Age and sex roles	Magic
Domestic discipline, hierarchies, sanctions	Religion
	Taboos
Political Economy	
Political organization, factions, clubs, associations, corporations	
Division of labor, taxation, tribute	
Political socialization, enculturation, education	
Class, caste, urban, rural hierarchies	
Discipline, police/military control	
War	

Superstructure

Art	Symbols
Music	Myths
Dance	Aesthetic standards and
Literature	philosophies
Advertising	Epistemologies
Rituals	Ideologies
Sports, games, hobbies	Magic
Science	Religion
	Taboos

Source: Harris (1979), pp. 52–54.

For Harris, one of the great advantages of the Principle of Infrastructural Determinism was that it created a logical set of research priorities. In explaining any given social or cultural practice, the anthropologist starts with the assumption that infrastructural conditions are determinant and proceeds to formulate and test hypotheses thusly. If infrastructural determinants cannot be identified after an extensive search, then the researcher may reasonably entertain structural conditions as causal forces. If this search also comes up empty, then—and only then—researchers may entertain the possibility of superstructural causation. Harris also attempted to answer the question why infrastructure should take priority over structure and superstructure. Infrastructure is primary, he contended, because it consists of those things that are most vital to human survival and well-being and that they themselves place priority on. Infrastructural conditions are also the parts of sociocultural systems that are subject to the most lawlike constraints. Harris puts it as follows (1979:58):

> Unlike ideas, patterns of production and reproduction cannot be made to appear and disappear by a mere act of will. Since they are grounded in nature they can only be changed by altering the balance between culture and nature, and this can only be done by the expenditure of energy. Thought changes nothing outside of the head unless it is accompanied by the movements of the body or its parts. It seems reasonable, therefore, to search for the beginnings of the causal chains affecting sociocultural evolution in the complex of energy-expending body activities that affect the balance between the size of each human population, the amount of energy devoted to production, and the supply of life-sustaining resources. Cultural materialists contend that this balance is so vital to the survival and well-being of the individuals and groups who are its beneficiaries that all other culturally patterned thoughts and activities in which these individuals and groups engage are probably directly or indirectly determined by its specific character.

H. Sidky (2004) has elegantly summarized Harris's Principle of Infrastructural Determinism in graphic form. Since we cannot improve on it, we present it as Figure I.I. Sidky has captured the model almost perfectly, showing not only how structure and superstructure can feed back to infrastructure, but also that Harris's model conceptualized relationships *within,* as well as between, his three major sociocultural components.

Individual versus Group Selection

Harris was frequently read and criticized as a type of functionalist. Certainly some of his early work, such as his analysis of the Northwest Coast potlatch, or his endorsement of Roy Rappaport's (1967) ultrafunctionalist analysis of Maring warfare, was strongly functionalist, and, we think, very dubious as a result. A number of the arguments in *Cows, Pigs, Wars, and Witches* (1974a) had a strong and rather uncritical functionalist cast. However, by the time of *Cannibals and Kings* (1977), just three years later, Harris had undergone a dramatic, if largely unacknowledged, shift in this aspect of his thinking. He had largely replaced functionalist with rational choice and methodologically individualist imagery. He had begun to explain cultural patterns largely in terms of their adaptive value for individuals rather than their adaptive value for societies. Harris said that (1979:60–61)

the selection processes responsible for the divergent and convergent evolutionary trajectories of sociocultural systems operate mainly on the individual level; individuals

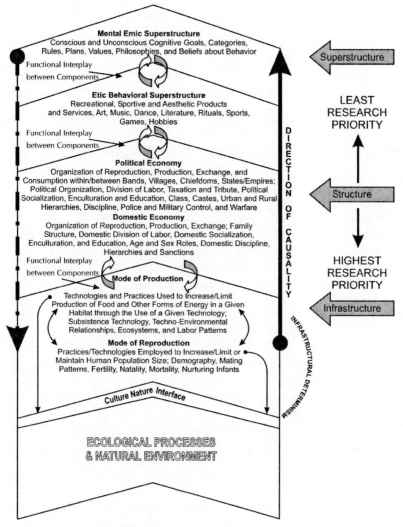

Figure I.1 The Principle of Infrastructural Determinism

Source: Sidky (2004), p. 362, Figure 14.5

follow one rather than another course of action, and as a result the aggregate pattern changes. But I don't mean to dismiss the possibility that many sociocultural traits are selected for by the differential survival of whole sociocultural systems—that is, by group selection. Because intense intergroup competition was probably present among early human populations, provision must be made for the extinction of systems that were bio-psychologically satisfying to the individuals concerned, but vulnerable to more predatory neighbors....

However, such group selection is merely a catastrophic consequence of selection operating on or through individuals. Cultural evolution, like biological evolution, has (up to now at least) taken place through opportunistic changes that increase benefits and lower costs to individuals.... If the sociocultural system survives as a result of patterns of thought and behavior selected for on the individual level, it is not because the group as such was successful but because some or all of the individuals in it were successful. Thus a group that is annihilated in warfare can be said to be selected for as a group, but if we want to understand why it was annihilated, we must examine the cost-benefit options exercised by its individual members relative to the options exercised by its victorious neighbors.... Altruism, to be successful, must confer adaptive advantages on those who give as well as on those who take.

We think that Harris's shift to an individualist form of cultural selectionism was exactly the right move. Unfortunately, the move was incomplete, for Harris still defended the notion of group selection and assumed that it was operating in some instances. Even though Harris recognized that such things as the defeat in war of one tribe by another is not a genuine form of group selection, he was still prone to accept genuine group selectionist arguments. Notice that in the quotation above Harris says that selection processes operate "mainly" on the individual level. As far as we know, Harris never disavowed his earlier functionalist explanations, and in fact he continued to be quite explicit in his view that people act so as to regulate population at the group level (Harris and Ross, 1987).

Darwinian Evolution and Human Behavior

Darwinian anthropology is an approach in which human social behavior and culture are ultimately explained as the result of human biological evolution. This approach contains the same theoretical foundations as sociobiology (Chagnon and Irons, 1979; Wilson, 1975, 1978), human behavioral ecology (Cronk, 1991a), and evolutionary psychology (Cosmides and Tooby, 1989; Barkow, Cosmides, and Tooby, 1992; Buss, 1999). Harris rejected Darwinian approaches and felt that they were antithetical to the cultural materialist paradigm. (He did accept optimal foraging theory [Harris, 1985:165–169, 1987b:74–77], which is a behavioral ecological approach with strong Darwinian roots, but he continued to reject sociobiology and evolutionary psychology throughout his career.) Harris maintained that Darwinian approaches failed to explain cultural diversity, failed to identify genetic bases for cultural traits, used a misplaced analogy with biological evolution, were methodologically inadequate, and failed to explain maladaptive behavior (Harris, 1979:Chapter 5, 1999b:Chapter 8).

Harris was adamant that the anthropologist's job is to explain both the similarities and differences in human cultural expression throughout the world and throughout history and prehistory. The biologically given commonalities of humans can only explain cultural similarities, he argued, thus missing the rich cultural diversity that is such an important part of the subject matter of anthropology (Harris, 1979:121, 126, 136). Culture is not the direct product of our genes, but an emergent property arising from the interactions of individuals (Harris, 1979:122). And this is why, he argued, sociobiologists have been unable to find genes that directly determine specific cultural traits (Harris, 1979:125). Harris also argued that culture evolves too rapidly for biology to influence it, and that the differences between genetic and cultural transmission meant that cultural evolution had to be fundamentally different (i.e., Lamarckian) from Darwinian evolution (Harris, 1979:134, 1999b:108). Another of Harris's objections was that in practice Darwinian anthropologists typically use measures of material economic success as proxies for reproductive success; therefore Darwinian anthropologists are practicing cultural materialism anyway (Harris, 1979:127, 1999b:104).

It is not difficult to counter many of Harris's accusations against Darwinian approaches. Harris's argument that genes for specific cultural behaviors do not exist was specious and a straw man if there ever was one. Darwinian anthropologists strongly emphasize the facultative and epigenetic nature of social behavior and cultural patterns. Indeed, it is recognized that even many clearly physical traits are expressed through complex interactions with environmental stimuli. If this is the case for physical traits, then it is so *a fortiori* with respect to cultural traits: Genetic predispositions are expressed in a wide range of ways under varying environmental influences (Cronk, 1999). Consequently, Darwinian anthropologists long ago gave up the search for strict one-to-one correspondences between particular genes and cultural forms, rendering Harris's objection moot. While Harris's observation that many Darwinian anthropologists have used economic rather than reproductive success as an index of adaptation is true, recent work has more explicitly linked behavior to reproductive success (Betzig, 1986; Chagnon, 1988; Gangestad and Simpson, 2000; Hawkes and Bliege Bird, 2002; Kaplan and Hill, 1985; Sellen, Borgerhoff Mulder, and Sieff, 2000).

Harris's point about the Lamarckian nature of cultural transmission is more difficult to counter, and much work is currently underway by Darwinian anthropologists to elucidate the implications of models of cultural transmission (Boyd and Richerson, 1985, 2005; Flinn, 1997; Henrich, 2002). Finally, the notion that because culture is emergent it is beyond explanation in Darwinian terms is based on an unnecessary fear of reductionism. Chemical compounds are the emergent properties of physical laws, but that does not mean that an understanding of physics is irrelevant to chemistry.

To some extent Harris undercut his own anti-Darwinian arguments by accepting the existence of human biopsychological constants, or, in others' terms, a human biogram. Harris's biogram includes the need for food, economizing behavior, the desire for mates, and social acceptance (Harris, 1979:62–64). It is actually not all that different from the biogram proposed by his sociobiological protagonist E. O. Wilson (1978:20–46). However, Wilson (1978:53ff., 1998:150) argued that complex behaviors could be explained as epigenetic traits—genetically based but responsive to environmental influence—and he included more in the biogram than Harris would ever have agreed to.

During the past 20 years, evolutionary anthropology has made many inroads in explaining a variety of complex behaviors, from favoring different offspring in direct proportion to their likely reproductive success (Borgerhoff Mulder, 1992; Cronk, 1999), to the relationship between social status and risk-taking behavior (Kuznar, 2002a; Winterhalder, Lu, and Tucker, 1999), to high sperm retention orgasms among university coeds (Simpson, Gangestad, Christensen, and Leck, 1999). Stephen Sanderson (2001a) has reviewed at length many of the research findings produced by Darwinian social scientists in the areas of reproductive behavior, human sexuality, sex and gender, family and kinship, economic behavior, social hierarchies, and politics and war. He is able to cite literally hundreds of studies demonstrating beyond any serious doubt that human behavior in these crucial areas has clear biological underpinnings.

While Harris stridently argued against what he feared was the biological reductionism of Darwinian approaches, some scholars in recent years have argued that the two paradigms can be synthesized. Azar Gat (2000a, 2000b) argues that Darwinian and cultural materialist approaches can be combined. For example, he points out that the proximate causes of warfare among foragers nearly always include competition over economic resources and that biologists have no problem applying evolutionary theory when analyzing the defense of territorial resources by nonhuman animals. Therefore, why should it be any different with the human animal, *Homo sapiens*? Sanderson (2001a) has proposed a much more extensive synthesis of cultural materialism and Darwinian social science that he calls Darwinian conflict theory. He describes Darwinian conflict theory as a "marriage of Darwinian biological materialism to the broader economic and ecological materialism and conflict theory that owes its ancestry to Marx and that has been continued by such leading anthropologists as Marvin Harris." "Sociobiology," he claims "is the ultimate form of materialist and conflict social theory, and other materialist and conflict theories must be grounded in it" (Sanderson, 2001a:143). Sanderson points out that Harris's admission of the existence of a basic human biogram means that he already had one foot placed squarely in the Darwinian camp. It is not a question of whether or not there is a human nature: Harris clearly thought that there is. It is a question of exactly what human nature consists of—of the specific content and dimensions of the biogram.

Harris's rejection of Darwinian modes of explanation was highly unfortunate and has stood as an unnecessary roadblock to the advancement of a more general, synthetic theory of society and culture. But even though Harris refused to take the Darwinian step, we can take it for him. Several papers in this collection suggest how cultural materialism can be extended and reformulated in a Darwinian way.

Harris on Theory and Praxis

Harris's major aim was to develop a coherent research strategy that would allow anthropologists and other comparative social scientists to explain the broadest array of cultural similarities and differences in the most parsimonious ways. He was primarily a theoretician, but he also was very politically engaged and thought that anthropology should seek not only to understand the world, but help to make it a better place. He was a tireless opponent of oppressive and exploitative social relations wherever and whenever they were to be found. Harris was very much on the political left, but he was not a radical. He did not condemn capitalism as an unreformable economic system, nor was he an advocate of socialism. He sought, in the words of many activists of the 1960s, "to work within the system." And yet, despite his criticisms of modern society and his advocacy of various types of social change (as in *America Now,* 1981), Harris was nonetheless attacked by left-wing anthropologists, Marxists in particular. The structural Marxist Jonathan Friedman (1974), for example, wrote a severe critique of Harris's cultural materialism, which he condemned as a kind of "mechanical" or "vulgar" materialism. And in one of the few instances a book of Harris's got reviewed in a sociological journal, the author of the review, Marxist sociologist Bernard Magubane, entitled his long review essay on *Cultural Materialism* "In search of an ideological alternative to Marxism" (Magubane, 1981). Magubane praised Harris for his brilliance and for his prodigious scholarship, but in the end Harris is found wanting on ideological grounds. Indeed, Magubane attributed a political motive to Harris's very formulation of cultural materialism (1981:72):

> Whether he likes it or not, cultural materialism, it must now be obvious, is an attempt to find ways of denying the necessity of transcending the *status quo.* The issue therefore reduces to this: How can social theory provide justification to deny the legitimacy of the struggle by the oppressed and poor classes? Here lies the whole art of conservative theory as represented in this instance by cultural materialism.

Magubane then goes on to say that "cultural materialism expresses also a vast satisfaction by its advocates with existing society" (1981:72). Magubane must be reading a completely different Marvin Harris than the contributors to this volume, for it seems to us that Harris was often profoundly *dissatisfied* with existing society (how Marvin must have winced when he read Magubane's review). That this is so is easily ascertainable from a great many of Harris's writings. If anyone was trying *not* to construct a theoretical or research strategy that would serve the purpose of justifying and reinforcing the *status quo,* it was Marvin Harris.

But if we read a little further into Magubane's critique we can see more precisely where the rub is for him. Harris, of course, was strongly opposed to the dialectical element in Marxian thought, which he called "the Hegelian monkey" on Marx and Engels's back. For Magubane, as for most Marxists, this is heresy. To quote from Magubane again (1981:73):

Harris has formulated a strategy ... that completely ignores historical process. He has selected examples eclectically and arbitrarily to "refute" the straw Marx that he created. The Marxist theory is clearly dangerous for Harris, in that it provides the masses of the oppressed humanity the key to understanding and struggling against their oppression. Consequently he set out to distort the categories, concepts, and methods which are the essence of dialectical materialism. Cultural materialism as an intellectual exercise amounts to counterrevolution in thought.

There is a straw man here, but it is not Marx. Presumably by "completely ignores historical process," Magubane can only mean "completely ignores *dialectical* process." If ever a social scientist stressed historical process, it was Marvin Harris. And if ever an intellectual exercise was *not* intended as one in counterrevolution, cultural materialism is that exercise.

Poor Marvin. He just couldn't win. Not only was he under constant attack from cultural idealists, but even those fellow materialists, the Marxists, had it in for him. Even though he was on the left, his sin was that he was not far enough on the left, and thus got (absurdly) branded as some sort of conservative. And even though he was a materialist, he dared to criticize the sacred dialectic of the Marxist canon, and thus once again was put beyond the pale. What all this really boils down to is that Harris was a maverick who was never comfortable with any party line, whether theoretical, methodological, or political. And that kind of stance will earn you a lot of enemies, to your left and to your right, behind you and in front of you. Harris once said, somewhere, in his disagreement with *both* sides of a debate, "A plague on both your houses!" That was the irrepressible and inimitable Marvin. Small wonder that he took a lot of flack!

A Superman of Anthropology

In a review of *Cultural Materialism,* the anthropologist Richard L. Currier calls Harris "a superman of anthropology" and points out that Harris's book does battle with "nearly every anthropological scholar who can conceivably be imagined to have a following" (1979:7). Elaborating, he says (1979:7):

Read this book, and you will enter a world of competing and mutually hostile world views, where true believers slug it out in the journal articles and scholarly tomes, each striving to best all contenders in complex mental combat.

This is a sport as exciting as it is bloody to its own devotees as professional football is to a different set of enthusiasts. And in this arena, Harris stands tall, like a gladiator, sword and shield held high, ready to take on all contenders.

Currier adds that Harris was often ruthless in his attacks and had a "zeal to unmask false prophets." And he marvels that *Cultural Materialism* "ranges so easily through the cacophony of competing paradigmatic voices or that demystifies their sacred litanies with such uncompromising effectiveness" (1979:7). Moreover (1979:7): "Among the paradigm masters of modern social thought.... Marvin Harris must be acknowledged a superstar. He is swifter than Claude Lévi-Strauss, more powerful than B. F. Skinner.

He can leap tall theories in a single bound. And as a critic of the theoretical follies of others, he is without equal in anthropology."

Harris was also an effective proselytizer of anthropology, popularizing it and its potential through books such as *Cows, Pigs, Wars, and Witches* (1974), *America Now* (1981), and *Good to Eat* (1985). Yes, that is the Marvin Harris all of us have known, love him or hate him. We are delighted to be able to honor and remember this great thinker and intellectual charioteer through the publication of this book. It was only death that could silence the voice of this warrior. Marvin, *Requiscat in Pace.*

Overview of the Chapters

Part I of this volume contains two papers that assess, in two different yet complementary ways, Marvin Harris's scholarly legacy. Using newly developed techniques in the field of information science, in Chapter 1 Pamela Effrein Sandstrom and Howard D. White characterize the work of Harris and demonstrate its influence in anthropology and cognate fields. The promising research methodology developed by White and colleagues at Drexel University to produce empirical CAMEO's (Characterizations Automatically Made and Edited Online) is used to profile Harris's publishing career. Through a series of tables and figures, the authors are able to visualize the intellectual and social networks revealed by the authors and concepts that Harris cites, and those who, in turn, cite him. Multiple CAMEO profiles of Harris as a focal author provide an objective look at the content and influence of cultural materialism as revealed by citation practices. Appropriately enough, Sandstrom and White's analysis turns scientific objectivity back upon Harris's science.

In Chapter 2, James Lett contends that there are significant theoretical limitations to cultural materialism that ultimately hinder its effectiveness as an explanatory approach. For him, the most important limitations involve ontological and theoretical problems with its fundamental theoretical principle, Infrastructural Determinism, and the lack of conceptual integration between cultural materialism and the natural sciences (especially evolutionary biology). Nevertheless, Lett argues that Harris deserves credit for monumental contributions to anthropological theory. Cultural materialism is based upon at least six fundamental premises that will have lasting value for anthropology: (1) anthropological theory should be thoroughly and exclusively grounded in the epistemology of science; (2) anthropologists should provide rebuttals to antiscientific arguments, whether those arguments originate inside or outside the discipline; (3) anthropological theory is strengthened when an integrated, four-field approach is maintained; (4) anthropologists should communicate their theories and research findings in clear, direct, and intelligible language; (5) anthropologists should seek to communicate anthropological knowledge to the general public; and (6) anthropology can and should play a role in championing social justice. Lett argues that Harris was an exceptionally creative, eloquent, and passionate advocate of each of these laudable positions, and that is where his enduring legacy will be found.

Part II considers the epistemology of cultural materialism. In Chapter 3, H. Sidky compares cultural materialism with the particularistic, interpretive, and literary approaches that emerged in anthropology in the 1980s and 1990s. Sidky highlights the differences between cultural materialism as a paradigm geared toward building a scientific understanding of the world and those approaches that espouse such goals as "narrative accounts of the particular" or "restructuring experience." Sidky subjects the claims of the new antiscientific anthropologists to a relentless attack, knocking down each one with impeccable logic and reasoning. In Chapter 4, Alan R. Sandstrom argues that cultural materialism is a fruitful research strategy for understanding similarities and differences among the world's cultures, although there are some theoretical problems with the approach that need to be addressed. In Harris's conception, sociocultural systems exhibit a rationality in the ways they adapt to the material conditions of existence. Left unresolved is the role of the individual in the dynamic functionalism of cultural materialism. During his career, Harris seemed to have moved from a more superorganic conception of sociocultural systems to one that focused on the cost-benefit calculations of individuals. A solution to the problem was suggested by Harris in his last theoretical writings when he implied that formalist economic theory could be used to better understand the behavior of individuals. Sandstrom contends that methodological individualism and the application of a rational choice model to the understanding of people's behavior in a variety of cultural contexts resolves many problems with cultural materialism and enhances its scientific potential. His chapter also examines why Harris was and continued to be such a divisive figure in contemporary cultural anthropology, and addresses problems in Harris's conception of the role of ethnography in the science of culture.

Part III contains three papers that represent applications of cultural materialism. In Chapter 5 James G. Peoples points out that some critics of materialism claim that historically contingent forces outweigh material forces, arguing that one cannot predict the content (specific behavioral patterns, ideological details) of a sociocultural system from knowledge of material conditions alone. Peoples contends that this critique seems unassailable unless a phylogenetic model of sociocultural change is adopted. Like biological species, sociocultural forms are surely products of their unique histories, but this fact does not rob materialism of its theoretical power. Indeed, comparisons between the historically related cultures of Nuclear Micronesia strengthen materialism by showing that diversification arises from common ancestral forms in accordance with the predictions of materialist theory. Peoples's chapter also suggests a solution to a major problem with materialist theory—how materially self-interested human actors can behave in ways that appear to be contrary to their interests.

In Chapter 6 P. Nick Kardulias claims that, by its emphasis on the physical record as the basis for understanding the past, archaeology is in many ways ideal for exploring the utility of the cultural materialist paradigm. Cultural materialism provides a programmatic statement that allows one to pinpoint the crucial components underlying social life. Ideological elements such as religion and philosophy are clearly secondary in nature and derivative in function from the more concrete aspects of culture that center on technology and economics, especially subsistence. This perspective is based on Harris's premise "that human social life is a response to the practical problems of earthly existence." Humans are seen as engaging in an ongoing attempt to improve their environment or to deal with demographic pressure by means of expanding the potential of the environment through the process of intensification, that is, increased exploitation of available resources in response to ecological shifts (both natural and cultural). Those individuals who adopt strategies yielding the greatest returns can be termed successful because of the advantages they garner for themselves, their kin, and their followers. When combined with elements of cultural evolutionism, the materialist perspective offers a dynamic way to examine the past. After discussing the appropriate theoretical constructs, Kardulias applies a materialist approach to the reconstruction of events during the transition from Classical Antiquity to the Medieval era at Isthmia, Greece, the site of an ancient Panhellenic sanctuary and a major Byzantine military installation.

Chapter 7, by Melvin and Carol R. Ember, reviews cross-cultural tests of the impact of the physical environment and economy on other aspects of culture, including child training, personality, and expressive culture (e. g., religion, art, beliefs). The authors show that, though Harris's theories were usually not cited in most of these studies, a large body of empirical evidence supports his view of the importance of material conditions for explaining culture. The chapter concludes with suggestions about specific propositions from Harris that could be tested cross-culturally in the future.

Part IV contains three papers that attempt to show how cultural materialism can be grounded in Darwinian social science and thereby deepened and improved. In Chapter 8 Lawrence A. Kuznar, William G. Frederick, and Robert L. Sedlmeyer examine the transition from relatively egalitarian band and tribal societies to hierarchical stratified chiefdoms and pristine states. The emergence of cultural complexity and social stratification was an important topic that ran through much of Harris's work. The authors point out that the consequences of this transition are clear: increased population growth, wealth inequality, and political centralization. However, the conditions that led to this transition are less clear. The authors explore the possibility that Darwinian principles, namely nepotism and the differential reproduction of high-status individuals, could have led to the unanticipated emergence of stratification and inequality. They use newly developed methods in computer modeling and simulation to test hypotheses about the rise of inequality in chiefdoms, and their approach brings together cultural materialist and Darwinian theory.

James W. Dow, in Chapter 9, claims that, although Harris saw cultural materialism as a research strategy equivalent to a paradigm in the natural sciences, this paradigm was developed rather dogmatically from Marx's idea that the material conditions of human existence preceded and determined social structure and ideology. In Dow's judgment, this is not how paradigms are developed in the natural sciences. Natural scientists develop them by sifting through and empirically evaluating competing theories. Nevertheless, Dow argues that there is wisdom in the cultural materialist point of view, which he believes comes from its relationship to both cultural and natural evolutionary processes. Material things have a fundamental impact on reproductive fitness and are evaluated by human beings in cultural terms relative to their impact on fitness. Therefore the material conditions of life can have a profound impact on the evolution of culture. For this reason, cultural materialism is a good research strategy for looking at the origins and development of cultural things. However, Dow tries to turn cultural materialism into a more scientific gene-culture evolutionary model, and he applies it to cultural patterns found in two populations of Otomí-speaking people of the eastern sierra of Hidalgo in Mexico. Using these two cases, he relates material conditions (infrastructure) to religion (superstructure). In the first case he shows how an agricultural subsistence system affects religious beliefs, and in the second he shows how demographic processes affect the advance of Protestantism.

Stephen K. Sanderson, a sociologist rather than an anthropologist (and the lone sociologist in the volume), had never heard of Harris or cultural materialism until several years after completing his Ph.D. His encounter with Harris's work was, however, a career-transforming event. After reading several of Harris's major works, Sanderson shifted from a relatively eclectic position to a materialist and evolutionary perspective and proceeded, in the 1980s and 1990s, to write several books that were guided by such a perspective. In time, however, Sanderson began to see significant weaknesses in cultural materialism. In Chapter 10 he provides a critique of both Harris's abstract theoretical model and his substantive theories, indicating which ones seem to have stood the test of time and evidence as well as which ones must give way to alternative explanations. For Sanderson, Harris's major failing was his inability to see that cultural materialism and Darwinian social science—whether called sociobiology, evolutionary psychology, or by some other name—need not be enemies. Despite some fundamental differences, they can be made compatible, at least at a general and abstract level. Indeed, Sanderson contends that they can be synthesized into an even more comprehensive paradigm that retains the core principles of cultural materialism but pushes them to a deeper level. He then goes on to outline the nature of the synthesis he has recently achieved, which he calls Darwinian conflict theory, and to illustrate it with respect to the evolution of social hierarchies in human societies.

Part V looks again at Harris's legacy. Chapter 11, by Robert L. Carneiro, explores the role Harris assigned to demographic factors in the evolution of society. Carneiro notes that Harris is not always explicit as to when population *density* turns into population *pressure,* and in fact generally avoids using the term "pressure." Carneiro contends that Harris sees population pressure coming into play when competition ensues over scarce resources during the early stages of chiefdom formation, but he still places at least as much emphasis on economic factors as on demographic or military ones in bringing chiefdoms into being. Harris seems to give more emphasis to population pressure once states begin to arise. He sees state formation occurring most readily in areas of environmental circumscription, where adverse conditions lead some societies to surrender their sovereignty to others. Nevertheless, Carneiro believes that Harris does not appear to fully embrace the coercive nature of the circumscription theory. In Chapter 12, David P. Kennedy explores not the work of Harris but rather the major theoretical strategies of Stephen Sanderson (evolutionary materialism and Darwinian conflict theory) and compares them with cultural materialism. He argues that Sanderson's attempts at building comprehensive theoretical syntheses have not been sufficiently distant from cultural materialism to qualify as being distinct from it. It is his contention that Sanderson's critiques are of specific theories developed using the research strategy of cultural materialism, rather than of the research strategy itself. Kennedy argues that Sanderson's primary contributions are improving and expanding theories of social change developed using cultural materialism, expanding the range of evolutionary phenomena typically explained by cultural materialism to include modern social change, and overcoming Harris's resistance to incorporating biological variables into the range of explanatory factors of sociocultural evolution.

In Chapter 13, Sanderson responds to Kennedy's critique. He agrees with Kennedy that evolutionary materialism is largely an extension and formalization of cultural materialism, rather than something completely new, but argues that there are two critical differences between the two paradigms insufficiently appreciated by Kennedy. Cultural materialism sees social evolution as a unitary process in which the same sets of variables explain social evolution throughout its entire range, whereas evolutionary materialism argues that different "evolutionary logics" operate in different historical epochs. In addition, evolutionary materialism conceptualizes "economy" as a singular entity rather than breaking it up into subsistence economy and political economy, as Harris does. With respect to Kennedy's claim that the basic principles of Darwinian conflict theory do not contradict those of cultural materialism, Sanderson argues that this is true in some respects but untrue in others. Harris's materialist explanations are often accurate proximate explanations that can be understood at an ultimate level in terms of certain biological predispositions. Nevertheless, some of Harris's materialist explanations are simply wrong and need to be replaced by Darwinian alternatives. Sanderson argues that much of the biological component of Darwinian conflict theory is highly inconsistent with some of the claims of cultural materialism, a point he thinks Harris would have readily agreed with.

Appendix A to this volume reprints two obituaries of Marvin Harris in order to give the reader a better feel for Harris the person. The first obituary was written by Douglas Martin for the *New York Times*. It is short and breezy. The second obituary, by two of Harris's former students and close followers, Maxine L. Margolis and Conrad Phillip Kottak, appeared in the *American Anthropologist*.

Harris published many books and dozens of articles and essays, both in scholarly journals and in such popular magazines as *The Nation* and *Saturday Review*. He also wrote a judicious number of incisive book reviews. His book production was clearly prodigious (some 18 in all, most of them translated into multiple languages), but his article production was not extraordinary in terms of quantity for a scholar of his stature. Harris was obviously a "book person" more than an "article person," something of an intellectual throwback in these days in which, as the evolutionary sociologist Gerhard Lenski once noted, most scholars "play the journal article game," publishing many articles but few, or in some cases, no books (alas, this seems to have become the royal road to tenure in the top departments). But Harris upholds anthropology's (like history's) goal standard and distinguishes himself among other social scientists by an enduring commitment to the monograph-length exposition (many analysts, including Hider [1996] strongly affirm that anthropology is a book-oriented discipline).

Pamela Effrein Sandstrom, a librarian and information scientist (and a coauthor of Chapter 1), has worked diligently to assemble as complete a bibliography of Harris's writings as seems humanly possible, and her heroic effort appears as Appendix B. This should serve as an extremely useful guide to those scholars who wish to explore the full range of Harris's writings over a fifty-year period. For devotees of Harris and cultural materialism, Sandstrom's bibliography is much more than a mere treat; it is virtually an orgiastic feast!

Part I

The Legacy of Cultural Materialism: I

Chapter One

The Impact of Cultural Materialism

A Bibliometric Analysis of the
Writings of Marvin Harris

Pamela Effrein Sandstrom and Howard D. White

Assessing the impact of a scholar on a field of study is daunting, especially when that scholar is as prolific and controversial as Marvin Harris. This chapter is the first in a volume aimed at appraising the significance of the cultural materialist research strategy to which Harris dedicated his life. We will document Harris's publishing career and demonstrate his influence in anthropology and cognate fields using bibliometric techniques developed by information scientists. These techniques are nicknamed CAMEOs, short for "Characterizations Automatically Made and Edited Online" (White, 2001). They make visible the authors that Harris cited and reveal the researchers who cited him in turn. They also suggest his topical range. By modeling the professional interests of Harris and those interested in his work, we glimpse into the social and intellectual structure of contemporary social and behavioral science and trace Harris's impact within and across disciplinary boundaries. This CAMEO portrait of Harris provides a systematic and empirically based look at the content and breadth of cultural materialism. It is designed to reflect the same scientific methodological requirements that were near and dear to Harris's research program.

We are able to create CAMEO portraits because scholars tend to cite their intellectual forebears and thereby trade in what Robert Merton (1968:56) called the "coin of recognition." Citation is a universal norm of science and scholarship that transcends material or epistemological allegiances (White, 2004). It reflects the social nature of science where research paradigms change systematically and an individual scholar's career relates to others to form a recognizable lineage of knowledge (see Merton, 1976; Cronin, 1984, 2005). Thousands of individual information-seeking behaviors and decisions about what to take heed of, read, and cite are recorded in footnotes and cited reference lists. These choices are constrained by a scholar's skills, a shared literature and disciplinary history, and the social organization of the scholarly workforce. The arrangements by which scholars keep informed and avoid information overload are adaptive features of a socioecological system of "public knowledge" (Wilson, 1977) and "external memory" (White, 1992). By framing these arrangements in a cost-benefit model, scholars' searching and handling of resources in libraries and information systems can be seen to follow the same behavioral ecological principles used by human and animal foragers as they exploit their natural environments (Sandstrom, 1994, 1998, 1999, 2001). CAMEO profiles are based on cumulative, empirical traces of scholars' decision-making behavior. Thus, the CAMEO profile of Marvin Harris is not a finished portrait but instead a work in progress as today's researchers and social thinkers either neglect or make new use of the past. Like archaeological evidence, however, the patterns detectable using bibliometric techniques tend to be robust and persist over time.

To portray Harris, we gathered bibliographic data on the output of his publishing career. He was a productive scholar who wrote eighteen books (thirteen solo authored, two coauthored, and three coedited volumes) and more than 100 articles, book chapters, and substantive comments. Harris gave interviews recorded in print, audio, and video formats, wrote entries for scholarly encyclopedias, regularly contributed columns to such periodicals as *Natural History* and *Psychology Today*, and prepared more than thirty book reviews for publication in the professional literature (e.g., *American Anthropologist, American Ethnologist, Man, Human Ecology, Ethnohistory, Hispanic American Historical Review, Political Science Quarterly, Social Forces, Academy of Management Review*) and the popular press (e.g., *Saturday Review, New York Times, Washington Post*). OCLC's WorldCat attests to Harris's stature as an author. This worldwide database of more than 60 million bibliographic records includes more than 140 records for multiple editions of his popular and scholarly books translated into at least seventeen different languages. Harris (1999b:11) himself identified the following books as among his "most influential":

> *The Rise of Anthropological Theory: A History of Theories of Culture* (1968b)
> *Culture, People, Nature* (seven editions, 1971–1997)
> *Cows, Pigs, Wars, and Witches: The Riddles of Culture* (1974a)
> *Cannibals and Kings: The Origins of Cultures* (1977)
> *Cultural Materialism: The Struggle for a Science of Culture* (1979)
> *Our Kind* (1989)

Appendix B to this volume provides a chronological listing of Harris's writings. We intend the bibliography to be complete and definitive but have found that Harris's writings are scattered and sometimes difficult to identify and locate. We now realize that the definitive compilation (and certainly others' commentaries on it) can only approach completion. The bibliography represents a compromise of a sort that Harris was willing to make but never ceased trying to improve upon.

Ego-Centered Citation Analysis

Despite the complexity imposed by the sheer growth in the number of documents and increasingly elaborate externalized systems of memory, the imperative to synthesize a field's literature, and the body of writing of a single scholar within it, remains a common goal of scholarship. (See Harris [1968b:614] on the "indigestible quantities of raw data" that threaten information systems and the importance of a nomothetic approach to summarizing literatures.) Characterizing the interests and concerns of anthropology in general during the second half of the twentieth century, including Marvin Harris's cultural materialism, would traditionally entail taking a bibliographic or editorial approach to the problem. After a massive, long-term compilation and close reading of a subject literature, the dedicated reader would emerge an expert. He or she would grasp the important names, publication outlets, keywords, dates, and other features that describe the area of interest. As an alternative strategy, a bibliometric approach is now possible using online information systems and graphical software to model—literally, visualize—the social and intellectual networks within a literature (White and McCain, 1989, 1997; also White and Griffith, 1981).

Bibliometricians, information retrievalists, and database designers deal with many types of relationships among people and literatures. One common aim they have is to produce accurate snapshots of the relationships among factors (such as authors, journals, subjects, references in a paper, citations to a paper, etc.) by creating visual images and other displays that can be readily interpreted by anyone who is interested in a subject domain or an individual who figures prominently within it. Much like the kinship diagrams used by anthropologists, the focal author of such an analysis appears at the center of the display, surrounded by other markers linked to ego (White, 2000:477).

We retrieved the data for our analysis of Harris's writings primarily from publicly searchable databases produced by the Institute for Scientific Information (ISI), now a division of Thompson Scientific. We used software specially developed to create profiles that measure the nature and scope of his output. We present several types of CAMEO profiles, each based on a set of indexing terms. For example, we have profiles of citations to the work of Harris and references he made to others that co-occur with subject descriptors, journal titles, and authors' names. These profiles reveal the extent of Harris's interdisciplinarity and breadth of his problem focus (White, 1996). By ranking these co-occurrence counts from high to low, CAMEOs produce distributions that describe the bibliographic context of Harris's work as well as its impact on researchers from anthropology and related fields. Most well-placed insiders or experts on the problems covered by Harris can readily interpret the CAMEO distributions of this work, although initially they may have been unaware of its full scope. Thus the profiles can be validated using emic criteria, that is, criteria meaningful to experts in the particular field of study. Equally important, they can be validated using etic criteria, that is, criteria agreed upon by observers abiding by international canons of scientific knowledge.

The distinction between emic and etic perspectives was itself the subject of an interesting bibliometric study that anticipated the present one. According to Harris, an emic perspective is one that takes the point of view of a member of the social group under study, while an etic perspective takes the point of view of the scientifically trained observer. Harris insisted as a cornerstone of the cultural materialist research strategy that emic and etic perspectives are epistemologically distinct and that they require different validation procedures. Insiders' perspectives may or may not agree with those of scientifically trained observers. According to Harris, the divergence between emic and etic perspectives is a measure of the degree to which the members of a social group are mystified by their shared beliefs. Thomas Headland convened a session at the 1988 annual meeting of the American Anthropological Association to explore these important analytical concepts. Originated by linguist Kenneth Pike (1954), the concepts were later elaborated by Harris (1964a, 1968b, 1976a) as powerful tools for the interpretation of cultural behavior and meaning systems. The expanded papers from the conference (Headland, Pike, and Harris, 1990) included Headland's citation-based analysis that documented how the usage of emics and etics had changed over a thirty-year period. The subjects of the 278 articles and books that employed these concepts from 1954 to 1989 illustrated that their impact spanned a wide range of disciplines and publications (see Headland, 1990:19, reproduced here in Table 1.1).

Anthropology and psychology dominate the list, but emics and etics have entered the lexicon of many other fields as well. In commenting on the symposium papers,

Table 1.1 Subjects of Articles and Books on Emics and Etics

Categories	References
Anthropology	74
Psychology	65
Linguistics	22
Cross-cultural research	18
Ethnography	17
Sociology	14
Medicine	13
Dictionaries	12
Education	12
Psychiatry	7
Translation	4
Management	3
Archaeology	2
Folklore	2
Economics	2
Religion	1
English	1
Other	9
Total	278

Source: Headland (1990), p. 19.

Roger Keesing claimed that cognitive anthropologists had ceased to regard the emic-etic distinction as relevant. Headland (1990:23) used empirical evidence to counter Keesing's claim, but the remark did serve to underscore the contentious nature of anthropology and the hazards of using technical language in an imprecise way. We argue that the distinctive epistemological statuses of emic and etic data continue to be of value to analysts in many social and behavioral science disciplines as well as to philosophers and historians of science (e. g., Jardine, 2004).

Maps such as those in Figures 1.1 and 1.2 provide additional insights into the structure and breadth of Harris's bibliographic environment. These display interauthor relationships from the perspective of journals analyzed by ISI's *Arts & Humanities Citation Index*. This database contains articles from more than 1,000 sources, augmented with selected articles from the social science journal literature, to cast a distinctly humanities-oriented light on Harris.

The first image is a Pathfinder network or PFNET (Schvaneveldt, 1990). It shows the major links between Harris and the 24 authors most frequently co-cited with him in an experimental database created by researchers at Drexel University. This database, a subset of the full *Arts & Humanities Citation Index*, contains about 1.26 million records of articles published in humanities journals during the ten-year period 1988–1997, including the authors and works they cite (White, 2000:487–488, 2001;

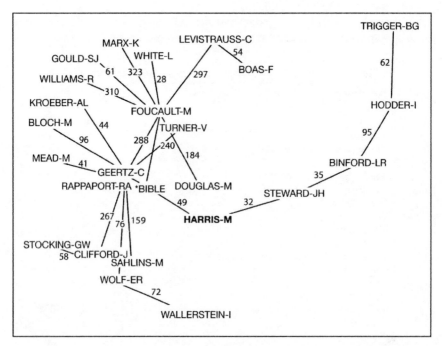

Figure 1.1 Pathfinder (PFNET) Map of Marvin Harris's Citation Image

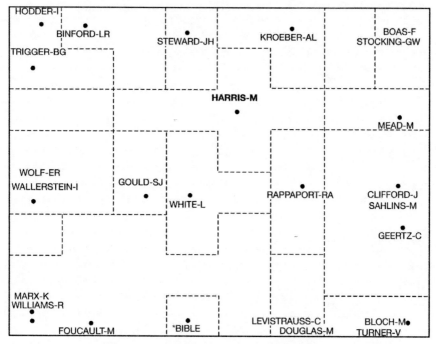

Figure 1.2 Kohonen Self-Organizing Feature
Map of Marvin Harris's Citation Image

White, Buzydlowski, and Lin, 2000). The second image is a Kohonen self-organizing feature map (Kohonen, 1989) of the same data (White, Lin, and McCain, 1998).

Using programming not yet available commercially from ISI through its Dialog or Web of Science interface, the input names for the displays are obtained in real time from articles that cite an input "seed" author—in this case, the 674 articles that cite one or more works by HARRIS M. (Citation data formatted by ISI contain only initials, never the full first names or middle names, which creates a validity problem that we discuss below.) The algorithm then finds how many articles in the 674 cites each author *with* Harris M—the co-citation counts. It ranks these other authors by their counts and extracts the top 24, as shown in Table 1.2. Next it systematically pairs the top-ranked authors and finds, in addition to their counts with Harris, the co-citation counts for every pair, which are then placed in a 25 x 25 symmetric matrix. The PFNET algorithm represents each author as a node and draws links to show only the *highest* co-citation counts between each pair of nodes. All less salient links are pruned away in a deliberate simplification. The numbers above the links in Figure 1.1 show these highest counts. Thus, although Harris is co-cited with everyone in the map, the PFNET reveals only the strongest connections in the citing literature.

Table 1.2 Marvin Harris's Citation Image in the Humanities Context, 1988–1997

674	HARRIS M
49	GEERTZ C
41	LEVISTRAUSS C
38	WOLF ER
37	SAHLINS M
34	DOUGLAS M
32	STEWARD JH
30	FOUCAULT M
29	CLIFFORD J
28	GOULD SJ
24	BINFORD LR
23	STOCKING GW
21	MARX K
21	BLOCH M
20	MEAD M
20	TURNER V
20	KROEBER AL
20	WHITE L
20	WILLIAMS R
19	BOAS F
19	TRIGGER BG
18	RAPPAPORT RA
18	WALLERSTEIN I
17	HODDER I
17	*BIBLE

While it is usual to conceive of co-cited authors not as actual persons but as *oeuvres* (in the singular, a writer's body of work taken as a whole; see White and Griffith, 1981:163), there is evidence that the links revealed by these measures often reflect not only intellectual relationships but also social relationships that range from acquaintanceships to coauthorships. In the decidedly limited bibliographic context of the arts and humanities, Harris's *oeuvre* is most frequently discussed alongside that of his theoretical opponent, Clifford Geertz, with whom he has been co-cited at least 49 times. For comparison, Figures 1.3 and 1.4 show similar PFNET and Kohonen maps with Geertz as the focal author. Geertz clearly figures prominently in the writings of many humanities scholars. He was cited in at least 2,183 articles, compared to Harris's 674, over the same ten-year period. Harris's 49 co-citations with Geertz are relatively insignificant compared to Geertz's much higher frequency pairing with postmodernist theoreticians, such as philosopher Michel Foucault (288 times co-cited), historian James Clifford (267 times co-cited), or sociologist Pierre Bourdieu (with whom Geertz is co-cited 263 times, although the number does not show up on the display because the Bourdieu-Foucault count of 532 is highest). Anthropologists identified with philosophical idealist or symbolist research programs who show up include Victor Turner, Claude Lévi-Strauss, Marshall Sahlins, and Mary Douglas. Many of the scholars associated with Geertz are prominent names in literary and cultural studies circles. (Both Harris and Geertz would be more properly mapped with data from ISI's *Social Sciences Citation Index,* which run from 1972 to the present. However, at the time our displays were made, only the test data from *Arts & Humanities Citation Index* for 1988–1997 were available in Drexel's mapping system.)

Alternate views of these same data in the Kohonen self-organizing maps allow for interesting comparisons of the intellectual milieus of Harris and Geertz. Like the PFNETs, the Kohonen maps in Figure 1.2 (for Harris) and Figure 1.4 (for Geertz) are automatically generated from the test database. They show each focal author surrounded by the other authors with whom they are most often discussed in the humanities context. Authors in closest proximity have the highest pairwise co-citation counts within the set of 25, and the size of their surrounding space represents the magnitude of their co-citation count. Multiple names sometimes occupy a larger single space, suggesting that hundreds of citing authors perceive them to share similar styles of work, research problems, or units of analysis (White and McCain, 1989:146). An advantage of this visualization technique is the ease with which meaningful dimensions can be discerned.

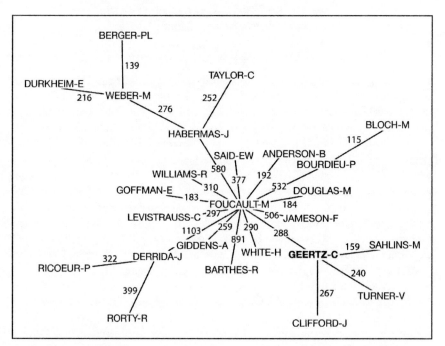

Figure 1.3 Pathfinder (PFNET) Map of Clifford Geertz's Citation Image

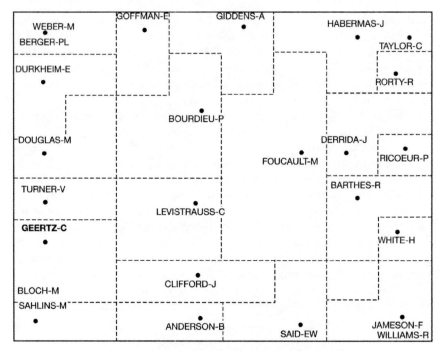

Figure 1.4 Kohonen Self-Organizing Feature
Map of Clifford Geertz's Citation Image

In Figure 1.2, Harris is surrounded by anthropology's founding figures Franz Boas, Alfred Kroeber, and Margaret Mead, along with the discipline's preeminent historian, George Stocking. Harris is aligned most closely with three cultural ecologists, his contemporary Roy Rappaport and early founders Leslie White and Julian Steward, with evolutionist-paleontologist Stephen Jay Gould located nearby. The upper half of the map is dominated by North American archaeologists Lewis Binford and Bruce Trigger along with British postprocessualist archaeologist Ian Hodder, whom Harris (1995b:64) critiques as one of the "influential sources of support for postmodernism in anthropology." The lower half of the map contains the names of well-known structuralist, interpretivist, or symbolist anthropologists (Claude Lévi-Strauss, Mary Douglas, Victor Turner, Clifford Geertz) whose research programs Harris frequently attacked. In the opposite corner are founding figure Karl Marx, British socialist and literary critic Raymond Williams, world-systems theorist Immanuel Wallerstein, and anthropologist Eric Wolf. Many of the names associated with Harris in this environment have made contributions to various cultural evolutionary models and theories of social change. The map thus portrays the "theoretical wellsprings of cultural materialism—Marx, White, and Steward—[who] represent three distinct but compatible traditions of materialist social theory: political economy, evolutionism, and cultural ecology" (Ferguson, 1995:34).

Two figures seem misplaced on the map's social theory axi materialists and Marxists on the left-hand side, and those whon ists and mentalists to the right. One is Michel Foucault, descri current top icon" (Harris, 1995b:72). It would appear to make b was reversed with that of structural Marxist anthropologist Maurice Bloch. ... although a self-proclaimed Marxist, wavered on the nature of infrastructural determinism, causing Harris to comment that "eclecticism propounded in the name of Karl Marx is still eclecticism" (Harris, 1979:229). Apparently the right side of the map is reserved for eclectics and other staunch adversaries of Harris, given the proximity of Clifford Geertz, James Clifford, and particularly Marshall Sahlins. One of Harris's favorite exercises was to root out evidence of theoretical laxity or inconsistency in identifying the causal variables of cultural similarities and differences. Humanities-oriented scholars, perhaps more tolerant of eclectic research strategies, may be more likely to mention Sahlins and Bloch along with Harris. They may also co-cite Foucault for his cultural studies connections with Marx and Williams and make other combinations that, like voting patterns, reveal empirically the connections that scholars make among authors that cluster together. Inspection of the PFNET display reveals the strong ties between distinctive clusters centered on Geertz and Foucault. Recall that these automatically generated visualization tools are based on repeated patterns of literature use over a restricted period of time. They are thus capable of approximating a synchronic view of a field's bibliographic structure. We hope that in the future ISI will develop the capability of generating such maps as a diachronic series to take advantage of the much more sizable, representative set of data in the Web of Science citation databases (see White, 2000).

Additional insight into anthropology's intellectual environment from the perspective of the humanities can be found in the Kohonen map for Geertz in Figure 1.4. Repeated citing of Geertz alongside the writings of other scholars places him at the far left-hand side close to many of the same names found on Harris's map. This interpretivist-symbolist anthropological cluster is aligned with founding fathers of the idealist paradigm, including Emile Durkheim and Max Weber, along with contemporary sociologist Peter Berger and symbolic interactionist Erving Goffman. Many prominent postmodern theorists show up on the map surrounding the Geertz–Lévi-Strauss–Foucault core, notably Pierre Bourdieu, Jacques Derrida, Roland Barthes, and Paul Ricoeur. At the top half of the map appear critical social theorists Anthony Giddens, Jürgen Habermas, Richard Rorty, and Charles Taylor. Marxist cultural studies proponents, literary critics, and philosophers arrayed at the bottom of the map in proximity to Raymond Williams include Edward Said, Frederic Jameson, and Hayden White. The map for Geertz may be more easily interpreted than that for Harris, and it serves as a guide to the postmodernist social theorists of both materialist and idealist orientation.

Wrestling with Methodological Issues

Before proceeding to the larger sample that expands this preliminary view from the humanities, let us first address several general problems with the methodology citation analysis and some special problems that emerged in analyzing cultural materialism's impact. From the outset, it was clear that common names pose difficulties as the focus of bibliometric analyses. We were forced to cope with the fact that there are numerous other publishing "M. Harrises" besides our Marvin Harris.

We made a preliminary retrieval and analysis of a subset of about 1,300 citations to Harris's work for a 2001 Central States Anthropological Society symposium on Marvin Harris organized by Lawrence Kuznar. Afterward we repeated our retrieval efforts, aiming to assemble a more complete set of the works citing Harris in the reference lists of articles, review essays, book reviews, editorials, and other published items in more than 8,500 international journals published from the early 1970s through June 2002. ISI's source journals are justifiably the top journals of record spanning the sciences, social sciences, and humanities. But by increasing the size of our retrieval set, we risked reducing its precision. Not only did we discover many more authors named "HARRIS M" who were not in fact Marvin Harris, but also found that numerous citations to Harris's work have been recorded simply as "HARRIS" with no initial. Disambiguating Harris in the online Dialog files required us to review more than 4,000 citations where the first author was listed as HARRIS M.

Examples of the wrong Harris cropped up in the pairing of the BIBLE with HARRIS M in Figures 1.1 and 1.2, for example. Although six of the seventeen articles referencing biblical passages did indeed cite one or more of Marvin Harris's writings (e. g., representative works include Marling, 1992; McGowan, 1994), the majority of these had actually cited writings by others, such as language scholar Martin Harris or Christian educator Maria Harris (e. g., see Manczak, 1991; Melchert, 1992). In the effort to retrieve information from all three ISI databases and not just the humanities sample, we experimented by pairing Harris with keywords from titles of his works, words (and variants) from the vocabulary of anthropology and cultural materialism, and Harris's University of Florida or Columbia University institutional affiliations. Others continued to be conflated with Marvin Harris despite these efforts, including British Amazonianist Mark Harris, American anthropologist Michael S. Harris, British psychologist Martha Harris (who wrote columns on kinship alongside Harris antagonist Mary Douglas), professor of entomology Marvin K. Harris, Michael Harris in library science, and even gospel musician Marvin Harris, to identify just a few. To be fair, none of these individuals were cited enough to affect results significantly. Anthropologist Marvin Harris is the only M. Harris whose raw citation count allowed him to be considered "well known beyond the discipline," that is, cited from 1,001 to 10,000 times. He did not, however, achieve the higher level of "world famous" on a proposed logarithmic scale of fame or reputation (see White, 2004:104–105). The others named Harris achieved such categories as "recognized in the specialty" (cited 11–100 times), or "well known in the discipline" (accruing 101–1,000 citations).

In our attempts to measure cultural materialism's impact across disciplines we uncovered Raymond Williams's explicit Marxist approach called "cultural materialism." The influence of this perspective is seen in the preceding visualizations as the interdisciplinary field of cultural studies. Harris was probably more chagrined than we were at the discovery of this logically connected but basically noninteractive literature (cf. Swanson, 1987). He began an encyclopedia article in *Encyclopedia of Cultural*

Anthropology with this priority claim for the concept: "Cultural materialism is a scientific research strategy or paradigm that prioritizes material, behavioral, and etic processes in the explanation of the divergent, convergent, and parallel evolution of human sociocultural systems. Its basic principles were first labeled and described in *The Rise of Anthropological Theory* [in 1968]," and furthermore, "The cultural materialism of postmodernist literary criticism has no affinity with the anthropological genre" (Harris, 1996:277). Others also acknowledge that Harris was the first to articulate the theory of cultural materialism (e. g., Simpson, 2000). In fact, very few works co-cite Williams and Harris even ceremonially (e. g., Wilson, 2002), much less engage the two perspectives to explore common ground. The exception is William Jackson's (1996) extended treatment of the culture concept within institutional economics. He acknowledges that "Neither Harris nor Williams cites the other's work, yet the two versions are broadly compatible; they are converging on the same middle ground" (Jackson, 1996:234). Raymond Williams's and Marvin Harris's convergence on cultural materialism is an excellent example of independent, multiple discoveries in the Mertonian sense.

In the past several years the Web-based citation indexes have become more readily accessible at large research libraries, and the Web of Science's scope of coverage is now much increased over the years that are accessible via Dialog's interface. Using the Web of Science it is now possible to trace Harris's impact back to the 1950s when he began publishing. Some institutional licenses with ISI go even further back in time. The distributions prepared for the present study are based largely on Dialog's version of ISI files, which cover the years only from 1972 on for the *Social Sciences Citation Index* (file 7), the *Science Citation Index* (from 1974, files 34 and 434), and the *Arts & Humanities Citation Index* (from 1980, file 439). These online databases are the equivalent of ISI's original printed indexes. An exception is our portrait of Harris covering the years 1955–2002, as we discuss below. We thought about reanalyzing the Harris co-citations so that we could include data from the 1950s and 1960s plus the last three years of data but in the end decided against it. We reasoned that the general patterns already documented would likely continue even if both older and newer materials were added to the mix. In fact this bibliometric analysis spans thirty years, a significant portion of Harris's productive career. Harris died in October 2001 and we chose mid-2002 as a logical cutoff for analysis. We note below when we deviate from this policy.

Among the difficulties we faced were duplications in the data. Although we used Dialog's RD process to remove duplicate records prior to downloading, we were unable to identify and eliminate all repetition. The magnitude of this problem is on the order of 200 records, contributing to an error rate of between one and two percent. We hired a computer science student to write a simple matching algorithm that would detect and remove duplicates. The program is similar to the one developed by Dialog. The program checked first authors (listed first in the AU field) against all other records, and for matching items it then compared the journal name (JN), the title (TI), and the list of authors and works in the cited references (CR) fields. The final set on which most of Harris's CAMEO is based contains 2,679 unique records for articles citing one or more of Harris's works between the early 1970s and mid-2002. Some of the results presented in Tables 1.2 to 1.4 add up to a slightly smaller or larger total number of records, depending on the integrity of the data contained in different fields of the ISI records.

Another difficulty that occurred in offline processing of downloaded records was ranking cited authors without also tabulating their cited works multiple times. For this analysis we were interested in author co-citation, that is, a count of articles that cite pairs of authors (Marvin Harris with others) in the sampling frame of ISI journals. Dialog permits the use of the RANK command, whereby thousands of cited references (CR) are transformed into cited-author (CA) data. It is designed to count each author's cited works only once per citing article in order to yield a portrait of a given author's relative position in a particular research context. Thus, instead of recording the number of times that individual works were cited, the programmer counted how many times any part of an author's *oeuvre* was cited in these 2,679 articles. For example, if two Harris works were cited in one article, the cited-author tally would be just one. The program thus mirrored Dialog's ranking algorithm to produce tabulations of cited and co-cited authors. ISI only recently added ranking of fields to the Web of Science interface. This long-awaited feature, called "Analyze," permits users to rank automatically up to 2,000 authors, journals, subjects, institutional affiliations, or languages, plus additional characteristics of the journal literature. However, it is cumbersome to build the body of cited references due to the heavy processing demand required to cross-list the thousands of authors' names attached to those cited references (and doing so requires use of the search history capability of Web of Science to intersect the sets of cited references). There remains no easy, automatic solution to the problem of producing co-cited author rankings, either to create interdisciplinary metanalyses, or simply to document interdisciplinarity (White, 1996).

Finally, we developed rules to combine obvious author allonyms, that is, legitimate name variants as well as common misspellings. For example, we combined counts for anthropologist Robert Carneiro under variants CARNEIRO RL, CARNEIRO R, CARNIERO RL, CARNIERO R, and CARNEIOR R. We decided against combining allonyms that might be ambiguous, with the result that we underestimate some authors' total citations. Thus, we combined Claude Lévi-Strauss's entries under LEVISTRAUSS C, LEVISTRAUS C, LEVISSTRAUSS C, and LEVISSTRAUS C to produce a total count for his name, but omitted numbers (always minor) that were recorded for LEVISTRAUSS L, LEVISTRAUSS, and LEVISTRAUS because we were not confident that the variants referred to the correct name. Cited authors with last names lacking first initials were combined only if no alternates existed with other initials (e. g., RADCLIFFEBROWN AR was combined with RADCLIFFEBROWN).

Marvin Harris in Profile

The CAMEOs shown in Table 1.3 characterize Harris's long-term research interests and provide a basis for understanding claims about his theoretical and disciplinary impact.

The first column reflects content markers drawn from Dialog's LC MARC–Books database (file 426, covering the years 1968–2002), in the form of the Library of Congress (LC) subject headings assigned to Harris's eighteen major books and edited works and at least sixteen later English-language editions. The table ranks "ethnology" and "anthropology" as the most frequently occurring descriptors, followed by "culture," "philosophy," "social evolution," and subjects as diverse as "food habits," "Marxist anthropology," "race relations," "witchcraft," "birth control," and "war and society." This

Table 1.3 Publication CAMEOs for Marvin Harris

Subjects of Books		Journals	
15	ETHNOLOGY	16	American Anthropologist
11	ANTHROPOLOGY	15	Natural History
7	CULTURE	11	Current Anthropology
6	PHILOSOPHY	8	Psychology Today
6	SOCIAL EVOLUTION	5	Journal of Anthropological
3	FOOD HABITS		Research
3	MARXIST ANTHROPOLOGY	4	Social Forces
2	ECONOMIC CONDITIONS	3	Human Ecology
2	EFFECT OF ENVIRONMENT ON	3	Sciences—New York
2	FOOD SUPPLY	2	Human Nature
2	HISTORY	2	Political Science Quarterly
2	HUMAN BEINGS	2	Southwestern Journal of
2	HUMAN EVOLUTION		Anthropology
2	LATIN AMERICA	1	Academy of Management
2	MISCELLANEA		Review
2	ORIGIN	1	American Ethnologist
2	RACE RELATIONS	1	Annual Review of Anthropology
2	SOCIAL CONDITIONS	1	Behavioral and Brain Sciences
2	UNITED STATES	1	Current Contents—Arts and
2	WITCHCRAFT		Humanities
1	AMERICA	1	Current Contents—Social and
1	BIRTH CONTROL		Behavioral Sciences
1	BRAZIL	1	Ethnohistory
1	CASE STUDIES	1	L'Homme
1	CITIES AND TOWNS	1	Man: Journal of the Royal
1	DEMOGRAPHIC		Anthropological Institute
	ANTHROPOLOGY	1	New York Review of Books
1	FERTILITY, HUMAN	1	New York Times Book Review
1	FOOD	1	Society
1	METHODOLOGY	1	Transactions of New York
1	MINAS VELHAS, BRAZIL		Academy of Sciences
1	MINORITIES		
1	MOZAMBIQUE		
1	NUTRITION		
1	PREHISTORIC PEOPLES		
1	PSYCHOLINGUISTICS		
1	SOCIAL ASPECTS		
1	WAR AND SOCIETY		

vocabulary summarizes at a glance the theoretical concerns and ethnological breadth of Harris's research in the United States, Brazil, Mozambique, and elsewhere.

Another of Harris's publication portraits appears under "Journals" in the second column of Table 1.3. This ranked list of 24 source journals indexed by ISI identifies where Harris published articles, critical commentaries, and book reviews. This portrait (and the next several, showing Harris's coauthors and the authors he cited) was validated using Harris's bibliography (see Appendix B to this volume); the 84 items in the bibliography that contributed to these profiles are identified with an asterisk [*]. This particular publication CAMEO draws on the longer range of years available via the enhanced Web of Science interface, tracing articles in the *Science Citation Index Expanded* (from 1955 to present), the *Social Sciences Citation Index* (from 1956), and the *Arts & Humanities Citation Index* (from 1975). We retrieved these records by matching unique keywords in Harris's titles to data in the title (TI) fields, and then ISI's "Analyze" feature to produce the ranked list of source (SO) titles.

Not all of Harris's journal publications that should have been recorded in the Web of Science could be found, however, which points to an additional source of bias or error in citation analyses. Some of Harris's most significant contributions were in the form of invited commentary in journals such as *Current Anthropology.* This important journal devotes significant space in each issue to its well-known "*CA* Star Treatment" forums. In this process, peer reviewers selected by the editors are asked to comment upon and critically review an original contribution submitted for publication in the journal, and the author of the article is given the opportunity to reply to the individual commentators. An example of an abbreviated type of *CA* treatment is the article published by Tim O'Meara (1997) entitled "Causation and the struggle for a science of culture," which featured just one extended "Comment" written by Harris (1997c). It was followed in a subsequent issue by further editorial remarks (see Adams, 1998). ISI's indexing practice is inconsistent with regard to commentary journals like *CA,* and Harris's six-page response to O'Meara's ten-page contribution was overlooked in the citation record (although O'Meara's and Adams's contributions were recorded). Upon first inspection of the "Harris Coauthors" distribution (see the next table), we were surprised by thirty-seven names listed with Harris as coauthors but who were actually his co-commentators. This is yet another example of an indexing error that we eliminated from the profile.

Author CAMEOs provide a different type of portrait from that drawn from Harris's cluster of coauthors. These CAMEOS are based on the authors whom Harris chose to cite over his career, as well as those who cited him. These personal networks reflect both *directed* (one-way) ties, and ties that are *undirected* (mutual or reciprocated among joint members) (see White [2001:620–622] for a discussion of the literature on social network analysis pertaining to author CAMEOs). Columns one through four of Table 1.4 reveal these personal networks, including:

1. Harris's *coauthors*;
2. the *citation identity,* consisting of the authors Harris cited;
3. the *citation image-makers,* consisting of authors who cited Harris, thus creating his citation image; and

4. the *citation image,* consisting of all of the authors co-cited by the image-makers with Harris.

The first column of Table 1.4, "Harris Coauthors," rank orders the authorship data in 84 journal articles picked up by ISI's enhanced Web of Science interface. As is

Table 1.4 Author CAMEOs for Marvin Harris

Harris Coauthors		Citation Identity	
84	HARRIS M	30	HARRIS M
5	DIVALE WT	9	DIVALE WT
3	BYRNE B	7	GOODENOUGH WH
3	CONSORTE JG	7	SERVICE ER
3	LANG J	4	BOAS F
1	MORREN GEB	4	CHAGNON NA
1	NAIR KN	4	GROSS DR
1	ROSS EB	4	LEE RB
1	VAIDYANATHAN A	4	LEWIS O
1	WILLIAMS DT	4	ROSS EB
		4	SANJEK R
		4	SIMOONS FJ
		4	TELLES EE
		3	CARNEIRO RL
		3	COTTRELL F
		3	DANDEKAR VM
		3	FRIED MH
		3	GANDHI MK
		3	HESTON A
		3	JOHNSON A
		3	KEESING RM
		3	KOTTAK C
		3	LEVISTRAUSS C
		3	MARX K
		3	MAYADAS C
		3	MITRA R
		3	NAIR KN
		3	PELTO PJ
		3	RAJ KN
		3	ROY P
		3	SAHLINS M
		3	SCHNEIDER H
		3	SKIDMORE T
		3	SPATE OHK
		3	SRINIVAS MN
		3	STEPHENS TM
		3	VAYDA AP
		3	WOOD CH
		1–2	421 others

Table 1.4 *(continued)*

Image-Makers		Citation Image	
31	HARRIS M	2,679	HARRIS M
31	MACKEY WC	463	SAHLINS MD
17	DIVALE WT	329	GEERTZ C
10	DIENER P	315	LEVISTRAUSS C
11	TRIGGER BG	278	MURDOCK GP
9	HAWKES K	275	STEWARD JH
8	SANDERSON SK	267	WHITE LA
7	CONEY NS	227	DIVALE WT
7	LENSKI GE	227	WOLF ER
7	LOVELL PA	215	CHAGNON NA
7	SHAPIRO W	214	RAPPAPORT RA
7	SIMOONS FJ	213	MARX K
6	BARKOW JH	211	KROEBER AL
6	BURGER HG	206	LEE RB
6	CARROLL MP	201	MEAD M
6	CHAGNON NA	201	SERVICE ER
6	CHICK G	199	LEACH ER
6	FISKE ST	194	CARNEIRO RL
6	GLICK P	191	MALINOWSKI B
6	HILL K	184	DOUGLAS MT
6	HIRSCHFELD LA	183	WILSON EO
6	JARVIE IC	179	FRIED MH
6	NAGEL J	173	VAYDA AP
6	TELLES EE	161	WEBER M
5	ADAMS RN	156	BOAS F
5	BIGLAN A	151	DURKHEIM E
5	BOYD R	145	BARTH F
5	CARR WJ	145	WAGLEY C
5	EMBER CR	142	VANDENBERGHE PL
5	FERGUSON RB	141	STOCKING GW
5	GRIGG D	140	EVANS-PRITCHARD EE
5	GROSS DR	139	GOULD SJ
5	HAYDEN B	136	KUHN TS
5	HOWE J	132	BINFORD LR
5	IBERALL AS	132	RADCLIFFE-BROWN AR
5	JOHNSON A	131	BOSERUP E
5	KAPLAN H	131	LOWIE R
5	LEAVITT GC	129	PARSONS T
5	MARKLEY R	125	GOODY JR
5	MASANI PR	125	TRIVERS RL
5	MUNTANER C	123	DAWKINS R
5	ROBKIN EE	122	ALEXANDER RD
5	SCHIFFER MB	118	NAROLL RS
5	SHANKMAN P	115	BENEDICT RF
5	SHERRY JF	115	WALLACE AFC
5	VANDENBERGHE PL	1–114	About 64,250 others
5	WERNER D		
1–4	2,735 others		

evident from this short list, Harris mostly worked alone. Harris's mentor and coauthor Charles Wagley is missing from the list even though he wrote one book about Brazil with him, in addition to a report and an *American Anthropologist* article, published in the 1950s but too early to be picked up by ISI. Eric Ross appears too, though he is credited for just the one article he wrote with Harris and not for their coauthored book nor the volume they coedited. Other collaborators whose works are invisible in this profile include Conrad Kottak, with whom Harris wrote on Brazilian racial categories, coeditors Morton Fried and Robert Murphy, with whom Harris published on warfare, and Thomas Headland and Kenneth Pike, who collaborated with Harris on the topic of emics and etics.

Ranked first at the top of all the distributions in Table 1.4 is Harris's name. It is almost inevitable that an author cites himself or herself more frequently than others. Thus, among the 84 articles that Harris authored or coauthored, he cited himself in at least 30 of them to create the "Citation Identity" registered in column two. Authors that he cited three or more times figure into this CAMEO profile, while 421 others cited only once are omitted from the distribution's long tail. The pool of singletons grows exponentially as the sample size increases (the number of omitted names is recorded at the end of each column). This pattern of citations means that the bulk of names in Harris's citing circle occupies an enormous periphery surrounding a small core of multiply cited authors. This fact reveals significant cross-boundary fertilization and innovation within the cultural materialist research strategy. The work of Diana Crane (1970, 1972) and other investigators working at the intersection of sociometric and bibliometric research provides evidence that information flows both to and from the periphery to alter the relations among participants and link old and new specialty concerns to one another.

Next, in columns three and four, Harris's "Image-Makers" and his "Citation Image" are presented. These are both robust CAMEOs based on Harris's 2,679 citations traced via Dialog's interface to the citation indexes from the 1970s to mid-2002. Recall that the main reason for confining our study to this thirty-year sample was the fact that it eliminated false associations with other publishing M. Harrises. The assumption is that scholars cite names together because they recognize that they have some subject or intellectual relationship and bearing on each other. A set of names is not a mere jumble but rather a well-structured network revealing a kind of consensual view formed by the aggregate perceptions of hundreds or thousands of citers over time (White, 2001:624). The two distributions presented are both based on articles that contain citations to Harris, but they differ from one another. The "Image-Makers" ranks the more than 2,700 authors contained in the author (AU) field, while the "Citation Image" is based on the more than 64,000 cited authors (CA) that appeared at least once in the cited reference (CR) field.

At or near the top of all of these CAMEOs appears the name of William Divale, Harris's coauthor in a number of papers and commentaries on the causes and consequences of male supremacy and warfare. Repetition of a name across different citation contexts is a sign of the importance of that person to the focal author. In addition to Divale, Napoleon Chagnon ranks high on all three lists. Chagnon was cited by Harris, cited him in turn, and was cited alongside him by others. Chagnon's relationship to cultural materialism is problematic, however. Chagnon's work on reproductive strategies among the Yanomamö in the Amazon is based on sociobiology, a research strategy that Harris relentlessly criticized for its biological reductionism. Harris and other cultural materialists preferred focusing on subsistence strategies and sources of protein to explain Yanomamö social structure, warfare, and infanticide. Although multiple-author CAMEOs require a degree of sophistication to interpret correctly, an individual's repeated appearance with an author reveals a kind of continuity between the focal author's self-identity and the image of that author viewed from the perspective of others.

The key names that show up encourage a closer reading. In each citation-based CAMEO, we can observe both Harris antagonists and sympathizers. High rates and breadth of citation and co-citation are indicators of a scholar's influence and impact, regardless of whether the association between a pair of names is a negative or positive one. (Collins [1998] shows that conflicts among intellectuals competing for attention are the norm in science and scholarship.) The top twenty co-citees that make up Harris's citation image (Table 1.4, column four) include Harris's critics and/or targets of criticism, notably Marshall Sahlins, Clifford Geertz, Claude Lévi-Strauss, Napoleon Chagnon, Elman Service, Edmund Leach, Mary Douglas, and E. O. Wilson. We also see interspersed the names of those whose research programs are compatible with or inform cultural materialism, including William Divale, Eric Wolf, Roy Rappaport, Richard Lee, and Robert Carneiro. Harris citees in column two include fewer founding figures than his co-citees in column four, although note that Franz Boas and Karl Marx are high on both lists. This difference is really an artifact of the article-based co-citation methodology, since most of Harris's eighteen books heavily cited most of these citation-image luminaries. In journals and numerous books, he cited Mohandas Gandhi, whose tracts on cow-love figured in Harris's analysis of the sacred cow in India and of taboos in general. Also evident in Harris's own citation identity are methodologists Roger Sanjek, Allen Johnson, and Pertti Pelto, as well as ethnographers and cultural ecologists such as Daniel Gross and Richard Lee, who did ethnographic fieldwork of interest to Harris.

In column three, the image-makers who cited Harris contain a number of researchers who are part of the larger debate over sociobiology. Sociobiology forms part of a multidisciplinary research specialty within the larger field of human behavioral ecology that spans anthropology, biology, and evolutionary psychology (for the results of a bibliometric analysis of the dimensions of this citing circle, see Sandstrom, 1998, 2001). Prominent on the list, along with Chagnon and Johnson, are key researchers in the field, including Kristen Hawkes, Jerome Barkow, Kim Hill, Robert Boyd, and Hillard Kaplan. People who figure in only one or two, but not all three, citing contexts may reveal interesting asymmetries in authors' citing relationships. These asymmetries suggest that reputation and intellectual seniority may predict whether citation ties will be reciprocated or not (White, 2001:625–626). High among the Harris image-makers is Wade Mackey, who publishes frequently on human sexuality in *Mankind Quarterly*. This journal, founded in 1961, publishes much controversial work on eugenicist connections among human biology, behavior, and culture (see the homepage at http://www/man-kindquarterly.org with justifications for the journal's objectives, editorial board membership, and content). Another author at the top of the list is Paul Diener, who for a period during the 1970s was a tendentious and ardent critic of cultural materialism. He has since faded away from the scene just as abruptly as he arrived. Although Harris engaged Diener in a few acerbic scholarly exchanges, he did not address authors like Mackey directly. It is clear that Harris, as noted in his *New York Times* obituary (see Appendix A), was often at the "storm center in his field."

The detailed list in the appendix to this chapter provides a fuller portrait of Harris's co-citees, and includes each individual's primary disciplinary and specialty area affiliations. This elaborated view of Harris's citation image includes the 182 authors who were co-cited with him 50 or more times but omits others who were co-cited less frequently. Proper forms of authors' names and their disciplines or specialties were identified using the American Anthropological Association's 2004–2005 *AAA Guide* to anthropology programs, and databases such as *Anthropology Plus, WorldCat, Biography & Genealogy Master Index,* and *Contemporary Authors.* Google and Wikipedia.com were also consulted as sources of last resort. A plus sign (+) following a name indicates that the author is a contemporary of Harris who has written in definitive support of the aims of cultural materialism, while a minus sign (–) indicates an ardent detractor of the approach (or someone Harris chose to attack in print). Founding figures in anthropology, sociology, biology, and other fields are designated with an asterisk (*). The many names without any indicators of allegiance or affinity are contemporaries who have not been overly visible in the published debate over cultural materialism. No effort has been made to indicate student–mentor bonds, a kind of consanguineal, as opposed to affinal, definition of the relationships that constitute the social organization of anthropology (on the importance of such bonds, see Collins, 1998). The assignment of pluses and minuses is admittedly impressionistic, as we could propose no suitable etic standard for validating these allegiances. Apologies are extended to overlooked allies and enemies.

Table 1.5 presents five descriptive portrayals to help set Harris's citation image in relief. The first column, labeled "Journals," identifies the primary outlets publishing articles that cite Harris's work. The list is headed by the top national and international journals of record in the field among an approximate total of 900 titles. They include *American Anthropologist, Current Anthropology, American Ethnologist, Journal of Anthropological Research, Man, L'Homme,* plus others considered to be anthropology's most influential journals according to ISI's *Journal Citation Reports. Annual Review of Anthropology* figures high in the list with at least 68 articles citing one or more of Harris's works. Column two, "Document Types," provides confirmation that the bibliographic review essay is prominent among the types of documents in which Harris is cited. Critical reviews serve an important function in establishing boundaries within fields and providing a basis for productive, cross-boundary synthesis. They also transform scholars' undirected searching outside their areas of expertise into a more efficient process for dealing with novel information. Reviews may substitute for a colleague's recommendation and are a more rewarding place for scholars to start than random encounters beyond the limits of their familiar territory. Harris contributed only one essay to this key journal during his career (his 1976 "History and significance of the emic/etic distinction"), but others found reasons to include Harris in their syntheses. A glance at the diversity of topics in this source alone points to Harris's place within a range of debates, for example: "Agrarian ecology" (Netting, 1974); "Anthropological economics: A question of distribution" (Gudeman, 1978); "Archaeology at the crossroads: What's new" (Trigger, 1984); "Conversation analysis" (Goodwin and Heritage, 1990); or "Conservation and subsistence in small-scale societies" (Smith and Wishnie, 2000).

High citation counts accrue for Harris in other journals that present research from anthropological subfields, including *Human Ecology, Human Organization* (applied anthropology), *American Antiquity* (archaeology), or *American Journal of Physical Anthropology.* Citations from mainstream linguistics journals are absent. Other problem or area specialties within anthropology appear as well, as is evidenced by journals such as *Anthropology and Education Quarterly, Ethos* (psychological anthropology), or *Plains Anthropologist.* Representative titles from outside anthropology that rank high on the list include *Behavioral Science Research, Social Forces, American Journal of Sociology, Behavioral and Brain Sciences, American Psychologist, Annals of the Association of American Geographers, American Historical Review,* and *Perspectives in Biology and Medicine,* to name just a few. The ranking of subjects assigned to these citing journals (see below) is a summary of the interdisciplinarity of articles in which Harris's work has been discussed.

While English-language journals dominate the rankings (a selection bias noted by many in ISI's high-impact journals), several core foreign-language anthropology titles also appear. The third column, headed "Geographic Locations," shows the affiliations of citing authors in English-speaking nations, but it points to a great diversity of authors located in nations outside of North America and Europe. In the column headed "Years," Harris's citation image is plainly visible as a steady increase of citations building up to its peak during the mid-1980s. This chronological account reveals the steady, regular pattern of attention paid to Harris and undermines the claim that his influence has already waned or is at risk of waning soon. It would be interesting to repeat the profile in the future or partition it diachronically into zones and show which particular works are being cited when.

The last portion of Table 1.5, "Subjects," shows the distribution of ISI subject descriptors assigned to the journals citing Harris. For clarity, subjects have been collapsed into broad categories without masking the details, with individual counts for related subjects shown in parentheses. Because an interdisciplinary journal may receive more than one such classification, the list is a fair depiction of the diversity of journals in which authors who cite Harris choose to publish. This diversity is a telling sign of Harris's own interdisciplinary reach. The social and behavioral sciences dominate the list, and anthropology is by far the predominant discipline attending to Harris's work. However, there is practically no subject within the wide spectrum of fields of study that has not been exposed to the precepts and research strategy of cultural materialism. These subjects include the whole of the humanities, law, education, natural science

Table 1.5 Marvin Harris's Citation Image CAMEOs Elaborated

Journals

145	American Anthropologist
141	Current Anthropology
68	Annual Review of Anthropology
54	Human Ecology
53	American Ethnologist
53	Journal of Anthropological Research
36	Man
30	Ethnology
30	Human Organization
28	Dialectical Anthropology
26	Anthropos
25	American Antiquity
23	L'Homme
22	Social Science Information
20	Anthropological Quarterly
20	Behavior Science Research
19	Behavior Analyst
19	Journal of Anthropological Archaeology
18	Social Forces
18	Social Science and Medicine
17	Comparative Studies in Society and History
16	American Behavioral Scientist
16	Ethnic and Racial Studies
16	Ethology and Sociobiology
15	American Journal of Sociology
15	American Sociological Review
15	Behavioral and Brain Sciences
12	American Psychologist
12	Anthropology and Education Quarterly
12	Ethos
12	Latin American Research Review
12	Mankind Quarterly
11	Human Nature: An Interdisciplinary Biosocial Perspective
11	Latin American Perspectives
11	Man in India
11	Plains Anthropologist
10	Annals of the Association of American Geographers
10	Journal of Social and Biological Structures
10	Journal of the History of the Behavioral Sciences
10	Kolner Zeitschrift fur Soziologie und Sozialpsychologie
10	Philosophy of the Social Sciences = Philosophie des sciences sociales
10	Science
9	American Historical Review
9	American Journal of Physical Anthropology
9	Journal of American History
9	Journal of the Royal Anthropological Institute
9	Perspectives in Biology and Medicine
9	Phylon
1–8	About 900 others

Document Types

2,217	Articles
312	Reviews (Including Review, Bibliography)
146	Book Reviews
80	Editorials (Including Editorial Material)
65	Notes
60	Letters
9	Discussions
4	Items about an Individual
1	Reprint
1	Abstract
1	News Item

Table 1.5 *(continued)*

Geographic Locations		Years		
1,960	U.S.A.	1972	52	
180	Canada	1973	48	
121	England	1974	65	
52	Australia	1975	78	
36	France	1976	76	
34	Germany	1977	85	
32	Federal Republic of Germany	1978	101	[rank 10 tied]
32	Netherlands	1979	107	[rank 8]
31	Israel	1980	111	[rank 6]
25	Brazil	1981	144	[rank 1]
24	Spain	1982	122	[rank 4]
21	India	1983	99	
18	Italy	1984	139	[rank 2]
15	New Zealand	1985	122	[rank 5]
15	South Africa	1986	130	[rank 3]
14	Norway	1987	98	
13	Scotland	1988	108	[rank 7]
12	Switzerland	1989	92	
11	Sweden	1990	91	
9	Belgium	1991	103	[rank 9]
9	Japan	1992	100	[rank 12]
8	Finland	1993	92	
7	Mexico	1994	101	[rank 10 tied]
7	Nigeria	1995	89	
6	South Korea	1996	75	
6	U.S.S.R.	1997	81	
6	Wales	1998	98	
5	Argentina	1999	87	
1–4	Removed 35 others (Armenia,	2000	98	
	Austria, Botswana, Chile,	2001	84	
	Colombia, Croatia, Denmark,	2002	20	[incomplete]
	Greece, Hong Kong,			
	Hungary, Iceland, Indonesia,			
	Iraq, Kenya, Macao,			
	Mozambique, Nepal, North			
	Ireland, Pakistan, Panama,			
	Papua New Guinea, Peoples			
	Republic of China, Peru,			
	Philippines, Poland,			
	Senegambia, Singapore,			
	Slovakia, Taiwan, Tanzania,			
	Thailand, Turkey, Uruguay,			
	Venezuela, Zambia)			

Table 1.5 *(continued)*

	Subjects
893	Anthropology
504	Sociology (327), Social Issues (36), Planning and Development (33), Demography (30), Family Studies (24), Urban Studies (19), Criminology and Penology (10), Rehabilitation (10), Social Work (10), Substance Abuse (5)
330	Psychology (112), Psychology, Social (45), Psychology, Clinical (40), Psychology, Experimental (36), Psychology, Developmental (25), Behavioral Sciences (19), Psychology, Applied (8), Psychology, Educational (5), Psychology, Biological (5), Psychology, Multidisciplinary (1), Psychology, Psychoanalysis (1), Psychology, Mathematical (1), Psychiatry (32)
236	History (177), History and Philosophy of Science (32), History of Social Sciences (27)
233	Social Sciences, Interdisciplinary (189), Social Sciences, Biomedical (39), Social Sciences, Mathematical Methods (5)
133	Area Studies (71), Ethnic Studies (51), Asian Studies (9), Oriental Studies (2)
114	Political Science (75), International Relations (33), Public Administration (6)
99	Environmental Studies (82), Ecology (9), Environmental Sciences (8)
88	Arts and Humanities (79), Art (7), Humanities, Multidisciplinary (2)
76	Archaeology
66	Medicine, General and Internal (12), Medicine, Research and Experimental (12), Neurosciences (14), Clinical Neurology (1) Nursing (7), Geriatrics and Gerontology (6), Endocrinology and Metabolism (4), Surgery (4), Obstetrics and Gynecology (2), Pharmacology and Pharmacy (2), Medicine, Legal (1), Cancer (1), Oncology (1), Toxicology (1)
65	Philosophy
62	Literature (24), Literary Reviews (14), Literature, Romance (9), Literature, African, Australian, Canadian (5), Literature, German, Netherlandic, Scandinavian (2), Literature, British Isles (2), Literature, American (2), Classics (4)
58	Business (30), Management (27), Business, Finance (1)
58	Education and Educational Research (54), Education, Special (4)
56	Economics
50	Law
49	Biology (39), Genetics and Heredity (9), Zoology (6), Botany (3), Bio-chemistry and Molecular Biology (2), Biotechnology and Applied Microbiology (2), Entomology (2), Cell Biology (1), Marine and Freshwater Biology (1), Physiology (1)
49	Geography
48	Religion
39	Multidisciplinary Sciences (including journals such as *Nature* or *Science*)
35	Information Science and Library Science, Computer Science, Cybernetics (4), Computer Science, Artificial Intelligence (1), Computer Science, Information Systems (1)
32	Public, Environmental, and Occupational Health (13), Public Health (12), Health Policy and Services (8)
27	Folklore
25	Language and Linguistics (22), Language and Linguistics Theory (2), Applied Linguistics (1)
23	Nutrition and Dietetics (17), Food Science and Technology (6)

Table 1.5 *(continued)*

	Subjects
20	Agriculture (5), Agricultural Economics and Policy (5), Dairy and Animal Science (3), Forestry (3), Plant Sciences (3), Veterinary Sciences (2), Veterinary Medicine (1) Fisheries (1)
17	Music
14	Women's Studies
12	Communication
6	Engineering (1), Engineering, Industrial (2), Aerospace Engineering and Technology (1), Engineering, Biomedical (1), Ergonomics (1)
5	Theater (3), Film, Radio, and Television (2)
4	Dentistry and Odontology (3), Dentistry, Oral Surgery, and Medicine (1)
4	Geology (3), Paleontology (1)
2	Physics (1), Nuclear Science and Technology (1)
1	Chemistry

fields such as biology and geology, applied fields such as medicine, engineering, and agriculture, and library and information science disciplines (to which we have both contributed Harris citations; in particular see Sandstrom and Sandstrom, 1995). The ubiquity of anthropological concepts such as "culture," "race," or "evolution" is due in large part to the efforts of Marvin Harris and to the thousands of scholars who have acknowledged his work and engaged his stimulating research strategy.

Anthropology at the Biting Edge of Controversy

Anthropologists have always engaged in critical self-appraisal about the status of their discipline and its relation to other fields. As Harris's fellow graduate student, Columbia University colleague, and frequent critic Robert Murphy noted:

> Modern cultural theory suffers from a diffuseness so great that it seems to subvert discourse within our scholarly community. Our theories range from sociobiology, at one extreme, through various kinds of materialism and old-fashioned functionalism to theories, at the other extreme, that locate the study of culture in language and meaning. One might hope that the protagonists of each doxology would illuminate our profession with constructive debate, but they speak past each other in a confusion of tongues; there is much talking but little dialogue. (Murphy, 1990:331)

Indeed, Harris wrote passionately, some say disparagingly, about research programs that are incommensurate, characterizing them as "ships that crash in the night" (Harris, 1991a). Harris noted that "anthropologists who carry out research in conformity with cultural materialist principles, to avoid controversy, often prefer not to label themselves as contributors to the cultural materialist corpus.

The unmarked influence of cultural materialism has been especially significant in American archaeology where, as one archaeologist has written: 'The principle of infrastructural determinism, of course, underlies modern archaeology, at least in North America' (Schiffer, 1983:191). An interest in cultural materialism among behavioral psychologists should also be noted" (Harris, 1991a:108–109).

We noted that Harris (1987d:517) referenced a forthcoming article, "Ships that crash in the night: Four paradigms," as "in press," due to be published in 1988 in the *American Anthropologist.* And yet the essay never came out in that flagship journal but instead appeared three years later as a chapter in an edited volume, *Perspectives on Behavioral Science: The Colorado Lectures* (see Harris, 1991a). The editor, Richard Jessor, a psychologist at the University of Colorado at Boulder, and director of the Institute of Behavioral Science, assembled a dozen essays on diverse issues ranging from ecology to metaphysics written by such luminaries as Herbert Simon and Noam Chomsky in order to explore the interdisciplinary boundaries and the promise of a unified behavioral science. Harris's erudite presentation, unlikely to have been widely read, characterized contemporary anthropology as a "complex and fractious collection of disciplines and subdisciplines" (1991a:70), which, at least within sociocultural anthropology and archaeology, offered no fewer than eight clashing paradigms based on distinctive epistemological and theoretical principles. He identified these as cultural materialism, cultural idealism, interpretive-phenomenological-postmodernist anthropology, postprocessualism, feminism, eclecticism, the new Marxist anthropology, and sociobiology. In a footnote (1991a:108, n.2), Harris cited approximately 50 empirical studies conducted within the cultural materialist research strategy.

Harris's monumental *The Rise of Anthropological Theory* (1968b) was the first extended articulation of the research strategy of cultural materialism and a partisan attempt (as he described it in retrospect) to outline a "specifically anthropological alternative to all forms of idealism, and to dialectical, Stalinist, and antipositivist as well as biological reductionist forms of materialism" (Harris, 1994:76). Harris complained (see Tavris, 1975:64) that professional anthropology journals in the U.S. ignored the book, even as the popular press and members of other disciplines took notice. Indeed, 170 reviews of Harris's books recorded as of November 2005 in the *Book Review Index* attest to the limited critical appraisal within anthropology of *The Rise of Anthropological Theory.* It was not reviewed by the *American Anthropologist* until six years after publication when a rather disjointed appraisal of it appeared. The review concluded, strangely, with the following: "Editor's note: This review's delay is not attributable to [the reviewer] Dr. Berger" (Berger, 1974:578). Journals and literary magazines that picked it up in a more timely fashion included *Atlantic Monthly, Science, Annals of the American Academy of Political and Social Science, American Sociological Review, American Historical Review,* and *Science and Society,* among others. To be fair, the journal *Man* in the United Kingdom reviewed it early on, and *Current Anthropology,* which many would argue is *the* scientific, four-field international anthropology journal of record, carried a timely "*CA* Book Review" treatment in which an international group of scholars from a variety of disciplines were invited to submit brief critiques based on prepublication copies of the book and a précis written by Harris (see Harris, 1968a). Of the 25 reviewers contacted, 16 responded in time for their comments to appear in the December 1968 issue. Criticize it they did, and Harris responded point by point with his usual incisive countercritique. One of the most timely, visible reviews appeared in the high-impact multidisciplinary journal *Science.* Written by historian George Stocking (1968:108), it gave the book an honest, "informational and critical" reading, and cast light on Harris's own polemical way of writing. Stocking accurately labeled the work "a historical brief for cultural materialism."

In 1991, the work was declared a "citation classic," having been referenced more than 685 times (see Harris [1991b] for his appraisal of its place in history). By late 2005, the book had become one of the most cited works by a contemporary anthropologist. According to the Web of Science, its citation count is approaching 900 in the mainstream journal literature. The number of references to it in books and other outlets cannot even be estimated. Harris's 1979 *Cultural Materialism: The Struggle for a Science of Culture* is also cited with remarkable frequency. That treatise has accrued a citation count of nearly 600 in journals across the spectrum of the sciences, social sciences, and humanities. Both of these books were reissued by AltaMira Press in 2001 just prior to Harris's death and included updated prefaces written by former students and colleagues. (The person responsible for this reissue was Mitchell Allen, AltaMira's founder and editor-in-chief, himself the holder of a Ph.D. in anthropological archaeology from Berkeley and an admirer of Harris.) The increased availability of these works to a new generation of scholars will likely stimulate interest in the cultural materialist research strategy.

Harris would probably have approved the following written by Murphy about his research program:

> Isaiah Berlin (1966) sorted career thinkers into two types: Foxes and Hedgehogs. The Foxes are people who have many ideas, folks like Clifford Geertz and myself. Our trouble is that after a while nobody knows where we stand, which only becomes a problem for us when they also no longer care. The Hedgehog, to the contrary, harbors only one idea, but it is a very BIG IDEA. This, of course, again describes Harris, who underwent a materialist Pentecost early in his career, which, in conjunction with his college behaviorism, became Cultural Materialism. He has stayed doggedly with this theory for 35 years, adding to it here and there, but never deviating one iota from its essential outlines. The theory, however, owes less to Karl Marx than to Jeremy Bentham, Adam Smith, and B. F. Skinner, and this may be why radical students in the 1970s and '80s turned instead to various types of Marxism—a movement already waning in the faddism that now besets our profession. (Murphy, 1990:331–332)

Harris himself consistently characterized cultural materialism as a Big Idea, whose scope spanned not only subdisciplines within anthropology, but the entire range of human history and social theory:

> Cultural materialism is a paradigm whose principles are relevant to the conduct of research and the development of theory in virtually all of the fields and subfields of anthropology.

Indeed, it has been guesstimated (Thomas, 1989:115) that half of the archaeologists in the United States consider themselves to be cultural materialist to some degree. For cultural materialists, whether they be cultural anthropologists, archaeologists, biological anthropologists, or linguists, the central intellectual experience is not ethnography but the exchange of data and theories among different fields and subfields concerned with the global, comparative, diachronic, and synchronic study of humankind: the origin of the hominids, the emergence of language and culture, the evolution of cultural differences and similarities, and the ways in which biocultural, mental, behavioral, demographic, environmental and other nomothetic processes have shaped and continue to shape the human world. (Harris, 1994:62)

Harris first laid out the key methodological requirements of cultural materialism as a coherent research strategy in 1968 in the concluding chapter of *The Rise*. He began with this passage in which he traced the closest antecedents to his formulation in Julian Steward's approach to cultural ecology:

The attempt to reconcile [Julian] Steward with [Leslie] White does not require further elaborations of a typology of evolutionism. The central question is to what extent the strategy employed by Steward corresponds to the cultural-materialist formulation which underlies White's evolutionary and energetistic pronouncements. It can be shown that Steward has led his contemporaries in actually applying cultural-materialist principles to the solution of concrete questions concerning cultural differences and similarities. Unlike White, Steward has sought to identify the material condition of sociocultural life in terms of the articulation between production processes and habitat. His cultural materialism resides in this pragmatic venture to which he himself gives the title "the method of cultural ecology." (Harris, 1968b:654)

Never deviating from his research program, Harris went on to comment that the production of cultural materialism itself requires an understanding of the economic forces that underlie different disciplinary traditions. The conscious association of cultural materialism with the natural sciences does not, as some social constructivists might argue, point to a deliberate attempt to deceive or persuade (e. g., Edge, 1979; Gilbert, 1977). Harris's observation simply points out that the search for nomothetic solutions to anthropological problems of significance requires authors to synthesize across and within disciplinary literatures. Our aim in this chapter is to trace whether Harris's cultural materialism does precisely that. As Harris stated:

Nothing would be more contrary to the general frame of reference advocated in this book than to explain the recent prominence of ecological studies as a result of Steward's personal influence. The mounting interest in techno-environmental and techno-economic relationships reflects a broad movement aimed at strengthening the scientific credentials of cultural anthropology within the prestigious and well-funded natural sciences. Cultural ecology, precisely because it links emic phenomena with the etic conditions of "nature" strengthens the association between social science and the "harder" disciplines. In a synchronic mode it thus promotes research involving cooperation with the general

medical sciences, biology, nutrition, demography, and agronomy, all of which enjoy high
levels of economic support. Applied diachronically, the ecological approach establishes
a similar set of ties between archaeology and numerous specialties within geology and
paleontology. The contemporary premium upon scientism thus makes the expansion of
cultural ecological research almost inevitable. (Harris, 1968b:655)

Through a logically consistent system of techno-demo-econo-environmental determinism, Harris sought to challenge the prevailing philosophical idealism of most
social theorists in favor of on-the-ground materialist explanations for every kind of
cultural phenomenon. Eric Wolf put it this way in his review of Harris's 1979 book
Cultural Materialism:

> The days are over when American anthropology was unified by a common concept of
> culture. Mentalists now battle the materialists for order of preference. The materialists
> cleave to the belief that human affairs are caused by the ways human beings cope with
> nature. . . . The mentalists, on the other hand, attract all those who believe in the primacy
> of Mind, who see humankind as spinning ever more complex webs of signification through
> autonomous process of the symbolic faculty. . . . Within this bimodal distribution of an-
> thropological stances, Marvin Harris is clearly King of the Peak of Materialism. King of
> the rival Mentalist Mountain is probably *le maître* Claude Lévi-Strauss who holds that it
> is thought which possesses men, rather than men possessing thought. (Wolf, 1982:148)

In his discussion of the causes of cultural similarities and differences, and due in
part to the sheer volume and range of the puzzling aspects of culture that he addressed,
Harris was at odds with most of his more narrowly focused colleagues. Harris offended
anthropologists whose works failed to transcend idiographic description or particularistic
causal analysis or who steered clear of generalizing theories. Harris consistently maintained
that, "Although I seek to be objective about rival paradigms, the grounds of objectivity are themselves relative to the categorizations, puzzles (*problematiques*), and basic
principles of one's own paradigmatic commitments (whether coherent and conscious,
or incoherent and unconscious)" (1991a:70). For Harris, the harm of eclecticism, which
others tended to equate with open-mindedness, was that it robbed anthropology of its
ability to identify causal factors in human social life. In eclecticism "causal priorities shift
from infrastructure to structure or superstructure relative to the society or topic being
studied, or . . . all the components of sociocultural systems—infrastructure, structure,
and superstructure—are simultaneously and equally determinative of differences and
similarities" (1991a:86). Anthropologists of all persuasions as well as scholars from other
fields rose to defend their programs against Harris. The debates became heated and raged
throughout the discipline and beyond, and they continue still. Through it all Harris
stood his ground and defended his position with wit and alacrity.

Harris often wrote that the role of the anthropologist was to solve the riddles or puzzles
of culture. His way of approaching the discipline flew in the face of scholars who spent
their time writing increasingly elaborate interpretations of cultural phenomena farther and
farther removed from the empirical world. It was philosopher of science Thomas Kuhn
(1970) who emphasized the puzzle-solving nature of scientific inquiry, and it was Harris's

intent to align anthropology with science by advocating that orientation to the work of the discipline. However, some anthropologists attacked Harris for the very range of topics ("trivial sociocultural phenomena") he addressed and claimed that he took a "defensive approach to problem selection" by jumping from puzzle to puzzle, which "dissipates the energy of cultural materialists and stultifies the development of substantive laws and theories" (Schiffer 1983:192). Harris said (in a personal communication in 1985 to Alan Sandstrom), that the most difficult task for cultural materialists was to draw connections between cause and effect. People rarely see cultural phenomena (trivial or otherwise) as subject to causation and are often surprised when the causative arrow is identified. Thus, for example, in his 1981 book, *America Now: The Anthropology of a Changing Culture,* Harris took pleasure in pointing out the causal connections among seemingly unrelated phenomena such as women's liberation, surly clerks, gays coming out of the closet, and reduced family size in the United States. Harris told Sandstrom that he expended his effort in identifying causative models so that other scholars could follow up and provide better empirical verification and refinement of them. Many of the essays in the present volume attest to the consistency and internal validity of Harris's research strategy.

Harris was himself a consummate boundary spanner in his personal use of the literature. He drew from a remarkable range of works belonging to different time periods and disciplinary perspectives. The breadth of his coverage can be observed in the 1,200+ cited references in *The Rise,* and in his bibliographies in subsequent works as well. Harris cannot be accused of ceremonial citation. On the contrary, he closely followed the arguments of those he cited and then, to the dismay or delight of his readers, used their words to hoist them on their own petard. The impact of this confrontational style and its role in marginalizing Harris was noted by a reviewer who compared Harris to B. F. Skinner:

> Both have been viewed as outside the mainstream of their respective fields. One difference is that Harris frequently cites his critics and opponents at length … whereas Skinner's publications are characterized by especially sparse reference lists.… Given the greater likelihood that authors read articles in which they are cited, it seems likely that Harris makes contact with a broader spectrum of anthropologists than do behavior analysts with mainstream psychologists. (Lloyd, 1985:281)

Harris was a force to be dealt with. The patterns of citation to and from other authors and the descriptive language associated with Harris's body of work reveal the remarkable scope of his comparative scientific research program.

Conclusion

What can we conclude from these intriguing portraits? Can we state that there is a distinctive school of cultural materialism, or address the claim by Harris detractors that he has not been widely influential? We do suspect that cultural materialism as a research strategy has not yet achieved the status of a school with a distinctive citing circle. Harris may enjoy less of a visible following precisely because the approach he has developed demands such wide-ranging, boundary spanning research—a costly and exhausting strategy for any scholar. The risk of being innovative in an interdisciplinary context is that one's innovations marginalize a scholar from easy identification with a constituency. Harris was aggressive and delighted in undermining anthropology's uncritical acceptance of philosophical idealism and atheoretical particularism. Only the brave or the politically naïve would call themselves cultural materialists, and Harris often shredded the arguments of his supporters with the same incisive vigor as those of his enemies.

Judging from citations of his work, Harris was a pervasive force in all subfields of anthropology and outside of the discipline. A lot of the attention comes from his detractors. He has truly been defined as much by adversaries as by supporters, and both show him as a significant force to be dealt with. This fact in itself is surely one definition of influence. We believe we have demonstrated that Harris's contribution to modern social theory is far from invisible or inconsequential. Harris's role has been to clarify confusing concepts and research perspectives, and to move the entire discipline of anthropology in the direction of empirical science—no small accomplishment.

Appendix: Marvin Harris's Citation Image in Focus

Co-Citees		Affinity for CM, Disciplinary or Specialty Affiliations
2,679	Harris, Marvin	
463	Sahlins, Marshall D	(–) anthropology, ethnology, French structuralism, Oceania
329	Geertz, Clifford	(–) anthropology, ethnology, symbolism, Islam
315	Lévi-Strauss, Claude	(–) anthropology, French structuralism, symbolism, South America
278	Murdock, George Peter	(*) anthropology, ethnology
275	Steward, Julian H	(*) anthropology, cultural ecology, South America
267	White, Leslie A	(*) anthropology, ethnology, cultural ecology
227	Divale, William T	(+) anthropology, Harris coauthor
227	Wolf, Eric R	(+) anthropology, history, ethnology, Europe
215	Chagnon, Napoleon A	(–) anthropology, sociobiology, Venezuela
214	Rappaport, Roy A	(+) anthropology, cultural ecology, New Guinea
213	Marx, Karl	(*) political economy
211	Kroeber, Alfred Louis	(*) anthropology
206	Lee, Richard B	(+) anthropology, cultural ecology, Africa
201	Mead, Margaret	(*) anthropology, ethnology, Polynesia
201	Service, Elman R	(–) anthropology, ethnology
199	Leach, Edmund R	(–) anthropology, ethnology, political anthropology, South Asia
194	Carneiro, Robert L	(+) anthropology, ethnology, cultural ecology, Brazil
191	Malinowski, Bronislaw	(*) anthropology, ethnology, Oceania

	Co-Citees	Affinity for CM, Disciplinary or Specialty Affiliations
184	Douglas, Mary T	(−) anthropology, ethnology, symbolism, religion
183	Wilson, Edward O	(−) biology, sociobiology
179	Fried, Morton H	(+) anthropology, ethnology, China, Harris co-editor
173	Vayda, Andrew P	(−) anthropology, cultural ecology
161	Weber, Max	(*) sociology, political economy
156	Boas, Franz	(*) anthropology, ethnology
151	Durkheim, Emile	(*) sociology
145	Barth, Fredrik	anthropology, ethnology, Pakistan
145	Wagley, Charles	(+) anthropology, ethnology, Brazil, Harris coauthor
142	Van den Berghe, Pierre L	(−) sociology, sociobiology, ethnology, Mesoamerica
141	Stocking, George W	history of anthropology
140	Evans-Pritchard, E E	(*) anthropology, Africa
139	Gould, Stephen Jay	(−) biology, paleontology, evolutionary biology
136	Kuhn, Thomas S	philosophy, history of science
132	Binford, Lewis R	archaeology, Mesopotamia, Mexico
132	Radcliffe-Brown, A R	(*) anthropology, Indian Ocean
131	Boserup, Ester	anthropology, economics
131	Lowie, Robert H	(*) anthropology, North America
129	Parsons, Talcott	(*) sociology
125	Goody, Jack (John R)	anthropology, ethnology, Africa
125	Trivers, Robert L	(−) biology, evolutionary biology, sociobiology
123	Dawkins, Richard	biology, ethology, sociobiology
122	Alexander, Richard D	biology, zoology, sociobiology
118	Naroll, Raoul S	anthropology, methodology
115	Benedict, Ruth F	(*) anthropology, ethnology, culture and personality
115	Wallace, Anthony F C	anthropology, ethnology, religion, culture and personality
113	Durham, William H	(−) biology, ecology, evolutionary culture theory
113	Johnson, Allen W	(+) anthropology, cultural ecology, methodology
113	Montagu, M F Ashley	physical anthropology
112	Goodenough, Ward H	(−) anthropology, linguistics, ethnoscience, Melanesia
111	Firth, Raymond W	anthropology, ethnology, economics, Oceania
111	Flannery, Kent V	archaeology, Mesoamerica
111	Godelier, Maurice	(−) anthropology, structural Marxism, ethnology, Melanesia
110	Gross, Daniel R	anthropology, economics, religion
110	Herskovits, Melville J	anthropology, ethnology, Africa
110	Murphy, Robert F	(−) anthropology, economics, ethnology, Brazil
110	Turner, Victor W	anthropology, religion, ethnology, Africa
110	Tylor, Edward Burnett	(*) anthropology
109	Bourdieu, Pierre	sociology, philosophy
108	Childe, V Gordon	(*) archaeology, prehistory, Europe
107	Freud, Sigmund	(*) psychology, psychoanalysis

	Co-Citees	Affinity for CM, Disciplinary or Specialty Affiliations	
106	Engels, Friedrich	(*)	political economy
106	Keesing, Roger M	(−)	anthropology, Oceania
104	Darwin, Charles	(*)	biology, evolution
104	Friedman, Jonathan	(−)	anthropology, Marxism
103	Trigger, Bruce G		archaeology, ethnohistory, North America
101	Foucault, Michel	(−)	philosophy
98	Harner, Michael J	(+)	anthropology, Aztec sacrifice
97	Foster, George M	(−)	anthropology, Mexico
97	Netting, Robert M		anthropology, cultural ecology, Africa
96	Cavalli-Sforza, Luigi L		biology, population genetics, sociobiology
94	Ross, Eric B	(+)	anthropology, cultural ecology, Harris coauthor
93	Kluckhohn, Clyde	(*)	anthropology, culture and personality, Navajo
92	Lorenz, Konrad Z	(−)	biology, zoology, ornithology, ethology
91	Campbell, Donald T		psychology, social psychology, methodology
91	Leacock, Eleanor B		anthropology, Marxism, sex roles
91	Lewis, Oscar	(−)	anthropology, culture and personality, Mexico
90	Popper, Karl R	(−)	philosophy of science
89	Giddens, Anthony		sociology, structuration
89	Levine, Robert A		anthropology, Africa
89	Morgan, Lewis Henry	(*)	anthropology, ethnology
89	Wallerstein, Immanuel		sociology, world-systems
87	Hymes, Dell		linguistics, North America
85	Degler, Carl N		history, race, slavery
85	Fortes, Meyer	(*)	anthropology, Africa
85	Mauss, Marcel	(*)	sociology, ethnology
84	Bennett, John W		anthropology, economic anthropology, cultural ecology
84	Lenski, Gerhard E		sociology, sociobiology
84	Whiting, John W M	(+)	anthropology, ethnology, culture and personality
83	Adams, Richard N	(+)	anthropology, cultural ecology, Latin America
83	Alland, Alexander, Jr.		physical anthropology, medical anthropology, race
83	Fox, Robin		anthropology, sociobiology
82	Boyd, Robert		biology, cultural evolution
81	Lewontin, Richard C		biology, evolutionary biology, genetics
80	Lumsden, Charles J		biology, sociobiology
80	Otterbein, Keith F		anthropology, warfare
79	Bateson, Gregory	(*)	anthropology, ethnology, psychiatry
79	Goffman, Erving	(*)	sociology, communication
79	Hamilton, W D		biology, evolutionary biology, sociobiology, kin selection
77	Bloch, Maurice	(−)	anthropology, structural Marxism, Africa
77	Mayr, Ernst		biology, evolutionary biology, ornithology
77	Ortner, Sherry B	(−)	anthropology, Himalayas
77	Redfield, Robert	(*)	anthropology, Mexico

	Co-Citees		Affinity for CM, Disciplinary or Specialty Affiliations
106	Engels, Friedrich	(*)	political economy
106	Keesing, Roger M	(–)	anthropology, Oceania
104	Darwin, Charles	(*)	biology, evolution
104	Friedman, Jonathan	(–)	anthropology, Marxism
103	Trigger, Bruce G		archaeology, ethnohistory, North America
101	Foucault, Michel	(–)	philosophy
98	Harner, Michael J	(+)	anthropology, Aztec sacrifice
97	Foster, George M	(–)	anthropology, Mexico
97	Netting, Robert M		anthropology, cultural ecology, Africa
96	Cavalli-Sforza, Luigi L		biology, population genetics, sociobiology
94	Ross, Eric B	(+)	anthropology, cultural ecology, Harris coauthor
93	Kluckhohn, Clyde	(*)	anthropology, culture and personality, Navajo
92	Lorenz, Konrad Z	(–)	biology, zoology, ornithology, ethology
91	Campbell, Donald T		psychology, social psychology, methodology
91	Leacock, Eleanor B		anthropology, Marxism, sex roles
91	Lewis, Oscar	(–)	anthropology, culture and personality, Mexico
90	Popper, Karl R	(–)	philosophy of science
89	Giddens, Anthony		sociology, structuration
89	Levine, Robert A		anthropology, Africa
89	Morgan, Lewis Henry	(*)	anthropology, ethnology
89	Wallerstein, Immanuel		sociology, world-systems
87	Hymes, Dell		linguistics, North America
85	Degler, Carl N		history, race, slavery
85	Fortes, Meyer	(*)	anthropology, Africa
85	Mauss, Marcel	(*)	sociology, ethnology
84	Bennett, John W		anthropology, economic anthropology, cultural ecology
84	Lenski, Gerhard E		sociology, sociobiology
84	Whiting, John W M	(+)	anthropology, ethnology, culture and personality
83	Adams, Richard N	(+)	anthropology, cultural ecology, Latin America
83	Alland, Alexander, Jr.		physical anthropology, medical anthropology, race
83	Fox, Robin		anthropology, sociobiology
82	Boyd, Robert		biology, cultural evolution
81	Lewontin, Richard C		biology, evolutionary biology, genetics
80	Lumsden, Charles J		biology, sociobiology
80	Otterbein, Keith F		anthropology, warfare
79	Bateson, Gregory	(*)	anthropology, ethnology, psychiatry
79	Goffman, Erving	(*)	sociology, communication
79	Hamilton, W D		biology, evolutionary biology, sociobiology, kin selection
77	Bloch, Maurice	(–)	anthropology, structural Marxism, Africa
77	Mayr, Ernst		biology, evolutionary biology, ornithology
77	Ortner, Sherry B	(–)	anthropology, Himalayas
77	Redfield, Robert	(*)	anthropology, Mexico

	Co-Citees		Affinity for CM, Disciplinary or Specialty Affiliations
59	Linton, Ralph	(*)	anthropology
59	Piaget, Jean	(*)	psychology
59	Whiting, Beatrice B	(+)	anthropology, psychology
58	Winterhalder, Bruce P	(+)	anthropology, behavioral ecology
57	Barkow, Jerome H		anthropology, evolutionary psychology
57	Gluckman, Max		anthropology, conflict theory
57	Sapir, Edward	(−)	linguistics, anthropology
56	Brown, Paula		anthropology, Oceania
55	Driver, Harold E		anthropology, ethnology, North America
55	Hobsbawm, Eric J		history, Marxism
55	Tyler, Stephen A	(−)	anthropology, linguistics
54	Frake, Charles O	(−)	anthropology, linguistics, ethnoscience
54	Freeman, Derek	(−)	anthropology, Polynesia
54	Williams, Raymond		literary criticism, Marxism, cultural materialism
53	Diamond, Stanley		anthropology
53	Fernandes, Florestan		anthropology
53	Hill, Kim R		anthropology, behavioral ecology
53	US Bureau of the Census		
52	Dumont, Louis	(−)	anthropology, India
52	Frazer, James G	(*)	anthropology
52	Myrdal, Gunnar	(*)	economics
52	Park, Robert E	(*)	sociology
51	Barry, Herbert		anthropology, methodology
51	Berlin, Brent	(−)	anthropology, ethnoscience
51	Freyre, Gilberto		anthropology, Brazil
51	Hardin, Garrett		biology, human ecology
51	Hawkes, Kristen		anthropology, behavioral ecology
51	Kottak, Conrad P	(+)	anthropology, cultural ecology, Harris coauthor
51	Wittfogel, Karl A	(+)	history, Marxism, China
50	Cohen, Abner		anthropology, Africa
50	Dalton, George	(−)	economics, economic anthropology
50	Goldschmidt, Walter R		anthropology, economic anthropology
50	Henry, Jules		anthropology, South America
50	Hrdy, Sarah Blaffer		anthropology, sociobiology
50	Neel, James V		medicine, genetics, South America
50	Sauer, Carl O	(*)	geography, Mexico, Caribbean
1–49	About 64,390 others		

Note: A plus sign (+) indicates a contemporary of Marvin Harris who has written in support of cultural materialism (CM), while a minus sign (−) indicates a detractor or someone Harris attacked in print. An asterisk (*) designates a field's founding figures. See text for further explanation.

Acknowledgments

We would like to thank Philip Johnson at Indiana University–Purdue University Fort Wayne (IPFW) for writing the Java programs to transform cited reference data into cited author data and create the ranked distributions for these CAMEO profiles. We also acknowledge the assistance of IPFW Document Delivery Services staff members Christine Smith, Shannon Johnson, and Graham Fredrick in obtaining copies of the writings of Marvin Harris from far and wide. We owe the greatest debt to our spouses, Alan R. Sandstrom and Maryellen McDonald, for generously sharing their insight, time, and patience, and we dedicate this work to Maryellen's memory.

Chapter Two

The Theoretical Legacies of Cultural Materialism and Marvin Harris

James Lett

Cultural materialism has many virtues, foremost among them its explicit appeal to the epistemology of science, but the paradigm is fundamentally flawed in ways that severely limit its usefulness as a guideline for future anthropological research and analysis. When anthropology finally emerges as a mature scientific discipline (one devoted exclusively to discovering *facts* and generating *theories* in the genuine scientific senses of the terms), the theoretical principles of cultural materialism will not play a major role. On the other hand, Marvin Harris was a proponent of several essential propositions that can serve as a blueprint for the construction of a mature science of anthropology. The legacy of cultural materialism will be distinct from the legacy of Marvin Harris.

The Legacy of Cultural Materialism

There are several fundamental difficulties with the paradigm of cultural materialism, as various critics have pointed out (Robarchek, 1989; Barkow, Cosmides, and Tooby, 1992; Magnarella, 1993; Sperber, 1996; O'Meara, 1997; Lett, 1997), but let me mention just four interrelated problems that seem to be especially damaging.

Problem 1: Cultural materialism is based upon a form of functionalism that lacks genuine explanatory power. As Barkow, Cosmides, and Tooby (1992:625) explain, cultural materialism is based upon a "present-oriented" or "future-oriented" form of functionalism that seeks to account for any particular phenomenon by asking, "How is it explained by the utility of its consequences?"—a question that makes the fundamental error of placing the consequence before the cause. Given that "causal explanations must necessarily focus on antecedent conditions," it follows that the "consequences of a phenomenon can be neither the cause of the phenomenon nor its explanation" (Barkow, Cosmides, and Tooby, 1992:625). The only form of functionalism that is tenable is a "past-oriented" form of functionalism, such as that found in evolutionary theory: "Darwin's theory of natural selection provides an explanation of how functional design can emerge from a nonforesightful causal process ... [based on the notion that] a design feature's functional consequences *in earlier generations* explain its presence in this one" (Barkow, Cosmides, and Tooby, 1992:625).

Even if Harris's Principle of Infrastructural Determinism claimed only to account for the *persistence* of cultural traits rather than their *emergence,* it would still lack explanatory power, because, unlike the principle of natural selection, it fails to identify a *feedback mechanism* with sufficient selective power to accomplish the task that is purportedly accomplished (Sperber, 1996:47–48). What, for example, is the feedback mechanism between a superstructural element such as religion and an infrastructural element such as the mode of production that is comparable to the feedback mechanism between protective coloration and reproductive success in a biological organism? There is a fundamental reason cultural materialism cannot provide a satisfactory answer to this question: Protective coloration and reproductive success are material phenomena, whereas religion and the mode of production are abstractions—which illustrates a second fundamental problem facing the paradigm.

Problem 2: Cultural materialism is not based upon an ontology of materialism. As Sperber (1996:10) observes, "Ontological questions have practical implications for anthropological research," and they include such questions as "what kinds of things are cultural things?" and "how do cultural things fit into the world and how do they relate to things other sciences are about?" He maintains that anthropology lacks well-developed answers to these questions, and that the paradigm of cultural materialism is no exception: "The difference between self-proclaimed materialists and those whom they accuse of idealism is that 'materialists' see representations [such as 'belief,' 'culture,' or 'superstructure'] more as *effects* of material conditions, while 'idealists' see them more as *causes* of material conditions" (Sperber, 1996:64). It does not matter in which direction the causal arrows are said to point—the problem is that both "materialists" and "idealists" imagine that material and nonmaterial "things" enter into causal relationships with one another, and that simply cannot occur. According to the ontology of materialism (as opposed to the ontology of dualism, for example), *everything* is material, including religious beliefs and modes of production. "From a truly materialist point of view," Sperber (1996:11) observes, "effects cannot be less material than their causes."

Cultural materialists are aware of this criticism, but the response they have offered is indicative of the ontological confusion inherent in their paradigm. Rather than describe the infrastructure, structure, and superstructure as material entities with material connections, cultural materialists maintain that cultural things are *both* material and nonmaterial: "[T]he identification and analysis of empirical (physical) but abstract, superorganic entities is a necessary and feasible component of sociocultural science" (Harris, 1997a:412). "[E]ven though some cultural things cannot be touched or seen," Harris argues (1999b:52), "they are nonetheless real." But what does "real" mean in this context? Harris (1999b:53) maintains that "as long as the model is constructed on an identifiable physical base and is built up according to explicit logical and empirical steps, it can lay claim to having a physical reality." This is hardly what "physical reality" means in the natural sciences, and it is hardly an unambiguous answer to the questions posed by Sperber and other critics of cultural materialism: *What kinds of things are cultural things, how do they fit into the world, and how do they relate to the things studied by other scientific disciplines?* The fact that cultural materialism is not based on an ontology of materialism leads directly to another fundamental problem: The paradigm cannot hope to identify causal forces, because "everything that has causal powers owes those powers exclusively to its physical properties" (Sperber, 1996:10).

Problem 3: Cultural materialism's causal principle (i.e., infrastructural determinism) does not identify agents or forces that have genuine causal power. Among anthropologists, Tim O'Meara (1997, 2001) is the scholar most responsible for developing this argument. Following the philosopher of science Wesley Salmon (1984), O'Meara (1997:405) "distinguishes 'causal processes' such as baseballs, windowpanes, and electromagnetic fields, which have causal efficacy in themselves, from 'pseudo processes' such as shadows and spots of light, which do not." He argues that "superorganic" entities (such as infrastructures, structures, and superstructures) are pseudo processes; they cannot possibly have causal efficacy because they are not physical entities. Bloch and Sperber (2002:727) concur on this point. In a recent article, they argue that nonphysical phenomena do not "possess causal powers" and that only "material events . . . can be invoked as causes and effects in naturalistic causal explanations." According to O'Meara, "Explanations of human affairs [such as those generated by cultural materialism] are necessarily faulty if they assert or imply that supraindividual or otherwise superphysical patterns or entities have causal efficacy in themselves"; instead, he argues, legitimate explanations of human affairs must be "limited to causal-mechanical explanations of the operations and interactions among individual human beings and other physical entities" (1997:408). Robarchek (1989:904) made this same point earlier when he argued that "any factor purported to have causal efficacy must in some way articulate with human motivational complexes if it is to find behavioral expression . . . [and that any] theoretical formulation that purports to offer a causal explanation of human behavior in terms of some extrinsic factor must explicitly specify the mode of this articulation."

O'Meara does not deny that cultural materialism identifies useful correlations among different types of events (such as the correlations between modes of production and forms of religious organization). Such correlations, however, are not indications of causal relationships. "Patterns of behavioral events in human affairs are not laws that 'determine' individual behaviors or their aggregates," O'Meara (1997:406) explains; instead, those patterns are simply "clues to the causal-mechanical properties of humans and their constituent parts." Identifying those causal-mechanical properties of humans entails identifying the evolved features of human minds and bodies, and those features have a physical reality in human anatomy and physiology. Thus, O'Meara (1997:410) concludes, "If only physical entities have causal efficacy by virtue only of their physical properties, then 'objective' or 'empirical' science literally means 'physical' science."

Many scholars have observed that the natural or "physical" sciences, unlike the social sciences, have achieved a high degree of mutual consistency, interconnectedness, and explanatory power stemming from a shared set of ontological and epistemological assumptions (Tooby and Cosmides, 1992:19; Sperber, 1996:10; Wilson, 1998:49–71). By insisting that its subject matter is unique to the social sciences, cultural materialism refuses to embrace that entire set of ontological and epistemological assumptions characteristic of the natural sciences, and it separates itself from the possibility of complete integration with the more successful fields of scientific inquiry. This reflects a fourth fundamental problem with the paradigm.

Problem 4: Cultural materialism is insufficiently grounded in biological evolution. The evolutionary processes that produced human beings are the same processes that have shaped the morphology, physiology, and behavior of all organisms on the planet. Thus understanding the selective forces that shaped human evolution is essential for understanding human nature—and understanding human nature is essential for understanding why humans behave the way they do (Boyd and Silk, 2000). Cultural materialism largely ignores the specifics of human nature and the details of human evolution. Instead, cultural materialism is content to posit the existence of four "biopsychological constants:" humans need to eat, they prefer to minimize the amount of work they have to do, they enjoy sexual intercourse, and they seek to increase the love and affection that others offer them (Harris, 1979:62–63).

In comparison to the expansive list of human universals identified by the newly emergent paradigm of evolutionary psychology (Brown, 1991; Barkow, Cosmides, and Tooby, 1992; Buss, 1999), the list suggested by cultural materialism is strikingly incomplete. Cultural materialism's raison d'etre is to explain the reasons for the similarities and differences among the world's cultures, but when it attempts to explain human universals without reference to the evolved details of human nature, it is doomed to failure. The Principle of Infrastructural Determinism will not explain, for example, the universality of violent male sexual jealousy, nor will it explain the fact that, on average, husbands are older than their wives in every society in the world. These human universals can only be explained by a shared human nature, and that shared human nature can only be explained by the evolutionary forces that shaped it.

Marvin Harris explicitly rejected the "neo-Darwinism" of evolutionary psychology; in the Boasian tradition, he remained "opposed to the application of these bioevolutionary principles to culture," and he continued to regard culture as a distinct ontological realm that must be understood in its own unique terms (Harris, 1999b:106). That was his major mistake. As Donald Brown (1991:6) convincingly demonstrates in his book *Human Universals,* "human biology *is* a key to understanding many human universals." Lacking sufficient "conceptual integration" with the biological sciences, cultural materialism cannot hope to achieve the same level of success enjoyed in the various disciplines of the natural sciences. The laws of chemistry may not be reducible to the laws of physics, but they are compatible with them; that degree of mutual consistency is characteristic of all the natural sciences, and it is largely responsible for their unparalleled success (Cosmides, Tooby, and Barkow, 1992:4). By declaring its subject matter to be a separate ontological domain, cultural materialism removes itself from the possibility of "consilience" with other realms of scientific knowledge. This is a fatal error, because Wilson (1998:53) is undoubtedly correct in observing that the "explanations of different phenomena most likely to survive are those that can be connected and proved consistent with one another."

Tooby and Cosmides (1992:23) describe the set of assumptions underlying cultural materialism as the "Standard Social Science Model," and they argue convincingly that this model "suffers from a series of major defects that make it a profoundly misleading framework." More than a decade ago, Marvin Harris (1994) asserted that "cultural materialism is alive and well and won't go away until something better comes along." Fair enough: Something better *has* come along. It's called evolutionary psychology, and it takes an epidemiological rather than a superorganic approach to culture (see Bloch and Sperber, 2002). It conceives of sociocultural phenomena as "ecological patterns of psychological phenomena" (Sperber, 1996:31), and the psychological phenomena to which it refers are the universal cognitive mechanisms shaped by human evolution. Cultural materialism was a brave, ingenious, and well-intentioned effort to achieve an objective understanding of sociocultural systems, but it will be supplanted by paradigms that apply the ontology of materialism and the epistemology of science more consistently, more thoroughly, and more productively.

The Legacy of Marvin Harris

Nevertheless, if Marvin Harris was wrong on several of the particulars about the best way to approach understanding and explanation in anthropology, he was right on virtually all of the principles. The work of Marvin Harris embodies at least six propositions that will prove to be of lasting value for anthropology.

Proposition 1: Anthropology should be thoroughly and exclusively grounded in the epistemology of science. Marvin Harris was not the first anthropologist to maintain this proposition (see White, 1949; Steward, 1955; Dole and Carneiro, 1960), but in the second half of the twentieth century he was its foremost proponent (at least among cultural anthropologists). The necessity of a scientific foundation for anthropology was the central theme of what was probably his most important book, *The Rise of Anthropological Theory* (Harris, 1968b), and it was the explicit goal of what was perhaps his second most important book, *Cultural Materialism* (Harris, 1979). *Cultural Materialism* is subtitled *The Struggle for a Science of Culture,* and that phrase aptly summarizes Harris's lifelong ambition.

Even if Harris made some errors when he applied the epistemology and ontology of science to cultural materialism, as various critics have alleged (e.g., Lett, 1990; Sperber, 1996; O'Meara, 1997), the definition of science that he propounded throughout his career was fundamentally sound. For Harris (1979:27), science was "an epistemology which seeks to restrict fields of inquiry to events, entities, and relationships that are knowable by means of explicit, logico-empirical, inductive-deductive, quantifiable public procedures or 'operations' subject to replication by independent observers." There are many other ways of expressing these essential ideas, of course (e.g., O'Meara, 1989; Lett, 1996), but the influence of Marvin Harris's conceptions (if not his exact phraseology) can be readily discerned in the work of most contemporary cultural anthropologists who identify themselves as scientific anthropologists (e.g., Gellner, 1988; Sangren, 1988; Appell, 1989; O'Meara, 1989; Reyna, 1994; Carneiro, 1995; D'Andrade, 1995a; Murphy and Margolis, 1995; Cerroni-Long, 1996; Spiro, 1996; Kuznar, 1997; Lett, 1997; Cronk, 1999).

Harris believed that anthropology would be irrelevant if it was not scientific, and he was right. In the Distinguished Lecture he delivered to the American Anthropological Association at its annual meeting in 1991, he reflected upon the unanticipated and revolutionary collapse of state communism in Europe in the late 1980s and early 1990s: "What do anthropologists have to say about all this? A branch of the human sciences that ignores these immense events, that interprets them exclusively in terms of relativized 'local knowledge,' or that derides the attempt to understand them in terms of nomothetic principles runs the risk of being confined to the backwaters of contemporary intellectual life" (Harris, 1992:295). It speaks well for anthropology that Marvin Harris enjoys many supporters on this point. Spiro (1986:278), for example, poses this pointed question: "For if, in principle, ethnographic studies ... can only contribute to unique understandings of this or that belief or custom or this or that primitive or peasant culture in all of its particularity, *what possible intellectual relevance might such studies have?*" (emphasis added). In the same vein, D'Andrade (1995a:4) observes that "anthropology without science is not much," and Carneiro (1995:14) comes to a similar conclusion: "For it is here, in ethnology, that broad theories are built and generalizations crafted; where the major questions of anthropology are asked and answered....What have postmodernists contributed to these great problems? Nothing." The problem with anthropology, Harris (1991a:83–84) was fond of saying, "is not that we have had too much of positivist social science but that we have had too little." He was right again.

Proposition 2: Anthropology should be resolute and resourceful in responding to competitive approaches based on irrationality, pseudoscience, and/or antiscience. Marvin Harris was a persistent and powerful critic of "obscurantism," the term he applied to the common set of assumptions underlying "astrology, witchcraft, messianism, hippiedom, fundamentalism, cults of personality, nationalism, ethnocentrism, and a hundred other contemporary modes of thought that exalt knowledge gained by inspiration, revelation, intuition, faith, or incantation as against knowledge obtained in conformity with scientific research principles" (Harris, 1979:316). He forcefully rebutted the challenge posed to scientific knowledge by Carlos Castaneda's Don Juan fantasies (Harris, 1979:319–324), and he warned about the moral and political dangers inherent in the rising tide of Evangelical Protestantism and other religious movements in the United States in the second half of the twentieth century (Harris, 1987a:141–165). Harris was unhesitant in confronting the errors of "ethnomania," or the irrational tendency of each racial and ethnic group "to pay far more attention to its own origins, history, heroism, suffering, and achievements than to those of other racial and ethnic groups" (Harris, 1999b:111), and he took great trouble to expose the myriad fallacies and shortcomings inherent in the antiscience of postmodernism (e.g., Harris, 1995b, 1999b:153–160).

Proposition 3: Anthropology should be a holistic discipline that integrates the methods and findings of the four subfields of archaeological anthropology, biological anthropology, cultural anthropology, and linguistic anthropology. In the later stages of his career, Harris (1994:62) opened one of his essays with a comment that expressed a long-held conviction: "At the outset, I wish to disassociate myself from the impression, sometimes carelessly and sometimes deliberately conveyed, that anthropology can be equated with cultural anthropology, or much less, with ethnography." He proceeded to argue that the strength of anthropology lay in the fact that cultural anthropologists, archaeologists, biological anthropologists, and linguists were involved in a collaborative effort to understand a wide range of interrelated problems, including "the origin of the hominids, the emergence of language and culture, [and] the evolution of cultural differences and similarities" (Harris, 1994:62). Harris's commitment to holism in anthropology was genuine and deep (Harris, 1997a). He was the author of a four-field introductory textbook, *Culture, People, Nature,* that was in its seventh edition at the time of his death (Harris, 1997b), and he served as President of the General Anthropology Division of the American Anthropological Association.

Proposition 4: Anthropology should be a discipline whose practitioners communicate in language that is clear, direct, intelligible, and unambiguous. Harris had no patience with sloppy, inexact, or pretentious writing. He was especially impatient with the typical writing style of postmodern anthropologists: "Their neobaroque prose style—with its inner clauses, bracketed syllables, metaphors and metonyms, verbal pirouettes, curlicues and filigrees—is not a mere epiphenomenon; rather, it is a mocking rejoinder to anyone who would try to write simple intelligible sentences in the modernist tradition" (Harris, 1999b:156–157). With the principal exception of *The Nature of Cultural Things,* which he published early in his career (Harris, 1964a), Harris almost always achieved his goal of writing simple intelligible sentences. You may not have agreed with what he said and you may not have liked him for having said it, but you rarely had trouble understanding what he meant to say.

Proposition 5: Anthropology should be a discipline whose practitioners reach out beyond the academy to communicate anthropological knowledge, perspectives, and insights to the general public. Among anthropologists, Harris was not only one of the leading theoreticians of his time—he was also one of the best-selling popular authors of his generation (Harris, 1974a, 1977, 1985, 1987a, 1989). On the whole, his trade books have stood the test of time well. *Cows, Pigs, Wars, and Witches* is still fun to read, full of provocative ideas and interesting connections, as is *Cannibals and Kings. Good to Eat* may be good to debate, as far as some anthropologists are concerned, but it is still good to read, as far as many in the general public are concerned (it certainly shows off to good advantage the anthropological penchant for cross-cultural comparisons and counterintuitive explanations). *Why Nothing Works* is still intriguing for its synthesizing overview of contemporary American culture, even if some of the details are becoming dated, and anyone who reads *Our Kind* will walk away with the accurate impression that anthropology is a varied, exciting, and dynamic discipline.

Proposition 6: Anthropology should be thoroughly grounded in a well-developed sense of morality that champions the cause of social justice. Marvin Harris was an uncompromising advocate of scientific objectivity, but at the same time he was also an unwavering proponent of humanistic morality. "I agree that scientific inquiry must be carried out in a manner that protects its findings from political-moral bias to the greatest possible degree," Harris (1999b:58–59) declared, "but this does not mean that scientific inquiry should be (or can be) conducted in a political-moral vacuum." He was proud of the fact that "science-oriented anthropologists have a long history of contributing to the struggle against racism, anti-Semitism, colonialism, and sexism" (Harris, 1999b:62), and he resented the fact that antiscientific anthropologists attempted to claim a more developed sense of morality for themselves: "To claim the political-moral high ground one must have reliable knowledge. We have to know what the world is like, who is doing or has done what to whom, who and what are responsible for the suffering and injustice we condemn and seek to remedy. If this be so, then science-minded anthropologists can plausibly claim that their model is not only moral but morally superior to those that reject science as a source of reliable knowledge about the human condition" (Harris, 1995a:424).

Conclusion

Marvin Harris was passionate about his convictions, and he could be uncompromising in their defense. He was, at times, dismissive of colleagues with whom he disagreed, and he did not suffer fools gladly. He was regarded by many of his critics as arrogant, but that may have been largely due to the fact that he was more intelligent, more articulate, more creative, and more productive than most of his critics. Even if Harris was wrong about cultural materialism (as, ultimately, I believe he was), he was right about the scientific and humanistic principles upon which he based his paradigm. Harris possessed an unusual combination of keen intellectual curiosity, acute intellectual capacity, and exceptional intellectual creativity, and he used all of his remarkable talents in trying to solve the riddles of culture. When even more satisfying solutions to those riddles are eventually developed, they will be developed by anthropologists who adhere to the fundamental principles Marvin Harris espoused.

If I may end on a personal note, I consider it ironic that so many of Harris's critics found his personality to be off-putting. I found him to be considerate, fair-minded, and capable of exceptional charm. When I was a graduate student at the University of Florida, Harris frequently conducted graduate seminars in his home, where he was a gracious and genial host. When he decided to change the venue for his seminars from the sterile concrete-block basement where the Anthropology Department was housed to his spacious glass-walled house set in the midst of a densely wooded lot, he fundamentally improved the tone of the course (and displayed his humanistic appreciation for the value of aesthetics in the process). In one of his seminars on anthropological theory, I submitted a term paper extolling the merits of interpretive anthropology (I was much younger then, and considerably more naïve and impressionable). In his evaluation of my paper, Harris offered these comments: "While ultimately unconvincing as far as I'm concerned, this is an excellent paper—thoughtful and thought-provoking." Those are the comments of a reasonable man who recognized the value of reasoned debate, and they provide a model that anthropology would do well to emulate.

Acknowledgments

I wish to thank James Dow, Nick Kardulias, Lawrence Kuznar, Joyce Lucke, Stephen Sanderson, and Homayun Sidky for the intellectual stimulation they provided at our session, "Marvin Harris and the Controversy Surrounding Cultural Materialism: Retrospective and Future Potential," at the 101st annual meeting of the American Anthropological Association in New Orleans in 2002. I am also indebted to my colleagues Robert Lawless and Tim O'Meara for their insightful readings of an earlier draft of this paper.

Part II

The Epistemology of Cultural Materialism

Chapter Three

Cultural Materialism, Scientific Anthropology, Epistemology, and "Narrative Ethnographies of the Particular"

H. Sidky

Marvin Harris was one of the most outstanding and controversial anthropologists of his time. He challenged us with his ideas, insights, and explanations for a wide range of what he called "riddles of culture." As for his publications and scholarship, he used a phrase in reference to Franz Boas's list of works that applies equally to his own creative output—"a torrent of books and articles [that] is well-nigh terrifying" (Harris, 1968b:252).

While some may disagree with his particular explanations and interpretations, with which he astonished, intrigued, baffled, or even tortured some members of the discipline, his steadfast vision of anthropology as a scientific enterprise *engaged* with the world is perhaps his lasting contribution to the discipline. The significance of this cannot be overestimated in these times in which anti-intellectualism, obscurantism, and irrationalism are booming endeavors inside the halls of American academia (Sidky, 2003:243–298).

This paper is not about the man and his career, but rather about the theoretical perspective he called cultural materialism (for a discussion see Sidky, 2004:336–393). Specifically, I wish to focus upon the epistemological orientation of this explicitly scientific perspective and its implications in terms of the conduct of anthropological research. Scientific approaches attempt to expand knowledge through the rigorous analysis of sociocultural phenomena and the systematic assessment of premises against the obdurate matrix of empirical data. The significance of this was noted by the philosopher Bertrand Russell (1961:782), who wrote that, "The concept of 'truth' as something dependent upon facts largely outside human control has been one of the ways in which philosophy hitherto has inculcated the necessary element of humility."

Cultural materialism is an explicitly scientific research strategy. As Eric Ross (1980a: xv) has pointed out, for cultural materialists science entails "the objective, comparative analysis of cultural similarities and differences which ... place the study of human behavior and thought within the province of a general evolutionary paradigm." The strengths and distinguishing feature of American anthropology, as I see it (and this is what attracted me to the discipline), derive from its scientific and evolutionary framework and holistic, cross-cultural, comparative approach.

In recent years, however, science has become a dirty word in some circles within the discipline. Antiscience writers reject the idea that sociocultural phenomena are amenable to rational scientific inquiry or that it is possible for anyone to develop understandings of the world that accord with an objective external reality. Thus, what I call *epistemophobia*, or a fear of knowledge and learning, is the order of the day. Why has this happened? Antiscience anthropologists (those espousing postmodern, hermeneutic, textual, interpretive, or cultural constructionist approaches) maintain that scientific anthropological paradigms failed to yield tangible results and have consequently collapsed and that the grand theoretical project of scientific anthropology is in shambles (Clifford, 1986:2–3; Marcus, 1986:263). These writers propose an alternative vision of the anthropological enterprise, one that they grandiosely tout as the "rearrangement of the very principles of intellectual perspective" (Herzfeld, 2001:2, 10). It would appear that there is now "a new and pragmatic understanding of epistemology" arising from a novel realization that science is merely a culturally constructed set of beliefs with no more validity, universality, or authority than any other way of knowing (Herzfeld, 2001:x, 2, 5, 9, 10, 22).

Science, reason, and rationality, which are the basis of what is pejoratively referred to as the West's "universalizing," "essentializing," "homogenizing" knowledge, are treated as the "folk knowledge" of Euro-Americans, or in the crudest form of the argument in anthropology, lies we tell about other people. Antiscience anthropologists assert that the privileged and prestigious position that science and scientific truths occupy is not because science works or because the scientific approach has contributed to a staggering growth of knowledge, but because of the West's political hegemony over the rest of the world. Truth, the reasoning goes, is based entirely on social conventions, and whose truth is heard and whose truth is silenced is a coefficient of power and coercion (Foucault, 1984:75). The West is powerful, hegemonic, and coercive; therefore its "truths" are privileged.

Given the novel (?) realization on the part of anthropologists regarding the cultural origins of science, the call is that all "voices," and all ways of knowing, or epistemologies, must be granted equal validity, legitimacy, and authority. The idea that it is possible to distinguish between different or contending claims to knowledge—the premise upon which science is based—is dismissed as an aspect of the West's hegemonic discourse. For antiscience anthropologists, the epistemological status of claims to knowledge is totally irrelevant in determining the veracity of such claims. This is because everything is "culturally constructed"; there are multiple realities, multiple equally valid truths (except science), and ethnography is "fiction."

Since advocates of the new vision deny that there are any criteria or epistemological procedures by means of which one can choose between different ways of knowing, how do they proceed? When we look past the thick smokescreen of jargon and impenetrable prose that characterizes antiscience discourse, we find that the antiscience advocates are guided simply by their own private political and moral values. Remarkably, what this enterprise amounts to is the reduction of the complexities of sociocultural experience to the antiscience writer's own personal and often oversimplified moral categories of exploitation versus resistance, with truth conflated with "good," provided by and suited to the analyst's own moralistic sensibilities (Sahlins, 1999). While writers espousing this view frequently express outrage and indignation toward scientific anthropologists for allegedly imposing their own "culture-bound" categories (i.e., scientific concepts) upon other cultures, they fail to recognize that they do the very same with their subjectively defined moral categories, which reflect merely the politics and values emanating from the spectrum of Euro-American culture these writers occupy (cf. D'Andrade, 1995a).

This ideological trajectory in the discipline against which Harris struggled throughout his career has vast implications for the anthropological enterprise. Enhancing the growth of knowledge has become an unfashionable and unethical exercise and has disappeared from the intellectual project of antiscience anthropologists. There is no new knowledge to be found here because the antiscience anthropologist herself or himself provides the "truth" (Salzman, 2001:136). These writers profess a self-righteous desire to "speak truth to evil" (Scheper-Hughes, 1995), but it is their own "truth" arrived at by means of special capacities and hermeneutic ingenuities with which they credit and privilege themselves and deny everyone else. Thus when the President of the United States remarks about "evil" and "evil doers," these writers react with contemptuous moralistic jeers. Yet they operate with absolute certitude regarding their own capacities to render judgments in terms of intrinsic categories of good and evil. But how does one know that something is good or evil? On empirical grounds? On rational grounds? Intuitively on the basis of the self-evident nature of good and evil? Differentiating between things designated as good or evil entails value judgments, and value judgments do not constitute judgments, but are merely "cheers or jeers," what philosophers refer to as the "Boo-Hooray theory of moral judgments" (Williams, 2001:91). This is the foundation upon which the antiscience anthropologists construct their intellectual enterprise.

Those advocating the new perspective avow that they have obliterated the once "axiomatic separation of theorizing scholar and ethnographic subject" or "the observer" and "the observed" (Herzfeld, 2001:2, 10). Scientific objectivity and objectively valid knowledge are mystifications and hallucinations, they avow, that have rightly been eradicated from the moral anthropology they propose as a replacement for scientific research. Objectivity, which is construed as transcendental and absolute objectivity (part of the antiscience writers' "straw man" argument about science), is relegated to a "professional discourse," which is in reality said to be "a language of power." Because objectivity is "bad," then so is the associated dimension of scientific research—making generalizations (D'Andrade, 1995b:406). Thus, as Abu-Lughod (1991:150–151) affirms, generalizations "can no longer be regarded as neutral description" and are therefore evil like oppression and power, with which they are inexorably intertwined. To avoid the morally questionable enterprise of making generalizations, it is mandated that anthropologists must write "narrative ethnographies of the particular," in other words, cleverly and experimentally written, subjective, idiosyncratic stories from the "bottom up" (Abu-Lughod, 1991:150–151). The so-called "rearrangement of the very principles of intellectual perspective" has therefore redirected the anthropological enterprise toward the same dreary dead-end road of particularism embarked upon decades ago by Franz Boas and his students and more recently by Clifford Geertz and his acolytes, with equally disappointing and dismal results (see Sidky, 2003:91–140, 199–242).

The shift toward "narrative ethnographies of the particular" entails the substitution of critical thinking and systematic and rigorous analysis with impressionistic anecdotal accounts. Narratives and anecdotes do not enhance knowledge. They are thick with bias and fulfill strictly ideological functions aimed at swaying audiences by appeal to emotion rather than evidence (Dawes, 2001:113). Narratives, storytelling, and poetry are in fashion and it appears that they are here to stay; and anthropology may yet make it as a literary field. But are storytelling and reciting poems anthropology?

The pseudopolitical project of the antiscience anthropologists hinges upon clever and ideologically tailored stories with "spaces" for "the voices of the Other." The aim of their enterprise is to use marginal knowledge of marginal communities (i.e., the stories and poems these anthropologists write), to question and destabilize "received values" of the dominant Western cultures (Herzfeld, 2001:5). Embracing "local knowledge" and the "native's point of view" are therefore offered as bold statements of political radicalism and militancy.

Some of the "superstars" of American anthropology are advocating the antiscience message, which Paul Gross (1997) aptly describes as a "flight from reason." The antiscience gurus have been well and widely received by colleagues and graduate students because their message holds the promise of liberation from the evils and fetters of "modernity." Their discourse is replete with statements about liberating "the Other," and liberating themselves. But astonishingly, this is a form of liberation hitherto unparalleled in human history—it is liberation on paper, in texts. According to the rhetoric, "to be written about as liberated is to be liberated" (Sapire, 1989). Gross and Levitt (1994:74) describe why antiscience writers have adopted this perspective:

> The idea that close attention to the words, tropes, and rhetorical postures of a culture gives one transmutative power over that culture finds acceptance for a number of reasons. First of all, it shifts the game of politics to the home turf of those who by inclination and training are clever with words, disposed to read texts with minute attention and to attend to the higher-order resonances of language. At the same time, it allows scholars of a certain stamp to construe the pursuit of the most arcane interests as a defiantly political act against the repressive strictures of society. This is exhilarating: it is radicalism without risk. It does not endanger careers but rather advances them. It is a radicalism

that university administrators and even boards of governors have found easy to tolerate, since its calls to arms generally result in nothing more menacing than aphorisms lodged in obscure periodicals.

As I have pointed out elsewhere, although this kind of feigned radicalism that reduces tangible earthly problems, such as oppression, exploitation, and slavery, to the level of textual analysis and writing styles may be beneficial for the academic in gaining tenure and promotion, it leaves the wretched of the earth to their own devices. This is a grotesque form of mystification and represents an abrogation of intellectual responsibilities.

There is a far more important reason for the popularity of the antiscience perspective than its chimerical promise of liberation and feigned radicalism and militancy. Those who espouse this perspective are "liberated" from the chore of learning science or undertaking the tedious task of actually conducting empirical fieldwork (cf. Fox, 1992:49). Moreover, the antiscience writer who repudiates the rules of logic, empirical evidence, validation, and standards of proof and disproof is freed from the responsibility of knowing anything and is at the same time empowered to say almost anything and never be shown to be wrong because his or her statements are immune to appraisal (cf. Reyna, 1994:576).

Thus unfettered from all conventions of scientific research and standards of scholarship, these writers happily render moralistic judgments and "speak truth to evil" on the basis of subjective, intuitive, impressionistic procedures, bolstered by the thought that their "moral" perspective alone is enough to suppress ethnocentrism and prejudice and guarantee greater insights (Sidky, 2003:384). Their message says nothing about the phenomena in question, but rather tells readers how to react emotionally to those phenomena (D'Andrade, 1995a:4). The objective is not to comprehend the world, but to advocate a particular vision of it that accords with some private political and moral agenda based upon the values of one stratum of Euro-American society. Such an enterprise translates into a kind of irrational and scientifically uninformed advocacy.

There are innumerable epistemological, theoretical, and ethical problems associated with this kind of anthropology (Gross and Plattner, 2002). As Harris (1995a:423) pointed out:

> It is a lack of scientific knowledge that places our politico-moral decisions in greatest jeopardy.... To claim the political-moral high ground one must have reliable knowledge. We have to know what the world is like, who is doing what to whom, who and what are responsible for the suffering and injustice we condemn and seek to remedy. If this be so, then science-minded anthropologists may plausibly claim that their model is not only moral but morally superior to those that reject science as a source of reliable knowledge about the human condition. Fantasies, intuitions, interpretations, and reflections may make for good poems and novels, but if you want to know what to do about the AIDS time bomb in Africa or landlessness in Mexico, neglect of objective data is reprehensible.

I wish to raise two questions with respect to the antiscience contentions: Are the assertions about science and scientific research based on evidence? Are they compelling? These assertions include the idea that science is merely another narrative, that science is a myth, that science is about absolute truths, that ethnography is fiction, that reality is culturally constructed, that there are no regularities in culture (hence a generalizing science of culture is untenable), that external reality is unknowable, and that scientific paradigms have collapsed due to their failure to yield results. In the remainder of this paper I shall provide a critical appraisal of these assertions.

Science as a Narrative

For the antiscience writers scientific discourse is merely a narrative that depends upon rhetorical ornamentation to persuade people of its authority and legitimacy. Science is portrayed as "'a kind of writing' minus the slightest possibility that it can get anything right" (Norris, 1997:7). This perspective fails to take note of the fact that one can learn physics, biology, mathematics, or astronomy without reading Einstein, Darwin, Newton, or Galileo (Sokal and Bricmont, 1998:196). The principles of aerodynamics and Mendelian genetics work no matter what languages are used in conveying those principles. As Reyna (1994:562) has pointed out in this regard:

> The propositions of an induction may be offered with considerable rhetorical fanfare. However, the persuasive effect of these statements depends upon whether canons of inductive or deductive logic have been appropriately applied and not upon their rhetorical ornamentation. [Antiscience writers have] confused the communication of scientific practices with the practice. Such a representation of science is a misrepresentation of it.

In science what counts are the factual and theoretical formulations, not the words used to convey those formulations. Writing and writing conventions (tropes, figurative devices, etc.) certainly have an effect, but not in the way suggested by the antiscience writers—otherwise, as Sangren (1988:411) has put it, "writers would be kings." By privileging texts over facts, thereby conveniently dismissing the empirical dimension of science, antiscience writers deceptively convert science into narrative, one narrative among others (Sokal and Bricmont, 1998:197).

Science as Myth

Scientific knowledge is not equivalent to the myths of a culture. There are no myths that postulate procedures with which to discriminate between earlier and later versions of those myths (Sokal and Bricmont, 1992:82). Scientific knowledge is altered in relation to empirical findings and science postulates procedures that are used to discriminate between alternative hypotheses. This is the significant difference between science and myth.

Science as Value-Free Knowledge

This conception is *scientism,* not science, and confuses "science as a critical judgment with science as revealed authority" (Lett, 1997:96; Sangren, 1988:420). As Lett (1997:96) has pointed out:

Science does not claim to be free of bias, error, or fraud; that is scientism. Science does not claim absolute certainty; that is scientism. Science does not claim that perception is simply a matter of passive reception; that too is scientism.... The notion of absolute truth is foreign to the epistemology of science. Truth, in science, has a provisional quality. A scientific proposition is considered to be true if it generates empirically supportable explanations and makes no false predictions. Scientific propositions and theories are never known to be true in any absolute sense, however.

What's more, most scientists do not entertain the misconception that science has all the answers, that it is the only way of knowing, or that it is a guaranteed way of getting at the "Truth." Nor do scientists promise "a permanent, utopian transcendence" (contra Tyler, 1986:134). As Harris (1995b:67) put it:

Science, with its counterintuitive, skeptical, provisional, and interminable dialogue, is exactly described as an intellectual system for comparing partial and probable truths. Science is less skeptical than postmodernism only in its refusal to concede that one partial truth is as good as any other. Science, unlike postmodernism, refuses to accept all partial truths as equally truthful. It denies that all truths are similarly constructed and equally partial. The question for the science-oriented anthropologist is not whether objective social science is possible, but how to judge whether one partial constructed truth is better than another.

Ethnography as Fiction

The problematic nature of the idea of ethnography as fiction has been astutely addressed by Appell (1989:196):

In this context are all ethnographies by their nature fictitious? Or only those purposefully created as interpretations of ethnographic reality? Or only those in error? ... But if ethnographies are fictions, are histories? Social histories? Are autobiographies? Biographies? Is a journalist's account of a bombing in Belfast or Beirut a fiction? Is the analysis of the enclosure movement by its very nature a fiction? If A and B both see X fire a pistol into Z's head, killing him, is their narrative of the event a fiction? An interpretation? If these statements are used to convict X, leading to life imprisonment, is not this sentence wrong since it is based on interpretation? Or is that itself an interpretation?

Appell (1989:196) elaborates upon the implications of the fictionalist perspective:

If we accept the fictionalist claim for ethnography, then there is no longer any need to train students to be aware of personal bias in observation, or of how one's own cultural constructs may lead one astray in the field. Courses in fieldwork now can be courses in creative writing. But if we accept this new definition of ethnography, we are also obliged to accept this claim as a possible fiction. The truth value of a statement by an interpretist or fictionalist must always be suspect because of his or her very claims on the nature of objective reality. Therefore, they should stop trying to convince the unconverted of their private reality since it cannot be shared.

Cultural Construction of Reality

Antiscience anthropologists' evocation of a radical diversity of cultures and the ideas of "multiple realities" and "multiple truths" is founded on the notion of "the cultural construction of reality." The idea of multiple truths, as Orans (1996:137) has observed, is used to justify epistemological free-for-alls and an "anything goes" approach in the pursuit of knowledge (see Sidky, 2004:19–23). This charter boils down to the following rationalization: I have my story/truth, you have your story, scientists have their story, my story is as good as anybody else's story (Harris, 1987a:14). Admitting this point renders superfluous the idea that claims to knowledge must be based upon evidence because "truth" is postulated to be merely a tag manipulated by contending groups to advance their own special political interests. Those who are obtuse enough to insist that propositions must be worded in such a way as to be verifiable and falsifiable are denigrated as sexist, ethnocentric positivists and unquestioned emissaries of the power-crazed ruling class (cf. Orans, 1996:137).

Antiscience writers would have a solid case if they could produce any evidence that reality is constructed in the manner they suggest. Simply stating that evidence is irrelevant does not absolve them of the burden of proof. And they have no proof. Careful scrutiny demonstrates that these writers have grossly exaggerated the idea of the cultural construction of reality. One might note that certain things are agreed upon, such as bits of metal or pieces of paper standing for value, particular combinations of phonemes standing for objects, places, and people, which might rightly be construed as culturally constituted (D'Andrade, 1999:88). There are also those things, such as gods and spirits, that are similar to agreed-upon things like coins, checks, names, and labels, but that have a weaker reality because for those who do not believe in them they are not real (D'Andrade, 1999:88).

However, these sorts of things do not encompass the whole of culture. As D'Andrade (1999:88) observes:

> In my experience as a cognitive anthropologist, I have found that many cultural models are simply descriptive and are strongly shaped by the ordinary world of normal perception.... Folk taxonomies in botany and zoology, the folk model of the mind, the categorizations of color, and numerous other cultural classification schemes seem to be strongly influenced by the structure of the world as normally perceived. So the statement that reality is culturally constructed is another of these partial truth arguments, in which a claim is made as if "culture is everything," and only on closer inspection does one find that the claim is much exaggerated—one part of culture is made to stand for the whole. I believe that people in other cultures most of the time inhabit the same reality as you or I do. Cultural reality is more often reality-shaped than culturally constituted.

What cultural constructionists have done is to substitute a partial truth for an absolute truth (D'Andrade, 1999:88). This entails the logical fallacy of composition.

There Are No Regularities in Culture

There is an overwhelming amount of historical, ethnographic, and archaeological evidence to refute the assertion that cultures are random entities unique unto themselves, and therefore that a generalizing science of culture is impossible. As Harris pointed out:

> Parallels and convergences in the evolution of New World and Old World political economies are difficult to dismiss as quirky stochastic effects (e.g., the independently evolved complexes surrounding ruling elites, use of preciosities consisting of rare metals and minerals, pyramids with hidden burial chambers, brother-sister marriage, human sacrifice, god-kings, astronomy, solar and lunar calendars, mathematics, etc.). Similarly, hundreds of studies based on the Human Relations Area Files or other large-scale comparative databases clearly demonstrate the nonrandom nature of sociocultural selection. (1999b:145)

External Reality Is Unknowable

According to this view, the template for scientific knowledge is not nature or an objective reality; rather, scientific truths are arrived at entirely by mutual agreement among sexist white men in white lab coats (science portrayed as an old white men's club), and those truths are then instilled by the aura of authority enjoyed by science. The premise behind this assertion is that it is impossible to obtain any reliable knowledge of the world, and an "external reality," if it even exists, is unknowable (Shweder, 1991:355–356).

The absurdities of this reality-doubting proposition become evident the moment it is applied to *all* aspects of our day-to-day ordinary experiences (Sokal and Bricmont, 1998:92). In daily affairs we account for "the coherence of our experiences" by assuming that the external world accords approximately with the impressions received by our senses. As Sokal and Bricmont (1998:53) point out, "even the most commonplace knowledge of our everyday lives—there is a glass of water in front of me on the table—depends entirely on the supposition that our perceptions do not *systematically* mislead us and that they are indeed produced by external objects that, in some way, resemble those perceptions." This is why we do not intentionally walk into walls, step in front of moving trains, or jump out of high buildings.

The practical rationality that guides our everyday life is not all that different from scientific rationality, as there is "a continuity between scientific knowledge and everyday knowledge" (Sokal and Bricmont, 1998:56). Listen to Sokal and Bricmont (1998:56) yet again:

> Historians, detectives, and plumbers—indeed, all human beings—use the same basic methods of induction, deduction, and assessment of evidence as do physicists or biochemists. Modern science tries to carry out these operations in a more careful and systematic way, by using controls and statistical testing, insisting on replication, and so forth. Moreover, scientific measurements are often much more precise than everyday

observations; they allow us to discover hitherto unknown phenomena; and they often conflict with "common sense." But the conflict is at the level of conclusions, not the basic approach.

It is true that no conclusions about an external reality can be proven with absolute certainty; however, they can be proven beyond reasonable doubt (unreasonable doubt will always remain) (Sokal and Bricmont, 1998:57). Using clever talk, antiscience writers have magnified unreasonable doubt and generalized it to all knowledge. The thousands of cases that demonstrate agreement between theory and experiment, often with remarkable precision, suggest not only that an external world exists, but also that science has acquired reliable knowledge about that world (Bernard, 1995:17; Sokal and Bricmont, 1998:57). Antiscience anthropologists are therefore deceptive, misleading, and intellectually dishonest when they state that such knowledge is impossible. Unable to support their assertions with evidence, these writers mask their subterfuge by resorting to derision and rhetoric. The antiscience discourse, as Fox (1992:55) has pointed out, is characterized by the "routinization of indignation" and the "politicization of theory," and angst concerning the hopelessness of the problem of knowledge (Gellner, 1992).

Paradigmatic Collapse

The assertion that scientific paradigms have failed due to a lack of results is one of the central manifestos of the antiscience movement in anthropology. However, as with their other declarations, antiscience anthropologists offer no evidence to support their case. Instead, the notion of paradigmatic collapse is presented as a self-evident truth on the authority of its expositors. Harris (1994:73) summed it up as follows:

> A popular myth among interpretationist science-bashers is that positivist anthropology deservedly collapsed because of its failure to produce a coherent body of scientific theories about society and culture. Marcus and Fischer for example assert that there is a crisis in anthropology and related fields because of the "disarray" in the "attempt to build general and comprehensive theories that would subsume all piecemeal research".... This implies that [antiscience anthropologists] have made a systematic study of the positivist corpus of theories that dealt with the parallel and convergent evolution of sociocultural systems. But they have not done this. It was only after World War II that nonbiological, positivist cultural and archaeological paradigms gained acceptance among anthropologists. In the ensuing years unprecedented strides have been made in solving the puzzles of sociocultural evolution through a genuinely cumulative and broadening corpus of sophisticated and powerful theories based on vastly improved and expanded research methods. The cumulative expansion of knowledge has been especially marked within archeology and at the interface between archaeology and cultural anthropology.... It is ironic, then, that at the very moment when anthropology is achieving its greatest scientific successes, anthropologists who have never tested the positivist theoretical corpus which they condemn hail the death of positivist anthropology and the birth of a "new" humanistic paradigm. Only those who know little about the history of anthropological theories could hail such a paradigm as "new," much less as a "reconfiguration of social thought."

Conclusion

In the absence of compelling evidence, prudent thinkers have ample justification based upon pragmatic evidence, everyday epistemology, and an overwhelming amount of data provided by anthropologists themselves to reject categorically the assertions of antiscience anthropology. Therefore, we may conclude as Cerroni-Long (1996:52) has, that "those anthropologists that go on telling stories or making poetry do so as [a] personal choice, not because the study of culture requires it."

I have grave concerns regarding the intellectual merits of any perspective that is inimical to the growth of knowledge. I also have great reservations about any intellectual enterprise in which claims to knowledge are immune to appraisal. Yet this is what the "rearrangement of the very principles of intellectual perspective" has yielded.

For Harris, anthropology was not about restructuring experience, storytelling, *epistemophobia,* or generating impenetrable discourses immune to appraisal and validation, but about enhancing our knowledge of the world and the operation of sociocultural systems through time and space by means of explicitly scientific formulations. The importance of this, to say it again, cannot be overstated. For cultural materialists the central aspiration of the discipline has been and remains

> the exchange of data and theories among different fields and subfields concerned with the global, comparative, diachronic, and synchronic study of humankind: the origin of the hominids, the emergence of language and culture, the evolution of cultural differences and similarities, and the ways in which biocultural, mental, behavioral, demographic, and environmental and other nomothetic processes have shaped and continue to shape the human world. (Harris, 1994:62)

Scientific research strategies are not useful because they guarantee absolute truths, free of subjective bias, error, or deception, but rather because science constitutes the best system created thus far for reducing bias, error, and deception (Harris, 1994:65). As Futuyma (1982:163) put it, the hallmark of science is not the question: "Do I wish to believe this?" but the question "What is the evidence?" The alternative antiscience anthropologists are touting is founded on the question: "Do I wish to believe this?" Here these anthropologists join the ranks of the proliferating "home-grown ayatollahs, born-again evangelists," self-styled messiahs, and an assortment of obscurantist gurus whose perspectives are based on this very same question (Harris, 1987a:14).

Scientific approaches operate on the assumption that our perceptions are subject to innumerable distortions and a host of "private perversions," as O'Meara (1995) has put it, which skew our views and bias our findings. This is where the "skeptical rigor of science comes in" (Sagan, 1993:21). Science is about detecting and eradicating errors, and expanding and advancing our understanding. As Sagan (1993:20–21) summed it up:

> Science thrives on errors, cutting them away one by one. False conclusions are drawn all the time, but they are drawn tentatively. Hypotheses are framed so they are capable

of being disproved. A succession of alternative hypotheses is confronted by experiment and observation. Science gropes and staggers toward improved understanding. Proprietary feelings are of course offended when a scientific hypothesis is disproved, but such disproofs are recognized as central to the scientific enterprise.

Of all the ways of knowing the world, the universe, and everything in them, science alone turns the critical judgment upon itself. As Harris (1979:27) elegantly put it, "In the entire course of prehistory and history only one way of knowing has encouraged its own practitioners to doubt their own premises and to systematically expose their own conclusions to the hostile scrutiny of nonbelievers."

Science consistently appeals to self-correcting epistemological foundations (Lett, 1987:21). Put differently, science is a systematic, self-correcting mode of generating knowledge (Kuznar, 1997:6). This explains the astonishing growth of knowledge in every field of investigation, including the study of human cognition and behavior and the operation of sociocultural systems, to which the scientific approach has been systematically applied for a length of time (Harris, 1994:73; Bernard, 1995:17). I contend, therefore, that the alternative presented by the antiscience writers—"rearrangement of the principles of intellectual perspective" or not—is not an alternative at all.

Antiscience anthropologists have spent close to twenty years deconstructing texts, uncovering "tropes," and analyzing "hybridities," "positionalities," "subjectivities," and identities in the "postcolonial," "postmodern" world. What have been the breathtaking breakthroughs in insight, wisdom, and sensibilities promised by those embarking on this venture? Not much in terms of substance. The antiscience anthropologists' unfortunate, mendacious, and self-serving enterprise has resulted in the obfuscation of theoretical and methodological issues, the politicization of theory, word games, factionalism and cronyism in anthropology departments, angst, derision, paralyzing *epistemophobia,* deficit of clarity, and massive damage to the discipline's intellectual integrity and standards of scholarship.

For his clarity of thought and unwavering endeavor to engage the world, tackle concrete earthly problems, and enhance our knowledge by developing a scientific anthropology, we owe Harris an immense debt of gratitude. Abandoning the endeavor to provide scientifically accurate accounts of the world is to risk the credibility of anthropology, the one discipline that by virtue of its subject matter should be at the center of the clash of cultures that threatens to embroil the world in violence, rifts, and divisions (Sidky, 2004:413–415).

Less flawed thinking, fewer explanations by "narrative," and greater effort toward "thinking straight about the world," as Gilovich (1991:6) has put it, is what is needed most in the discipline at this critical historical juncture. I therefore urge anthropologists to carefully assess the central epistemological issues in the antiscience alternative before they pack up their methodological tool kits and take up storytelling and reciting poetry as the practice of a politically relevant anthropology in the new millennium.

Chapter Four

Cultural Materialism, Rational Choice, and the Problem of General Ethnography

Marvin Harris and the Struggle for Science in Anthropology

Alan R. Sandstrom

> A cultural materialist perspective is open enough to tolerate individual agency, social structure, and human biology as distinct influences on economic or other behavior.
>
> —*William A. Jackson* (1996:241)

FEW ANTHROPOLOGISTS ARE NEUTRAL about cultural materialism. A brief experiment will illustrate. Find a group of anthropologists and mention the phrase cultural materialism or the name Marvin Harris, founder of the research strategy, and observe the effect. A few will shake their heads and smile but a majority will react with indignity and pained expressions on their faces. Some will walk away in disgust. Cultural materialism comes out of a respected tradition in anthropology and general social science and so its power to divide the discipline is noteworthy. Marvin Harris is at the same time one of the most despised and respected modern anthropologists.

In this chapter, I would like briefly to discuss Harris's standing in anthropology and outline some reasons why his colleagues react so strongly to his influence. In the interest of full disclosure, I view cultural materialism as one of the most comprehensive and interesting theories to come out of anthropology in the last forty years. No scientific theory is perfect or complete, however, and I will identify some problems I see with the research strategy and suggest approaches that will help resolve them. In short, I want to defend general (descriptive) ethnography against implied cultural materialist critiques and, more importantly, advocate rational choice theory as a key to unleashing the full potential of cultural materialism as a universal explanation of cultural similarities and differences. Harris died in 2001 while still in relatively good health (his death resulted from complications that developed after surgery) and, quite likely, with several more important publications in him. It is my hope that volumes such as this one will encourage social scientists to engage themselves with Harris's substantial contributions to the scientific understanding of culture.

Harris relished intellectual combat and he would be disappointed to find people in too much agreement. In true scientific fashion, he saw his work as a challenge to others to do better (Harris, 1994). It is in this spirit that I will discuss what I find to be an ambiguity at the heart of his conception of cultural materialism. It is an ambiguity that lies at the center of all functionalist theories of human social life and it involves the complex relationship between the individual and the collectivity. The fact that Harris struggled with this key contradiction is testimony to his insight and vision but also of his dogged, some might say stubborn, determination not to change the original vision of cultural materialism. My solution involves the highly controversial approach that includes methodological individualism and a rational actor model. Harris would undoubtedly vigorously disagree with my suggestions, but I offer them with the aim of improving the scientific rigor of cultural materialism and that goal is consonant with his life's work. I will begin with Harris's difficulties with his colleagues.

Cultural Materialism as Taboo Research Strategy

I would like to recount three brief anecdotes that reveal something of the power of Harris's thought. Several years ago, I was a member of the J. I. Staley book prize committee of the School of American Research in Santa Fe, New Mexico. The Staley Prize is arguably the most prestigious award granted for books published in anthropology. We were a committee of about six or seven and we had to read a stack of books and through our deliberations decide which one would get the prize that year. As we sat down for our first meeting, two committee members announced that they would resign if we even discussed a book by Marvin Harris as a contender. After offering a brief defense of Harris's work, I asked what it was they found so offensive. I was met with silence and a look that must have been reserved for people who announce that they have a highly contagious and usually fatal disease. I was dumbfounded that we were not permitted even to consider Harris for this honor.

The second anecdote involves undergraduate education and preparation for graduate work in anthropology. At Indiana University–Purdue University Ft. Wayne, where I teach, we require a capstone seminar in the history and theory of anthropology for our majors, a large number of whom go on to graduate school. We devote one week to cultural materialism in the seminar, but the writings of Harris come up often throughout the semester. A few years ago, one of our majors was accepted into Case Western Reserve University to pursue graduate training in medical anthropology. One of the initial required courses was on the history and theory of anthropology. The newly hired faculty member in charge handed out the syllabus and our student asked where cultural materialism fit into the course. A look of shock came over the faculty member and he stated, "Cultural materialism is an illusion found only in one person's head." The student was devastated and ended up dropping out after earning her master's degree.

My final anecdote involves a colleague who is relatively new to our anthropology department. He received his Ph.D. several years ago and he was told by his advisors that if he mentioned Marvin Harris even once during his qualifying examinations he would fail. I am not exaggerating in the slightest. Of course, after receiving his degree he made it a point to read Harris on his own and has now become a devotee of cultural materialism.

In many anthropological circles, Marvin Harris and cultural materialism have achieved the status of taboo. As A. R. Radcliffe-Brown (1965[1939]) pointed out, analysis of taboo areas often reveals something important about the central features of a social system and so the way Harris and his works are treated within anthropology should tell us something significant about our field. Why do so many anthropologists revile cultural materialism? Why has it entered the realm of topics that are undiscussible? Is Harris so incredibly incompetent or wrongheaded that he is a pariah, beneath contempt like some racist ideologue or apologist for imperialism?

There are a number of reasons for the studied neglect of Harris's work and I would like to mention just a few of them. First, Marvin Harris was a combative person who was a formidable opponent in a scholarly debate. On the negative side he could be mockingly aggressive (see for example his 1974 review of John Honigmann's edited volume *Handbook of Social and Cultural Anthropology* [Harris, 1974b]). On the positive side, he had a way of stripping away the impenetrable rhetoric that so many scholars use to cloak their confused thought, and of revealing fatal flaws in theoretical positions. His 1975 article "Why a perfect knowledge of all the rules one must know in order to act like a native cannot lead to a knowledge of how natives act" practically in one blow demolished the ethnoscience perspective that was so popular at the time. When Claude Lévi-Strauss offered a structuralist analysis based on supposed dialectical inversions of the meanings of clams in Bella Bella myth, Harris wrote "Lévi-Strauss and the clam" (1976b), in which he demonstrated the arbitrary, antiempirical, and fundamentally confused nature of this type of analysis. When Lévi-Strauss's British defender Edmund Leach responded with a structuralist analysis of traffic signals, Harris entitled a section of his chapter on structuralism in *Cultural Materialism* "On the road with Edmund Leach" (1979:197–200) and showed that Leach's analysis was completely contradicted by empirical data on this topic. Harris was a clear writer who used wit effectively to deflate pretension and obfuscated thought. This ability did not endear him to a number of his social science colleagues.

Harris introduced behaviorism into anthropology and advocated a materialist research strategy to understand culture. He thus called into question a discipline saturated with philosophical idealism whose advocates conceptualize culture as socially shared values, worldviews, and meanings, and who give causal efficacy to these mental abstractions. In a series of now famous studies on India's sacred cow, food taboos and preferences, warfare, human sacrifice, witchcraft, women's liberation, and the effects of the transition from a manufacturing to a service-and-information economy, Harris based his explanations not on culture as ideology but rather on material conditions and how people solved the pragmatic problems of daily life. He focused on body movements and behavior in relation to technological and environmental constraints and opportunities, and he avoided explanations that were based on the ways that people create meaning or that resulted from the shared ideas or values of a group. In effect, he marginalized culture as it was understood by a majority of anthropologists and made it an epiphenomenon of behavior. Thus Harris in effect seemingly undermined one of the most important contributions of anthropology to the social sciences—the concept of culture. It is no wonder that Harris alienated a large segment of professional anthropologists.

Much of Harris's writing is a spirited defense of the role of science in the understanding of human social life. His embrace of materialism and behaviorism is an attempt to improve the scientific status of anthropological generalizations and theoretical explanations. He stressed that scientific knowledge, while firmly situated in specific historical contexts, transcends cultural differences. In a discipline that is suspicious of ethnocentrism, Harris asserts that the institutionalization of science is one of the great gifts to the world from the Euro-American tradition (1979:27). He points out that while scientific knowledge is always provisional, it provides the only hope for people to transcend their own tribal, gender, class, or cultural affiliations. Otherwise, people are doomed to repeat their own myths with no way to evaluate one set of assertions over any other set. Harris stood against extreme cultural relativism, moral or ethical relativism, and, above all, eclectic research strategies that relativized theoretical perspectives. Paradigms should clash and theories should fight it out to the death in the arena of empirical studies until only the best among them is left standing. No more Mr. Nice Guy—it is to be a fight to the death (Lawrence Kuznar, coeditor of this volume, has written a thorough and effective defense of scientific anthropology based partly on the work of Marvin Harris [Kuznar, 1997]).

Many anthropologists with a postmodernist leaning now assert that science is simply one aspect of Euro-American ideology and that it has no more claim to truth than the prevailing ideology of any other culture (Kuznar, 1997:144–152, 177–189; Sidky, 2004:24–28, 392, 395–411; Sidky, Chapter 3, this volume). For them, to use science in anthropology is to perpetuate the old colonial order with any attempt at objective analysis but a thinly disguised excuse for neoimperial domination. The reliance on science seems to some to vindicate nineteenth-century claims to the superiority of the Euro-American axis, while, in contrast, a morally superior radical relativist stance recognizes the worth of each culture as a product of the human spirit. According to the postmodern creed, cultural anthropologists should evoke rather than try to represent culture in their writings because evocation "frees ethnography from *mimesis* and the inappropriate mode of scientific rhetoric that entails 'objects,' 'facts,' 'descriptions,' 'inductions,' 'generalizations,' 'verification,' 'experiment,' 'truth,' and like concepts that, except as empty invocations, have no parallels either in the experience of ethnographic fieldwork or in the writing of ethnographies" (Tyler, 1986:130). Rhetorical flourishes often stand in for convincing argument: "Neither the scientific illusion of reality nor the religious reality of illusion is congruent with the reality of fantasy in the fantasy reality of the postmodern world" (Tyler, 1986:135). These and similar sentiments are meant to supplant an ethnographic record based on more than 100 years of painstaking research among the world's cultures.

To the radical relativists, Harris appears to be a throwback to the bad old days of ethnocentrism and imperial domination. Equally damning, the antiscience crowd sees Harris's embrace of the search for scientific, objective knowledge of human behavior to be an abdication of the imperative to help people overthrow oppressive regimes that deny people their rights and dignity (e.g., Scheper-Hughes, 1995). Objectivity is seen as another guise to empower elites and hide human suffering under an illusion of value-free knowledge. Critics ask, How can objective knowledge address the great moral questions of our age? In short, Harris is condemned for his moral defense of science as a means to liberate people, while at the same time he is condemned for advocating objective knowledge in the service of science. The so-called anticolonialists find very little that is good about cultural materialism.

In sum, Marvin Harris attacked all of the major schools of anthropology, leaving few unscathed. He introduced materialism and behaviorism in a discipline devoted to philosophical idealism and the search for meaning, and he advocated science in a period when science has come to be seen by many as bourgeois ideology that oppresses "the Other." And he championed objective knowledge about social life when objectivity is suspected to mask imperialism. Perhaps worst of all for the sensitive egos in academia, he published a number of successful books for public consumption and best-selling textbooks in anthropology. No wonder cultural materialism is taboo and the mention of Marvin Harris's name sends shivers down the spines of so many people on book prize panels and Ph.D. examination committees.

Cultural Materialism: Potential and Problems

I will not review the basic principles of cultural materialism here. There are several excellent summaries of the research strategy including those by Stephen Sanderson (1990:153–166, 1999b, 2001a:110–119, 2007:172–183) and H. Sidky (2004:353–393) (see also Kuznar and Sanderson, Introduction to this volume), while Harris (1979:5–114) himself provides a very clear description of the approach with plenty of examples. It is gratifying to see that scholars are beginning to take another look at this research strategy (e.g., Dawson, 2002; Sanderson, 1999b, 2001a; Sidky, 2004) and over the years many have stepped forward to defend Harris in the sometimes vicious debates over his work (Berger, 1976; Ehrenreich, 1981, 1984; Johnson, 1984; Leeds, 1978; Magnarella,

1982, 1984; Price, 1982). At least two edited volumes have been devoted to Harris and his work (Ross, 1980c; Murphy and Margolis, 1995). However, as mentioned above there are some things that I find troublesome about cultural materialism and I will discuss two of these in a moment. But at great personal risk, I would first like briefly to make the case that Marvin Harris and cultural materialism have been very helpful to anthropology and it is time that we remove the taboo and begin to discuss and evaluate what he has done for the discipline.

One of the criticisms parroted constantly by critics is that cultural materialism is too simple or mechanical to capture the complexities of human social life. This view is invariably held by those who have not read Harris's work, or who have never actually tried to apply the research strategy. Marvin Harris is easy to criticize because he writes and thinks very clearly (Sidky, 2004:367). Many anthropologists, foremost among them myself, have benefited immensely from works such as *The Rise of Anthropological Theory* (1968b) and *Cultural Materialism* (1979), not only because of the perspective outlined in these important books, but also from the way Harris masterfully critiqued alternative research strategies. Such arcane topics as the emic-etic distinction, dialectical reasoning, French structuralism, and structural Marxism, as well as such extremely controversial and highly volatile research strategies as sociobiology, are made transparent in Harris's writings. He clarified major questions in cultural anthropology and offered many materialist explanations for sociocultural phenomena based on analysis of empirical data. In some of these explanations he was shown to be incorrect, but that is the whole point. He offered testable hypotheses, clearly stated, that invited debate. This clarity in itself is a revolution in a field such as anthropology that is filled with murky theory and opaque writing. Just compare any paragraph from Harris with the incoherent and obscurantist writings of many vocal postmodern critics of scientific anthropology, and the difference is startling.

In my view, anthropology has benefited from a dose of behaviorism and materialism. Why do we uncritically accept the conceptions of culture of Talcott Parsons and his followers that restrict it to the realm of ideology and meaning? Before Parsons, culture covered a much broader area of human experience including actual behavior, objects made by people, demographics, and technology. Why restrict our studies to meaning systems and ideology and relinquish to other disciplines the study of what people actually do? Look at how many kinship studies have been published by anthropologists and at how few authors bother to match the analysis of kinship ideology with what people actually do on the ground. When idea and act are compared, the ideational realm often seems to be a weak predictor of how people behave. The accusation that Harris neglected ideology in favor of environment and technology is simply false. Much of his writing is focused on explaining such aspects of ideology as food taboos, religious beliefs, shared ideas about kinship, racial categorization systems, witchcraft beliefs, and gender ideologies. Harris writes: "Surprisingly little attention has been devoted toward explaining why the purely ideational definition [of culture] is a good thing. After all no one has sought to define culture as exclusively behavioral. Wouldn't it be best to accept both ideas and behavior as our starting point?" (1999b:29). This statement reveals that Harris is not the hardened behaviorist caricatured by the critics.

Harris's defense of science in social science is a much-needed antidote to the nihilistic postmodernism that has passed for scholarship in recent years. Systematic empirical studies guided by coherent scientific theories will stand the test of time and lead to the accumulation of positive knowledge about human social life. They have already done so, despite vigorous denials to the contrary (see the dismissals discussed in Harris [1994:73] and Bernard [2002:15–16]). Just look at how far we have come since the days before scientific ethnography. Where will antiscientific research strategies such as Geertzian interpretivism, Lévi-Straussian structuralism, or postmodernism lead us? Certainly not to a greater understanding of the causes of the similarities and differences among the world's cultures. The examination of textual strategies in ethnographies, looking at anthropologists as writers, attempting to evoke culture, writing poems about "the Other," or entering into dialogues with people in the field will not of themselves produce positive knowledge about the origins and functions of social systems. Without positive knowledge of social life we have no way of producing information that can be used to benefit people. Despite its anticolonial zeal, much of the antiscientific writing coming out of postmodernism works to the benefit of worldwide political, social, and economic elites (see DaMatta, 1994). If all knowledge is socially constructed, then there is no objective information to counter elite definitions of the world and only the elite will have the unimpeded power to create reality for the rest of us (see this point debated in Sandstrom and Sandstrom, 1995, 1998, 1999; Nyce and Thomas, 1999; Thomas and Nyce, 1998).

There are problems with cultural materialism as a research strategy but they are correctable, just as specific cultural materialist theories to explain social phenomena are correctable. That is how science should work. The critics of the research strategy outnumber its supporters. Some find the perspective too restrictive and not eclectic enough (Service, 1968; Staniford, 1976; Heinen, 1975) while others dispute the materialist stance and wish to substitute philosophical idealism or reliance on dialectical analysis (Sahlins, 1976; Diener, Nonini, and Robkin, 1978; Diener and Robkin, 1978; Diener, Moore, and Mutaw, 1980). Harris has been criticized for being a heterodox Marxist (Friedman, 1974; Bloch, 1975) and some anthropologists argue against cultural materialism as a research strategy because of its use of the universal pattern of infrastructure–structure–superstructure (Adams, 1981; Westen, 1984). Harris's development of the emic-etic distinction that is central to cultural materialism has come under attack (Fisher and Werner, 1978; Hardman, 1985), and at least one critic seems to complain that the research strategy takes some of the romance out of anthropology (Wolf, 1982). As discussed below, Harris has also been criticized for not taking human biology sufficiently into account (Sanderson, 2001a:143–147, and Chapter 10 this volume).

One disagreement I have with Harris is that he was opposed to writing holistic descriptive ethnographies in favor of narrowly focused, problem-oriented studies designed to gather data to solve a specific puzzle. I do not think that he ever actually wrote against general ethnography but he advised me personally against my plans to write a theoretically informed but basically descriptive ethnography of the Nahua of Mexico on the grounds that research should be undertaken to solve a specific research problem. I believe he fully understood that all description is based on a theory, even if unstated, partially formulated, or not fully conscious. However, some ethnographies are more clearly theoretical than others. Harris's ethnographic work in India is an excellent example of his views of ethnographic research. He went to gather information on the place of cattle in the Indian ecosystem in order to provide a cultural materialist solution to the problem of the sacred cow complex. He did not go there to gather data on kinship, politics, or any of the other standard topics that often occupy ethnographers. One could argue that his study lacked sufficient context specifically because it ignored these other variables.

However, Harris was interested in the causes of sociocultural phenomena and so a study that stops at simply showing context is not of theoretical interest. Following some philosophers of science he restricted his efforts to the solution of cultural puzzles, or "riddles" as he called them (Harris, 1974a). In the hands of Harris, cultural materialism is harnessed to explain why there are sacred cows or why it is that some groups of people love pork and others abhor it. I would defend general descriptive ethnography on the grounds that it is useful to cultural materialists specifically because it provides the background context so necessary to understand even narrowly focused puzzles. It also supplies fundamental information on groups that have never been documented and thus provides a crucial baseline of cultural data. Because scholars had written general ethnographies on cultures in India, Harris could look at the specific set of variables that interested him as a scientist and not have to provide masses of information that informed his topic of research. I think that ethnographies are also useful for helping to define the scope of sociocultural factors found in a culture area. Community studies in particular are important because they provide information on the social units in which most people spend their lives (see Sandstrom, 2000:117–118). They also give a more complete picture of how social systems operate and produce distinctive lifestyles. I support holistic ethnography but only time will tell if such work will continue to have a future.

In my view, a more serious problem with Harris's conception of cultural materialism and one that goes to the heart of many persistent and widespread controversies in the social sciences and in social philosophy is the whole issue of the nature of the economy. Developing a coherent perspective on the economy has occupied thinkers from Aristotle to modern economists and other social scientists and there is little evidence that a consensus is developing. At issue are serious and difficult-to-resolve conceptual and philosophical matters including the relation of the individual to the collectivity, conceptions of human nature, the basic principles governing human social life, cultural relativism, and the role of science in understanding the human condition. The arguments are complex and challenging to summarize, but within anthropology many key issues were revealed in a debate that raged during the 1960s and 1970s between the so-called substantivists and the formalists (see LeClair and Schneider, 1968; Wilk, 1996:3–13). I would like to describe selected aspects of the debate that are relevant to Harris and cultural materialism. I will argue that because each position represents a distinct worldview and research agenda, the debate cannot be resolved strictly on evidential or logical grounds but that each side can be evaluated based on the criterion of fruitfulness. I will also argue that while Harris shifted his position on the substantivist-formalist debate he ultimately remained on the wrong side of the issue and cultural materialism suffered as a result.

Substantivism and Formalism

The modern substantivist position is associated with the writings of Karl Polanyi and his followers. In several publications (e.g., Polanyi, 1947; Polanyi, Arensberg, and Pearson, 1957) Polanyi asserted that there are two fundamental and incompatible meanings of "economic" (he referred specifically to microeconomics). The formalist meaning derives from modern economic theory and is based on analyses of the behavior of presumed rational actors operating in market-oriented, capitalist societies. Economists developed theories of decision making to apply to a specific type of actor in a specific type of society. The substantivist meaning of economics, on the other hand, is focused on the ways that people depend on nature and on their fellow societal members to satisfy their material wants. For substantivists, the economy is embedded in the larger social structure. Substantivist economists might describe technology, social institutions, systems of reciprocity, and customary practices for producing and exchanging food and other material items. All societies have a substantive economy but only certain societies have a market. Harris could not be more in the substantivist camp when he writes: "But economic analysis is properly a matter of a system of production and distribution: of energy, of time and labor input, of the transformation, transportation, mechanical and chemical interplay between a human population and their habitat and of the distribution of the products of this interaction in terms of energy, especially food energy, and the mechanical and biological apparata upon which all these processes depend" (Harris, 1968b:563).

In his popular introductory anthropology textbook, Harris approvingly quotes the radical substantivist George Dalton, who defines economy as "a set of institutionalized activities which combine natural resources, human labor, and technology to acquire, produce, and distribute material goods and specialist services in a structured, repetitive fashion" (Dalton, 1969:97; quoted in Harris and Johnson, 2002:99). Substantivist economics is inductive in approach, is associated with functionalism and cultural relativism, and is believed by its adherents to be the only way to describe and analyze noncapitalist, traditional cultures (Wilk, 1996:6–9). It is easy to see that the substantivist perspective on the economy is highly consonant with mainstream cultural anthropology and functionalist sociology.

The formalist position can be divided into a number of variants but they all have in common the conviction that formal economic theory developed to understand capitalist market-based economies can be applied fruitfully to analyze people's behavior in any culture, including traditional, noncapitalist ones (Wilk, 1996:9–11). This line of reasoning began with the Enlightenment writings of Adam Smith and is perpetuated today by most economists and by social scientists trained in economic theory. On the surface, the proposition underlying the formalist approach sounds unlikely to be valid. Do individuals who are Eskimo, Lakota, Ashante, and Kiriwina of the Trobriand

Islands, for example, allocate their resources in a rational manner like the people on Wall Street and in other financial capitals of the world? The proposition may appear preposterous. But the basic idea is the reasonable assumption that people, regardless of cultural affiliation and whether or not their society is market based, will use their reason to increase benefits (no matter how defined) and reduce costs (no matter how defined) with the idea of increasing their own overall level of utility. From this perspective, economics is a decision-making discipline and it applies anywhere and anytime that people make strategic choices.

For formalist Lionel Robbins, "Economics is the science which studies human behavior as a relationship between ends and scarce means which have alternative uses" (Robbins, 1972[1932]:16). The formalist approach is based on the deductive study of individual rational choice (see below), the conviction that science can transcend cultural particularity, and the idea that people everywhere experience limitations on their ability to cut costs and increase benefits. Because scarcity is a fundamental condition of human existence, people are forced to make strategic decisions in how they allocate their resources. The formalist approach is not widely embraced in contemporary social science for several reasons: It focuses on individual decision making seemingly at the expense of the collective society or culture; it is seen as the unconscious projection onto traditional peoples of an image created by capitalist societies of an unpleasant, grasping, maximizing human being ("economic man"); and it contradicts the inductive bias of most social-scientific research (Pellicani, 1995; Wilk, 1996). While a formalist approach to economic anthropology is mentioned by Harris (Harris and Johnson, 2002:99), cultural materialism is clearly wedded to substantivist economics. Although Harris is often considered to be a radical adherent of science and therefore marginal to mainstream anthropology, he is quite traditional within anthropology in his commitment to substantivist economics.

It is easy to see why formalist economics is rejected by so many social scientists, particularly those interested in cross-cultural research. It is seen by many as a departure from orthodoxy and a contradiction of accepted truths about the role of culture in human life. Most economists working in market-based societies measure utility as the acquisition of some easily quantified material item, such as money or land. Without such a convenient measure and a formal market to determine price, their models do not seem to apply. What about societies where money is not in use or land is not commodified within a system of property rights? As mentioned above, Robbins defines economy as the allocation of scarce means toward alternative ends. Nowhere in that definition is there any mention of what means are used or what the ends are that actors are seeking. A key insight from formalist economic anthropology is that individuals optimize or try to increase many types of value, some material and some nonmaterial. Even in a society with an all-pervasive market system, such as the United States, people do not spend all their means maximizing money. People differ in what they want. Leisure time, prestige, a sense of community involvement, a well-tended garden, cooking skills, a powerful motorcycle, or the esteem of friends and colleagues are all scarce items that people may allocate their scarce means to increase. Some people avoid risk. Others embrace it. Robbins Burling states that economic anthropologists should not do with respect to non-Western societies what economists do with respect to our own, that is, restrict their analyses to material wants (Burling, 1962:805ff.; cited in Schneider, 1974:97). It is in understanding these nonmaterial values that motivate people where social sciences such as anthropology can make a significant contribution to the expansion of economic theory (see Ruttan, 2001:24; Jackson, 1996).

Probably the best example of the fruitful expansion of economic theory beyond the obvious material gain is seen in the development of exchange theory in sociology (see Homans, 1968; Blau, 1964). Based on utilitarianism, exchange theory seeks to understand how humans employ maximizing strategies in contexts outside of those traditionally defined as economic. When people interact they routinely exchange values in order to gain rewards. The values exchanged may include deference, respect, interest in another person, time, or advice. These values are scarce in that they are not freely given. People experience them as rewards and they tend to continue the behavior that elicits them. People's interaction patterns are structured around strategies to elicit rewards and in this sense they are economic (see Schneider, 1974:97–156; Sanderson, 2001a:99–102). Thus, the overall effect of the formalist perspective is to see economizing as an aspect of all behavior and not restricted to provisioning and exchanging of valued material goods. Homans states that "a process of exchanging behavior, rewarding and costly in different degrees, in which the increment of reward and cost varied with the frequency of the behavior" generates group structure or what social scientists call a social structure in equilibrium (Homans, 1968:120–121). In sum, Homans sees social exchange as the atom of social systems.

In a summary statement on economic anthropology published more than thirty years ago, Scott Cook (1973) pointed out that, despite influences from Marx and an emphasis on production and exchange, cultural materialism and the larger subfield of cultural ecology in general developed independently of economics. Cultural materialism came out of scientific traditions studying biological adaptation to the environment, whereas economics derives from more strictly social-scientific pursuits. "The separate trajectories of economic anthropology and 'cultural materialism' certainly merit the attention of the historian of anthropological thought; their divergent courses of development were set by 1900, and only seventy-odd years later ... do they show signs of converging" (Cook, 1973:816). Cook goes on to criticize Harris's formulation, and states, "By submerging the socioeconomic concept of production in the cultural-adaptive concept of technology, the cultural materialist approach has prevented itself from recognizing the role of production as a means for integrating cultural ecological and evolutionary interests with the study of economic anthropology and the economic field proper" (1973:820). Cook ends his detailed summary by advocating that scholars develop "a conceptual framework and a set of explanatory principles that integrates, rather than segregates, the ecological and economic branches of anthropological inquiry" (1973:851).

To be fair, cultural materialism developed in isolation from the formalist position, but under Harris it certainly began by embracing substantivist economics. However, during his career, Harris seems to have moved toward a more formalist position as he continued to develop the research strategy of cultural materialism (Sanderson, 2001a:113). In a review essay published in 1974, Harris was highly critical of Cook and his approach to economics by noting, "Cook and Dalton began the substantivist -formalist argument, which as far as I was concerned, hopelessly muddled the basic strategic alternatives confronting economic anthropology" (1974b:180). In short, Harris did not recognize as significant the whole issue of whether people economize regardless of cultural affiliation. Because he did not see it as a problem, he floated between substantivism and formalism when, in fact, they are incompatible research strategies based on distinctive epistemologies.

One unfortunate feature of the formalist approach that reduces its popularity among academics, anthropologists in particular, is that it is invariably, and I think unfairly, associated with a conservative economic and political perspective. Marx rejected the utilitarian basis of neoclassical economics (Wilk, 1996:89–90) and saw the field as a bourgeois science that served the interests of ruling elites. The idea that people everywhere seek to maximize utility is to project onto "the Other" our own cynical view of humans that is rooted in capitalist acquisitiveness. In my view, despite significant disagreement with my position among contemporary anthropologists, there is no necessary connection between formalism and political stance. The formalist perspective sees a fundamental similarity among all peoples. Despite great cultural variety, at a profound level human beings are the same. It strikes me as blatantly ethnocentric to assert that only people in market economies allocate their resources rationally. It is the substantivists who have created a false image of non-Western people. In a denunciation of substantivist pretense, Harold Schneider wrote:

> We have allowed ourselves to suppose that they ["the Others"] live in a world purified of economic problems. Relations among them, we assume, are personal rather than economic, so no one ever competes with anyone else for scarce goods. Wants are traditionally specified, because a process of natural selection has balanced ecological opportunities and human preferences so that there is no sense of scarcity or want. Each person desires only that which is in sufficient supply to satisfy unvarying demand. The economy is of the subsistence type, meaning that every household always produces in sufficient quantity to satisfy the needs of its members, and trade is therefore unnecessary except as social activity. There is no innovation in production or consumption because these are dictated by tradition. (Schneider, 1974:209–210)

This stereotyped image of non-Western people has no basis in empirical fact anywhere and it is in no way more accurate than the image underlying the formalist position of human nature based on rational choice. The formalist approach is compatible with capitalism but it is equally compatible with a socialist economy or, for that matter, any type of economic or political system (Heinen, 1975:453).

The Individual and the Social Group

One key problem faced by many social theorists, including cultural materialists, is defining the relation between the individual and the collectivity. In the functionalist tradition, the collectivity or social level of analysis is superorganic, that is, it exists above and beyond the individual and obeys laws of its own quite apart from the will or consciousness of the individuals who comprise it. Conceived in this way, the social sciences are not about people but rather about the social systems in which people live. The social system is the unit of analysis and the behavior of individuals is understood in terms of it. Society creates the individual and not the reverse. Such a view leads social theorists to explain behavior by reference to the social superorganic (see Pellicani, 1995). For example, one might say that Native Americans of the Northwest Coast culture area participate in the famous potlatch because it is part of their culture. It is easy to see that this statement is not an explanation but the working out of a tautology: Culture is what people think or do and what people think or do is explained as the result of culture. The goal of cultural materialism is to get beyond tautology and to explain what causes something like the potlatch to exist in the first place or at least to explain why the practice continues to survive. The problem is that functionalism (even dynamic functionalism) is itself grounded in a type of tautology that, while scientific in intent, does not admit scientific causation.

Cultural materialism is functionalist in conception and it is clear that Harris spent his whole professional life struggling to reconcile the actions of the rational individual actor with the constraints of the collectivity, as well as in trying to identify causation in human social life. In *The Rise of Anthropological Theory* he praised eighteenth-century thinkers such as Giambattista Vico and Montesquieu for their "particular construal of the superorganic evolutionary process" that underlies social development (Harris, 1968b:26). But, according to Harris, at the same time their views on the place of the individual undermined their achievements: "The great luminaries of the eighteenth century struggled toward the concepts which unlock the secrets of superorganic causality only to be beaten back by their implacable dedication to the power of individual rational choice" (1968b:43). In *Cultural Materialism,* Harris states that the universal pattern of infrastructure, structure, and superstructure constitutes a system. He writes, "In this regard, cultural materialism is compatible with all those varieties of functionalism employing an organismic analogy to convey an appreciation of the interdependence among the 'cells' and 'organs' of the social 'body'" (1979:71). In these statements, and in many more that could be cited, Harris clearly views his research strategy as functionalist in conception.

At the same time, evidence exists in his writings that he recognized the problems entailed in leaving out of the equation individual humans and their behavior. He states, "It is essential to the task of constructing cultural materialist theories that one be able to establish a link between the behavioral choices made by definite individuals and the aggregate responses of sociocultural systems. One must be able to show why one kind of behavioral option is more likely than another not in terms of abstract pushes, pulls, pressures, and other metaphysical 'forces,' but in terms of concrete biopsychological principles pertinent to the behavior of the individuals participating in the system" (1979:60). In case there is any ambiguity about the matter, he writes, "Just as a species does not 'struggle to survive' as a collective entity, but survives or not as a consequence of the adaptive changes of individual organisms, so too do sociocultural systems survive or not as a consequence of the adaptive changes in the thought and activities of individual men and women who respond opportunistically to cost-benefit options" (1979:61). He almost approaches a formalist position at one point when declaring, "There are whole universes of phenomena concerning ownership and exchange in price-market settings, for example, which must be approached by means of the categories and models by which economists describe and predict monetary inputs and outputs, capital investments, wages and prices, and so forth" (1979:65). More recently, Harris wrote that if causes produce regularities in sociocultural evolution, it is not because mysterious forces impose their will on people. "Rather it is because individuals who are confronted with similar constraints and opportunities tend to make similar choices regarding their self-interest" (1995b:76). In a 1996 encyclopedia entry on cultural materialism, he writes of individuals "who respond to the cost-benefit balance associated with alternative means of satisfying ... biopsychological needs" (Harris, 1996:280). These last statements fit in with a formalist position regarding culture and the economy.

However, although Harris was able to escape the hopeless quagmire of dialectical reasoning in Marxist thought (see Harris, 1979:141–164), he was not able to free himself completely from Marx's insistence that rational choice is a corrupt product of capitalist market mentality. Earlier he had written, "No informed critic of the historical-materialist position could confuse the utilitarian doctrines of classical economic theory with the research strategy associated with Marx.... Historical materialism as proposed by Marx did not consist of attempts to explain particular sociocultural systems by reference to individual economic motivations" (1968b:565–566). Cultural materialism was inspired by Marx and perpetuated the deep suspicion of the rational actor in history. Harris stated that, "In a modern anthropological formulation, it is the technoenvironmental and technoeconomic conditions in which the human population finds itself which demand priority of analysis because there exists overwhelming evidence that these are the parts of the total sociocultural system which in the long run and in most cases swing social structure and ideology into functional conformity" (1968b:566). Clearly, over the span of his career in his theoretical writings, Harris moved from a materialist dynamic functionalism based on Marx to embrace a conception of real people making rational choices in their particular historical context. However, to my knowledge he never actually employed formalist theory in any of the cases where he applied cultural materialism to solve cultural puzzles. His solutions were all functionalist in the cultural ecological mode of analysis. Nowhere is this dilemma more clearly revealed than when early on Harris noted that Marx wrote about masses of people throughout history making choices that are "not only 'irrational' but positively contradictory to their own 'enlightened self-interest'" (1968:565). But he adds that irrational ingredients are "nonetheless 'functional' features of the particular sociocultural systems in which they are found" (1968b:565). Referring to individuals caught up in these systems, Harris wrote, "Whether this means that they are rational in terms of the actors' short- or long-term 'goals' (whatever these are) is a philosophical issue into which we need not venture" (1968b:565).

Rational Choice

It is my contention that it is precisely this philosophical issue that social scientists must venture into if we are to rectify the shortcomings in the cultural materialist research strategy. I think that it is time that we get past the contradiction of the individual versus the collectivity and recognize that selection, whether biological or cultural, operates on the individual. Furthermore, we need to embrace the formalist position that people will act (or at least try to act) rationally on their own behalf, or at least we must proceed to establish explanatory models identifying the causes of sociocultural phenomena based on the explicit assumption that people actively aim to cut costs and increase benefits. The coeditor of this volume, Stephen Sanderson, is one of the few recent social theorists to embrace cultural materialism and he, too, wants to combine it with rational choice theory. He links rational choice to social exchange and notes that it is incompatible with the functionalism of Emile Durkheim and Talcott Parsons. He reduces rational choice theory to four basic principles (Sanderson, 2001a:102):

1. Actors are rational calculators who establish a hierarchy of preferences.
2. Rational calculations are always subject to constraints, including scarce resources, opportunity costs, and institutional factors.
3. Actors always possess limited information.
4. Rational choices made by actors are aggregated to produce social outcomes.

There are several clarifications that need to be made in this model. First, each actor has his or her own hierarchy of preferences and, second, the means and goals vary individually. There is also the presumption that actors with similar means in similar contexts will share means and goals. However, the degree to which means and goals are shared is an empirical question and cannot simply be assumed in advance. The goals of rational choice are specific to the individual and cannot be judged outside of that individual's context and beliefs. Believers in a religion, for example, are rational to make offerings or engage in other exchanges with the spirit realm even though these actions may appear irrational to nonbelievers. Rationality itself cannot be determined absolutely but must be understood in the context of a specific decision-making model (Schneider, 1971:205). Finally, individuals acting in their own interest in the short term may set in motion consequences that will be ecologically, socially, politically, or economically disadvantageous in the long term. For example, it may be rational for farmers in India to have many children for any number of pragmatic reasons. However, such decisions in the aggregate and over the long run may lead to disastrous results that eventually cancel out short-term advantages.

It is often the case that the rational actor has to take the strategies and actions of other actors into account. As previously mentioned, social exchange theory is based on the give and take of people interacting with each other. But more pointedly, there are many situations where one person's choice directly affects the outcome of another person's choice. To handle these special cases, the mathematician John von Neumann and the economist Oskar Morgenstern created mathematical models and laid the groundwork for a subset of microeconomics called game theory (see Wilk, 1996:63–64). A simple example is a game like Monopoly, in which players compete with each other, but there are many cases in real life where people must take the strategies of others into account in their decision making. For example, postmarital residence practices in the United States are overwhelmingly neolocal. That this is so will figure into the calculations of each newly married couple. Following what others do and have done in the past is based on the decision to conform. Even when practices become normative, there is still the decision of whether or not to obey the society's dictates. In short, norms are another one of the many factors that decision makers must take into account when allocating scarce resources. The recognition that norms can be a factor in how rational actors make decisions is an important way that anthropology can help broaden and make more inclusive, and thus more realistic, narrowly conceived definitions of rationality employed by economists.

Regarding the critical question of whether people in other cultures are rational, Cook states, "The general consensus of contemporary studies focused on this issue seems to be that preindustrial tribesmen and peasants, together with men [or women] in industrial societies who earn their living in the market economy, are 'rational' in their economic conduct" (Cook, 1973:842–843; see Isaac [2005:14], who agrees that the formalists won in the end). He is careful to point out that context is critical in understanding why certain decisions and not others are made by people, but that the means-to-end rationality is similar regardless of the society in question. Cook even goes on to state that all fields of social interaction require decisions, thus reinforcing the formalist conception that economizing is an aspect of all behavior and is not restricted to production and exchange of material products. For Cook, the link between the culture and the individual is the process of production. He concludes that, "it is through their organized productive effort in a given natural environment that human populations provision themselves with the material means of social reproduction; and it is through the forces and organization of production that the 'rationality' of ecological selection operates in the process of sociocultural adaptation" (Cook, 1973:850).

For Harris and the cultural materialists, the sociocultural systems in which people live exhibit a rationality with regard to how they adapt to the requirements of a given environment. While this position is plausible, social systems cannot act on their own behalf; only individuals have this ability. From the formalist perspective, it is the individual who acts rationally to increase his or her own utility. Thus, the rational actions of individuals must cause key variables in the social system to stay within tolerable limits. If these limits are consistently breached, deviation amplification may cause the social system to fail. In the words of one critic, "Cultural materialism lacks a theory of the relation between individual action and infrastructural determinants that can account for the convergence of aggregate behavior and material demands" (Westen, 1984:652). Use of microeconomics has the potential to make Harris's analyses more precise and to clarify the difficult-to-understand relationships between the infrastructure, structure, and superstructure. Regarding the cultural materialist analysis of the sacred cow complex of India, one economist has written, "Harris's interpretation would have carried more conviction, at least among economists, if he had employed the more formal tools of microeconomic analysis and a conventional statistical test of his hypothesis" (Ruttan, 2001:18).

Before proceeding, I want to acknowledge that rational choice theory has come under severe criticism from some economists and other social scientists, and for me to advocate it as a corrective for cultural materialism appears to fly in the face of many current trends. A repeated criticism is that the perspective presents an unrealistic portrait of human beings as omniscient supercalculators with infinite time and resources to maximize their utility rationally (Selten, 2001:14–15; Klein, 2001:103–121). In real life, people can be bundles of contradictory thoughts and emotions relying on wishful thinking and magical solutions to problems and are not always models of cold calculating maximizers. Time can affect decisions. For example, people may continue to pursue deleterious or even fatal habits such as smoking cigarettes when they know that the costs of such behavior are put off into the distant future. Moreover, the theory of the rational actor provides no way to explain why people have the preferences they exhibit and act upon (Sanderson, 2001a:106–108). It also assumes that all preferences can be ranked, even though clearly some are incompatible, and that humans have a single, stable conception of utility, when they likely do not. The whole question of human emotion is also left out of the equation. Then there is the problem that rational actor theory is vulnerable to the charge of tautology: We only know what people's preferences are by their choices and the choices they make reveal their preferences. Put another way, we assume that actors are rational allocators, but then take their allocations as evidence of their rationality. In this conception irrationality is an impossibility. In real life people often have no objective basis for making decisions, they have no ranked preferences, and they make wrong choices (Wilk, 1996). These and many additional criticisms of the rational actor approach seem to vitiate any contribution that microeconomics may make to cultural materialism (see Gigerenzer, 2001:40–41).

An attempt to correct deficiencies in the rational actor model was proposed by Herbert Simon in the mid-1950s and the effort is being carried forward in the work of several contemporary social scientists. Simon pointed out that rational actor models focus on the outcomes of decisions and he proposed instead to analyze the processes of how decisions are actually reached. The approach is called *bounded rationality* but, unfortunately, over the years the phrase has been used very loosely and it has lost much of its precision (Gigerenzer, 2001:37; Gigerenzer and Selten, 2001:4–6; Selten, 2001:15–16). In fact, to date there is no unified theory of bounded rationality and so the approach is still in the process of being explored and developed (Gigerenzer and Selten, 2001:8). Bounded rationality looks at decision making, but without optimization, utility, and even probabilities playing a role. It tries to unite psychological factors in decision making with what adherents call *ecological rationality*. People decide using "aspiration levels" as guides and "fast and frugal heuristics" in the search for cues to direct their choices (Simon, 1957). They do not base most decisions on cold calculations of cost and benefit. An aspiration level is "a value of a goal variable that must be reached or surpassed by a satisfactory decision alternative" (Selten, 2001:13). Thus, Simon labels decision making based on aspiration level as *satisficing* rather than maximizing. A fast and frugal heuristic is a guiding suggestion from the natural or social environment that allows a person to choose without going through the process of calculating costs and rewards. An actor is ecologically rational when environmental and heuristic structures are matched (Gigerenzer, 2001:37–38, 46–48). Bounded rationality takes decision making out of the realm of cognition and places it in the psychological, emotional, and environmental context of real human beings.

Bounded rationality dispenses with cost-benefit calculation and sees decisions as being based on other factors, such as adhering to cultural norms, conformity to common behavioral patterns or expectations, imitation of prestigious people, intuition, emotional response, following algorithms developed over long-term evolutionary time scales, and being influenced by sociocultural interactional processes (Henrich, 2001:997; Henrich, Albers, Boyd, Gigerenzer, McCabe, Ockenfels, and Young, 2001:343–346). All of these examples appear to circumvent maximization calculation and seem reasonable and consonant with the influences real people experience when making choices. It is important to note that bounded rationality is conceived to be domain specific, and that a given example of decision making is not generalizable to other domains or situations (Gigerenzer and Selten, 2001:7). In this regard, it differs from rational actor models in which social scientists attempt to define universal mechanisms of decision making.

Cultural transmission theory (Boyd and Richerson, 1985, 2005; Richerson and Boyd, 2005; Henrich, 2001) is an attempt to apply bounded rationality to understanding the diffusion of innovations and how information is passed between generations. It is seen by its proponents as an alternative to rational choice theory and the application of microeconomics to the understanding of sociocultural phenomena. It begins with the argument that research strategies such as cultural materialism are based on "individuals opportunistically selecting among cultural/behavioral variants according to their cost-benefit ratios" (Henrich, 2001:996). Presumably these variants are then passed on to future generations and are the basic mechanism of cultural evolution. The cultural transmission adherents claim that in fact culture traits that are passed between generations do not conform to this model. In a process called *biased cultural transmission* they purport to show that traits passed on over time do not relate to costs and benefits of alternative behaviors: "Although the biased cultural transmission processes ... do involve the transfer of information among individuals, this imitation process does *not* directly involve the transmission of ... information used by individuals to evaluate costs and benefits of alternative practices" (Henrich, 2001:1008). In another publication, Henrich and his coauthors offer three examples where culture can be seen consistently to trump cost-benefit calculations of rational actors: systems of reciprocity and cooperation, mate selection, and food choice (Henrich et al., 2001:347–348). They purport to show that the ways people cooperate or engage in reciprocity are controlled by cultural norms and not cost-benefit calculation. The famous Kula ring described by Malinowski comes to mind. They also claim to demonstrate that mate selection is controlled by factors such as arbitrary kinship rules, and that food choice varies around the world according to cultural preferences rather than rational thought. The overall point of this work is that mechanisms of bounded rationality must be used to account for the content and evolutionary trajectories of culture.

A thoroughgoing critique of bounded rationality is beyond the scope of this chapter, but I would like to mention several troubling features of the approach. In the formalist approach, actors are assumed to be rational insofar as they allocate scarce resources to achieve alternative ends, but it is not necessary to understand the precise mental mechanisms of decision making for the approach to work. Formalists identify key factors that influence how people decide in a given situation and, following a deductive approach, measure the outcomes of their decisions. They then make predictions about people's behavior based on the changing situation or the introduction of new factors in the decision-making environment. In true deductive fashion, the theory is tested by the accuracy of the predictions and not by increased understanding of the mechanisms by which actors make decisions. The deductive approach avoids the possibly insurmountable problem of connecting hypercomplex brain function with behavior and takes into account all noncognitive factors identified by bounded rationalists, assuming that people try to maximize utility and, given a specified set of factors, the decisions that people make are predictable. Deviations from the predictions require the researcher to revisit the decision-making context and identify intervening variables. This deductive approach often appears to skirt key issues and does not seem very satisfying to researchers in largely inductive sciences such as anthropology. However, economists are able to predict behavior with varying degrees of success by employing this approach, and because of their successes they are in heavy demand by government and industry. Functionalist anthropologists, on the other hand, rarely get beyond description and have very limited ability to predict behavior. Adherents of bounded rationality are also unlikely to overcome particularism and to be able to predict behavior or produce generalized knowledge that could be used to guide policy. Formalist economics may be tautological, but tautologies can be very instructive and, like mathematics, they may be used to create whole new realms of knowledge.

In my view, the decision-making factors being explored by bounded rationality theorists are very interesting but they in no way undermine the research strategy of the formalists. A microeconomist would be very interested in identifying conditions that lead decision makers to imitate prestigious people, follow cultural norms, or become emotional. Following those behaviors constitutes a decision on the part of the actor and they cannot be defined as a nonrational alternative to calculating costs and benefits. This is one area where anthropologists could help to broaden the scope of microeconomic analysis beyond the usual focus on quantifiable material items. At any rate, surely some behavior engaged in by people is based on strict cost-benefit analysis. By allowing no optimization or rational calculating in the way people think, the bounded rationality theorists are removing any possibility that social scientists could identify causal factors that explain human behavior. They see people as responding to innumerable qualitatively different factors at multiple simultaneous levels that are totally removed from individual utility. Bounded rationality seems to be like the substantivism of old in that it is highly descriptive and cannot explain the similarities and differences in people's behavior exhibited in cultures throughout the world.

It is interesting that throughout their writings the bounded rationalists constantly explain people's choices by reference to payoffs, benefits, or advantages. Even they cannot completely avoid the conclusion that people in general try to cut costs and increase benefits, the basic assumption underlying the formalist position. They criticize Harris for basing cultural materialism on individuals evaluating the disadvantages and advantages of specific types of behavior. We have seen above that, although Harris seemed to embrace rational-actor mechanisms in his theoretical writings, he never employed them in the applications of his research strategy, so it is difficult to know the origin of this criticism. Henrich et al. (2001) cite systems of reciprocity and cooperation, mate selection, and food choice as prime examples of nonrational culture trumping rational choice. By listing numerous examples from around the world of various food taboos and preferences, they make it seem that culture is completely nonutilitarian and infinitely variable. But food taboos and preferences are specific practices linked to real people in very definite contexts. As Harris himself has shown, detailed local ethnographic study would have to be undertaken to determine if indeed a food was preferred or prohibited for a reason. The same point holds with respect to explaining systems of reciprocity and cooperation and mate choice. Surely some parts of a culture transmitted from generation to generation contain critical information that helps people increase their utility and reduce their costs. Henrich (2001) seems to assume a sort of generalized and universally agreed upon definition of utility while ignoring possible local needs and understandings. For example, people may reject a cultural innovation that appears to outsiders to be beneficial but that is inconsistent with a critical element of people's lives. Factors such as maintaining ethnic identity, avoiding dominant group violence, or sustaining crucial trading relationships may cause people to reject seemingly beneficial innovations. Contexts can be complicated and in their decisions people have to take multiple variables into account.

Rational Choice and Social Structure

Perhaps the best way to approach the difficult issue of reconciling rational choice with social structure, at least in the short term, is to segregate the two research strategies according to the type of problem to be solved. When the aim is to investigate individual behavior, formalist models can be applied, with social factors such as norms or rules viewed as among the constraints faced by decision makers. I believe that it is a mistake to assume that people automatically obey the dictates of their social system, although many functionalists seem to make that assumption. It is common for people to skirt the rules, and I would say that it is even more common during periods of cultural change or crisis. Individuals can easily rationalize their choices, redefine their options, or view themselves as innovators who no longer are obliged to conform to social expectations. When, on the other hand, researchers aim to investigate the social system, they can use cultural ecological or cultural materialist strategies to understand the causes of superorganic phenomena. However, the two approaches, rational choice and functionalism, are not necessarily incompatible. I suggest a two-track approach so that social scientists can proceed with their research agendas while keeping in mind that the ultimate goal is to develop causal links between the individual rational actor and the social system in which he or she operates. In one of his last statements on the issue, Harris asks the key question concerning the relation between the individual and the collectivity and provides the following answer: "So what is the ontological relationship between culture and the individual? It seems to me that the answer lies in accepting and combining both viewpoints, working up from the individual to the higher-order abstractions and then back down to the individual again" (Harris, 1999b:55–56). Such a strategy is not unprecedented in science: Individual subatomic particles are indeterminate at some levels but in groups they become a mathematical certainty. Rationality is such that individual behavior may appear to be incomprehensible until it is placed in the context of the social group.

Understanding the links between cultural materialism and economizing behavior is far more complex than it appears. As previously noted, Sanderson has embraced rational choice theory and the formalist perspective on the economy. He writes, "It is my contention that the formalists are right ... that people's wants are infinitely expandable and that people everywhere behave rationally and are driven by self-interest" (Sanderson, 2001a:250). Sanderson's definition of the economy is designed to apply to both the substantivist and formalist schools: "Economic systems involve the production, distribution, and exchange of goods and services that people want and find valuable" (2001a:249). However, he argues (2001a:250) that the profit motive is not found in all societies, which appears to support the substantivists' position. Sanderson also finds value in Sahlins's classification of types of reciprocity (2001a:270–276), which fits with a more substantivist conception. Formalists usually see means-to-ends rationality as universal regardless of context and regardless of what is being maximized. It is interesting that Sahlins is a leading advocate of substantivist economics. The reason for the apparent contradictions is that Sanderson is developing a theoretical approach called Darwinian conflict theory, which is rooted in sociobiology (see Sanderson, Chapter 10 in this volume). Thus, he attempts to explain human behavior by referring to biological predispositions and tendencies that are genetically based. People economize in order to increase overall biological fitness and to enhance reproductive success, not just economic utility. Or, to put it another way, Sanderson bases overall utility on biological imperatives.

It is well known that Harris was strongly opposed to sociobiology and made powerful arguments against it (e.g., Harris, 1979:119–140, 1991a:101–108). He certainly agreed that all humans have biologically based drives and predispositions and he even identified some of these, including the need to be active and the need for love and affection (Harris, 1979:63–64). But he was fundamentally opposed to explaining cultural similarities and differences around the world in terms of this common human biological heritage. Cultural similarities and differences are instead caused by variations in techno-econo-demo-environmental features of the world's human groups. Harris appreciated that sociobiology is firmly based in science but he disagreed with it as a research strategy: "Cultural materialism and sociobiology have similar epistemologies but radically different theoretical principles" (Harris, 1979:141). I think part of the problem is that he feared a return to arguments from the turn of the twentieth century based on racism, sexism, and eugenics. Perhaps a key difference between Sanderson and Harris on this issue is that Sanderson, while not denying the role of material factors in explaining cultural differences and similarities, wants to expand the human biogram to include more genetically based traits. It is interesting that Sanderson does implicate ecological and economic factors in his discussion of the causes of aggression, polyandry, and cross-cousin marriage (Sanderson, 2001a:121–124). Cultural materialism versus sociobiology is a debate within the scientific tradition that ultimately will be resolved by empirical research.

Idealism and Materialism

One apparent feature of the formalist position that may have caused Harris to hesitate before embracing it as a causal link between human agency and cultural adaptation is its presumed association with philosophical idealism. Cook asserts that substantivists are philosophical materialists while the formalists "find that the method of conventional economic theory is compatible with their idealistic epistemology" (Cook, 1973:803). Cook does not further explain the reasoning underlying this statement, and so it is difficult to evaluate the claim. Apparently, his point is that formalists view the behavior of individuals as the maximization of ranked values or levels of utility and, therefore, as in the idealist tradition, ideas or values are said to be causally prior to observable behavior. As a resolute materialist, Harris would never admit an idealist research strategy into his theoretical perspective. But, early on, Harris did address this problem, albeit only in passing. In the 1974 review article referred to above, Harris criticized Cook for putting the substantivists in the materialist camp. Citing a study he had published early in his career entitled "The economy has no surplus?" (1959), in which he criticized the idealism of the substantivist economists Karl Polanyi (1947; see also Polanyi, Arensberg, and Pearson, 1957) and Harry Pearson (1957), he wrote, "Yet when I published my article . . . it was to object specifically to the idealist position taken by Pearson and Polanyi when they insisted that ideology, not material conditions, provided the opportunity for surplus production" (1974b:180). I think Harris concluded that there is no necessary link between economics, regardless of how it is defined, and either idealism or materialism.

I am not convinced that formalism is necessarily linked to philosophical idealism. In the first place, thoughts are as real as any material object and cultural materialists have long recognized this fact. Thoughts are directly observable as biochemical brain processes, and they can be indirectly approached through people's descriptions. But thoughts remain internal to the individual and can have no effect on the social group unless they result in bodily action. Because we make plans and itineraries and then act on them, it seems logical that thought precedes action but that thoughts themselves have no cause. However, plans are never created from nothing but "are drawn from the inventory of recurrent scenes characteristic of a particular culture. The issue of behavioral versus mental determinism is not a matter of whether mind guides action, but whether mind determines the selection of the inventory of culturally actionable thoughts" (Harris, 1979:60). In short, the values we maximize and the strategies we employ in the process are largely given by the social traditions of the group that derive, according to theorists like Harris, from material causes.

Criticisms of Cultural Materialism

James Lett (Chapter 2, this volume), a former student of Harris, presents what he views as four fundamental flaws of cultural materialism. These shortcomings derive from Lett's conversion to evolutionary psychology, which he regards as a master paradigm that will better answer the scientific questions addressed by cultural materialism. I paraphrase here the shortcomings identified by Lett with a brief response to each.

1. Cultural materialism is based on a form of functionalism that lacks genuine explanatory power. Harris's research strategy fails to identify a feedback mechanism between superstructure, structure, and infrastructure that could account for the power to select one cultural trait over another. *Response*: Elucidating the relationship between the individual and the collectivity is indeed a fundamental problem with functionalism. The problem is resolved through the application of formalist economic theory to understand how individuals maximize their utility, causing cultural systems to change in response to the changing conditions in which they operate.

2. Cultural materialism is not based upon an ontology of materialism. What kinds of things are cultural things? *Response*: Real human beings acting in response to the constraints and opportunities of the material world create and maintain a repertory of shared thoughts and actions that are empirical realities. Thoughts, religious beliefs, kinship systems, and the other elements associated with culture may be abstractions but they are material and empirically analyzable (Harris, 1999b:52–54).

3. Cultural materialism's Principle of Infrastructural Determinism does not identify agents or forces that have genuine causal power. *Response*: Human beings behaving to maximize their utility within the constraints and opportunities of the material world have causal power.

4. Cultural materialism is insufficiently grounded in biological evolution. *Response:* This seems to me to be an empirical question. Only further research will tell whether sociobiology or cultural materialism will be better able to explain the similarities and differences of the world's cultures.

I believe that many of the problems that people have identified with cultural materialism can be addressed by the application of formalist economic theory to the behavior that anthropologists witness and record in the field. There is an understandable lack of precision in how the infrastructure, structure, and superstructure are defined and said to be interrelated (see Ferguson, 1995). Precisely how is infrastructural causation realized? People always have choices, even in areas of social life surrounded by norms. But the norms themselves are just another factor individual actors must take into account when they engage in strategies to increase their utility. To uncover what causes the norms, we need to seek detailed information on the total context in which actors strategize to increase their utility.

Formalist researchers can make a serious contribution to explanations of human behavior by providing quantified information on how people allocate their scarce means to achieve alternative ends, as well as by providing detailed descriptions of the context in which such decisions are made. It is at this step that general ethnography can be extremely useful. Once an understanding of the basic static system is achieved, the researcher should then examine what happens when the situation in which the actors operate changes in some way. The researcher should be able to document modifications in people's strategies in response to the changed circumstances in which they are behaving. By specifying what decisions are made and why, it should be possible to predict people's behavior as they strive to achieve their alternative goals. It is the maximizing behavior of real actors that provides the link between the individual and the collectivity. It is the individual rational actor responding to opportunities and constraints whose behavior creates the social system that in turn may feed back and become a factor in future decisions.

Rational-actor modeling based on an expanded definition of economic behavior offers a way out of the functionalist tautology that Harris struggled against his whole professional life. The idea of the rational actor may be seen simply as a heuristic and not a statement of deep conviction about human nature. The measure of success of such a formulation will be how fruitful the analyses based on this assumption prove to be. A sample of detailed budgets of individual households among farmers in India may provide the specific reasons why cattle have become sacred. It may also help us understand why it is that, despite their being sacred, they are systematically culled in response to ecological contingencies (Harris, 1974a:28–30). After all, Harris revealed that the strong religious injunction against killing cattle is routinely violated by farmers as they attempt to reduce material costs and increase material benefits. By specifying the set of changing conditions, we may be able to identify with precision factors that lead people to change their strategic allocations and the behavior that accompanies them. In the end, I think that Harris will be proven correct. It is the material conditions that have causal priority in explaining why people economize the way they do.

It is time to go beyond our unstated assumption that people in other cultures are so different from people in the West that they are incapable of making or disinclined to make rational decisions or behave economically. I believe that many development projects throughout the world have failed because of the myopic view that the local people cannot think for themselves. Time and time again throughout history, people have transformed their whole economic and social life in the pursuit of increased utility when given an opportunity that falls within their understanding and their technological capacities. For example, new crops and farm animals have been adopted throughout the world when technical knowledge, transportation, and markets were within people's reach. Centrally planned economies may have faltered because they failed to take into account the rational actor. Central planning and the rational actor are not necessarily based on contradictory philosophies, but the one must take the other into account if individuals and the system are to succeed. Even ethnic identity can be understood as a rational response to political economic factors and competition among groups for resources (Sandstrom, in press).

Marvin Harris was one of the most important and controversial American an-thropologists in the second half of the twentieth century. His work has a scientific integrity that suits it well to address the great intellectual questions of our age. Cultural materialism is also positioned to contribute to some of the great moral debates of the day by providing empirical information on the range of human behavior and causal explanations of sociocultural phenomena. Harris set before himself the immense task of developing a scientific research strategy that would explain the range of cultures throughout the world. He tried to do for social theory what Darwin did for biology. Harris's task was more difficult by far because of the complexity of the subject and the fact that people are conscious actors in the whole cultural drama. I would say that he did a remarkable job. Cultural materialism is a work in progress and it is incumbent on us to continue to build on the edifice that Harris created. As William Jackson suggests in the epigram at the beginning of this chapter, cultural materialism is a kind of master paradigm that could be given even greater strength by incorporating inputs from biology and microeconomics. We should take up Jackson's challenge and try to do better. In my view, the key to improvement of the strategy is to combine rational actor modeling with infrastructural determinism. If you object, do better! By any measure, it is time to remove the taboo from Marvin Harris and his works.

Acknowledgments

I want to thank C. J. Bolster, John Sandstrom, Lawrence A. Kuznar, and Pamela Effrein Sandstrom for reading earlier drafts of this chapter and for making many suggestions for improvement. I am also grateful to Stephen Sanderson for his judicious copy editing and attention to stylistic detail.

Part III

Applications of Cultural Materialism

Chapter Five

Materialist Particularity in Nuclear Micronesia

A Pre-Postmodernist Theory of Cultural Evolution

James G. Peoples

Challenges to Materialism in Anthropology

CHALLENGES TO CULTURAL MATERIALISM come from a variety of perspectives. Some mistrust its search for generalized explanations for human sociocultural systems. They hold that the forces affecting human life depend largely on the local culture with its unique and particular past. Other critics hold that the materialist effort to explain sociocultural systems dehumanizes people. They believe that materialists treat people as automatons who respond adaptively to unfilled stomachs but are mostly unconcerned with empty worldviews.

Anthropological materialists have effectively countered these challenges (e.g., Harris, 1978, 1999b; Kuznar, 1997; O'Meara, 1989, 1997). However, it seems to me that other critiques have more merit. One such challenge is that materialism is overly deterministic. There are several variants of this critique, including the view that materialism discounts the independent causal power of mental/psychological factors and the opinion that materialism is a linear theory. A more compelling variant of the overdeterminism criticism is the challenge that materialism is inadequate because historical contingencies are so common that material forces cannot have the causal power we attribute to them. *Historical contingency* implies that sociocultural forms are so frequently and so powerfully affected by essentially random events that the impact of material forces is muted. Even if material forces do in fact have great causal power, random historical events strike societies often enough that material processes fail to produce regular patterns of differences and similarities. There are echoes of "chaos theory" in this critique—small random fluctuations in exogenous events interfere with law-like interactions in complex systems. Similar debates exist in biology in the form of the historicists' challenge to the adaptationists.

Two other challenges materialists should take seriously are old ones. One concerns the relationships between ideas and patterns of behavior. The most enduring objection to materialists is that we downplay the independent power of ideas and beliefs to shape behavior. Materialists have responded by arguing that the material payoffs from behavior are more likely to shape ideas and beliefs in the "long run" and in the "majority of cases." Thus, material cost-benefit ratios were at the heart of Harris's (1977) materialist explanation of both sacred cows and abominable pigs, although his arguments were unfortunately burdened by macrofunctionalist assumptions. Materialists often do in fact treat beliefs, values, worldviews, and the like as by-products or rationalizations of material conditions (Harner's [1977] account of Aztec human sacrifice may be the most disparaged example).

Viewing some ideas as caused by behavior is not problematic—ideas may in fact rationalize actions and they are in fact subject to selective pressures (Boyd and Richerson, 1985; Sperber, 1996). Too often, though, materialists treat the relationship between ideas and behaviors mechanically: If a behavior has net material benefits, ideas arise and persist that make it likely to continue over generations. How the behavior produces the given ideas, and how these given ideas persist despite numerous rival ideas, is unspecified.

Another classic challenge is the ability of materialism to predict sociocultural forms from environmental, technological, demographic, and other conditions. The resolution of this issue depends mainly on the level of abstraction one adopts (or tolerates). If our concern is very general patterns and relationships, materialist approaches fare well. Is it not true that the cultures of hunter-gatherers differ greatly and in patterned ways from those of intensive agriculturalists? Is it not true that the two major transformations in human cultural existence followed the two major transformations in human technoeconomic existence, namely, agriculture and industry? But if one insists on explanations of the detailed contents of customs and beliefs, then our explanatory standard is raised and materialists have a tougher job—there are just too many particularities. Materialists usually do have a hard time explaining the specific content of ideas (Sahlins, 1976) and accounting for why behavior x is chosen over behavioral alternative y (the "functional equivalents" issue).

In sum, three of the more compelling challenges to materialist approaches in anthropology are:

- showing how historical contingencies may reduce the power of material forces to affect change
- specifying how material forces produce and retain materially useful ideas
- predicting the content of specific ideas and behaviors

In this chapter, I argue that these challenges are partly overcome by comparing peoples whose languages, cultures, and perhaps genes have a fairly recent common ancestor. Such peoples comprise a phylogenetic unit (see below): In the past, all the peoples were one people. Their cultures are studied using the method of controlled comparison. With controlled comparison, we do not deny or ignore historical contingencies. But their effects can be more easily untangled, for some contingencies occurred prior to the separation of the peoples and these are of no analytical interest. We recognize that the behaviors and beliefs of the peoples we study cannot be predicted in detail. But if the peoples comprise a phylogenetic unit, then the behaviors and beliefs they hold in common are taken as historical givens, allowing us to more easily study how baseline behaviors and beliefs were affected by material forces after their separation.

This chapter applies the methodology of controlled comparison to a region of the western Pacific known to linguists and specialists as Nuclear Micronesia. First I describe briefly the benefits of controlled comparison. Then I summarize recent research on the prehistory of the Pacific as a necessary prelude to documenting that the peoples of Nuclear Micronesia comprise a phylogenetic unit. I discuss the Nuclear Micronesian chiefdoms, selectively focusing on inequalities between chiefs and subjects. Next, I propose a processual model for the growth of chiefly power out of an original cultural baseline. The model assumes that people reach ordinary conclusions from their social experiences, given their preexisting ideas and beliefs. Finally, I make some new arguments about how the model might explain some of the diversity in chiefly control and power in Nuclear Micronesia.

On Controlled Comparison

Conceptually, the method of controlled comparison is simple. One chooses a sample of societies based on two criteria. First, the societies share a common historical ancestry, here meaning that the various peoples once shared a single language and culture (based, of course, on available evidence). Second, the common ancestor was sufficiently distinctive that its "descendant" societies are, as a group, distinctive. Ordinarily the distinctiveness of the ancestral society arose as a consequence of a period of relative isolation, during which it evolved unique characteristics. The societies in the sample may or may not be geographically contiguous (Eggan, 1954).

Within the group of descendant societies, any cross-societal similarities in the ethnographic present usually are assumed to exist because of common origin, not because of convergence, limited possibilities, or chance. There is no necessity to explain the similarities, which are historical givens. For example, if all are ranked societies, then ranking is assumed to have been present in the ancestral society as well and requires no separate explanation. (This does not preclude an explanation, but the method does not require it.) Ideally, direct evidence of the presence of social ranking in the ancestral society will exist from linguistic comparisons or archaeological data. Where they exist, such comparisons and data may allow a partial reconstruction of some aspects of the ancestral society, as has been done for Polynesians (e.g., Kirch and Green, 2001).

With the similarities derived from common origin as a backdrop, one contrasts the societies, looking for differences and, especially, whether the differences are patterned. Differences might originate from many sources, including historical contingencies after the time of separation, random innovations in technology and ideas, and relationships with environmental factors such as resource abundance or topographic features. Materialists are likely to hypothesize a systematic relationship between environmental and sociocultural differences, so will focus especially on possible relationships between ecological factors and sociocultural differences.

Advantages over indiscriminate comparisons—that is, comparisons made without attention to historical relationships between the sample societies—are clear. The latter face the problem of determining the independence of cases ("Galton's problem"): If an indiscriminate sample includes three Athapaskan peoples, do we count each case separately (N = 3) or do we collapse all three into one case (N = 1)? Are any similarities between the Athapaskan peoples due to convergence, common ancestry, or diffusion? With controlled comparison, we do not worry about whether the societies represent independent cases: We know that, historically speaking, they do not. But controlled comparative researchers usually are more interested in the differences between them, so each society legitimately is a single member of a sample. Of course, we may still have difficulty in defining whether "a" society is only "one society," or whether one or multiple "polities" exist, but such issues exist in all ethnological studies.

Further, controlled comparison allows materialist researchers to reduce the chances that historical contingencies obscure structures and patterns that emerged from material relationships. Certainly material causes operate probabilistically rather than deterministically, a concession Marvin Harris made throughout his career to idealists, particularists, eclectics, and antiscientists generally (compare Harris [1968b] with Harris [1999b]). Contingencies of the distant past (temporally prior to divergence) are controlled for, and in fact may account for the similarities in the societies. Contingencies since the time of divergence may still obscure structures and patterns, but at least we can be more confident about what our materialist models do and do not explain.

In brief, the method of controlled comparison is the closest naturalistic observers are likely to come in the real world to laboratory conditions. Its value has been recognized by many researchers for diverse peoples, including the Athapaskan peoples, the Maya, the Bantu, and the Polynesians (see Boyd, Borgerhoff Mulder, Durham, and Richerson [1997] for a critical review and examples). Polynesian societies, in particular, have been favored subjects for scholars as diverse as the early Sahlins (1958), Kirch and Green (2001), and Diamond (1997).

Controlled comparison requires good evidence that the societies under scrutiny evolved from a common historical ancestor with distinctive sociocultural characteristics. In the ideal case (although perhaps rare in real cases), the societies remained isolated from significant contact with unrelated societies after their dispersal. Following Kirch and Green (2001), I call the societies that share common ancestry a *phylogenetic unit* (Boyd et al. [1997] discuss some complexities).

In the absence of written records, three kinds of evidence establish the existence of a phylogenetic unit: (1) independent ethnographic studies showing close similarities in the traditional cultures; (2) archaeological data suggesting uniformity of artifact types and stylistic forms over the region during prehistory; and (3) linguistic comparisons revealing that the peoples speak languages that form a distinct subgroup. Similarities in physical features such as blood types, dentition, and facial structure might also indicate common ancestry, provided they distinguish the peoples from neighboring populations. Physical data (including data on MtDNA) are most relevant if they suggest an absence or rarity of gene flow between the peoples of the culture area and other peoples. Little or no interbreeding increases the probability that peoples in the sample were relatively isolated after their separation from other peoples. Controlled comparison does not require genetic isolation, however.

Pacific Prehistory

Archaeological and linguistic research since the 1980s has resulted in a fundamental reconceptualization of the cultural regions of the Pacific Basin. Most of us learned that there are three "culture areas" of the Pacific: Melanesia, Polynesia, and Micronesia. Although still taught to undergraduates in most area courses, this tripartite division of Oceania does not reflect the probable prehistoric, linguistic, cultural, or biological relationships of Pacific peoples. Most notably, it is very clear that "Melanesia" does not form a meaningful linguistic or cultural unit. Nor do its incredibly diverse peoples represent a phylogenetic unit in any other sense, including the biological one. "Polynesia" has more historical and linguistic reality and remains a meaningful term. With respect to its historical relations, the islands usually labeled "Micronesia" are intermediate between the other two traditional groupings, as discussed later.

If there is a viable high-level distinction within the Pacific, it is not between the Melanesians, Micronesians, and Polynesians. Rather, it is between the earliest inhabitants of Near Oceania and the later arriving peoples of Remote Oceania (Kirch, 1997, 2000). The larger, geologically complex islands of Near Oceania extend eastward from New Guinea through the Bismarcks, to the Solomon archipelago as far east as the island of San Cristobal. All other Pacific islands, including the Santa Cruz islands, Vanuatu, New Caledonia, and all of Polynesia and Micronesia comprise Remote Oceania (see Figure 5.1).

This dual classification of Oceanic islands and peoples is based on biogeographical, linguistic, and archaeological evidence, summarized as follows.

Biogeography

The diversity of indigenous flora and fauna is far higher in Near Oceania, where islands are generally much larger and arose from geologically complex materials. Islands are also in much closer proximity and most are intervisible, making it possible to spot potential destinations. For millennia, humans lived in Near Oceania from diverse wild plants, animals, and fish. Later in prehistory, New Guinea people were the probable originators of several important cultigens, possibly including sugar cane and taro.

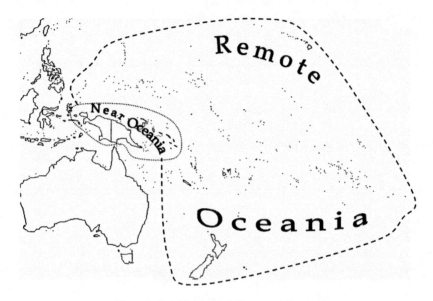

Figure 5.1 Near and Remote Oceania

In Remote Oceania archipelagos are mostly separated by hundreds of miles of ocean, with currents and winds that are not favorable for discovery by seacraft voyages from west to east. Virtually all the edible plants of Remote Oceania were taken to the islands by early human settlers. On present evidence human settlement of Remote Oceania did not occur until suitable cultigens and a viable maritime voyaging and fishing technology appeared in the Pacific.

Linguistics

Linguists divide Pacific languages into two categories: Austronesian and Nonaustronesian (sometimes called "Papuan"). Austronesian (AN) is a very widespread family of languages, spoken by indigenous peoples from the Malagasy Republic off the coast of east Africa to Easter Island and the Hawaiian islands in the far reaches of Polynesia. Within Remote Oceania, from the Santa Cruz groups to the archipelagos east, north, and south, all indigenous languages are AN.

As the term suggests, Nonaustronesian (NAN) is negatively defined. It refers to over 700 Pacific languages that are unrelated to those of the Austronesian family. All NAN languages of the Pacific occur in Near Oceania. They are so different from one another that linguists cannot agree on the number of families within the NAN category.

Austronesian languages also occur in Near Oceania, largely on the coasts of New Guinea and in the Bismarcks and Solomons. Indeed, there are over 400 languages of

AN represented in the Pacific. However, except for the westernmost of the Caroline islands, all AN languages of the Pacific belong to a single major branch of the AN family known as *Oceanic*. Oceanic, in turn, has at least nine smaller branches (Pawley and Ross, 1995). All but two of these smaller branches occur entirely in Melanesia (as the term is traditionally defined). The two that occur outside Melanesia are also the two that are the most widespread in terms of ocean distances (but not land areas) encompassed by their speakers: Nuclear Micronesian and Central Pacific (see Figure 5.2).

What do these relationships between languages suggest about Pacific prehistory? The enormous diversity of the NAN languages, confined to Near Oceania, point to a lengthy human settlement. Whether the diversity represents multiple settlements or in situ diversification is unresolved. In contrast, all languages of Remote Oceania are related, despite the enormous ocean distances separating many of their speakers. This suggests a more recent human colonization. In short, assuming that the diversity of languages is greatest in regions that humans have occupied the longest, humans have lived in Near Oceania far longer than in Remote Oceania.

Comparative linguistics also suggests several migrations into the Pacific, all almost certainly from southeast Asia. The earliest was by the ancestors of the modern-day NAN speakers, probably involving diverse origins and multiple migrations over several

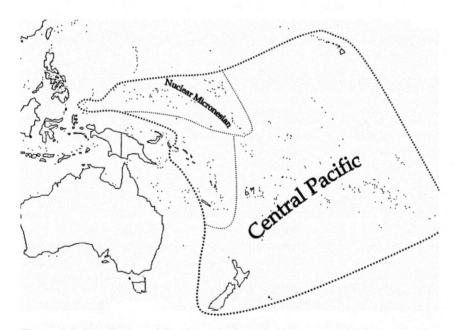

Figure 5.2 Distribution of the Oceanic Branch of Austronesian in the Pacific, Showing the Nuclear Micronesian and Central Pacific Subbranches

Note: some Oceanic languages also occur along the coasts of New Guinea and surrounding islands.

millennia. On present evidence, the descendants of the first settlers remained entirely in Near Oceania. The later migration(s) was by the ancestors of the modern-day AN speakers. When they moved into the region they initially settled many of the same islands as the NAN peoples. As peoples separated, their ancestral language diversified and eventually developed into the nine or more major branches of Oceanic. When they sailed into the huge expanse of Remote Oceania, Oceanic speakers were the first humans to have arrived—or, at least, to have left evidence of their settlement.

The geographic origins of Oceanic languages are debatable. Because languages of the AN family are concentrated in southeast Asia and the Pacific, and because most evidence suggests that southeast Asia is the immediate homeland of AN, scholars formerly believed that the Oceanic branch of AN originated somewhere in southeast Asia. But many linguists now seem to favor an immediate origin of Oceanic and its several branches in eastern Melanesia, somewhere in the Solomon Islands and/or the Vanuatu region.

Archaeology

The preceding indirect history inferred from comparative linguistics is reinforced by more direct evidence from archaeological work, which offers the twin advantages of actual physical remains and absolute dates. Archaeological data also suggest that humans settled Near Oceania much earlier than any part of Remote Oceania. Specifically, there is firm evidence of human presence in New Guinea by about 40,000 BP, in the Bismarck archipelago by about 30,000 BP, and in the Solomon island chain prior to 20,000 BP (Kirch [2000] is the most accessible recent source of precise dates and detailed information). However, there is no firm current evidence for human occupation of any island of Remote Oceania until around 3200 BP. Although the movement into Remote Oceania represents the last prehistoric human colonization of a world region, the widely scattered archipelagos of Remote Oceania were colonized remarkably rapidly: the Fijian, Samoan, and Tongan islands by around 3000 BP, the rest of tropical Polynesia by 1200 BP, eastern Micronesia by 2000 BP, and almost all the rest of Nuclear Micronesia by 1000 BP.

In broadest terms using rounded dates, humans lived in Near Oceania for 30,000 years prior to moving further eastward or northward around 3000 BP, but in the next 2,000 years people had colonized and adapted to all the archipelagos of Remote Oceania.

Interpretation

The most credible (although far from firmly established) interpretation of linguistic and archaeological evidence is that the people who settled Remote Oceania were a different people from the long-established residents of Near Oceania. Specifically, around 4000 BP new peoples entered the Pacific from southeast Asia, carrying new genes, new languages, new voyaging and subsistence technologies, new ways of adapting to tropical islands, and new ideas.

The newcomers spoke one or more languages of the AN language family, previously not present in the Pacific Basin. At first they settled the coastal regions of Near Oceania, where they coexisted for a millennium or more with the NAN peoples who were already there. At least one of their languages diversified into a new branch of AN, called *proto-Oceanic* by linguists. They also developed a distinctive pottery tradition called Lapita (analyzed in detail in Kirch [1997]). The root and tree crops carried by their ancestors adapted to new ecological circumstances, while the people perfected methods of farming the land and fishing the waters. They learned to manufacture some of the world's finest sailing canoes and to develop unique ways to navigate the oceans.

Between 4000 and 3000 BP, speakers of one branch of the Oceanic languages, called Central Pacific, migrated eastward into the distant archipelagos of Fiji, Samoa, and Tonga. Centuries later, their descendants settled the far-flung archipelagos even further to the east and north. Traces of their common biological, linguistic, and cultural heritage persisted after their dispersal into the remotest regions of the ocean. After contact with explorers from other continents in the late 1700s, they became known to the outside world as the Polynesians.

Within another millennium, almost certainly prior to 2,000 years ago, the ancestors of the speakers of another branch of Oceanic, known as Nuclear Micronesian, migrated northward. Whether they first settled the high volcanic islands of Kosrae, Pohnpei, and Chuuk, or the atolls of the Marshalls or Kiribati, is at present unclear. In all likelihood, the tiny atolls of the western Carolines between Chuuk and Yap were the last islands to be settled, probably from Chuuk and surrounding islands (see Figure 5.3). (Rainbird [2004] provides the most recent overview of Micronesian prehistory.) Like their Polynesian phylogenetic cousins, even as Nuclear Micronesians colonized new islands and diversified, glimpses of their common ancestry persisted into modern times.

Nuclear Micronesia as a Phylogenetic Unit

Nuclear Micronesia refers to those islands of eastern and central Micronesia that form a distinct subgroup of the Oceanic branch of the AN language family. Figure 5.3 identifies the major islands and island groups referred to in this chapter. Notice that, based on differences in language and culture, three of the better-known archipelagos are not part of Nuclear Micronesia: the Marianas (including Guam), Palau, and Yap. The Marianas and Palau appear to have their closest historical relationships with southeast Asia. Yap has linguistic affinities to Nuclear Micronesian islands to the east, but its historical relationships have yet to be firmly established.

Historical and ethnographic information on the inhabitants of these islands has accumulated for over 150 years, but most work on prehistory and languages has occurred since the 1970s. In the remainder of this section, I limit the description to evidence from historical linguistics, archaeology, and ethnology that is most relevant for my subsequent arguments. The three types of evidence for the classification of Nuclear Micronesia as a legitimate phylogenetic unit are summarized as follows.

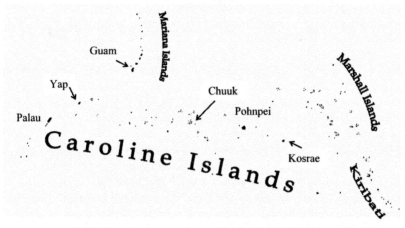

Figure 5.3 Islands and Archipelagos of Micronesia

Language Relationships

Specialists in Pacific languages coined the phrase *Nuclear Micronesian* to refer to one of at least nine higher-order subgroups of the Oceanic branch of the large AN family of languages (Pawley and Ross, 1993, 1995). Another, and better-known, subgroup of the same order of inclusiveness is *Central Pacific,* which includes Fijian, Rotuman, and all the Polynesian languages. Linguistic evidence supports ethnological and archaeological evidence that some, but not all, peoples of the Caroline, Marshall, and Gilbert islands share common origins, and therefore comprise a phylogenetic unit (see Kirch and Green, 2001:65). The islanders of the Marianas chain (including Guam) and Palau (Belau) appear to have migrated directly from southeast Asia. Their languages are not even part of the Oceanic branch of AN. The origins of the Yapese people are controversial, though recent work suggests they may share origins with other Caroline islanders to the east. The rest of the Caroline islanders, the Marshallese, and the peoples of Kiribati speak some Nuclear Micronesian language.

How many Nuclear Micronesian languages exist? There are probably at least fifteen (Bender et al., 2003). The main issue, of course, is whether some islanders speak a "separate language" or a "dialect." The greatest linguistic diversity is in the eastern islands: Kiribatese (Gilbertese), Marshallese, and Kosraen are clearly separate languages, although there are dialects of the first two and Kosraen exhibits some linguistic anomalies (Kenneth Rehg, personal communication). Pohnpeic probably includes three or four languages: the volcanic high island of Pohnpei itself and those of three nearby atolls, Mokilese, Pingelapese, and possibly Ngatikese. Chuuk (formerly Truk) and the central and western Carolinian low islands form a dialect chain, which is usually taken as evidence both of a more recent common origin and of frequent inter-island trade and intermarriage. Chuuk and the central and western low islands of the Carolines may contain as many as eleven languages, all members of the Chuukic ("Trukic") subgroup of Nuclear Micronesian (Bender et al., 2003; Bender and Wang, 1985; Jackson, 1983; Marck, 1994).

Although work is ongoing, current linguistic evidence suggests there are five major subgroups of Nuclear Micronesian: Kiribatese, Marshallese, Kosraen, Pohnpeic, and Chuukic. Figure 5.4 shows the locations of these subgroups. Pohnpeic includes three or four languages and Chuukic includes ten or more languages that form a dialect chain encompassing the central and western Carolines (Bender et al., 2003). Theoretically, the ancestral language of the Nuclear Micronesian subgroup split into these groups after the peoples became more isolated from one another, although inter-island voyaging skills and technologies allowed some islanders to maintain regular contact (Rehg [1995] discusses some linguistic implications). The split(s) probably did not occur at the same time; for example, proto-Chuukic and proto-Pohnpeic probably diverged after the latter split from Kosraen, Kiribatese, and/or Marshallese. Future research by Pacific linguists using the comparative method may reveal more details of the subgroups within Nuclear Micronesian (Bender et al. [2003] provide the most recent reconstructions). My subsequent arguments do not require such details.

Archaeological Findings

Research allowing meaningful comparisons of Micronesian prehistory began only in the late 1970s. The first conference attempting to bring together archaeological scholars was not organized until 1987, in Guam (Hunter-Anderson, 1990). Many issues therefore remain unresolved, though some research deals with prehistoric sequences of political evolution (e.g., Bath and Athens, 1990; Cordy, 1986; Ueki, 1990).

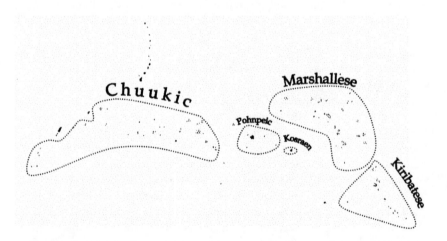

Figure 5.4 Nuclear Micronesian Languages and Language Groupings
Note: Yapese is not considered Nuclear Micronesian here.

Most archaeologists agree that the earliest evidence for human settlement in eastern Micronesia is the late first millennium BCE (Rainbird, 2004). Historical Micronesians manufactured no pottery, but in the 1980s several archaeologists discovered pottery fragments in the lowest levels of archaeological sites on Chuuk, Pohnpei, and Kosrae, dated to within a couple of centuries of CE 1 (Athens, 1990a, 1990b; King and Parker, 1984). In manufacturing techniques and style, Micronesian pottery resembles that of the late Lapita, a type that most archaeologists believe accompanied the initial spread of the early Austronesian speakers into Remote Oceania (Kirch, 1997).

Thus, both linguistic and archaeological evidence link the central and eastern Micronesian peoples to the Austronesian dispersal into Remote Oceania. The precise archipelagos from which eastern Micronesians migrated are debatable. The southeast Solomons and/or northern Vanuatu are leading candidates.

Which Micronesian islands were settled earliest is likewise uncertain. Legends on some islands recount that they were settled from a place called *Kachaw* (*Katau*). Some interpret this place as Kosrae island, but Goodenough (1986) argues persuasively that *Kachaw* is more likely to have been a legendary "sky world." Some of the earliest radiocarbon dates are from the northern Marshallese atoll of Bikini, but their accuracy is questionable (Rainbird, 1994, 2004:86–87).

Sociocultural Similarities

Given their apparent common ancestry, Nuclear Micronesian peoples shared numerous sociocultural features, of which the following are most important for my future discussion. The people relied on tropical root and tree crops and marine resources for their subsistence, with no indigenous livestock (pigs and fowl were postcontact introductions, although widespread today). Kinship ties through females were emphasized in ranking and property inheritance, although Kiribatese kin reckoning was more complicated. Kin groupings above the levels of nuclear families included extended families, matrilineages, and matriclans (again, Kiribati cannot be so simply categorized). Individuals and kin groups were most commonly ranked on the ideological basis of genealogical seniority: Within a single generation, older siblings were superior to younger siblings, whereas over the course of several generations the descendants of older descendants were superior in rank to the descendants of younger siblings. Chiefs were ubiquitous and largely hereditary, with authority to direct public works and coordinate labor on public projects and with some (highly variable) powers of overlordship of land and marine resources and control of public labor. The relative social rank of a matriclan varied with success in warfare, with narratives about clan fissioning, and with legends about the historical priority of settlement, with earlier arriving clans considered superior in rank to later arriving clans. Most matriclans included lineage segments, ranked on the basis of genealogical seniority such that members of senior lineages were superior to their juniors. Members of groups ideologically considered junior owed some kinds of material payment (first fruits or tribute), service, and formal social obeisance to their seniors. Public feasting was a means to celebrate life crisis events, validate rank, and enhance status.

Nuclear Micronesian Chiefdoms

The peoples who first dispersed among the eastern and central Micronesian islands brought along their ancestral languages, customs, and beliefs. This ancestral society almost certainly included hereditary distinctions in social rank. Historical linguists have reconstructed morphemes in proto-Oceanic (the common ancestor of all Nuclear Micronesian and Polynesian languages) indicating status differentiation. Whether status differentiation should be equated with a "chief-subject" distinction is arguable, but most likely hereditary differences in social rank were present in the ancestral society. Proto-Oceanic kinship terms also have been reconstructed. Notably for present purposes, the kin terms distinguish younger and older siblings and there is a special term for oldest child (Hage, 1999; Hage and Marck, 2002; Lichtenberk, 1986; Pawley, 1982; Pawley and Ross, 1995). With due caution, this suggests that genealogical seniority was a principle of the ancestral Micronesian society, just as of historically known Micronesian societies.

As the humans bearing and transmitting this ancestral culture spread out and colonized islands and archipelagos with diverse topographies, land and lagoon areas, rainfall patterns, typhoon and tropical storm hazards, and so forth, the culture changed. Fortunately, the method of controlled comparison does not require a separate explanation for the ancestral traits of cultures that comprise a phylogenetic unit. It does require that we try to explain whatever variation arose after the geographic dispersal of the ancestral population.

Materialists hold that the relevant features of the natural environment are important—commonly, the most important—influences on the evolution of variation. If the variation arose from a common cultural/historical baseline, then recognizing the importance of natural constraints is in no sense environmental determinism. Along with the critics of materialism, we recognize that the environment "influenced a preexisting culture"—it did not "determine" each element of this culture either piecemeal or systemically, but affected how people adjusted to the material world. There is plenty of room for "human agency"—nature does not exert its influence on automatons, but on persons with motives and emotions who find meanings in symbols and rituals.

In the remainder of this paper, I propose and apply a model describing how varying degrees of chiefly power evolved from the ancestral culture on different islands and archipelagos, depending on environmental circumstances. I suggest how varying island geographic and ecological conditions affected the ability of chiefs to sustain control over resources and people. Related theoretical arguments for political evolution in Nuclear Micronesia have been proposed by Alkire (1978), Cordy (1986), Knudson (1970), Mason (1968), and myself (Peoples, 1990, 1992, 1993).

In my view, the most important general process in cultural evolution is intensification, defined as the attempt to control environments to increase production. In turn—in the long run and in the majority of cases—intensification is driven by the inherent tendency of human population numbers to increase over long time spans (a bold statement, I recognize, but one well supported by humanity's past). Some environments cannot accommodate sustained population growth, so people either disperse into adjacent lands (or islands) or are held at low densities by diseases or other Malthusian forces. Other environments, though, can be refashioned by generations of people applying their labor, knowledge, and tools to increase carrying capacities. Long-term population growth forces increasing intensification. In turn, intensification accounts for most major transformations in human societies, including the development of agriculture (Cohen, 1977) and civilization. Among scholars who have championed the theoretical importance of intensification are Harris (1977, 1979), Earle (1997), Johnson and Earle (1987), Sanderson (1999b), and Diamond (1997).

As mentioned earlier, Micronesian subsistence was based on horticulture and fishing and political organization fell into the comparative type known as *chiefdoms*. An operational definition of chiefdom is provided by Earle (1997:14): "A chiefdom is a regional polity with institutional governance and some social stratification organizing a population of a few thousand [actually only "a few hundred" on some Micronesian atolls and atoll archipelagos] to tens of thousands of people." In most chiefdoms, "institutional governance" was vested in the holders of a series of titles, known as *chiefs*, with the following features:

- chiefs are strongly hereditary (defined on the basis of genealogical distinctions);
- chiefs have (variable) rights to deny access to some resources to their subjects;
- chiefs collect and distribute resources ("redistributive" exchanges dominate in the public arena);
- there is greater or lesser development of chiefly hierarchy, commonly including distinctions between "greater" (high) chiefs and "lesser" (local) chiefs;
- chiefs are owed social obeisance from their subjects.

This conception of chiefdoms is undoubtedly biased toward the Pacific chiefdoms I know best—those of Polynesia and Micronesia—but the argument may have wider relevance.

Like their (metaphorical) cousins in Polynesia, Micronesian chiefdoms were variably stratified. In the Central and Western Carolines social distinctions between chiefs and subjects were largely honorific. Although families and large kin groupings were ranked, the important distinction was between hereditary chiefs and their families and everyone else. In Pohnpei, Kosrae, and the Marshalls chiefs had powers and privileges comparable to those of some of the more stratified Polynesian archipelagos. On these islands, chiefs apparently had the power to punish their subjects, allocate natural resources, organize labor both for public projects and their own purposes, enjoy special consumption prerogatives, collect large amounts of tribute, and maintain large physical structures for their material pleasure and as symbols of their status and power. Moreover, there were at least three levels of social hierarchy, with a principal chief, lesser chiefs, and commoners. Hierarchical organizations in Micronesia were enormously complicated, especially in Pohnpei (Riesenberg, 1965; Petersen, 1982), Kosrae (Peoples, 1985), and at least some of the Marshall islands. The five political units of Pohnpei featured an enormous proliferation of titles at both the level of the chiefdom and the sectional divisions within it, a pattern that has persisted into the present.

The rest of this chapter proposes a general model for the evolution of stratification in chiefdoms and briefly applies it to Nuclear Micronesian societies.

Stratification, Self-Interest, and Ideology

Most existing ideas about stratification fall into two broad types, functionalist (or consensualist) and conflict (or coercive). (Lenski [1966] is still an excellent summary of these models.) Functionalists emphasize the societal-level benefits of inequality, such as redistribution of resources, organization of cooperative labor, and nonviolent resolution of disputes. Conflict theorists emphasize the advantages of stratification to elite groups and individuals, based on factors such as exploitation of labor and control over production and exchange. Most conflict approaches argue that elites (including "chiefs") control life-sustaining or culturally valuable resources, use this control to establish a power base, and manipulate the power base to their own advantage. Nonelites (including "subjects") may receive benefits also, but these generally are interpreted as side benefits or as necessary costs of maintaining power.

With respect to chiefdoms, the argument of conflict theorists that stratification arises from control over resources is beset by two main problems. First, in the absence of *significant* differences in the capacity for military force between chiefs and their subjects in chiefdoms (as contrasted with states), how is control initially acquired and subsequently maintained? Second, how does control over resources become transformed into power over individuals and groups, given that the latter generally have alternatives to submission? Many existing answers fall into two main categories: self-interest and ideology. *Self-interest* implies that chiefs are able to control the conditions of the lives of their subjects in important ways, so the latter go along because they have no alternatives that are genuinely viable (i.e., the costs of noncompliance are too high). Because of their control and power, chiefs constrain the actions of subjects, making it in the self-interest of subjects to conform to the interests and wishes of chiefs. *Ideology* implies that subjects accept chiefly control because of shared beliefs and values that legitimize chiefly prerogatives, even though such beliefs and values are contrary to subjects' material self-interest. Ideology is a necessary component of theories of stratification in chiefdoms to the extent that chiefly control over resources and actual force or threat are insufficient to constrain the actions of subjects. (Earle [1997] takes a different approach, but our conclusions are similar.)

Clearly, one drawback of ideological explanations is their assumption that subjects for some reason hold beliefs and values that significantly harm their material self-interest. (Some anthropologists have fewer problems with such an assumption than we materialists do.) Often subjects appear gullible or ignorant, chiefs manipulative or conspiratorial. Yet it is well established that subjects commonly do, in fact, hold beliefs and values that assist chiefs in controlling resources. These beliefs and values include such notions as genealogical entitlement, supernatural sanctions, divine right, and subjects' subjective overvaluation of the services of elites. (Presumably, people learn these ideologies as part of socialization, which need not imply that ideologies are never questioned.) I agree that ideologies are powerful and necessary sources of chiefly control, although I do not agree that they alone are sufficient. The question *for materialists* is: How do subjects come to hold such beliefs and values?

I propose a causal connection between chiefly control over resources and prevalent ideologies. The connection, though, requires neither conscious manipulation by chiefs nor gullibility by subjects. Rather, ideologies arise out of the normal, everyday social experiences of subjects as they encounter chiefly control. The mere existence of resource control promotes ideologies of acceptance and subordination, even where chiefs themselves do not actively promote such ideologies. Resource control is thus translated into power. But the probability of this happening depends on the material conditions of life, as I shall try to illustrate for Nuclear Micronesian chiefdoms.

Here I simply assume chiefly control over resources, irrespective of its origins (see Diamond [1997] for a clear and wide-ranging explanation of the connections between cultural change and environmental conditions). Such control is not ubiquitous, of course, and did not seem to exist among most foraging and many horticultural peoples. It did seem to exist in the ancestral societies of Nuclear Micronesians, as discussed earlier. Where it exists, resource control can originate through a variety of historical mechanisms, including temporal order of settlement, spatial differences in environmental quality and productivity, intergroup conflict (which *some group* ultimately wins), or sheer luck. The interesting theoretical question is not the *multifarious origins* of resource control, but the patterned mechanisms by which it *persists* over many human generations.

What resources do chiefs commonly control? Johnson and Earle (1987) provide a useful list, which I shamelessly modify for my own purposes. In regions where intensification of land use is sufficiently high, people (1) must deal with periodic resource fluctuations, (2) have to cope with competition from other groups, (3) make capital investments to improve productivity, and (4) experience resource deficiencies. To solve such problems, human communities (1) seek to reduce risks by producing surpluses that are *stored* for lean times, (2) form alliances that result in a need for *protection* from rivals within and enemies without, (3) invest in *technologies to increase production,* and (4) engage in *essential trade* with other communities. These responses involve new ways of organizing economic activities that, in turn, provide new opportunities for some individuals and groups to achieve control over life-sustaining or -enhancing resources.

To Johnson and Earle's list, I add two others: First, some land areas (for Micronesia, including sea coasts, wet lowlands for taro, and valleys) are more amenable to human manipulation than others. Specifically, some lands are more responsive to human labor input and technological investment than other lands. In Marvin Harris's language, they are more *intensifiable.* Individuals or groups who historically have (or who are able to acquire by actual conflict or threat) control over these lands are likely to have advantages over others. Where those who have lost resources are unable to escape the victors, then control over nature is likely to be translated into control over people as well, as Carneiro (1970) realized in his seminal article on the origin of states.

Second, those who acquire control over resources are likely to try to exert influence over the means of communication and the content of information. The obvious connection here is to ideology—the "ideas of the ruling class" may become widespread and incorporated into generalized cultural knowledge. Another connection, though, is to the kinds of culturally encoded information that appears in the public arena, in the form of highly visible symbols such as monuments and objects of art.

In summary, under intensification, some specific resources, once controlled by chiefs and their supporters, can be used as a power base. Such resources include

- stored foods, whose distribution chiefs control or influence
- protective services, which can be withheld
- technologies to improve productivity, to which access can be restricted
- essential trade relations and/or networks, which can be monopolized or re-strained
- the most desirable land and other productive areas, which can be occupied and intensified
- means of communication and content of culturally encoded information, which can potentially be used to increase power.

Of course, the relevance and relative weighting of these resources vary from chiefdom to chiefdom. As Johnson and Earle (1987:16–18) point out, solving adaptive problems is helpful to communities and potentially to their individual members. However, solutions also increase the probability that some group will control the resources, and thereby raise the *potential* for significant inequalities to develop. Here I propose a general process by which such inequalities persist over cultural evolutionary time.

Consider a nonstandard interpretation of redistribution, for example. It is ordinarily seen as either an organized way to aid subject communities according to their needs (functionalists) or as a mechanism to direct surplus into the hands of elites (conflict theorists). But control over redistribution also is a political tool of chiefs, for by strategic collection and allocation of food and valued objects they can earn support of key constituencies (including lesser chiefs and subjects of the latter). Acting in their *self-interest*, some lesser chiefs seek to persuade high chiefs to direct greater shares of the polity's resources to themselves, which leads them to cooperate with high chiefs. Their cooperation is witnessed by others and becomes part of the social experience of other lesser chiefs and the subject population at large. Would-be rival chiefs and subjects observe that high chiefs have a lot of support, further encouraging their own acquiescence to chiefly control and power. Over time, this social experience is explained in ways consistent with previously existing cultural assumptions and worldviews. These become elaborated into the ideas and beliefs social scientists call *ideologies*.

A causal diagram portrays the general argument succinctly (see Figure 5.5). The aim is to show how low levels of stratification develop into higher levels by processes of interaction that generate (Barth, 1966) subordination by means of both self-interest and ideology.

Given an initially low degree of resource control, high chiefs/families can increase their future rewards if they are able to restrict access to resources and allocate them according to their own interests. But whether they are able to do so depends on other factors. Two such factors are the effects of chiefly resource control on their subjects and lesser chiefs, and whether the latter react by resistance or acquiescence.

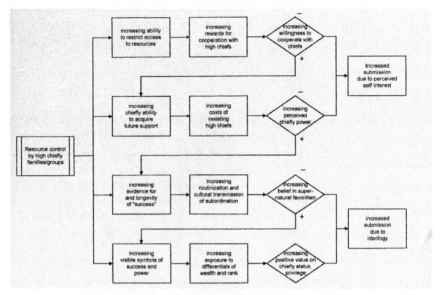

Figure 5.5 Social Processes Leading to Chiefly
Power by Self-Interest and Ideology

In return for increased rewards from redistribution, some lesser chiefs submit because they receive direct benefits from cooperation with high chiefs. Other lesser chiefs (and their subjects) socially experience the cooperation of their social and political peer group as an enhanced ability of higher chiefs to acquire support by maintaining or attracting allies, now or in the future (see Barnes [1988] for the general argument). The costs or risks of resisting the control of high chiefs over important resources increase, either in the perceptions of lesser chiefs and subjects or in actual political contests. Lesser chiefs perceive the acquiescence of their peers of coequal rank as making higher chiefs more powerful, so various subject groups perceive it as in their interest to continue to submit. Others—those who receive few material benefits from chiefly control—nonetheless submit because chiefly success at holding allies makes resistance too costly or risky. In a few words, self-interest leads to increasing chiefly power because some receive direct rewards from submitting to and cooperating with chiefs while others interpret the observed submission or cooperation of their coequals as evidence of chiefly power. (This process is portrayed in the top half of Figure 5.5.)

All else equal, this process increases the ability of chiefs to maintain power or remain successful over generational time by encouraging the development of beliefs that have an ideological character. Subject groups become familiar with and accustomed to subordination, leading to the cultural transmission of ideas (following Boyd and Richerson, 1985) that support subordination. Such ideas may be interpreted as chiefly power resulting from favoritism by the gods, or as sanctioned by Heaven, or as descent from a Sun Goddess, or as a divine right to rule. In order to demonstrate, maintain, and/or increase control, chiefs adopt visible symbols of their success and power (think of sumptuary wealth objects, Olmec or Rapa Nui stone heads, Hawaiian feather cloaks, funeral mounds from around the world, temples and other architectural monuments, and so forth). Such material symbols of wealth, power, rank, and other valued attributes leads subjects to attach positive value to chiefly status, power, and privilege. In some cases, subjects must believe that chiefly sponsored monuments and the like are a form of public service.

In sum, two specific forces make it in the self-interest of subjects to submit: rewards to some lesser chiefs and subjects from cooperation and alliances with high chiefs, and the costs (including the perceived risks) of resistance by would-be resistors that arise from their social experience. Given control, chiefs can reward supporters, and such rewards raise the perceived costs of resistance to potential nonsupporters.

Similarly, two specific ideational factors contribute to the evolution of an ideological basis for submission: beliefs in supernatural favoritism and the effects of prolonged exposure to material symbols of power and privilege. Both, I suggest, result from ordinary processes of human life, that is, social experiences and the conclusions humans commonly draw from these experiences. For example, the ancient Austronesian concept of *mana* ("spiritual power") that explained success or "effectiveness" in objects or artifacts was transformed in Polynesian chiefdoms into "power" that was granted to chiefs by deities. If *mana* explains success and certain people become successful, then it logically follows that over generational time subjects will come to believe that successful people have *mana*. Chiefly people themselves certainly can easily believe it and need not conspire among themselves to convince others. Frequent exposure to visible material symbols of power and privilege has a comparable impact on widespread perceptions of what is desirable, as advertisers in the modern world know very well.

Of course, even should such processes contribute to chiefly power, there are many ways by which these processes can be interrupted by events, such that the process leads to the unraveling of chiefly control rather than the maintenance of it. Readers can think of several questions: Why don't lesser chiefs who receive rewards from higher chiefs use those rewards to help themselves become "the" high chief? Why will allocating rewards to supporters not make other groups even more resentful and rebellious, rather than more subordinate?

My responses to such objections are as follows: First, sometimes rewards to one group will cause resentment and rebellion among other groups, or lead to the unraveling of chiefly control through some other process. Empirically the most common organizers of such overthrows are not the lowest-ranking subjects of some high chief, but some other lesser chief who wishes to wrest control of the chiefdom from his rival—often a brother or other close relative. So what will strategically smart high chiefs do? They will allocate rewards so as to weaken opponents and strengthen supporters. Surely higher chiefs are as smart as anthropologists insofar as they recognize that those who receive rewards may use the additional resources to organize opposition. Therefore, they allocate rewards (and administer punishments) to reduce this possibility. Like anthropologists, chiefs sometimes make mistakes.

Second, when their strategies misfire, the common result is chiefly replacement, not change in form; usually it is the chief(s), and not the chiefdom, that is overthrown.

Rival chiefs want to acquire power and privilege by controlling more resources. When they succeed by violent conflict, symbolic contest, threat, intrigue, or even persuasion, the chiefdom persists as a form of political organization. Indeed, those chiefdoms that survived long enough to be studied firsthand by ethnographers had experienced a process of political evolution, during which less stable mechanisms of establishing control were replaced by more stable mechanisms. (If readers wish to call this process "selection," I have no objection.) In terms of the process portrayed by the causal diagram, long-term stability occurs whenever circumstances allow the process to run its course. In other circumstances, which may well be most circumstances, chiefs are unable to sustain or increase control. The chiefdom collapses as a political organization, or the chiefdom stays "simple" rather than becoming "complex" (following the typology of Johnson and Earle [1987]). New World scholars of such places as Chaco Canyon, Cahokia, and Mesoamerica may be familiar with so-called arrested evolution and collapse.

Third, if the argument is empirically applicable, this last point implies that different forms of the chiefdom evolve according to how far the process runs its course or is interrupted by events. If the process shown by the causal diagram reflects real-world processes that occurred in actual chiefdoms, then we should be able to learn something about differences between chiefdoms by considering the circumstances that interrupt the process. On the causal diagram, these are the paths by which lesser chiefs and subjects submit as the result of self-interest and ideology. What keeps these processes from running their evolutionary course? This brings us back to Nuclear Micronesia.

Application

Nuclear Micronesian islands provide enough diversity in political organization and social inequality to investigate these ideas. Here my application includes mainly the Caroline islands (excluding Palau and Yap due to their different ancestry), with brief references to the Marshalls and Kiribati. Archaeological and linguistic evidence strongly indicate that the initial settlers of these islands brought a "simple chiefdom" with them from their homelands in eastern Melanesia and/or Western Polynesia. Over time, as islands and archipelagos with diverse environmental characteristics were settled, the chiefdom evolved into various forms.

In the Western Carolinian atolls and other low islands, chiefly rank persisted, but chiefly economic and social prerogatives few (Alkire, 1965, 1977). In the two high islands of the Eastern Carolines, Pohnpei and Kosrae, "rank" distinctions evolved into "class" distinctions, or nearly so (Riesenberg, 1968; Peoples, 1985). Although Chuuk is also an archipelago consisting of several high islands within a common lagoon, in its political organization Chuuk resembled its low island neighbors to the west more than the other two high islands. It is sometimes viewed as an anomaly—a "simple chiefdom" persisting in an environment more similar to those of the two high islands where "complex chiefdoms" developed. (Peoples [1990] is only partly successful in explaining Chuuk.) Further east, in the scattered atolls of the Marshalls, at least some multi-atoll polities existed, with chiefs collecting tribute from subject atolls by long-distance canoe voyages.

Between islands and island groups, environmental, geographical, and meteorological conditions varied substantially. There are the obvious differences between "high" and "low" islands, with all they imply for land areas, diversity of soils, topography, potential productivity, ability to withstand natural hazards, and so forth. But even between low islands, considerable variability existed in land areas, reef/lagoon areas and productivities, rainfall averages and variations, and typhoon and tropical storm incidences (Alkire, 1978).

I suggest that such ecological variability affected political variability between Micronesian chiefdoms by favoring or interrupting the social processes that generate different degrees of chiefly control and power. Stated differently, political evolution (whether of "chiefdoms" or other representatives of anthropological typologies) is an outcome of processes that are affected by natural conditions. But such conditions are not determinative in a linear or absolute sense. Rather, they affect human societies by making certain kinds of social processes necessary, probable, possible, difficult, or impossible. The processes portrayed in the causal diagram are the ones I discuss here. Space permits only a few suggestions, presented baldly and without supporting details (no doubt much to the horror of Micronesian specialists, along with my use of the ethnographic present tense).

Consider first the impact of substantial differences in the quality and productivity of land on a single island or small archipelago. Where differences in the quality of land are most pronounced within a single island, control over the most productive lands is more rewarding to chiefs and access to such lands or their products is more rewarding to subjects. Lesser chiefs and their subjects lacking such resources seek them by cooperating with high chiefs (in my model), or through threat or actual violent rebellion. Intra-island ecological differences are greatest on the three high islands, so the rewards of maintaining control over productive lands (e.g., wetlands best suited for taro production, coastal areas with productive fishing) are greatest there. Pohnpeian and Kosraen high chiefs had the right to allocate use of lands in their polities among lesser chiefs and subjects, and they sponsored dozens of regularly scheduled ceremonial feasts at which huge quantities of food were consumed and distributed. Two of the main reasons for feasts were to provide occasions for chiefs of various levels to acquire and maintain political support and to provide subjects with a way to demonstrate loyalty by making contributions to chiefly activities through labor and tribute. Lesser chiefs and subjects were rewarded for their loyalty with titles and access to resources, as is best documented for the very complex system of ranked titles on Pohnpei (Riesenberg, 1968). Feast customs also existed on the Western Carolinian low islands, where they also had competitive elements. But without the major differences in productivity found on high islands, feasts had a more honorific character. Feasting customs almost certainly were found in the ancestral (Austronesian) culture(s) of the islands. Kosraen and Pohnpeian feasts and titles were ways of rewarding supporters (by high chiefs) and publicly demonstrating loyalty and competing for chiefly favors (by subjects). They not only were important means of communicating (advertising) chiefly power and control, but also of signaling the likelihood of future cooperation.

Second, consider the possible effects of population size. Population numbers may favor or interrupt political processes, especially insofar as greater or lesser numbers

of people interact with geographical features. As Barnes (1988) has sho
power will be more successful if they can persuade would-be enemie..... .....,
that they have a sufficient amount of popular support such that resistance is futile,
risky, or too costly. Chiefly control of resources can be strengthened by controlling the
knowledge that low chiefs and subjects acquire about the amount of support a high
chief can count on. Chiefs want people to *think* they are powerful and have support,
because doing so helps them to *become* powerful and *maintain* or *increase* support. So
chiefs should attempt to convince people of their power by activities such as ostentatious displays, demands for obeisance, punishments for offenses tempered by mercy
if offenders are contrite, public displays of resources, development of special "respect
speech," and other visible symbols of success and power. Kosraen and Pohnpeian chiefs
used all these ways to advertise their power, to make people think they were powerful.
In Kosrae, and centuries ago in Pohnpei, such advertisements included the construction of enormous basalt walls around their compounds. Power thus has some of the
attributes of a shared fiction—power is something that people believe a powerholder
possesses, but he or she possesses it partly because almost everyone believes it. I suggest that many of the expenditures of chiefs on visible public symbols are designed to
persuade and convince.

In Nuclear Micronesia (and perhaps elsewhere), the larger the population subject
to chiefly control, the better the chance that such a shared fiction can persist. Reduced
interaction and communication between all the subgroups and communities that
make up the entire population strengthens the ability of powerholders to retain power.
Likewise, the more dispersed the population over the landscape, the more difficult
islandwide communication will be. *If important,* this process contributes to the greater
complexity of chiefdoms on high islands, for their populations were far greater and
the communities more dispersed over the landscape than on low islands. Subjects on
more spacious, more geographically diverse, and more populous high islands were more
likely to perceive chiefs as more powerful than subjects on low islands. And because
of these perceptions, chiefs were, in fact, more powerful. Here we see the possibility
that natural conditions affected political evolution by influencing the ability of subject
communities to share information with one another.

Balancing this process, however, is a counterprocess, for access to information is
double-edged: The chiefs' own ability to acquire information about activities among
their subjects is lower if the population is larger and more dispersed. This is an especially
strong political force if the local culture values concealment of knowledge, as did the
people of Pohnpei (Petersen, 1993) and perhaps other islands. Kosrae, with 42 square
miles of land area, was a single polity under a single high chief at the time of contact.
Pohnpei, with over 120 square miles of land area and a substantially larger reef area,
likewise was a single polity under a legendary despotic ruler until a few hundred years
ago. It broke up into the five independent polities (separate chiefdoms) that existed at
contact, each with two parallel lines of high chiefs, numerous sections, and a labyrinth of
lesser titles (see Riesenberg [1968] for a discussion of the traditional system and Petersen
[1982] for information about an historical split of a section). Perhaps Pohnpei was too
large for a single paramount chief to exercise control over its land and people.

Third, consider the possible implications of the relative longevity of chiefly control. The longer a given chiefly line of descent (e.g., a matriclan) or family remained in power, the more likely subjects were to adopt ideas and beliefs with an ideological character. Given the widespread human tendency to interpret "secular" success as indicative of "supernatural" favor, over generational time chiefly families will be seen as spiritually powerful (e.g., as having *mana*). Any circumstance or event that interrupted a particular chiefly line's resource control and power would decrease the probability that such ideas and beliefs would become routinized and culturally transmitted. In an island environment, one class of such "circumstances" are natural hazards such as storms and insufficient rainfall.

Within Nuclear Micronesia, the frequency and intensity of tropical storms and typhoons increases from east to west, with the westernmost atolls the most seriously and frequently affected—so much so that some smaller atolls were abandoned and their people sought refuge with clanmates on other atolls (Levin, 1976). In these low islands, the most common cultural rationales for between-clan rankings were historical priority of settlement and past success in warfare. High-ranking clans on one atoll often had lower rank on other atolls (Alkire, 1965; Alkire and Fujimara, 1990; Goodenough, 1986). Because inter-island voyaging for trade, visiting, and refuge was frequent, there were plenty of opportunities for residents of one island to take note of the differing clan rankings of other islands, and to communicate those rankings to their home islands. Under circumstances of variable inter-atoll clan rankings and frequent opportunities to observe relative clan rankings on neighboring atolls, the chances that a chiefly family or a particular clan would be perceived as endowed with power because of their supernatural connections was decreased.

Perhaps a similar process applies to the Marshall Islands. Scholars generally agree that chiefly control and inequality was greatest in the south and least in the north, paralleling the distribution of rainfall. So far as is known, the Marshalls never were unified into a single polity, but in early postcontact times a chief was able to exert control over many atolls and collect tribute from their inhabitants (Tobin, 1958). My impression is that chiefly control and power waxed and waned often in the Marshalls, sometimes being limited to one atoll, sometimes encompassing several (the temporal complexity in the Marshalls is discussed in Carucci [1988]). If so, the argument here is that the transformation of beliefs into powerful ideologies was interrupted periodically by natural hazards, including periods of low productivity related to rainfall amounts and fluctuations. Similarly, in Kiribati (formerly the Gilbert Islands), rainfall decreased from north to south, as did the power of chiefs.

In the atolls of the western Carolines, the northern Marshalls, and the southern Gilberts, then, most Micronesian scholars believe that inequality was lower and chiefly control and power less than on Pohnpei and Kosrae. Interpreted in terms of the model presented here, one reason for this pattern is that the success of *particular* chiefly lines did not last long enough for a belief in supernatural favoritism to become a powerful political ideology in the culture of the inhabitants. In these three archipelagos, I suggest that geographic conditions affected the degree of stratification and chiefly power partly by affecting the longevity of control by particular clans or kin groups. Longevity of control by a single family, clan, or other group is surely more difficult to achieve in some environments than in others.

Ideologies *arise* from a variety of sources, some of them historically contingent, but they *persist* because of social processes that are rooted in the material conditions of life. The ability of specific groups to sustain control over resources over multigenerational time varies according to material conditions. Under some conditions, control fluctuates over time and ideologies remain weak or wither. Under other conditions, control is more enduring and ideologies become both powerful and general. Ideologies do indeed have a contingent character—their specific content cannot be derived from material forces, for such content is historically given and depends on complex and usually unknowable historical events, perhaps from the deep past of a particular people. Yet this contingency of content does not remove ideologies from the influence of material forces.

Conclusion

Controlled comparison offers materialists at least two advantages. First, it allows more effective responses to several valid challenges (see the introduction) made by nonmaterialists and antiscientists. Second, anthropological data are overwhelmingly gathered naturalistically. With no ability (or desire) to control the conditions under which people live or lived, we should seek opportunities where nature and/or history have provided us with such controls. Among cultures that comprise a phylogenetic unit, history provides us with a common cultural baseline, whereas nature provides us with the variable ecological conditions that materialists believe are such an important source of diversity. The argument and application presented in this chapter is an example of materialist particularity: Like other kinds of materialism, it compares; like particularism, it admits uniqueness and revels in diversity.

The specific ideas in this chapter have the advantages of being explicit, comparative, and of specifying conditions under which different levels of chiefly control and inequality will develop. Whether they also are realistic (depicting real-world processes) and applicable in Nuclear Micronesia and elsewhere, I leave to the judgment of others.

Acknowledgments

Jan Smith, Ross Cordy, Lawrence Kuznar, and Stephen Sanderson commented on the theoretical points in this chapter. I am to blame for any errors of fact, misrepresentations, conceptual sloppiness, or inanities.

Chapter Six

Linking Past and Present

Cultural Materialism, Archaeology, and the Medieval Transition in the Aegean

P. Nick Kardulias

By its emphasis on the physical record as the basis for understanding the past, archaeology is in many ways the ideal candidate for exploring the utility of the cultural materialist paradigm. Cultural materialism provides a programmatic statement that allows one to pinpoint the crucial components underlying social life. Ideological elements such as religion and philosophy are clearly secondary in nature and derivative in function from the more concrete aspects of culture, those centering on technology and economics, especially subsistence. Those individuals who adopt strategies yielding the greatest energy returns can be termed successful because of the advantages they garner for themselves, their kin, and their followers. When combined with elements of cultural evolutionism, the materialist perspective offers a dynamic way to examine the past. After a discussion of the theoretical framework, I use a materialist approach to study the building of public monuments during the transition from Classical Antiquity to the Medieval era at Isthmia, Greece, the site of an ancient Panhellenic sanctuary and a major Byzantine military installation.

This study attempts to bring an anthropological perspective to the historical archaeology of a complex period in the Greek past. In so doing, it may be possible to comprehend more clearly the nature of the social transformation that occurred at the close of Classical times. Traditionally, discussion of the transition from Late Antiquity to the Early Byzantine period in the Aegean region has focused on the fate of Classical urban culture. Scholarly opinion is divided as to whether the Classical polis and its constituent institutions (i.e., a governing *boule* or council composed of aristocratic landowners, a monetary economy, elaborate public works, and a complex hierarchical social structure) emerged intact from the disruptive events of the third to sixth centuries CE. Some argue that the collapse of city life devastated the social fabric of Antiquity and left in its wake smaller settlements that lacked key features of Greco-Roman civilization. Other scholars see an unbroken historical thread connecting all of Greek history. Over the past two decades a consensus has emerged that argues that the break between Classical and Byzantine occurred in the seventh century rather than the fourth or fifth centuries CE, and that it was a more gradual process than previously believed. As one key scholar has noted, "it should be clear that the process of the 'medievalization' of early Byzantine settlement was a long and complex one and that an evolutionary model is to be preferred to explain the change rather than the usual catastrophy [sic] model" (Gregory, 1992:252). The present study uses an evolutionary materialist perspective to examine the Byzantine Fortress at Isthmia in eastern Greece in order to understand social change during this critical period, first at the level of the site and then at the level of the region.

The site of Isthmia in the northeastern Peloponnesos of Greece has occupied a strategic location since Antiquity (Figure 6.1). Situated at the southeastern corner of the Isthmus of Korinth (Figure 6.2), it commands the major land route from central to southern Greece. Virtually all land traffic into and out of the Peloponnesos had to traverse the Isthmus near this site (Wiseman, 1978:50–51). Perhaps in part due to this geographic prominence, Isthmia enjoyed an international reputation in Antiquity as one of the four major Panhellenic sanctuaries. The Temple of Poseidon and the associated complex of public facilities, including other temples, a stadium, baths, and a theater (see Figure 6.3), attracted visitors from all parts of the Greek world, and later, from many areas of the Roman Empire, to engage in festivals with religious, athletic, and musical components. The biennial Isthmian Games were just one of a number of events celebrated there. Isthmia was also the site of major political events. Alexander the Great announced his Asian campaign there in the fourth century BCE, and Emperor Nero visited the site as part of his grand tour of Greece in the first century CE.

The predominantly ceremonial nature of Isthmia underwent significant alteration in the fourth and fifth centuries CE. At that time, the construction of the Hexamilion, a defensive wall stretching the entire breadth of the Isthmus from the Gulf of Korinth to the Saronic Gulf, signaled a shift in orientation (Gregory, 1993a). Bastions anchored either end of this monumental wall, with a large fortress just east of the Sanctuary of Poseidon at Isthmia to house a major garrison. This project was part of a grand strategy of defense for the entire northeastern Peloponnesos, if not the whole of southern Greece. Beyond this immediate goal, there is evidence that the construction of these fortifications formed part of an empirewide strategy of containment (Cheetham, 1981:15–16; Luttwak, 1976). Over the succeeding centuries, the Fortress and Hexamilion were occasionally refurbished in order to meet various military threats. In the interim periods, people occupied parts of the Fortress and farmed the surrounding area.

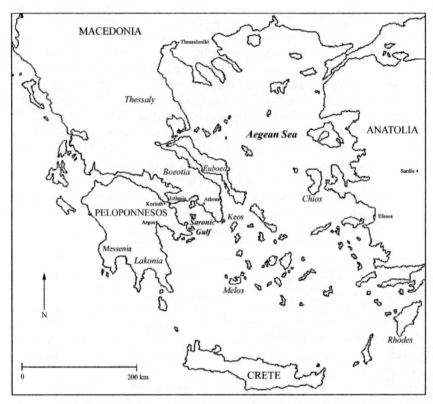

Figure 6.1 Map of Greece and the Aegean Region Showing Location of Isthmia and Other Key Sites of the Late Roman and Early Byzantine Periods

In order to begin filling in the rather sparse image of Byzantine Isthmia, further fieldwork concentrated on the later portions of the site. Since the Fortress had not been fully investigated, a key goal of the research was to determine the layout of structures there in order to compare the level of building activity at Isthmia over time. Geophysical survey and surface collection were conducted in each of the two main field seasons (1985 and 1986); further brief investigations occurred intermittently between 1988 and 2001. These studies revealed the presence of up to ten buildings, and a garrison of 1,200–1,700 men (Gregory and Kardulias, 1990; Kardulias, 1992, 2005).

The concept of transition is central to this study. The issue involves how to examine culture change in the past. Key questions include the following: Does social change tend to be abrupt, with new technologies, modes of behavior, and ideas becoming dominant in a brief period of flux? If so, what are the causes of such revolutionary changes? If, on the other hand, culture change is gradual, how do we account for the dramatic differences that seem to characterize periods separated by short time spans? What is the role of the individual in social change? These and other related questions

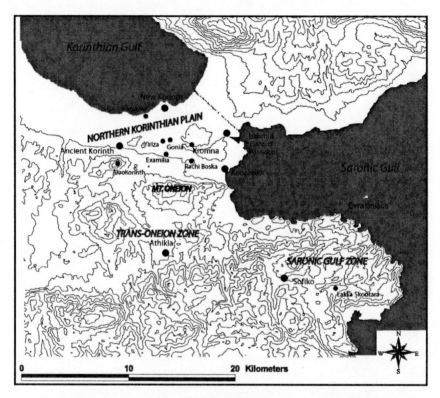

Figure 6.2 Map of the Korinthia Showing Isthmia and Other
Key Sites (modified from original in Eastern Korinthia
Archaeological Survey [EKAS] archives)

have consumed historians, archaeologists, and anthropologists for decades. The model of social change adopted in this study is evolutionary or developmental in form. Change occurs through the accumulation of cultural innovations that feed off each other. This does not mean, however, that change occurs only through the interplay of historical forces or trends. While it is true that humans do not act in a cultural void, they also must be seen as independent actors and innovators. Humans are the agents of social change, not just media for the expression of inanimate cultural processes. This study characterizes transition as directed by humans toward some perceived benefits.

Isthmia, with its long history, provides a good setting to examine the problem of transition or social change in the Aegean region (see Randsborg [1990, 1991] for discussion of the issue in a Mediterranean context). I suggest that the entire sequence of occupation at Isthmia is amenable to an evolutionary materialist treatment, that the periodization applied here and elsewhere in Greece is useful as a heuristic tool, but it often belies the complex relationships that tie events together. However, the focus of this study is the transition from Late Antiquity to Early Byzantine at Isthmia. This

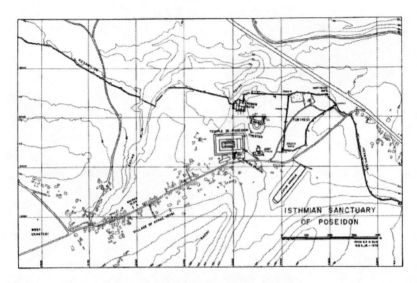

Figure 6.3 Plan of Isthmia Showing Location of Various Structures and
Features of the Landscape (Ohio State University
Excavations at Isthmia [OSUEI] archives)

site offers good evidence for these phases and can aid in resolving some of the issues
concerning the shift that occurred at the end of antiquity.

Theoretical Perspective

The approach employed herein borrows from cultural materialism as developed and
espoused by Marvin Harris (1968b, 1979; see also Haas, 1982), and cultural evolutionism (see Boyd and Richerson [1985] and Johnson and Earle [1987]). In their search
for nomothetic, generalizing laws to explain social phenomena, these two approaches
attempt to deal with human behavior on a universal, cross-cultural scale.

Cultural Materialism

Harris's concern is to present a "basic research strategy" that has parallels to the theory
of biological evolution developed by Darwin. As he has stated (1968b:4):

> I believe that the analogue of the Darwinian strategy in the realm of sociocultural phe-
> nomena is the principle of techno-environmental and techno-economic determinism.
> This principle holds that similar technologies applied to similar environments tend to
> produce similar arrangements of labor in production and distribution, and that these in

turn call forth similar kinds of social groupings, which justify and coordinate their activities by means of similar systems of values and beliefs. Translated into research strategy, the principle of techno-environmental, techno-economic determinism assigns priority to the study of the material conditions of sociocultural life, much as the principle of natural selection assigns priority to the study of differential reproductive success.

Harris leaves no doubt as to what he perceives to be the ultimate motivating factors behind human behavior. This perspective is based on "the premise that human social life is a response to the practical problems of earthly existence" (1979:ix). Humans are seen as engaged in an ongoing attempt to ameliorate their environment or to deal with demographic pressure by means of expanding the potential of the environment through the process of intensification, that is, increased exploitation of available resources in response to ecological shifts (both natural and cultural).

There are two entrenched laws humans must face. First, people must expend energy to obtain energy. Second, the human ability to produce children exceeds the ability to obtain energy for them. Harris suggests that the best humans can do is to seek a balance between reproduction on one hand, and the production and consumption of energy on the other. He then argues that cultural evolution, like biological evolution, has occurred through opportunistic alterations that increase benefits and lower costs to individuals. Success of a group depends on the success of the individuals who comprise it (Harris, 1979:56, 60). The implications of this thesis for the understanding of past human societies center on the notion that most people engage in activities that they believe will enhance their material position in the world.

Cultural Evolutionism

How to model culture change is, of course, a major issue for archaeology, historic or prehistoric. As Harris notes, "The tension between the unique and the recurrent exists in every field that concerns itself with diachronic processes. Evolution is the record of how out of sameness differences emerge" (Harris, 1979:79). With this statement Harris captures the basic thrust of historical transformation. The purpose of the present study is to demonstrate that Early Byzantine culture was an outgrowth of its Late Antique roots, that the trajectory of development is comprehensible because human action in all periods is governed by similar forces, and that evolutionary theory, specifically as it relates to architecture, offers an elegant interpretive framework to explore those processes at a particular site.

Since energy is indispensable to human survival, Leslie White saw a causal thread connecting technology to all facets of society, from the material to the ideological. White (1949:365) is emphatic about the direction of the relationship:

The roles played by the several subsystems in the culture process as a whole are not equal by any means. The primary role is played by the technological system. This is, of course, as we would expect it to be; it could not be otherwise. Man as an animal species, and consequently culture as a whole, is dependent upon the material, mechanical means of adjustment to the natural environment. Man must have food. He must be protected from the elements, and he must defend himself from his enemies. These three things he must do if he is to continue to live, and these objectives are attained only by technological means. The technical system is therefore both primary and basic in importance; all human life and culture rest and depend upon it.

The fundamental truths that White enumerates in this passage are essential to the argument of the present study. Evolution for White involved the increasing capacity to capture and use energy.

In sum, many scholars argue that culture can provide either stability or innovation, and thus offers humans an immensely rapid and flexible response system (Figure 6.4). The ultimate impact of accumulated short-term decisions transforms society as particular choices prove more beneficial than others (that is, as they are adaptive). But we must realize that most of the decisions people make are conservative, that is, they try to maintain a particular system or set of relationships that they favor. However, their efforts to do so actually introduce some changes that lead to incremental realignment of the system, rather than its wholesale replacement. Even when systems are planned, the results are rarely predictable; witness the intent and effect of socialist systems in Eastern Europe. Conrad Kottak (1999:33) compares this aspect of culture to Romer's Rule "that an innovation that evolves to *maintain* a system can play a major role in *changing* that system. Evolution occurs in increments. Systems take a series of small

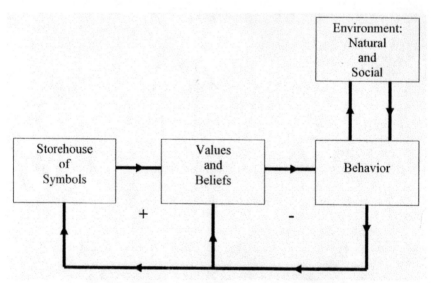

Figure 6.4 A Model of Culture Emphasizing the
Decision-Making Aspects as Critical to Adaptation

Note: Negative feedback (-) inhibits change and positive feedback (+) encourages change.
Source: Mark Shutes, personal communication, 1984.

steps to maintain themselves, and they gradually change." In a similar way, I suggest that decisions ancient Korinthians made concerning various aspects of their lives (especially as they related to architecture) were drawn from an array of choices, but they could in no way envision all of the long-term consequences of those decisions; energy considerations influenced these decisions (see Abrams [1989, 1994] for the connection to architecture).

Stephen Sanderson (1990) has offered an excellent overview that makes clear the link between cultural materialism and social evolutionism. First he notes that many social scientists fail to distinguish *evolutionist* from *evolutionary* approaches. Evolutionist models explain change as the result of a "logical unfolding" that generates progress. Evolutionary formulations "attempt to explain changes as responses to particular requirements imbedded in specific historical situations" (Sanderson, 1990:3). Cultural materialism is an evolutionary approach in which "adaptation is a concept that principally relates to how individuals make choices under particular kinds of material constraints" (Sanderson, 1990:5). Furthermore, evolutionary models allow for retrogression, that is, evolutionism can encompass the decay or collapse of complex social systems into simpler forms—precisely one of the key points of the present study.

As Sanderson (1990:160) has pointed out, Harris conceives of adaptation as acting on individuals whose choices determine the nature of a culture: "The selection processes responsible for the divergent and convergent evolutionary trajectories of sociocultural systems operate mainly on the individual level; individuals follow one rather than another course of action, and as a result the aggregate pattern changes" (Harris, 1979:60). Furthermore, Harris's view of adaptation is quite similar to the formalist approach: "Cultural evolution, like biological evolution, has (up to now at least) taken place through opportunistic changes that increase benefits and lower costs to individuals" (Harris, 1979:61). Many critics of such cost-benefit models argue that humans also act on the basis of emotion as well as logic, and often make choices that are clearly not in their material best interest. Robert Frank (1988) offers a solution to this problem with his commitment model. He notes that, although people often act from emotion in a manner that is contrary to their short-term self-interest (that is, irrationally), such behavior can in fact have long-term benefits (and thus be rational):

> There are many problems that purely self-interested persons simply cannot solve. They cannot make themselves attractive for ventures that require trust. They cannot threaten credibly to walk away from unfair transactions that will increase their wealth. Nor can they deter aggressors when retaliation would be prohibitively costly. Nor can they make credible commitments in intimate personal relationships.
>
> All of these problems are important.... The problems require that we tie our hands, and the emotions have just the desired effect. We have also seen a variety of plausible means whereby others might discern our predispositions. It is not necessary that we be able to judge everyone's character with complete accuracy. The commitment model requires only that we be able to make reasonably accurate judgments concerning people we know very well.
>
> Most of us believe we have this capacity. If we are right, it follows that noble human motives, and the costly behaviors they often summon, will not only survive the ruthless pressures of the material world, but even be nourished by them. (Frank 1988:255–256)

Frank's approach supplements rather than supplants the model of the economic formalists. As many formalists have noted, people make choices about nonmaterial as well as material items, and thus invest in elements of great emotional value (for example, prestige and status).

The materialist, rationalist perspective represented by Harris, evolutionism, and the formalists provides a comparative framework that attempts to transcend differences of time and space. In this way, events that transpired at Isthmia in various periods can be examined in a uniform fashion. Although activities at the site varied in the different historical eras, these events can all be understood in terms of people carrying out actions they deemed to be most likely to provide the greatest benefits. For example, the establishment of the Sanctuary and its embellishment conferred certain advantages on residents of Isthmia and neighboring communities, including employment in construction; maintenance and servicing of the facilities; the economic windfall resulting from the celebration of festivals drawing large crowds with the concomitant demands for food, drink, and lodging; and the prestige associated with a Panhellenic center. It is little wonder that several poleis vied for the honor of controlling this Sanctuary. By the fifth century CE, political, religious, and economic conditions dictated a new scenario. Survival was best served by the construction of fortifications, and to expedite this activity many of the structures in the Sanctuary were dismantled to provide building material. Rather than viewing this event as symbolic of the disaffection with pagan religion, reflected in the irreverent treatment of sacred edifices, it may be more profitable in some ways to suggest that people were still acting in essentially the same way by attempting to maximize their potential for survival. The expression of the adaptive strategy changed because other environmental (cultural, in this case) factors had changed. Perhaps in this way the span of events at Isthmia can be viewed as an evolving pattern of adaptation by the residents.

Some researchers have applied a number of evolutionary principles to architecture, thus allowing us to evaluate the humanly constructed environment in a dynamic fashion. While there is an extensive literature on this subject, I will concentrate on the work of several key scholars. The architect and city planner Constantine Doxiadis (1968) coined the term "ekistics" to describe his efforts to understand human settlements as integrated wholes. In his view, architecture responds to the changing needs a society faces:

> We live in a developing world, and the only justification for architecture is its connection with the overall evolution of society. For our purposes we may define this as the expression of all the forces which influence the creation of buildings, bearing in mind that the architect is conditioned by economic as well as by aesthetic, by social as well as by technical, by political as well as by cultural considerations. If we view architecture as a part of the overall development taking place around us we shall understand how much it is conditioned by environmental factors, factors that must seriously be taken into account. (Doxiadis, 1963:88)

Doxiadis's concern is with the need to adapt modern architecture and city layout to the requirements of twentieth-century life, but his ideas are applicable to earlier periods, in particular the notion that buildings reflect the political and economic fortunes of a society. He contends that one of the major differences between ancient and modern architects is that the former were concerned only with a single settlement, whereas their modern counterparts have regional and national concerns (Doxiadis, 1963:97). Here I believe Doxiadis seriously underestimated the role played by the ancient builder. As many historians have demonstrated, military and civilian structures in national building programs often exhibited considerable integration in planning and function. This issue aside, Doxiadis (1968:21–22) offers a comprehensive approach. He stresses the examination of the physical layout of a settlement in order to gain insight into the significant human interactions contained within it.

Bruce Trigger (1990) offers an important assessment of the role architecture plays in sociopolitical complexity. He notes that monumental architecture, the scale and orna-mentation of which often exceed necessary functional requirements, is uniformly present in all complex societies. In addition, he observes that while people attempt to minimize their expenditure of energy in attaining their goals, large-scale architecture seems to be wasteful and appears to obviate a purely materialist explanation of the phenomenon. But there is a solution to the conundrum. Trigger (1990:126) suggests that conspicuous consumption in the form not only of architecture but also of burial rituals, art, calendrics, and other elements did serve a very practical function: All of these things represented a massive energy investment that demonstrated and reinforced the social distance separat-ing the upper and lower classes. To the elite, the expenditure of energy in large public buildings served the function of solidifying its preeminent position.

Elliot Abrams (1989, 1994) provides an explicit statement of the importance of architecture in the study of cultural evolution. Like Trigger, he focuses on the energy involved in construction as an indicator of societal complexity. In a very clear statement he proposes to "describe and explain the process of changing energy expenditure in architecture through time" (Abrams, 1989:53). Since the control of energy resources can be measured objectively, it is possible to compare the relative status of societal complexity at different times or between different groups (Cheek, 1986:50). For example, a decline in the construction of monumental buildings should mirror the collapse of a complex cultural system. To operationalize this approach archaeologically, one must translate energy into architectural equivalents. One of the most basic means of accomplishing this is to determine work rates and person-days expended in the construction of particular structures. Erasmus (1965) and Abrams (1994) conducted a series of timed experiments in Mexico and their figures provide a baseline for measuring energy invested in large-scale architecture. Table 6.1 provides a summary of their estimates for the energy expenditure required to prepare certain architectural elements; the figures from Erasmus's (1965) study incorporate procurement, transportation, and construction costs.

Energy and Architecture at Isthmia

The estimation of energy investment in architecture at Isthmia provides a quantified measure of resource expenditure. From an evolutionary standpoint, a society that wastes its resources on nonessential activities in a period of stress (e.g., a fluctuating

Table 6.1 Work Rates Based on Timed Experiments

Activity	Person-days
Rubble masonry	5.25 p-d/m^3
Finished masonry	12.25 p-d/m^3
Sculpted stone surface	3 p-d/1000 cm^2
Shaped wood surface	8.3 p-h/m^2
Grass roof construction	p-d=2.95+.16 (area)
Rooftile production	
Making tiles	1 p-d/100 tiles
Firing	2 p-d/500 tiles
Excavating soil	1 p-d/m^3

Sources: Erasmus (1965); Abrams (1989). The figures refer to the number of person-days (p-d) required to accomplish particular tasks. For example, 5.25 p-d are needed to build 1 m^3 of rubble masonry; the rate includes the time needed to procure, transport, and prepare the raw materials and to undertake the actual construction. The figures for sculpted stone and shaped wood surfaces refer only to the manufacturing stage. The other factors are self-explanatory.

environment), or that misapplies resources in an effort to address a known problem, undermines its own viability. Strategic choices about the allocation of resources have a major impact on the form of a particular social structure. Abrams (1989:57) notes that heavy investment in monumental public architecture is a sign of emerging state-level polities. I would add that such investment also tells us about the maintenance of complex societies.

The purpose of this exercise is to evaluate and compare the conditions at Isthmia in the Early Roman period (first and second centuries CE), when there was general stability in the Empire, and in the early fifth century CE after an era of political and economic upheaval. Some scholars argue that significant changes occurred in the fifth century CE, but most believe that the seventh century was the critical period (Haldon, 1990). While the latter period certainly was a time of significant change, similar events marked the late fourth and early fifth centuries CE. Alaric's raid into the Peloponnesos in CE 395 may have triggered the collapse of Isthmia as a major pagan Sanctuary (Beaton and Clement, 1976). Thus, the shift that Haldon (1990) identifies was in part based on trends that developed earlier. In addition, it is clear that the nature of the site changed significantly between the two periods represented in the following analysis. The Early Roman sanctuary gave way to the Late Roman/Early Byzantine military complex. I intend to demonstrate that energy investment in the two periods was essentially unchanged despite the shift in emphasis. As a result, I argue for system maintenance in the fifth century despite significant differences in the outward appearance of the site. Most historians now agree that imperial institutions were still firmly in place in the Eastern Empire in the fourth and fifth centuries. The present study proposes some additional support for this view in terms of monumental public construction at one site.

For this quantitative comparison I concentrate on the central part of the Roman Sanctuary and the Early Byzantine Fortress (Figure 6.3). I calculate energy expenditure in person-days (p-d) of work, based on the timed experiments conducted by Erasmus (1965) and Abrams (1989, 1994:41–55). Since the structures in the Sanctuary represent different periods of occupation, not all will be included in the present analysis. I calculated estimates for the *stoas* that formed the *temenos* boundaries, the Palaimonion complex, and several smaller features (Figure 6.5). I excluded the Temple of Poseidon because the structure dates to the fourth century BCE, and, despite maintenance costs, the main resource expenditure falls well outside the Early Roman period. Roman construction at the site also included the bath, theater, renovation of the later stadium, and several building complexes east of the *temenos*. I do not consider these other structures because work in the center of the Sanctuary represents a concentrated effort to reestablish cult activity after a period of disuse (Broneer, 1973:67), and thus is most equivalent to the intense building that characterized the construction of the Fortress; in addition, information is incomplete about many of the other buildings. To balance this limited focus for the Early Roman period, I calculate figures for the Fortress wall only, and omit consideration of the numerous, but incompletely preserved, structures in the interior, the defensive outworks, and the massive Hexamilion. For the purposes of this type of

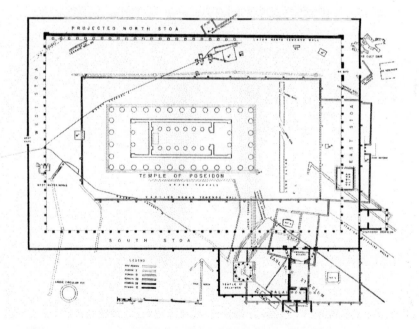

Figure 6.5 Plan of the Central Part of the Roman Sanctuary

Source: Broneer, 1973. Reprinted by permission of the American School of Classical Studies at Athens.

analytical comparison, the units of study are acceptably comparable. Another important consideration is the number of years during which people erected the various structures. Major building programs in the Roman Sanctuary covered a period of about 170 years, from the late first century BCE when construction resumed under the auspices of the Roman colony at Korinthos (Broneer, 1973:67–68), to the time of Pausanias's visit (ca. CE 160). The Fortress, on the other hand, was built over a period of several years (ca. five years for the whole Hexamilion system). The gradual vs. intense nature of these respective activities suggests differential concentration of resources in the periods under consideration. Military exigencies almost certainly dictated massive allocation of resources for building the Fortress; the fact that the state could marshal such quantities of materials and manpower quickly is in itself an indication of its continuing power.

Table 6.2 displays the figures derived for the Sanctuary. I took measurements for the various structures from Broneer (1973). Wherever reconstructed heights or thicknesses were not provided, I used the preserved dimension, so the estimates must be viewed as conservative. For purposes of differentiating work rates, I consider entablature pieces as sculpted blocks that require considerably more time to complete than plain building blocks. Estimates of roof construction include time to erect the timber frame and put

Table 6.2 Energy Expenditure in the Central Part of the Sanctuary of Poseidon at Isthmia during the Roman Period

Structure	Volume/Area x work rate	Total person-days
Roman Altar		
Rubble masonry	35.35 m^3 x 5.25 p-d/m^3	186
Finished masonry	3.05 m^3 x 12.25 p-d/m^3	37
Roman Temenos Wall		
Finished masonry	89.6 x 12.25	1,098
Stoas		
Foundation		
To excavate	226.72 m^3/(2 m^3/p-d)	113
To fill	226.72 x 5.25	1,190
Floor	149.3 x 12.25	1,829
Back wall	944.16 x 12.25	11,566
Columns (n = 78)		
Column blanks	71.76 x 12.25	879
To carve	575.56 m^2 x 3 p-d/1000 cm^2	17,267
Entablature		
To prepare blocks	98.8 x 12.25	1,210
To carve	247 x 3 p-d/1000 cm^2	7,410
Roof		
Cross beams	2.56 m^2/beam x 8.3 p-h/m^2	
	21.25 p-h/beam=2.66 p-d/beam	
	2.66 x 156	415
Rafters	4.8 m^2/rafter x 8.3	
	39.8 p-h/rafter=4.98 p-d/rafter	
	4.98 x 78	388

Table 6.2 *(continued)*

Structure		Volume/Area X Work Rate	Total Person-Days
	Roof tiles		
	Making tiles	6552/100	66
	Firing tiles	6552/500	13
	Roof construction	2.95 + .16(2150.80)	347
Palaimonion			
	Temple of Palaimon		
	Podium		
	Rubble	140.80 x 5.25	739
	Veneer	32 x 12.25	392
	Columns (n = 11)		
	Blanks	8.4 x 12.25	103
	Carving	71.5 m² x 3 p-d/1000 cm²	2,145
	Entablature		
	Blocks	10.70 x 12.25	131
	Carving	17.84 x 3 p-d/1000 cm²	535
	Roof		
	Making tiles	748/100	7
	Firing tiles	748/500	1
	Construction	2.95 + .16(36.3)	9
	Enclosure wall	98 x 12.25	1,201
	Ritual pits		
	Soil removal	30.94 m³/2.6 m³/p-d	12
	Stone lining	6.7 x 5.25	35
	South building	31.5 x 12.25	386
	Road	48.8 m³/9.6	5
Statues		360 p-d x 64	23,040
Stelae and Inscribed Blocks		90 p-d x 5	450
Southeast Propylon			
	Finished masonry	52.8 x 12.25	647
	Columns (n = 4)		
	Blanks	3.68 x 12.25	45
	Carving	29.52 x 3 p-d/1000 cm²	886
Total			74,783

Note: In the central column, the first figures indicate the volume or area of the particular material from each structure (left column) as calculated from data in Broneer (1973); the second figures indicate the work rates for dealing with the material. The third column (far right) gives the total estimated p-d required to accomplish each of the tasks; figures are rounded to the nearest whole number. For columns and entablature, the first line provides the energy required to provide blanks or blocks, and the second line indicates the time needed to carve the pieces into the final form. Estimates for the number of rafters, beams, and rooftiles are based on reconstructions in Broneer (1973).

on ceramic tiles. I use Abrams's (1989) formula for the construction of a grass roof, so the figures are conservative. The road consists of a bed of crushed stone across the length of the sacred area. The pits in the Palaimonion are rectangular holes with crude stone linings; the figures reflect the time needed to dig the pits and position the stones. Pausanias (1964:II.1.7–9, II.2.1) mentions twenty-one statues of gods and other mythological figures, and also notes that an unspecified number of portrait statues of athletes lined one side of the Sanctuary. Sturgeon (1987:9) suggests that the ten statue bases along the north side of the Sanctuary may be those Pausanias noted for the athletes; in addition, she identifies Roman-period fragments that represent another thirty-three statues (Sturgeon, 1987:131–155) for a total of sixty-four statues, although there almost certainly were more (see Drees [1968] for a discussion of the number of statues at Olympia, another Panhellenic sanctuary). The discovery of Phidias's atelier at Olympia (Drees, 1968) and the workshop at Nemea where bronze statues were cast (Miller, 1990:63) supplement the limited evidence for the production of statuary at Isthmia (Rostoker and Gebhard, 1980). Scranton (1969:32–33) noted that the wages paid to sculptors who prepared the figures (each of which was about two feet high) for the Erechtheion frieze in the fifth century BCE was sixty drachmas. At a typical wage of one drachma per day, each figure required sixty p-d. Since most of the statues at Isthmia were lifesize, I multiplied the p-d estimate by six (three times higher and two times wider to equal a lifesize statue) to compensate for the increased mass of each piece. I estimate 360 p-d for each statue. I also estimate that each commemorative stela and decorative inscribed block required one-fourth the effort of a lifesize statue. A number of such stelae must have adorned the Sanctuary. Two stelae (Clement, 1974) and three intricately carved entablature blocks were reused as paving slabs in the road through the Northeast Gate (total of five pieces).

Table 6.3 presents the figures for the Fortress. While there is some variation in wall thickness, Gregory (1993a:135) states that the average is 2.3 m, which represents about eight Roman feet, of which the ashlar blocks make up 1.2 m (0.6 m on either side) and a cemented rubble core the remaining 1.1 m. I calculated separately the work rates for the curtain walls and the towers because of the differences in height and the space necessary for the stairwells and storage sections in the towers. Although the towers differ somewhat in configuration, based on Gregory (1993a) I used a minimal figure of 6 m per side; height to

Table 6.3 Work Estimates for the Construction of the Isthmian Fortress

Feature	Volume of material x work rate	Total person-days
Curtain walls without towers		
Rubble	4552.02 m³ x 5.25	23,898
Finished masonry	5842.86 m³ x 12.25	71,575
Towers (n = 19)		
Rubble	1244.88 m³ x 5.25	6,536
Finished masonry	3570.48 m³ x 12.25	43,738
Total		145,747

Source: The volume of material data is derived from Gregory (1993a). The p-d estimates are rounded to the nearest whole number.

the fighting platform was 9 m, and the parapet wall rose 2 m above that. On wall sections between towers, height to the fighting platform was 5.7 m, with an additional 2 m on the outer face for the parapet wall (Gregory, 1993a:135). The wall perimeter measures 728 m.

The figure of 74,783 p-d required for the construction of the main portions of the Roman-era Sanctuary does not include all of the features in the area bounded by the *temenos* wall. I omitted both other known structures and features (a bath, water lines, theater, and stadium from the Roman period, and the Byzantine Hexamilion) and buildings known only from a reference on an inscription (Broneer, 1973:113) to maintain a level of comparability. So the energy expenditure figure from Table 6.2 represents only the core of the Roman Sanctuary. Similarly, the energy estimate for the Fortress reflects only the most visible part of the military complex, and excludes the numerous internal structures (up to ten large buildings—see Kardulias [1992]), the Hexamilion, and temporary structures erected in the ancient *temenos* (Broneer, 1973:96–98). Although not exactly equivalent, the central Roman Sanctuary and the Fortress provide bases for comparison. The p-d figures suggest a heavier building investment in the fifth century than in the second century CE. This situation speaks directly to the issue of societal maintenance and change.

While the functions of these buildings certainly differed, the massive investment in the Fortress is a clear indication of the ability to marshal substantial resources, and thus suggests the continued existence of a complex centralized political organization, as some historians have noted (Haldon, 1990). In constructing the fortifications, the Early Byzantine decision makers altered the external form and function of buildings at the site; as conditions played out over the next 150 years, their choice proved to have adaptive significance as the Korinthia withstood a series of assaults. In the difficult period of the seventh century, the site witnessed yet another shift as people took up residence in the ruins of the Bath and the Fortress (Gregory, 1993b). There is clearly a decline in construction at Isthmia in this period, but people continued to use available structures. The imperial government decreased its efforts in peripheral areas like Isthmia, but expended substantial energy at major centers such as Thessaloniki and Constantinople. This realignment of priorities was a reaction to political and military realities. That the Byzantine state was able to withstand considerable external pressure, in the form of raids and large-scale attacks by Slavs, Persians, and Arabs, and to expand in subsequent centuries, reflects the cultural resilience modeled in Figure 6.4. Evolutionary and materialist theory informs us that change is part of a continuum of human behavior. What we see at Isthmia is that the sociopolitical core was essentially unchanged between the second and the fifth centuries despite decisions to invest in different types of public architecture. Energy investment clearly drops in the seventh century, with no evidence of monumental construction at Isthmia, but substantial use of the site continued, as reflected in the considerable quantities of "Slavic" pottery found in the Fortress and the Bath (Gregory, 1993b). What we see, then, is a decline in architectural investment, but a continuity in site usage.

Discussion

Based on the preceding material, I derive a model of culture change that has the following elements:

1. The least effort principle guides human behavior. Humans must, at some level, be concerned with the efficient expenditure of energy. This principle relates directly to the universal human capacity for rational choice. People will select those options that seem to be in their best interest, that is, that provide them the most benefits at the lowest cost. The benefits include both material and nonmaterial items; the latter include status and prestige.

2. The principles of the Darwinian evolutionary model are applicable to social change. The change is nondirected, but people do make efforts to provide an orientation by dealing with immediate problems; in so doing, their actions have long-range consequences, many of which are unforeseen and thus introduce the nondirected component. Changes are often incremental, but the cumulative effect can be far-reaching. From Joseph Tainter (1988) we learn that collapse has positive elements, or at the very least is understandable as an option for a society undergoing significant stress.

3. Architecture reflects these individual and societal concerns. Since practical factors are primary, one cannot proceed with monumental undertakings without making important choices about the disposition of limited resources. The investment of vast resources in large building projects reflects social complexity with hierarchical organization. Such complexity persisted from Late Antiquity into the Medieval period, even though the precise overt manifestation of the phenomenon changed. I do not deny that Byzantine and Late Antique culture differed, but to characterize the transition as an abrupt break or dissolution is of little assistance in determining the process of change. What is of interest is not the shift in emphasis on architectural function, but the degree to which energy investment in construction continued, when it changed, and why it did so.

Examination of the historical and archaeological evidence provided by proponents of abrupt discontinuity (Foss, 1975, 1976; Kazhdan and Cutler, 1982) suggests that this perspective is not an adequate explanation for what transpired in the Aegean region between the fourth and seventh centuries. Also unsatisfactory is a simple version of continuity that sees a direct reflection of ancient Hellenic culture in Byzantine and modern Greek societies. This notion of continuity makes of the Byzantines little more than caretakers of the ancient legacy. The present study emphasizes continuity, but with the Byzantine people as active participants in retaining some key elements of Late Antique culture while altering other aspects to meet their particular needs. I call this perspective "modified continuity" and it entails certain assumptions. Foremost is the notion that people are motivated by self-interest, that is, they act to satisfy a set of perceived needs, material and nonmaterial (Frank, 1988; Homans, 1968; Lenski, 1970:32–34; see Randsborg [1990, 1991] for the period in question). This is true of humans in all time periods and provides a common ground by which contemporary scholars can assess the actions of past peoples. Another underlying assumption is the primacy of infrastructural components (for example, mode of production, practical political considerations of power) over superstructural ones (that is, religion, ideology). In other words, the pragmatic, concrete considerations of the material world determine the tenor of any historical period, with a symbolic overlay that justifies the system. Religion and other ideological components of social life are derivative from and not causative of human action. People manipulate symbolic systems, including religion and ideology, to aid them in achieving certain desired ends. The cultural materialist perspective of Marvin Harris (1974a, 1977, 1979) and the microeconomic principles of formalist economic anthropology (Homans, 1968; Burling, 1962) are the bases for these key assumptions.

Appended to this materialist viewpoint is the definition of culture as a flexible response system used by humans in the complex process of adapting to the physical and cultural environment. As noted above, culture is not a fixed, static set of rules that provides people with an unvarying blueprint for reacting to the world, but is rather a dynamic information system that people constantly change; people tap and add to its reservoir of knowledge. Culture consists of the adaptive strategies used by humans and, thus, changes as human needs and the environment change. This view of culture derives from cultural ecology and its offshoots (Moran, 1982; Netting, 1977), and has strong connections to evolutionism. The evolutionary paradigm has proved its utility to archaeology in a number of studies (Bettinger, 1991; Dunnell, 1989, 1992; Neff, 1992; O'Brien, 1996; O'Brien and Holland, 1992, 1995; Rindos, 1984; Rosenberg, 1994; Teltser, 1995; Trigger, 1998), although there is continuing vigorous debate over the best specific approach (Broughton and O'Connell, 1999). For my purposes, the selectionist approach (Dunnell, 1980) offers a useful way to examine the actions of past peoples. In brief, "humans are subject to the process of selection just as is anything else organic" (O'Brien and Holland, 1995:177). Furthermore, there is the effort to determine why particular adaptations or cultural features become dominant in particular periods. If we begin with the idea that "artifacts represent solutions to roadblocks that our ancestors encountered" (O'Brien and Holland, 1995:192), we can extend the model to other aspects of technology and behavior. As part of the quest to resolve various problems, ancient Korinthians invested heavily in monumental architecture at various times. When that option held fewer benefits for various reasons, the people ceased such work in the Sanctuary, and shifted focus to the fortifications. In the seventh century, abandonment of the Fortress reflects disinvestment by the imperial government at a time when it needed to concentrate resources elsewhere, while the squatters who moved into the military installation and the Bath (Gregory, 1993a, 1993b) did so to take advantage of existing structures, an adaptation that allowed them to expend energy on chores other than house construction.

Another important consideration is the degree to which we can generalize issues of structural deterioration. I believe Adams (1988:24–25) is correct in stating that the decay of complex structures rarely occurs simultaneously across the entire structure. As a supplement to Adams's notion, decline in one area is often compensated by reassignment of resources to another. I contend that changes at Isthmia in the fifth to sixth centuries are aspects of such a realignment, a reordering of priorities, or what Lenski (1970:89–90) calls intrasocietal selection. As Lenski points out, the choices people make over a period of time create a "definite progression of organizational forms" that modify older structures to meet new demands. In the process, the structures (especially the economic and political systems) are gradually transformed.

Examining Isthmia with such a model provides a necessary balance between the extreme continuity and discontinuity positions. The transition from Late Antiquity to Early Byzantine is only one phase of an ongoing process that includes all of Greek history. When we talk of Classical Antiquity or the Classical polis system, we often describe the diagnostic phenomena at some arbitrary point in time and make that reference point characteristic of all periods. There were changes in urban culture throughout Antiquity, and the alterations in the Aegean region and at Isthmia during the fourth to seventh centuries CE are extensions of this flux. In the region as a whole, certain elements of that urban system were maintained while others were changed to accommodate the altered conditions of the period. The environmental conditions (social and natural) of the period selected for a system in which residents abandoned certain traits of Classical urban culture. The public buildings of the polis (baths, temples, *stoas,* theaters, and so on) proved to be excessive burdens; reduction in scale enhanced survivability (financial, economic) of many cities. In addition, the central administration focused much of its architectural efforts on the capital in Constantinople. In some cases, other forms co-opted their functions (e.g., churches replaced temples).

At Isthmia these conditions translated into an abandonment of the Sanctuary and the systematic dismantling of its structures. The precise date of the Sanctuary's demise is a matter of some debate. Beaton and Clement (1976) suggest cult activity at Isthmia terminated abruptly in CE 395 when Alaric's raid destroyed most of the site. Gebhard (in Catling, 1988:22) places the demise in the mid-third century. Rothaus (1993) has found evidence for cult activity as late as the sixth century in the Korinthia and at least to the late fourth century at Isthmia. Excavation in the periphery of the Sanctuary has revealed some evidence concerning this issue. For example, work in the Roman Bath indicates that the structure was in use into the fourth century (Gregory, 1995; Gregory and Kardulias, 1989). *Spolia* from the Bath were used in the fortifications that were erected ca. CE 410–420 to answer the threat of barbarian invasions (Clement, 1975; Gregory, 1993a:142). Byzantine military engineers made considerable use of *spolia* at Isthmia (Broneer, 1971:102). The extent of the practice had a dramatic impact on the appearance of the Sanctuary. We know from Pausanias (1964:II.1.7) that the Temple of Poseidon was intact and functioning in the second half of the second century CE. Yet when various travelers visited the site in the seventeenth century and later (Leake, 1968[1830]; Wheler, 1682), no traces of this large structure remained on the ground. In fact early researchers, such as Monceaux (1884, 1885), mistook the Fortress for the *temenos* wall of the temple. Broneer's (1953, 1971) work demonstrated conclusively the location of the temple and the core of the Sanctuary, even though his excavations in the area of the *temenos* revealed a singular lack of the numerous architectural members from the temples and associated structures. Such a thorough disappearance was evidently not due to natural disasters, since other ancient structures in the region had withstood the ravages of time. The Temple of Zeus at Nemea, for example, described by Pausanias (1964:II.15.2) as in a poor state of repair, remained a visible monument throughout the Medieval period and into modern times (Miller, 1990:13).

Although it is difficult to assign particular blocks to specific ancient buildings, many reused blocks have appeared in the fortifications. The Northeast Gate of the Fortress incorporates an earlier Roman arch and also contains numerous other reused blocks (Gregory and Mills, 1984). The base of the Gate's north tower contains a number of voussoir blocks from some circular structure (Gregory, 1993a:57–59); a large rectangular marble block, used as a paving slab for the road through the Gate, was originally a monument commemorating the victories of one Lucius Kornelios Korinthos in various musical competitions (Clement, 1974). A series of column drums served as a ceiling in the entrance to Tower 15 of the Fortress (Figure 6.6). Excavation in the area around Tower 14 of the Fortress yielded the following pieces of the Temple of Poseidon: two building blocks from the foundation of the interior colonnade, a geison block, and a fragmentary mutule (Broneer, 1971:104, 115, 135–136). A segment of the Hexamilion near the Roman Bath contains a wide array of ancient blocks: column drums, triglyph-metopes blocks, and Doric capitals (Gregory, 1993a:43–44). Vitruvius (1926:I.5.8) and the anonymous author of the military treatise *De Re Strategica* (Köchly and Rustow, 1885:10.3) both advocated such use of *spolia*. Since *spolia* did not provide sufficient material for the task of constructing the Fortress, the Byzantines also quarried stone near the walls. Gregory (1993a:116–117) identified one such quarry near the east Fortress wall; removal of the blocks from the limestone bedrock minimized the transport distance and steepened the approach to the wall. Additional material may have come from the ancient quarries several kilometers west of the site from which derived much of the stone for the original ancient buildings in the Sanctuary (Hayward, 1996).

Some scholars might argue that this use of *spolia* marks a fundamental shift in perspective that separates the Late Antique mindset, and thus the society that fostered it, from the Early Byzantine. I suggest that it was largely material conditions that dictated a shift in strategy. The changes in the physical aspects of the site reflect a change in the adaptive strategy of the area's occupants and the central government to enhance

Figure 6.6 View of Entrance to Tower 15 of the Fortress
Showing Column Drum Used as Lintel Block

Source: Photograph by the author

survival. Even this transition reflects a consistent pragmatic orientation. Although ritual behavior was important at Isthmia from the founding of the Sanctuary down to the late fourth century CE, a variety of other activities provided the foundation for the various religious, athletic, and theatrical events. Planning and execution of the various Sanctuary construction projects required considerable resources and skills in architectural design, financing, organizing labor, stone masonry, and a variety of other vocations. Maintenance of the facilities and festivals also required considerable administrative expertise and monetary outlay. The benefits of controlling the Sanctuary were, I suggest, primarily practical in providing such things as income from gifts and visitors and employment. The prestige associated with control of the Sanctuary also had a pragmatic component. The greater the reputation of the various festivals conducted at the site, the more likely it was that large crowds would attend and enrich Korinthian coffers. John Salmon (1984:403) notes that the Isthmian Games were the only Panhellenic festival under the direct control of a major polis and Korinthos made the most of this economic opportunity. I do not wish to deny the importance of religious motivations. Rather, I simply do not assign them primacy.

In tearing down ancient structures, the people of the fifth century pursued an activity they estimated would help them overcome certain immediate problems. In a similar manner, cities such as Efesos, Sardis, and Korinthos that contracted in size did so to adjust to current conditions. The people found that maintenance of the status quo was counterproductive and so they pursued innovations; in terms of the culture model (Figure 6.4), they adopted new values, which in turn permitted restricting the size of the community because they probably found unbearable the cost of maintaining an indefensible system of extensive walls. The intent was not to create a "Byzantine" type of community, but in the long term the new strategies altered the appearance of Classical cities, such as Korinthos. Nor was the dismantling of ancient monuments always an expression of Christian hostility toward pagans. Saradi-Mendelovici (1990) demonstrates that, while persecution of pagans and destruction of their buildings did occur, Christians also often displayed a positive attitude toward pagan monuments, many of which they actively preserved. She also attributes the regular use of marble from ancient temples in Christian buildings to "convenience and financial motives" (Saradi-Mendelovici 1990:52), an argument fully supported by the present study.

The practical considerations entailed in this perspective are perhaps more evident in discussing the Fortress. The construction of the fortifications was an outgrowth of security concerns in a period of foreign incursions. The need for defense was pressing. To expedite completion of the walls, ready sources of stone, such as the buildings of the Sanctuary, were used (Figure 6.7). Major rebuilding episodes in the sixth and fifteenth centuries (Gregory, 1993a:144, 147–148) reflect similar processes of decision making based on practical considerations. Time, effort, and money were invested to secure material benefits. The failure of these attempts to block invaders does not obviate the rational, ends-oriented process in which the builders engaged.

The change in the character of the site from primarily religious to military in orientation can thus be viewed from the perspective of people acting to maximize their benefits at the minimum cost. As a Sanctuary, the site was failing to meet the immediate

Figure 6.7 Section of Hexamilion Wall ca. 5 Meters
North of Roman Bath Showing Use of Spolia

Source: Photograph by the author

needs of people in the northeastern Korinthia in the fourth and fifth centuries CE. The new challenges confronting them required a change in strategy, which is reflected in construction of the fortifications. The use of prepared stone is more efficient than quarrying new blocks, and so the temples and other structures were mined to provide building material. While modern scholars may decry this destruction of architectural treasures, the ancients had to make practical choices and acted accordingly. If the Sanctuary had not been so violated prior to the fifth century, it was because the site served a practical function and residents saw it was in their interest to maintain the structures, or, after the cult place was abandoned, that there was nothing to be gained by destroying the buildings. As such, the Sanctuary buildings can be seen as idle assets that were put to use by the government when a particular need for them arose. The change that occurred at the site can be described as part of a series of activities that are understandable in such pragmatic terms.

The events at Isthmia did not occur in a historical vacuum, and thus comparison with other sites is necessary and instructive. The excavations in Athens provide excellent comparanda to assess the nature of the transition. It is undeniable that monumental construction in the Agora declined in Late Antiquity. Several authors view the Herulian raid of CE 267 as the critical event that began Athens's decline from a Classical polis to a medieval town. Thompson and Wycherley (1972:210) note the destruction of the ancient administrative structures (Bouleterion, Tholos, Metroon). While they are uncertain what buildings replaced these civic offices, both the institutions housed there and the economy of the city suffered a decline. Frantz (1988:3) places greater emphasis on the Herulian raid as a watershed event, suggesting it marks "clearly the end of the ancient city and its transition to the status of a minor provincial town ... with life disrupted to such an extent that the old pattern could never be resumed." While clearly significant, the raid was probably not cataclysmic. In the late fourth and early fifth centuries CE, the Agora experienced a building spurt that, while it did not reestablish the ancient pattern and style, clearly reflects a rejuvenation of significant proportions. In addition, a number of important visitors and scholars graced Athens in the seventh century CE and speak to its continued vitality: St. Gislenus and Theodore of Tarsus (later Archbishop of Canterbury) both studied philosophy there in the mid-seventh century, and Emperor Constans II stayed in Athens during the winter of 662–663 (Thompson and Wycherley, 1972:216).

Furthermore, not all cities in the Aegean area experienced the transformation uniformly as a decline. Preferable to the "great break" perspective is one that stresses a "continual process of cultural transformation" (Rautman, 1990:14; see also Kaegi, 1989), what I would call an evolutionary development. Frank Trombley (1985) demonstrates the persistence of Euchaita as an urban entity in Asia Minor during the seventh century. James Russell's (1986, 2001) work at Anemurium indicates continued strong urban activity at the same time that Sardis and other Anatolian cities experienced a drop in monumental construction and other civic activities. In general, though, a transformation of some significance occurred between the fifth and seventh centuries. John Haldon (1990:92–117) attributes the changes to the loss of fiscal, economic, and political autonomy. The reduced status of towns led directly, he argues, to the decrease in size, population, and complexity witnessed in Anatolian and Greek urban settlements. Haldon's emphasis on structural, rather than external factors (i.e., invasions) permits a clear delineation of the forces at play. Accompanying the deemphasis on cities was the increased importance of villages as administrative units, the landowners of which formed the core for revenue collection by the state. This process had begun at least by the sixth century (Haldon, 1990:138–139). Haldon's penetrating analysis focuses on attempts by the Byzantines to deal with a fluctuating situation. He states that the major response centered on efforts to reestablish the efficacy of the worldview that had been buffeted by various events in the sixth and seventh centuries. While I concur that a search to reaffirm basic cultural values occurred (positive feedback loop in Figure 6.4), one cannot lose sight of the basic material causes (for example, the need to provide security and a stable subsistence base) that underlay the abstract cultural conceptions. It is not that Haldon disregards these material causes, but he argues that the Byzantines acted on the basis of a constructed worldview, a series of perceptions. I see a somewhat more direct link between material causes and cultural behavior, but in general I find Haldon's approach quite useful. The "whole" he refers to that makes individual behavior comprehensible (Haldon, 1990:439) is culture. Haldon allows for significant regional variation in changes to settlements. In addition, the process he describes, with the possibility of alternative strategies, fits the evolutionary model outlined above.

Conclusion

This study has used archaeological evidence to tell us something about the people who inhabited the site of Isthmia in a transitional period. The site did not exist in isolation. The number of people resident in the military installation certainly had a significant impact on regional agricultural, manufacturing, and commercial activity. As representatives of the central government, they symbolized the political concerns of the imperial polity. The troops probably played both disruptive and constructive roles during their stay. The goal is to envision the inhabitants of the region as actively involved in a living, interactive system. The rudimentary analysis of architectural energetics attempted here is a starting point toward that goal. I suggest that a materialist perspective goes a long way toward helping us discern some markers of the past in a more comprehensible manner than other approaches.

Viewed from such a perspective, the historical transition to the Early Byzantine period is less one of discontinuity than of continuity. The elements of change were carried out within the context of societal adjustments rather than total realignment. Another important point in considering conditions at Isthmia during the period of change is the multidimensional nature of the site before and after the construction of the fortifications. In Antiquity, cultural activity at Isthmia encompassed more than the rituals and festivals. The large West Cemetery and domestic quarters in the East Field and on Rachi attest to the presence of a sizable resident population. The dyeing facilities on Rachi demonstrate the presence of an important commercial enterprise (Kardara, 1961). As described above, the various festivals also had a substantial economic component. The nature of the road system made Isthmia a central transportation node. After the construction of the Fortress in the fifth century many of these features remained significant. The selection of Isthmia as the location of the Fortress undoubtedly had much to do with the site's command of the roads along the eastern part of the Isthmus. Occupation of the Fortress alternated between a military garrison and civilian residents from the fifth century on. The Fortress was an important component in the local settlement system, both as a residential area and as a last refuge in periods of duress. A series of economic links certainly bound the Fortress garrison to the local community since the maximum contingent (about 1700 men) probably was not self-sufficient in terms of many important commodities, such as food and pottery. The Fortress and Sanctuary thus both exhibited a diverse array of activities even though they are often each identified with only one primary function. The nature of some of these activities changed in significant ways between the fourth and fifth centuries, but the site always supported a variety of human behavior.

The size of the Byzantine Empire precludes any simple solution to the problem of understanding how that society adapted and changed through time. Evolutionary and materialist theory provide significant insights into this process of culture change. The data from Isthmia offer evidence for the importance of regional variation in providing loose parameters that allowed people leeway to make adjustments they deemed necessary under various conditions. In a general way, these data tend to support a revised form of the continuity thesis. Even if Classical urban culture was eclipsed suddenly in Anatolia, and the evidence is by no means unequivocally in support of this interpretation, we must entertain the possibility of a different outcome in Greece. As more Byzantine sites are examined, perhaps this phenomenon of regional variation within a general cultural context will become increasingly apparent. Perhaps then Byzantine society will be seen as a dynamic successor to the ancient legacy, which it adapted to its own particular needs. I suggest that people were not fundamentally different. Continuity is evident in the constant human drive to secure economic and other benefits; adaptive behaviors can result from these actions. As Darwin noted (1928[1859]:437), "there is a Struggle for Existence leading to the preservation of each profitable deviation of structure or instinct. The truth of these propositions cannot, I think, be disputed."

Acknowledgments

I thank Andrew Womack for his assistance in formatting the text and preparing the figures. I am also grateful to the American School of Classical Studies for allowing me to reproduce Figure 6.5.

Chapter Seven

Effects of the Physical and Social Environment on Culture

Results of Cross-Cultural Tests

Melvin Ember and Carol R. Ember

Some YEARS AGO, Marvin Harris (1996:279) noted that "hundreds of studies based on the Human Relations Area Files or other large-scale comparative databases clearly demonstrate the nonrandom nature of sociocultural selection." The evidence is even more overwhelming now, and it is increasing at a geometric rate. For this and other reasons, many in anthropology and the other social sciences believe that culture is generally (but not always) adaptive. This paper selectively reviews worldwide cross-cultural studies that explicitly test hypotheses about cultural adaptation. We discuss how particular aspects of cross-cultural variation have been linked statistically to particular conditions and variables in the physical and social environment. Many of the results reviewed here suggest how new research could add to our understanding. We briefly describe these possibilities as we go.

We hope that our discussion will stimulate new efforts to test for adaptationist explanations of cultural variation. In addition to studies addressing new questions, we need studies that put together what previous studies have found. Do all of the known predictors work independently and cumulatively? Which are more important? Which are redundant? A cross-cultural study allows us to test explanations against each other. A field study may not be able to do that because it lacks one or more of the suspected determinants. In addition to facilitating multivariate tests, the major advantage of a cross-cultural study is that it can produce more generalizable conclusions than other kinds of study. A field study, or even a regional comparison, cannot produce a result that is generalizable to the world *with a measurable degree of confidence* (M. Ember, 1991). The most efficient way to discover the generalizability of a result is to conduct a worldwide cross-cultural study, which is not hard to do (for a primer, see C. R. Ember and M. Ember, 2001). One should not be dismayed by the fact that the units of analysis (cultures, societies) are different in size or complexity, so long as they fit the same operational definition (M. Ember and C. R. Ember, 2000).

Ever since Ellsworth Huntington (1919) wrote about the superiority of cultures in temperate climates, which many in social science saw as justification of North European and North American hegemony, cultural anthropologists (with the exception of cultural ecologists) have often been loath to consider the possible effects of environment on culture. And though cultural ecologists may generally argue for cultural adaptation in particular societies or regions, their arguments are often not generalizable, not translatable into hypotheses that could be tested on data from a worldwide sample of cultures. In contrast, cross-cultural researchers (mainly coming out of anthropology, psychology, and sociology) generally assume that certain aspects of culture are or were adaptive in their particular environments, and they have tested hundreds of adaptationist hypotheses. But we are still very ignorant about cultural causality—only about 1,000 cross-cultural studies have been published so far. Much or even most of the unexplained cultural variation could be measured using existing ethnographic materials. (The HRAF Collection of Ethnography—in paper, microfiche, and now on the Web—was invented to facilitate such studies, by providing easily retrievable information on a sample of the world's cultures. And the annually growing eHRAF Archaeology can facilitate studies of cultural evolution and devolution.) Because we restrict ourselves here to results of hypothesis tests, we do not try to summarize the largely descriptive results in Binford's (2001) magisterial survey of hunter-gatherers.

We start with studies of the possible effects of variables in the physical environment. Then we turn to possible effects of the social environment, which we divide into macrolevel and microlevel variables. Macrolevel variables include such things as size of the linguistic/cultural group, population density, and war and peace. By microlevel variables we mean such things as family context and child rearing.

All too often, different sets of researchers do not interact or read the other's research as much as they should. Even with similar research interests, we tend to keep up with different journals. Cross-cultural researchers from anthropology, psychology, and sociology may not know much about what evolutionary biologists and evolutionary psychologists have been investigating about humans, even though both sets of researchers often use the same cross-cultural databases. We ourselves plead guilty to this bias; it is difficult to keep up with everything relevant. But it is our impression that the same is true vice versa: Evolutionary biologists and psychologists may not be very conversant with what has been accomplished by other kinds of cross-cultural researchers. So this paper may provide a bridge between the two research traditions, even if it is more one-way than it should be.

An earlier review of worldwide cross-cultural research, by Carol R. Ember and David Levinson (1991), mentioned that studies by biologists and psychologists testing evolutionary theories probably comprised the fastest growing segment of the cross-cultural research literature at that time. To increase the likelihood of all kinds of researchers knowing about what others have done, the Human Relations Area Files is planning to build an online database of results of cross-cultural hypothesis tests. With the participation of many of the researchers themselves, who will be provided with a template so that they can plug in the details of their own and related studies, this database may be accessible on the Web within a few years. This should make it easier for all kinds of cross-cultural researchers to keep up with the work of others.

One last introductory remark needs to be made. Statistics textbooks often tell us that correlation does not necessarily mean causation. But this caveat may not apply to cross-cultural tests of possible environmental effects. Even though the measured variables for a single case pertain to more or less the same time period, we could still be testing a causal hypothesis. This is because the cultural variation measured is less likely to precede the environmental variation measured than vice versa. For example, we know that smaller populations are more likely to prohibit all types of first cousin marriage, presumably because the likelihood of inbreeding, and the deleterious effects of it, is greater in smaller as compared with larger populations (M. Ember, 1975). The reverse causality is less plausible: How could the absence of first cousin marriage come first and then produce a smaller breeding population? So a cross-cultural result that links cultural variation to variation in the environment (here the social environment) may be more plausibly interpreted as identifying the environment as cause than as identifying culture as cause. This may generally be true of studies showing how environment predicts culture. And note too that cross-archaeological tests, using archaeological indicators of environmental and cultural variables, could confirm the presumed causal (temporal) ordering of the variables.

Effects of the Physical Environment

In our review of the possible effects of the physical environment we consider the effects of climate, natural disasters, and epidemics caused by introduced diseases. Cross-cultural studies have linked climate to postpartum sex taboos, sleeping arrangements, how babies are carried, and even some aspects of language. Natural disasters and food shortages have been linked to avoidance of heterosexuality, preference for thinness or fatness, and frequency of warfare. Epidemics of introduced diseases predict such aspects of social organization as residence and cousin marriage.

In a paper titled "Effects of climate on certain cultural practices," John Whiting (1964) was probably the first cross-cultural anthropologist to conduct a systematic worldwide investigation of the possible effects of the physical environment. He showed that rainy tropical climates are associated with diets presumably low in protein, and that such diets predict long postpartum sex taboos. The suggested explanation was that kwashiorkor, the protein deficiency disease that is common in the rainy tropics, would favor extended lactation (which would maximize the baby's chance to survive) and therefore a cultural prohibition on the resumption of intercourse for at least a year after the baby's birth would also be favored (to allow for extended lactation). Needless to say, there may be other causes of long postpartum sex taboos. Whiting himself pointed to the difficulty of carrying two or more infants in a nomadic foraging society. Also, it is possible that if men fear sex with women, which is not uncommon cross-culturally, that may reduce the frequency of marital sex. A low frequency of sex might function like a postpartum sex taboo and also extend the interval between conceptions. (See C. R. Ember [1978] for a cross-cultural study of men's fear of sex with women.)

Whiting (1964) also showed that winter temperatures predict sleeping arrangements, which predict other cultural variation, as we shall see. Husband and wife tend not to sleep together when the average "winter" temperature is above 50 degrees Fahrenheit (10 Centigrade). In contrast, the baby tends to sleep with the mother when the average winter temperature is above 50 degrees F. Whiting thinks that husbands and wives sleep separately in warm climates to keep cooler. Of course, this consideration does not explain why babies sleep only with mothers in warm climates. That has not yet been investigated. With regard to why babies are kept separate in cold climates, Whiting suggests that by sleeping in its own cradle, crib, or sleeping bag, the baby stays warmer. Keeping the baby warm in cold climates should be selectively advantageous, other things being equal.

Sleeping arrangements are highly correlated with how babies are moved around and where they are left. If average winter temperatures are below 50 degrees F, infants are usually placed in cradles for carrying or resting and they are often swaddled. Where temperatures are warmer, babies are typically carried in slings and shawls and spend much of their time in close body contact with the mother or another caretaker (Whiting, 1981). The 50 degree isotherm may be a significant predictor of many things. According to Whiting, Sodergren, and Stigler (1982), the 50 degree isotherm has been a serious barrier to migration—the languages belonging to a particular language phylum tend not to be distributed on both sides of this isotherm.

Later, in our discussion of possible effects of microlevel variables in the social environment, we shall see that long postpartum sex taboos and mother-child sleeping (and related carrying/resting arrangements for babies) appear to have important consequences for personality, many of which may relate to what evolutionary biologists and psychologists refer to as male-male competition.

Temperature has been shown to predict certain aspects of a culture's language. In warmer climates, languages have proportionately more consonant-vowel syllables and more sonorous sounds (Munroe, Munroe, and Winters, 1996; Munroe and Silander, 1999; Munroe, Fought, and Fought, 2000; Fought, Munroe, Fought, and Good, 2004). The word "mama" has two consonant-vowel (CV) syllables; the word "appearance" has none. Sonority has to do with audibility at a distance—the vowel "a" has higher sonority than the vowel "i" and vowels are more sonorous than consonants. The CV syllable presents maximal contrast and is more audible at a distance than other syllables. Munroe and his colleagues theorize that people in warmer climates will generally spend more time outdoors and communicate at a distance more often than people in colder climates. They argue that it is adaptive for the languages in warmer climates, where more conversation is out of doors, to have syllables and sounds that are more easily heard and recognized at a distance. Density of plant cover interacting with climate also influences sonority (C. R. Ember and M. Ember, 2000).

Now we turn to some effects of famines and severe food shortages, many of which are strongly affected by natural disasters.

Famines and severe food shortages may be partially produced by social factors, especially in societies like modern Ethiopia where class and ethnic groups have differential access to food and other resources. But in the sample we have used for our research on resource uncertainty and warfare (C. R. Ember and M. Ember, 1992a, 1992b), famines and food shortages seem to be strongly correlated with unpredictable but expectable natural disasters that destroy food supplies (e.g., droughts, locust infestations). No one has yet done a study to compare the relative effects of natural disasters and social inequality on the likelihood of famines and food shortages. Multivariate analyses could be easily done with the coded data now available (Dirks, 1993; C. R. Ember and M. Ember, 1992b).

It has been suggested that resource scarcity selects for a positive valuation of fatness in women. But new evidence indicates that the causality is more complicated. In the absence of food storage, resource scarcity seems to favor a preference for thinness, which may be an advantageous way for the group to conserve group resources (C. R. Ember, M. Ember, Korotayev, and de Munck, 2005).

With respect to possible effects on sexual behavior, Carol Ember (1978) found that males fear heterosexual sex in societies that have a history of food shortages and famine. For example, the Enga of New Guinea believe that "each act of coitus increases a man's chances of being contaminated; ... every ejaculation depletes his vitality, and overindulgence must dull his mind and leave his body permanently exhausted and withered" (Meggitt, 1964:210). The fear of sex among the Enga and other societies is consistent with the theory that such beliefs should be found where population increase would exceed required resources (Lindenbaum, 1972). Werner (1975) found that famines and food shortages also predict tolerance of homosexuality, which would also reduce pressure on resources (assuming that the reproductive rate is lower with more homosexuality). Societies that are more tolerant of homosexuality do have more abortion and infanticide (Werner, 1979), which is consistent with the idea that homosexuality is more tolerated where there is less desire for children (because of pressure on resources?). But men's fear of sex with women and tolerance of homosexuality are not predicted by the same child-rearing conditions, and so it doesn't necessarily follow that men are more likely to engage in homosexual behavior if they are afraid of heterosexual sex. We need more research to untangle the possible causal chains.

In our research on warfare, we found that a history of unpredictable natural disasters that destroy food supplies is an extremely strong predictor of higher frequencies of war. This and other evidence supports the theory that people may go to war mostly to cushion themselves against the possibility of shortages that they expect but cannot predict or control. While this finding appears to be consistent with the idea that population pressure predicts warfare, we found that *chronic* scarcity is not at all predictive, which suggests that the fear of loss is a more powerful motive than actual loss of resources. We found no cross-cultural support for the Divale and Harris (1976) theory that a shortage of women increases the likelihood of war. (For our various results, see C. R. Ember and M. Ember, 1992a.)

The mythology of a culture may also be influenced by a history of unpredictable resource scarcity. A cross-cultural study by Alex Cohen (1990) found that unprovoked aggression is likely in the folktales of societies that are subject to unpredictable food shortages. The folktales may reflect reality; after all, a serious drought may seem capricious, not possibly provoked by any human activity, brought on by the gods or nature "out of the blue." Curiously, societies with a history of unpredictable food shortages hardly mention natural disasters in their folktales, perhaps because disasters are too frightening. Still, the capriciousness of unpredictable disasters seems to be transformed into the capricious aggression of characters in the folktales.

Some physical environmental conditions are implicated in the emergence of certain kinds of social organization. We first consider the probable effects of depopulation caused by newly introduced diseases.

Particularly in the New World and the far islands of the Pacific, which were relatively isolated from the main population centers in the Old World, the expansion of Europeans brought diseases to which local populations had little or no resistance. In many of these areas, enormous numbers of people died in the first generation after first contact with the European colonists and imperialists. Almost always, the first contact antedated the time focus of our first ethnographic reports. Indeed, our image of aboriginal culture in many areas of the world may be false or distorted in many respects, inasmuch as the first ethnographic reports (by missionaries and others, as well as by professional anthropologists) often describe adaptations to the new diseases and the resulting depopulation. For example, cross-cultural research (C. R. Ember and M. Ember, 1972) supports the hypothesis, suggested by Elman Service (1962:137) on the basis of work by Gertrude Dole and Robert Lane, that most cases of bilocal residence (residence with or near the husband's *or* wife's kin) may have developed because of depopulation. The suggested explanation is that depopulation so reduces the feasibility of invariable or nearly invariable unilocal residence (patrilocal, matrilocal) that couples are forced to live with whichever spouse's close relatives are still alive after the epidemics. Implicit in this argument, it should be noted, is the assumption that in noncommercial societies people are usually obliged to live and work cooperatively with kin in order to make a living. This assumption is consistent with the results of a cross-cultural study predicting neolocal residence, that is, residence apart from kin (M. Ember, 1967).

Among foragers (hunters, gatherers, and/or fishers), other conditions besides depopulation predict bilocal residence. A high degree of rainfall variability around a low mean also predicts bilocality, as does community size under 50 (which correlates with the rainfall pattern just mentioned—see C. R. Ember [1975] for these results and the sources of the original ideas). The suggested explanation for bilocality among foragers is that a combination of different residence patterns is an adaptation to changing availability of resources in different localities and chance fluctuation in the sex ratio of small local groups. You choose as a couple to live where you can find enough kin, on either side, to cooperate with, and you change your place of residence (which may mean moving to another band) when resources become less available because of less rainfall where you were.

Possibly because the Mbuti and !Kung San are very well-known hunter-gatherers, many in anthropology assume that bilocal or flexible residence rules (which the Mbuti and !Kung both had as of the 1950s and 1960s) was characteristic of hunter-gatherers. But this is not correct. Most hunter-gatherers in the ethnographic record (particularly as of the times they were first described) are patrilocal; they almost always live with the husband's kin (C. R. Ember, 1975). The cross-cultural results strongly suggest, then, that bilocality occurs under identifiable special circumstances (particularly depopulation due to diseases introduced by expanding Europeans) and is not characteristic of any stage of culture.

In societies with more than 1,000 and less than 20,000 people (counting children), depopulation also predicts that one or more types of first cousin marriage will be allowed (M. Ember, 1975). Generally, in smaller but not tiny societies (not less than 1,000), first cousin marriage is completely prohibited, which is consistent with the implications of inbreeding theory. (Societies that have small breeding populations, and therefore have a high likelihood of cousins marrying, should generally prohibit such marriage; and they do.) But depopulation may induce people to relax their prior taboo on first cousin marriage in order to have enough mating possibilities, even though first cousin marriages are likely to have lower reproductive rates. After all, some births are more advantageous than none. In depopulated societies that have recently relaxed the taboo on first cousin marriage, it may be that elders would have to encourage first cousins to marry, which may be why preferences for first cousin marriage are likely in depopulated societies, and in others (such as Bedouin Arabs) where local groups can also be suddenly reduced in size (by the uncertainties of pastoral life, etc.).

Effects of the Social Environment

With regard to the possible effects of the social environment we distinguish between such macrolevel environmental variables as population size, population density, social complexity, type and frequency of warfare, and such microlevel environmental factors as the family setting. Let us first turn to macrolevel variables in the social environment and their apparent effects on cultural variation.

Population size and density appear to predict some aspects of social organization, including kinship structure, type of warfare, and cousin marriage. In preindustrial societies, social complexity appears to predict higher fertility, increased parental hostility to or indifference toward children, and higher levels of corporal punishment of children. The presence of war appears to increase the likelihood of unilineal descent groups. And societies with high male mortality in warfare (as well as high pathogen stress) have higher levels of polygyny. Internal war in particular appears to favor patrilocal residence, lineage organization, fear of heterosexual sex when the internal war involves marrying enemies, and exclusion of women from planning or participating in combat.

Societies with more than 20,000 people or so tend to have at least some internal warfare—organized fighting between communities belonging to the same society or language group. Small societies tend to have purely external warfare, except for dispersed hunter-gatherer and island societies for whom the distances involved may make it disadvantageous to engage in purely external warfare. C. R. Ember (1974) has argued that people in nonstate societies may be able to maintain internal harmony, or resolve internal conflicts without resort to war, only in a population limited in size and extent (dispersion). When the senior author was in American Samoa doing fieldwork, he was frequently approached by strangers who said: "I heard about your dancing in Fitiuta." They might have lived in a village 60 or more miles from Fitiuta, and on another island, but they had heard about him. His dancing might have been especially amusing, but he prefers to think that every adult in a population of 20,000 might hear about events in the society. Is a population not exceeding 20,000 a "magic number" marking other kinds of transition as well? Future studies may tell us.

Another study suggests that there may be correlates of another number, this time a population of 9,000 or so. Very small societies (fewer than 9,000 people), if they have unilineal (patrilineal, matrilineal) descent groups, are likely to have a moiety system (C. R. Ember, M. Ember, and Pasternak, 1974). That is, the society is divided into two maximal descent groups. (The word moiety derives from the French word *moitié*, meaning "half"). Lévi-Strauss (1969:75) and other "structuralist" anthropologists have paid a lot of attention to societies with moiety systems as if they were somehow special, expressive of a tendency in humans to think dualistically. But if there were such a tendency in humans, wouldn't nearly all societies show signs of it? Very few societies have moiety systems, so it is hardly likely that some imagined universal tendency could explain a phenomenon that seldom occurs. Indeed, the results described by Ember, Ember, and Pasternak (1974) indicate that the number of maximal descent groups in a society increases with societal size, which suggests that societies with moiety systems are not particularly special, just very small.

There are other signs that small population size may make a difference in cultural variation. As suggested above, smaller but not tiny breeding populations, as indicated by low levels of political integration and the absence of communities with more than 5,000 people, seem to favor the extension of the familial incest taboo to all first cousins (M. Ember, 1975). The theory is that in small but not tiny breeding populations the chances of marrying a first cousin (and the deleterious consequences of such marriages) are relatively high. Therefore natural selection should tend to favor the prohibition of all first cousin marriage. Melvin Ember (1975) presented an algebraic model suggesting that the prohibition of familial matings (between siblings, between parent and child) may have been invented and become universal after breeding isolates began to increase considerably in size. Increasing size of isolates would have allowed more accumulation of harmful recessives in the gene pool, and consequently would have made it possible for people to notice that familial *and* first cousin matings had much lower reproductive rates than other matings (see the various solutions of the model in M. Ember, 1975). When would isolates have begun to grow larger? Certainly after the emergence and spread of agriculture, when we know from the archaeological record that local groups began to proliferate, and possibly even before that when Mesolithic peoples began to settle down because they had begun to exploit more stationary resources such as shell fish.

Population density seems also to predict the importance of agriculture as compared with other modes of subsistence. Density may even be a stronger predictor than the agricultural potential of an area (Pryor, 1986). The theory—following Boserup, Cohen, and Flannery—is that increasing density reduces the amount of land available for foraging (Pryor, 1986:884), so natural selection should favor the adoption or invention of agriculture when the marginal productivity of agriculture exceeds that of foraging (hunting, gathering, fishing).

Over the years, many researchers have suggested that crowding produces more aggression, particularly perhaps in captive populations. But the evidence is equivocal. Bolton and Vadheim (1973), in a comparative study of East African societies, found the opposite relationship: More homicide correlates with lower density. Their theory is that higher homicide rates are related to factors that produce more hypoglycemia, as among the Qolla in the Peruvian highlands who were previously studied by Bolton (1973). Bolton and Vadheim found that low animal and vegetable protein in the diet and disease stress, both of which presumably increase the likelihood of hypoglycemia, predicted higher homicide rates in East Africa. And Jonathan Freedman (1975) collected evidence suggesting that crowding by itself has little or no effect on rates of aggression. To clarify the situation, we need systematic cross-cultural and cross-national studies that test the alternative explanations against each other. Coded cross-cultural and other tabulated data are available to make the required multivariate tests.

Higher population densities are the hallmark of high societal complexity. In a broad sense, societal complexity can be thought of as part of the social environment that people have to respond to, and that culture may be adapted to. In any case, we know that societal complexity is related to many aspects of culture. We mention only a few here.

More complex societies tend to score higher on parental rejection of children, that is, hostility or indifference toward children (Rohner, 1975). Exactly why this is so is not clear, but there are several possible reasons. First, people may have less leisure time with increasing cultural complexity, and less leisure may increase the irritability of parents (and hence hostility or indifference toward children). Think of people who have to work at more than one job in order to earn a living. Or think of women who have to juggle child care and wage work outside the home. Second, many investigators have found that less help with child care from others predicts less warmth toward children (Whiting, 1960; Minturn and Lambert, 1964; Rohner, 1975; Levinson, 1979). A related finding, alluded to above, is that commercial exchange or a money economy predicts living apart from kin or neolocal residence (M. Ember, 1967). If people do not live with or next door to kin, they may find it difficult to rely on others for child care. Third, greater parental rejection is perhaps related to having more children. A study by C. R. Ember (1983) found that societies with intensive agriculture have significantly higher fertility than societies with horticulture or nonintensive agriculture. More complex societies (with more children), in addition to displaying more hostility toward children, are likely to emphasize compliance in child rearing and to punish their children physically (Barry, Child, and Bacon, 1959; Ellis, Lee, and Petersen, 1978; Petersen, Lee, and Ellis, 1982; Hendrix, 1985).

A recent multivariate study indicates that corporal punishment of children may prepare them psychologically for living in a society with native or imposed (e.g., colonial) power inequality; corporal punishment is also more likely where nonrelatives help raise children, and (in nonpacified societies) where there is undemocratic decision making and a culture of violence (C. R. Ember and M. Ember, 2005b).

More complex societies, particularly more stratified societies, are also more likely to restrict premarital sex (C. R. Ember and M. Ember, 2005a:346–347). But as Broude (1975, 1976) notes, this effect is not as strong as less time spent in close body contact with a caretaker. The effect of cultural complexity cannot be that strong: Witness the changing premarital sex norms in our own society in recent years. Clearly society is not getting less complex! We think it is likely that we shall soon see studies that clarify the predictors of less versus more premarital sex.

We now turn to the possible effects of variables relating to war and peace.

Melvin Ember (1974a) presented evidence that high male mortality in war is strongly correlated with more than occasional polygyny. And in societies with information on sex ratio, more than occasional polygyny is associated with an excess of females, as is expectable given the male mortality in war. These findings suggest that natural selection might favor polygyny as a way to maximize reproductive rates in societies with an excess of women.

We are aware that evolutionary biologists and psychologists may think that both polygyny and high male mortality are joint consequences of a high degree of competition among males for females. But there is no evidence that competition among males is greater in societies with an excess of women. If anything, the degree of competition should be lower because women outnumber men. And if it is a universal that males compete for females, why don't all societies practice polygyny? We think the sex ratio explanation provides a parsimonious answer: not all societies practice polygyny because the condition mainly favoring it, i.e., an excess of women, is not universal. The sex ratio explanation also accounts for why more complex, socially stratified societies tend to lack polygyny, even though the richer males in them have the resources to attract and support multiple wives. We suggest that the reason such societies tend to lack polygyny is that they have lower male mortality *proportionately* in war. Why? Because they have standing armies that do the fighting in war. Most men in the society do not participate in combat, and only a small proportion of them die in war. Thus, the sex ratio can stay more equal in stratified societies, and therefore polygyny is not necessary to ensure that most women marry and have children. Of course, this explanation of polygyny assumes that natural selection generally favors things that maximize the reproductive rate. This may not always be true in the modern world, but it probably *was* true for most societies described in the ethnographic record.

Note too that complex, socially stratified societies generally have commercialized economies, in the ethnographic record as well as in the modern world. This means that at least some women can support themselves by selling their labor or products and therefore any excess women do not have to be married. This consideration certainly fits the modern world. But it doesn't fit noncommercial societies. Judging by the ubiquity of polygyny as well as obligatory remarriage (levirate and sororate) after the death of a spouse, it appears that most or nearly all adult men and women have to be married in noncommercial societies.

Low (1990) has suggested that the presence of more pathogens makes it selectively advantageous to have more genetically variable offspring. Assuming that polygyny (particularly nonsororal polygyny) maximizes that variability, high pathogen stress should predict more polygyny. The cross-cultural evidence supports this expectation.

Polygyny is also associated with internal war (war within the society or language group). Fighting within the society appears to result in high male mortality in warfare, which we know is associated with polygyny. Otterbein (1968) suggests that the presence of fraternal interest groups, as indicated by patrilocal residence, explains the association between internal war and polygyny. (He doesn't consider the sex ratio explanation of polygyny.) We disagree with Otterbein's argument for two reasons. First, when we added patrilocal residence to a multiple regression analysis, it is far from being a significant predictor of more internal war, controlling for other predictors (C. R. Ember, M. Ember, and Russett, 1992). Second, the "fraternal interest group" theory does not account for polygyny in societies with purely external war, which generally have matrilocal rather than patrilocal residence (and therefore by definition lack fraternal interest groups). Localized groups of related men do not occur in matrilocal societies; the husbands who have moved in with their wives are not generally members of the same lineage or clan. Some matrilocal societies have polygyny anyway, probably because they have an excess of women. The polygyny in those societies, by the way, tends to be of the sororal variety; the cowives are sisters. For why sisters may be more prepared emotionally than nonsisters to share their husbands, see M. Ember (1973).

In nonstate societies, the presence of warfare together with unilocal (patrilocal or matrilocal) residence appears to favor the development of patrilineal or matrilineal descent groups, respectively (C. R. Ember, M. Ember, and Pasternak, 1974). The theory is that in nonstate societies a lineal (one-sex) rule of descent provides unambiguously discrete groups of people for unambivalent collective action in competitive situations. In bilateral or ambilineal societies, by contrast, kin groups are overlapping and nondiscrete, and individuals have conflicting loyalties with respect to which particular set of kin they should act with in competitive situations. So unilineal descent groups should be likely in unilocal societies with warfare. And they are.

There are some nonstate societies whose communities change in size and composition throughout the year. This means that members of your kin group may not always be around. In such societies, it seems that age-set systems develop to provide social units for fighting whatever the time of year and wherever one happens to be (Ritter, 1980). Age sets are groups, usually of males, who are initiated together, receive a group name, and graduate together through a succession of life stages, one of which is usually called "warriors." When you are raided for animals, you can always find age-mates nearby to help you repel the raiders, or to follow them to recover the animals taken away.

As we have noted, warfare (organized combat between territorial groups from bands and villages on up) can occur within the society or language group (which we call internal war) or may only involve people from other societies (which we call purely external war). A society may have both types of warfare. The presence of internal war predicts various aspects of social organization, including patrilocal versus matrilocal residence (M. Ember and C. R. Ember, 1971), avunculocal residence (in the presence also of matrilineal descent; see M. Ember, 1974b), and contiguous unilineal descent groups and the reckoning of descent through known genealogical links (the descent groups we call "lineages"; see C. R. Ember, M. Ember, and Pasternak, 1974).

The theory that provided the impetus for these studies is based on the assumption that families faced with fighting close to home would want to keep their most loyal defenders at home or close by, ready to be quickly mobilized for defense. With internal war, we argue that sons are more likely to be loyal defenders than sons-in-law (who may be from enemy communities). Hence families would want their sons to stay close after they marry (thus patrilocal residence). Internal war, we further argue, would also favor males staying close to a larger group of unilineal kin (usually patrilineal). And if they live contiguously, they are likely to remember their precise genealogical links and hence lineages will be present. Avunculocal residence also occurs with internal war, but only under the circumstances of prior matrilineal descent (all avunculocal societies are matrilineal) and high male mortality because of war. If warfare changes from purely external to at least partly internal, families would want to keep their matrilineally related males together. Melvin Ember (1974b) argues that such a switch may be preferred at least for a time, rather than an immediate switch to patrilocality and patrilineality. If male mortality increases with the emergence of internal war, a man could mobilize more matrilineal than patrilineal male relatives, because there would be more males nearby who were related through his mother and sisters (who could remarry after their husbands are killed). Males related patrilineally would not be as numerous because the higher male mortality would translate into fewer males descended from males who had died in war. This is of course assuming that males are killed more often than females in warfare, which we think is generally the case in the ethnographic record.

We should note that Divale (1974) has a different theory of matrilocality. He thinks that recent migration explains matrilocality. According to his theory, purely external warfare is a consequence, not a cause, of matrilocal residence. (See C. R. Ember [1974] for a critical evaluation of the Divale theory and evidence that seems inconsistent with it.) Suffice it to say here that Divale's theory does not explain patrilocality; it just assumes that it is normal (which it is). And it doesn't say why a migrating group would deliberately adopt matrilocal residence in order to preclude internal war. Divale assumes that matrilocality does that by dispersing related males, who if not dispersed would be likely to engage in internal war. Clearly, we need a multivariate study and/or some cross-historical data to help us choose between the two theories. Since they postulate opposite temporal orderings, they cannot both be correct.

Marriages usually occur between people who speak the same language, and therefore internal warfare often means that people marry their enemies. (More precisely, they marry people from groups who were enemies in the past and who might be enemies in the future.) Marrying enemies is significantly associated with men's fear of sex with women, with babies sleeping closer to their mothers than to their fathers (C. R. Ember, 1978), and with other aspects of husband-wife aloofness (Whiting and Whiting, 1975; but see Broude, 1983). Internal warfare and marrying out of the community (local exogamy) are associated with strict rules prohibiting women from participating in war or handling weapons (Adams, 1983). The theory is that women coming from enemy communities (which would happen with patrilocal residence) are likely to have a conflict of interest when it comes to war between their natal and marital communities, and therefore males try to keep them ignorant of military plans. If you are afraid of intimacy with your wife, she would be less likely to hear about such plans because you would not be spending much time with her. Higher frequencies of rape may also be found in societies with internal war, male domination of political decision making, and separation of the sexes (cf. Sanday, 1981a, 1981b; Otterbein, 1968, 1979).

Although the microlevel social environment (e. g., family context, child rearing customs) is not usually thought of as "environment" when evolutionary issues are discussed, some of the findings in this area are of interest because they may relate to issues discussed by evolutionists. We pay particular attention here to the effects of father absence in creating "hypermasculine" behavior.

A large body of literature in psychology and a considerable number of cross-cultural studies have suggested that boys growing up without fathers early in life or with relatively absent fathers tend to show hypermasculine behaviors (e. g., violence, boasting) later in life (for references, see Munroe, Munroe, and Whiting, 1981). Some theorists (e.g., J. W. M. Whiting and B. B. Whiting, 1978) suggest that boys may exaggerate their masculine behavior because of conflict about their unconscious feminine identification. In the cross-cultural research literature, several cultural features are used to indicate the likelihood of early unconscious feminine identification, including exclusive mother-child sleeping, baby sleeping closer to mother than to father, mother carrying child in sling or shawl, and little father-infant contact as indicated by fathers sleeping apart from infants (and mothers). Although the results of early cross-cultural studies were equivocal, a recent study indicates that low father salience does increase the likelihood of male aggression, i.e., homicide and assault (C. R. Ember and M. Ember, 2002).

If the competition theory of polygyny were correct, we should find that hypermasculine males have higher reproductive rates, and not just in the F-1 generation. Chagnon's (1988) results for the Yanomamo are supportive but problematic, we think, because he did not calculate reproductive rates for the men who had been killed. Many of those men may have been killers themselves. If they had lower reproductive rates (because they died early) than killers who lived longer, but were included in the computation, the reproductive difference that Chagnon thinks he found between killers and nonkillers might be nonexistent.

Parenthetically, we are obliged to call the reader's attention to the atypicality of the Yanomamo in two respects. First, the particular group of Yanomamo described by Chagnon had an *excess* of men together with polygyny, a combination that is extremely unusual in the ethnographic record. Second, in contrast to most societies with very frequent internal warfare, the Yanomamo described by Chagnon did not have localized patrilineal descent groups. They should have had such groups, judging by the fact that patrilineal descent groups (particularly lineages) are very likely when there are frequent wars between villages within a society (C. R. Ember, M. Ember, and Pasternak, 1974). But the Yanomamo didn't have such groups. Why we cannot say, except that their wars may have mostly involved villages not near each other. In any case, the Yanomamo described by Chagnon are quite anomalous, viewed cross-culturally.

Returning to the issue of supposedly hypermasculine behavior, it is possible that the psychological explanation is not alternative to the male-male competition explanation. Draper and Harpending (1982) have argued that aspects of child rearing and the presumably resultant hypermasculine behaviors are parts of an adaptive strategy (at least for males) that they call the "cad" as opposed to the "dad" strategy. So in their view the psychological explanation provides the mechanism required for a more complete explanation of the presumably adaptive "cad" strategy. But we still need evidence that it is adaptive over time. And the psychological and competition explanations should still be pitted against each other in multivariate analyses of cross-cultural and/or individual-level data.

Conclusion

From the point of view of cross-cultural research, cultural materialism is alive and well as a theoretical orientation. Most cross-cultural researchers are cultural materialists, and they (and their studies) are increasing in number geometrically. They are materialists because they look first to the physical and social environment for explanations of cultural variation, on the assumption that culture is mostly adapted to the physical and social environment. The growth in the cross-cultural research literature is now fueled by various kinds of researchers—cultural anthropologists, evolutionary biologists and evolutionary psychologists, comparative archaeologists, and other social scientists. The word seems to be getting out that it is not hard to test an explanation cross-culturally. You don't need to apply for a large grant to do a cross-cultural study. You do have to have the patience to read and measure variables in ethnography (which is facilitated by the HRAF Collection of Ethnography). Measuring variables that are described in those records is even easier now because you can quickly retrieve the information you need from the Web. You still need to devise measures of the variables you are interested in. But that task is not hard, and there is guidance available (C. R. Ember and M. Ember, 2001). If we want to keep cultural materialism alive and well, all we have to do is continue testing our explanations. And the test of choice is the cross-cultural one, which is the most generalizable and most efficient way to discover how cultural variation may be adapted to physical and social environments.

So let's go to it, in the spirit of Marvin Harris. All we can lose is our ignorance!

Part IV

*The Darwinian Challenge
to Cultural Materialism*

Chapter Eight

The Effect of Nepotism on the Evolution of Social Inequality

Lawrence A. Kuznar, William G. Frederick, and Robert L. Sedlmeyer

The transition from relatively egalitarian hunter-gatherer societies to more complex societies characterized by stratification and inequality has always been a central concern of anthropologists. Lewis Henry Morgan (1974[1877]:560) ended his pioneering work on social evolution with a consideration of how the concentration of property among elite chiefly lineages in his stage of Upper Barbarism led to inequality. Frederick Engels (1972[1891]:223) built upon Morgan's foundation to argue for the formation of a class-based society where economic privilege and social inheritance were united. Modern anthropologists have maintained this interest in explaining the origins of inequality during the transition from foraging bands to complex, hierarchical societies (Carneiro, 1981, 1998; Johnson and Earle, 1987; Price and Brown, 1985; Read, 2002).

In this chapter, we explore the fundamental processes that may account for the transition from band-like levels of inequality, to the more extreme levels of inequality that become entrenched in complex, highly stratified societies. We take advantage of agent-based modeling techniques in computational social science that allow more flexible exploration of the consequences of competing theoretical propositions. This flexibility is leveraged to compare and contrast Darwinian theories of human social evolution with more economically focused cultural materialist theories. We demonstrate that social inequality and class societies can emerge as the unintended consequence of nepotism and the differential reproduction of culturally successful individuals.

The chapter proceeds as follows. First, we review key cultural materialist arguments for the rise of complex societies and class-like hierarchy. We then demonstrate the pervasive character of wealth and class inequality in complex societies. Next, we describe new developments in computational social science that allow for both synthesis and testing of competing hypotheses. We detail our own computational model, and describe its results. The chapter concludes with a discussion of the implications of these results for understanding the evolution of inequality.

The Emergence of Cultural Complexity

Cultural complexity accompanied the Neolithic revolution, the transition from small mobile foraging societies to settled village societies and the eventual domestication of plants and animals (Childe, 1951). Brown and Price (1985) provide a useful summary of what the Neolithic revolution entailed based upon a review of prehistoric cases from North America, Europe, and the Middle East. Their synopsis is reinforced by data from South America (Burger, 1995; Nuñez, 1983; Quilter, 1991) and Africa (Haaland, 1995). The cultural complexity that accompanied the Neolithic transition included increased population density, increased settlement size, sedentism, permanent residential structures, permanent ceremonial grounds, elaboration of art styles, increased trade in exotic materials, and more pronounced wealth inequality (Brown and Price, 1985:437–438). The earliest sedentary societies were most likely organized along tribal lines, with allied lineages and kin groups cohabiting because of the draw of productive resource zones (Brown and Price, 1985), and because of population pressure and social circumscription as human populations increased (Binford, 1987; Brown and Price, 1985; Kuznar, 1989; Sanderson, 1999b).

While human social life certainly changed dramatically after the Neolithic transition, and the stage was set for even more dramatic increases in population and wealth inequality, the levels of wealth inequality were probably not that dramatic and no elite hierarchy could claim hereditary control of wealth. Scholars, however, recognize a fundamental change in human social life with the advent of the first chiefdoms (Carneiro, 1998; Sanderson, 1999b). Chiefdoms are complex societies in which a lineage or clan comes to dominate others to the point of being able to extract tribute (Carneiro, 1970:735). When this subordination occurred as the result of warfare and raiding, it led to the development of both wealth and settlement hierarchies in which paramount chiefs and their kin inhabited a centrally located village or town, militarily dominating surrounding villages or towns and exacting tribute from their local leaders (Carneiro, 1991, 1998).

Sanderson (1999b:68–88) provides a useful overview of theories concerning the emergence of chiefdoms. First, he notes the strikingly parallel ways that such transformations have taken place worldwide, arguing that such parallels indicate that general theoretical models are needed to explain them (Sanderson, 1999b:69). Sanderson (1999b:72) rejects more ideationalist and symbolic theories on the grounds that they ignore the very obvious role of the production of basic goods necessary to support elite polities. He divides theories of chiefdom formation into conflict theories, which posit the evolution of chiefdoms as the result of conflicts within and between polities, and functionalist theories, which posit the evolution of chiefdoms as the result of the broad social benefits they provide, such as irrigation or the regulation of trade. He points out that functionalist theories fail to account for the differential benefits that accrue to elites, casting doubt that cultural complexity and chiefdoms emerge as the result of an altruistic desire of the powerful to help the weak (Sanderson, 1999b:86). Instead, Sanderson points out that materialist theories that focus on how social forms emerge from competition between individuals and corporate groups (for example circumscription theory) hold more promise and are more consistent with archaeological and ethnohistoric data.

Marvin Harris accounts for the origin of the chiefdom, and eventually the state, in the activities of big men, which he refers to as "intensifier-redistributor-warriors" (Harris, 1979:95), "worker-entrepreneurs" (Harris, 1977:118), "food managers," and "redistributors" (Harris, 1977:104, 113). Harris largely avoids functionalist traps by noting that, while big men facilitate and encourage increased production, they do so for their own benefit, and those whose aid they inveigle provide it for their own benefits (Harris, 1977). Harris details how, in time, self-aggrandizing big men acquire the use of force and transform a mutually (if not equally) beneficial relationship into one of domination. Importantly, he stresses that, in contrast to functionalist analyses, individuals need not and probably were not consciously aware of the long-term consequences of their actions, which would transform essentially egalitarian societies into elite-dominated hierarchies (Harris, 1977:122). Given his well-known aversion to sociobiology (Harris, 1979), Harris takes pains to avoid appeals to Darwinian forces, such as drives to reproduction and nepotism. However, both his data and his rhetoric belie an evolutionary basis for the emergence of chiefdoms. In this regard, Harris invokes a "drive for prestige" that preferentially motivates big men rather than others (Harris, 1977:111). Also, some of his key examples make clear that opportunities for sex and reproduction were central to the motivation of both chiefs and their followers. He points out that Trobriand chiefs acquired as many as two dozen wives, and the Bunyoro chiefs of central Africa maintained large harems (Harris, 1977:109, 115).

The male supporters of chiefs likewise received reproductive benefits, whether it was the polygynous ménages of the Bunyoro chief's brothers or the sexual favors bestowed upon warriors in the Solomon Islands. In fact, the ability to provide sexual partners appears to be an historical requisite for power among Solomon Island chiefs. Quoting Douglas Oliver's informants on their *mumi*, or chief, Harris (1977:108) notes, "If the *mumi* did not furnish us with women, we were angry.... All night long we would copulate and still want more. It was the same with eating." If Harris wants his explanation to be devoid of Darwinian underpinnings, then why are there so many references to copulation? Would not food or some other form of material gain have been enough? The requisite supply of women is actually reminiscent of suggestions made by Harris's principal sociobiological nemesis Napoleon Chagnon (1983, 1988), who argues that the desire to acquire and control women is central to tribal warfare.

Finally, it is apparent from Harris's examples that kin ties and nepotism are central to the motives and successes of chiefs, indicating the influence of nepotistic tendencies in human behavior. For instance, Harris notes that a chief's ability to play the role of provider depends on ties of kinship more than anything else, and all of his examples demonstrate the close support of kin and the chief's reciprocity for their aid; in no case do nonkin figure prominently in a chief's support (Harris, 1977, 1979). Therefore, Darwinian principles do not contradict Harris's cultural materialist explanation, but rather may be the foundation for it.

Complex Inequality: The Empirical Evidence

Some controversy surrounds the use of the term *egalitarian* in anthropology (Salzman, 1999). It cannot be taken to indicate strict equality, because there is always some degree of inequality in wealth, access to mates, and social status; at best equality only ever exists as equality of opportunity. This is amply borne out when quantitative measures of status and equality are applied to actual groups. It is striking that, in our research, no matter what measure of value is used—cost of house construction, money, beads, access to mates, hunting returns, gathering returns—there is never anything like complete equality. Furthermore, inequalities typically have S-shaped oscillations as one moves from the poorest to the wealthiest individuals in a society. We have documented these S-shaped, or sigmoid, wealth distributions among nonhuman primates, foragers, chiefdoms, ancient kingdoms, modern states, and even in the current global economy (Kuznar, 2001, 2002a, 2002b; Kuznar and Frederick, 2003, 2005a, 2005b; Kuznar and Gragson, 2005.).

The flattened areas of the S-shaped curves represent wealth-based classes. Economists and anthropologists have proposed that individuals on the border between classes should exhibit risk-taking behavior (Friedman and Savage, 1948; Winterhalder, Lu, and Tucker, 1999), and empirical findings from studies of peasant societies support this proposal (Cancian, 1972, 1989). Individuals in such positions have more to gain (entrance into a higher social class and a better material standard of living) than to lose (staying in the same class) by taking risks. We have correlated risk taking on these class borders with political activism, collective violence, and terrorist recruitment (Kuznar, Sedlmeyer, and Frederick, 2005; Kuznar and Frederick, 2003). Since the determinative factor in risk taking is being on the cusp of a class boundary, rather than simply being poor, the approach allows us to predict dissatisfaction and risk taking by some wealthy individuals, as well as complacency of some poor ones.

We have discovered two fundamental wealth distributions in human economies. The comparative method, in which societies representing different levels of socioeconomic integration are compared as though on an evolutionary scale, provides a sense of the transitions in inequality that accompanied the Neolithic transition and the rise of chiefdoms and the state (Sanderson, 1999b:88–94). A simple sigmoid curve is typical of small-scale forager societies, and consists of an S-shaped (sigmoid) oscillation around a linear increase in wealth. These oscillations are defined as quasiperiods because true periods oscillate around zero, whereas our periods oscillate around increasing lines or curves. Figure 8.1 represents the hunting success rates of men in a Ju/'hoansi community in Botswana (Kent, 1996), whose quasiperiods depict three "classes" of

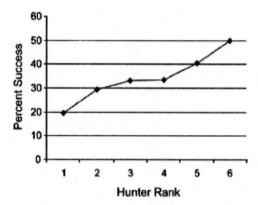

Figure 8.1 Ju/'hoansi (!Kung) Hunter Skill Distribution
Source: Kent (1996).

hunters: a few individuals who are superior in talents and abilities, a "middle class" of individuals who are average, and a few individuals at the bottom who are very poor hunters (Kuznar, 2002a; Kuznar and Gragson, 2005).

The other distribution, which we call "expo-sigmoid," consists of an overall exponential increase in wealth with sigmoid oscillations around this curve (Kuznar, Sedlmeyer, and Frederick, 2005; Kuznar and Frederick, 2003). Figure 8.2 shows a classic expo-sigmoid distribution for the Kapauku village of Botukebo (Pospisil, 1964), which could be considered an incipient chiefdom (Pospisil, 1972:45). The expo-sigmoid distribution is typical of complex societies such as chiefdoms, ancient kingdoms, modern states, and even the current global economy (see Kuznar and Frederick [2003] and Lewis [2004] for examples). Two features of this distribution are significant. Since convexity (concave upwardness) of a wealth distribution curve correlates with risk taking, it follows that societies with expo-sigmoid wealth distributions are likely to experience substantial social unrest because they will contain many individuals who are dissatisfied with the status quo. Second, there are always steps, or sigmoid oscillations, around this curve. These steps create alternating convex and concave distributions of wealth, and consequently alternating risk-taking and risk-averse sectors of a population, conditioned by the general risk proneness of an expo-sigmoid population. The most common pattern is for the masses to have one sigmoid quasiperiod (indicating an impoverished class and a middle class), and the elites to have their own sigmoid quasiperiod (indicating class distinctions even among the wealthiest).

Clearly, a fundamental shift in the nature of inequality accompanies the shift from small-scale band-level societies to chiefdoms, and this pattern has since been preserved in human economies. The central question we address in this chapter is, "What fundamental processes create the expo-sigmoid wealth distribution, its concentration of material wealth in the hands of a few, and its corresponding potential for social unrest?"

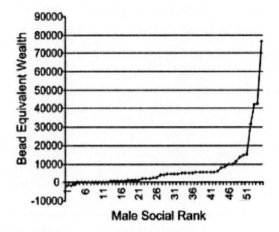

Figure 8.2 Kapauku Net Worth Wealth Distribution in Glass Beads
Source: Pospisil (1972).

Explaining Expo-Sigmoid Wealth Distributions:
Darwinian Possibilities

What is the significance of wealth inequality for social evolution, especially the evolution of chiefdoms and states? Is it cause or consequence? For Sanderson (1999b) it is both, although he gives more emphasis to stratification as a cause of political evolution than to the reverse. For theorists like Carneiro (1970:735), on the other hand, social stratification is the result of political subordination. Conquerors acquire greater wealth and use heredity to bequeath it to their descendants; when these conquerors have a monopoly over the use of force, class distinctions of rulers and ruled become strongly entrenched (Carneiro, 1991:175; 1998:35). Perhaps unwittingly, Carneiro has departed from a strict ecological/materialist explanation and has invoked a human evolutionary tendency to favor kin—nepotism. Both Sanderson and Harris recognize the pervasive role that nepotism plays in chiefly rule. Furthermore, Harris asserts that the evolution of chiefdoms and states is to a large extent an unanticipated consequence of individual maximizing behavior: "What I find most remarkable about the evolution of pristine states is that it occurred as the result of an unconscious process" (Harris, 1977:122). Harris is referring to economic behavior, but unconscious processes could also have been involved in the development of chiefdoms and eventually pristine states if they were the result of reproductive decisions. We pose the question, "Could nepotism and related Darwinian influences be sufficient to produce the kinds of inequality typical of chiefdoms and necessary for the formation of the state?"

Nepotism is the favoring of kin, especially close kin (Alexander, 1974). In many ways, nepotism is the first principle of human political interaction. In hunter-gatherer bands, sibling alliances stand at the core of band political organization (Gurven, Hill,

Kaplan, Hurtado, and Lyles, 2000; Lee, 1979). In tribal Amazonian societies, kinship alliances structure intratribal violence and intertribal warfare (Chagnon, 1990). In more complex chiefdoms, powerful lineages not only come to dominate other lineages, but eventually dominate other chiefdoms as well (Carneiro, 1998). In modern conflicts as well, nepotism is often a contributing cause (Collier, 2000). Nepotism is a pervasive tendency in human behavior, and any attempt at understanding human interaction must take it into account (Betzig, 1986).

Cultural success refers to individuals' fulfillment of the most important goals of their society, and those who achieve cultural success tend to have higher reproductive success (Irons, 1979). The definition of success is contingent to some extent upon particular social and cultural settings, but it is significant that in the vast majority of cases success is defined as the acquisition of material wealth and the ability to dispense it; consider the examples of chieftainship reviewed above. Cultural success theory has been most successful when applied to traditional, preindustrial societies. It helps to explain why good hunters enjoy increased reproductive success in foraging societies (Hawkes, 1993; Hawkes and Bliege Bird, 2002; Hawkes, O'Connell, and Blurton Jones, 2001b; Smith and Bliege Bird, 2000), patterns of violence in tribal societies (Chagnon, 1988), fertility in pastoral societies (Mace, 2000), and the extraordinary reproductive success of chiefs and kings throughout history (Betzig, 1986). In light of these findings, a model of preindustrial wealth accumulation should certainly incorporate cultural success.

Computational Social Science and Agent-Based Modeling

Computational Social Science (CSS) employs formal mathematics, and especially agent-based modeling (ABM) techniques, for social theories (Bankes, Lempert, and Popper, 2002; Berry, Kiel, and Elliott, 2002; Kohler, 2000; Sallach, 2003). These models typically represent classes of agents who interact with one another and produce emergent phenomena such as migrations, social structures, and epidemics (Kohler, 2000; O'Sullivan, 2004; Sallach, 2003; Sallach and Macal, 2001). As two pioneers of this new approach argue, simulation provides a crucial first test of a social theory; if you can grow it you may be able to explain it (Epstein and Axtell, 1996:20). If you cannot grow a simulated society despite your ability to control factors in your virtual world, then your theories are likely wrong, or at best badly misspecified.

Agent-based models are computer programs that allow individual agents to interact with their environment and other agents according to programmed rules (Epstein and Axtell, 1996). Researchers test theories of environmental influence or social interaction by programming these conditions and rules into the model, and then seeing if the model produces life-like results (Kohler, 2000; Sallach, 2003).

A dichotomy has emerged in ABM research between simple abstract models and complicated realistic models (see Sallach and Macal [2001] for a general discussion of the issue). Robert Axelrod (1997) advocates the KISS (Keep It Simple Stupid) approach in which researchers keep parameters at a minimum to facilitate exploring relationships among a few abstract and general variables. Other researchers favor relatively more detailed and realistic models (Carley, 2002; Kuznar, in press). We see a role for both, and have developed complicated, detailed "high-fidelity" models of pastoral/peasant interaction in the Middle East and Darfur, Sudan (Kuznar and Sedlmeyer, 2005; Kuznar, Sedlmeyer, and Kreft, in press), as well as simpler models focused on abstract relations among a few parameters (Kuznar, Sedlmeyer, and Frederick, 2005; Kuznar and Frederick, 2005a, 2005b). Given the abstract and general nature of arguments for the evolution of inequality, we have adopted the simpler KISS approach in this chapter. In order for us to apply ABM to the evolution of inequality, it needs to instantiate basic aspects of theorized social interactions proposed by Darwinian anthropologists and cultural materialists. We use a model we have developed for modeling risk-taking behavior, RiskTaker, to instantiate these elements.

Simulating the Evolution of Inequality

Harris and Sanderson see the rise of chiefdoms as the unintended cumulative result of individual behaviors. Therefore our modeling effort will reflect this methodological individualism, and our basic agents will represent individuals who have the capacity to reproduce, be reproduced, gain wealth, and inherit wealth. In keeping with Axelrod's KISS approach, we will keep these rules as simple as possible in order to minimize results that are artifacts of programming and to focus most fundamentally on basic interrelationships. The key elements of RiskTaker include time, wealth as an indicator of social status, demography, a model of agent interaction, and the dynamic exchange of wealth and change in individual social status.

Time. Each iteration roughly represents a year, although given the abstract nature of this simulation, caution should be exercised in interpreting model results in terms of actual years passed. We ran each simulation for 200 iterations (memory problems developed after this point in some models), and we did 5 sample runs for each experimental case to monitor divergent results due to nonlinear and stochastic effects.

Wealth. The wealth variable in RiskTaker can be considered any culturally appropriate form of wealth or power over which individuals would compete in a particular society. We use a simple sigmoid wealth distribution with one quasiperiod (a single oscillation) to initialize RiskTaker.

Demography. For simplicity's sake, our agents will be sexless, and have the capacity to reproduce at a rate of 2 percent per iteration (roughly 1 year equivalent), consonant with growth rates observed among traditional foragers (Kaplan, Hill, Lancaster, and Hurtado, 2000). RiskTaker begins with 24 agents, simulating an initial population in a foraging band. Agents do not die, but each initial agent serves as the founder of a lineage.

Agent Interaction: The Coordination Game. We model agent interaction with a game theory model variously referred to as the Stag hunt, or coordination game (Battalio, Samuelson, and van Huyck, 2001). Social scientists use this model because it has multiple Nash equilibria, which makes it a realistic model of the outcomes of human interaction (Alvard and Nolin, 2002; Battalio, Samuelson, and van Huyck, 2001; van Huyck, Battalio, and Beil, 1990). In the coordination game, both players benefit most by cooperating or joining a coalition. The players each earn a lower payoff if they both defect. The sucker's payoff is the one a player receives if her partner defects, and the temptation payoff is the one her defector receives. In our version of the coordination game, the temptation payoff equals the payoff when both players defect, indicating that the temptation to defect on a cooperating partner is not very great. These relative payoffs allow two Nash equilibrium solutions: Either both players defect or both cooperate.

The coordination game models situations in which benefits from cooperation are reasonably attained, as in sharing of hunting returns, cooperation in dividing prizes, or joining groups that can attain a public good that benefits its members. The coordination game, however, also has a solution in which both players defect on one another, modeling the possibility of defection from and dissolution of coalitions, which is also observed human behavior. Competing game theory models, such as the Prisoner's Dilemma, have only one solution in which both players defect (Axelrod, 1997). While modeling purely adversarial interactions, the Prisoner's Dilemma fails to capture mutually beneficial cooperation, without which human societies could not be sustained (Alvard and Nolin, 2002). The Nash optimum of the coordination game is to play a mixed strategy of Join and Defect, as our agents do in these simple simulations. Assuming a relatively open society for starters, we randomly assign agents for game play. Such a scenario approximates small-scale face-to-face societies.

Experimental Treatments

Baseline. We first establish a baseline by simply running the model with no effects from our theories of interest—nepotism, cultural success, or reproduction.

Nepotism. Nepotism occurs in two ways. Parents benefit from kin by earning payoffs from the coordination game proportionate to their inclusive fitness: Payoff = payoff*inclusive fitness, where inclusive fitness is calculated as the discounted genetic reproduction of one's relatives (Alexander, 1974). Offspring inherit 50 percent of parents' wealth, capturing nepotistic benefits from ancestors to descendants. In this manner, we capture both the benefits of being born into a large, wealthy lineage, and the recursive benefits to lineage members of the addition of another agent to their kindred.

Cultural Success. Cultural success is modeled by making fertility a function of wealth. Fertility is increased by increasing an agent's probability of reproducing (Pr. reproduce) = agent's wealth/MAX, where MAX = highest-status agent's wealth. The wealthiest agents always reproduce.

Complex Nepotism. In this experiment, we combine the effects of nepotism and cultural success to provide a slightly more realistic simulation.

Results

Experiment 1: Baseline. This experiment did little to alter the fundamental simple sigmoid wealth distribution (Figure 8.3a).

Experiment 2: Nepotism. Nepotism had an unexpected result on the evolution of wealth distributions. Fundamentally, it made the distribution more linear and more

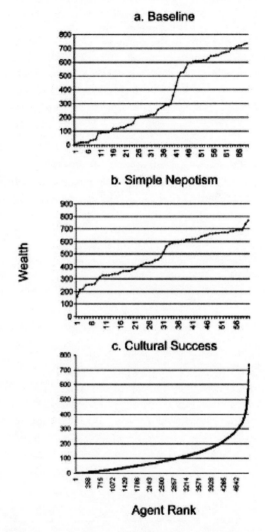

Figure 8.3 Experimental Results of Simulation:
Baseline, Simple Nepotism, Cultural Success

equal through time (Figure 8.3b). We suspect that this was because of interacting effects of allowing agents with many kin to earn more, but also allowing their offspring to inherit more, spreading wealth throughout the simulated society. In none of our empirical research have we seen wealth distributions like these, raising doubt that nepotism alone could effect the transition in inequality that accompanies the rise of chiefdoms.

Experiment 3: Cultural Success. Cultural success had the obvious effect of enhancing the fertility of the wealthiest agents, but because there was no provision for their offspring to inherit differentially, the experiment resulted in a vast underclass of poor. The resulting wealth distribution is essentially an exponential curve from poorest to wealthiest individuals, but without the sigmoid oscillations that define social classes, and that we have previously seen empirically (Figure 8.3c). Given this experiment's inability to produce sigmoid variations, cultural success alone is probably insufficient to account for the rise of class-based inequality within chiefdoms. The influence of cultural success, however, did dramatically increase the reproductive fitness of the wealthiest agents, and consequently population increased over time.

Experiment 4: Complex Nepotism. The combined effects of nepotism and cultural success in this experiment resulted in an expo-sigmoid wealth distribution characteristic of complex societies. The resulting distribution has distinct concave and convex sections (Figure 8.4). These sections are created in two ways. First, the abundant descendants of high-status individuals tend to accumulate as a second-tier "noble class," reproducing the demographic seen in ancient states or even the emergent chiefly society of Kapauku (see Figure 8.2). Second, relatively impoverished agents, as well as their offspring, tend to remain poor, leading to the long "tail" in the distribution of wealth. As with the cultural success model, enhancing the wealthiest agents' ability to reproduce led to an overall increase in population through time.

Discussion and Implications

Fundamental Darwinian propositions about human reproductive and nepotistic behavior can account for the rise of complex forms of class-based inequality. However, it takes the combined effects of both nepotism and cultural success to produce class-based inequality. The fact that these fundamental tendencies can produce expo-sigmoid wealth distributions is a vital first step in testing these Darwinian principles—we can

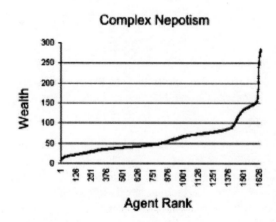

Figure 8.4 Experimental Results of Simulation: Complex Nepotism

grow it. However, further research is necessary to exclude alternatives. We conducted runs based on purely economic factors, such as the rich get richer (stacking earnings in proportion to agents' wealth), and these purely cultural materialist simulations failed to produce expo-sigmoid distributions. Therefore, we have preliminary evidence that Darwinian principles are probably necessary to account for the evolution of class-based inequality.

One implication of this simulation exercise is that we were able to produce an emergent socioeconomic phenomenon, expo-sigmoid wealth distributions, by modeling individuals' reproductive behavior. This reductionism has the appeal of grounding higher-level emergent economic phenomena (that may very well have unique properties) in lower-level biobehavioral phenomena, therefore grounding cultural materialist explanation in more fundamental behaviors.

By comparing the results of these simulations to our other work, we can derive other implications, both theoretical and practical. The research that eventually led us to simulation was a series of empirical studies and formal mathematical models of risk-taking behavior. We consistently found that individuals who were willing to take risks were located in convex sections of material wealth distributions; these individuals have more to gain than to lose in such situations (Kuznar, 2001, 2002a, 2002b; Kuznar, Sedlmeyer, and Frederick, 2005). This was true across the broadest array of social, religious, and economic conditions. In the end, the character of material wealth distributions has an undeniably profound effect on individuals' behavior.

We can predict several effects from the emergence of expo-sigmoid wealth distributions with the transition to chiefdoms. The overall exponential distribution of wealth produces a situation where an increasingly larger proportion of people in a society will have material cause to challenge those in power. Furthermore, the sigmoid oscillations produce classes with sharp boundaries, and these sharp boundaries are where we predict the most intense risk-taking behavior to occur. Other research we have conducted confirms that agents in convex sections tend to aggregate in coalitions, and these coalitions are potentially volatile due to the risk proneness of their agents (Kuznar, Sedlmeyer, and Frederick, 2005). Empirical research confirms that agents in such real-world coalitions are responsible for social unrest and collective violence, including political coups and popular rebellions (Kuznar and Frederick, 2005a, 2005b). Therefore, expo-sigmoid wealth distributions generate an environment conducive to social unrest, and create segments of the population containing individuals particularly motivated to challenge elites and willing to coalesce to do so. Such a situation is a formula for constant turmoil, and in fact, chiefdoms are characterized by political instability. The only way for a particular elite to maintain control will be through the use, implied or actual, of force. This constant threat of force is a defining feature of what anthropologists define as the state (Carneiro, 1970:733). Even in our relatively peaceful society, most people voluntarily pay their taxes, but the severest of penalties await those who willfully refuse. In this manner, the ultimate evolution of the state and its systems of taxation and standing armies and police forces was rooted in evolved behavioral tendencies that grew expo-sigmoid wealth distributions and reaped their fruits of discord, as well as increased reproductive fitness and prosperity.

Chapter Nine

Coevolutionary Materialism

James W. Dow

THE THRUST OF HARRIS'S THEORETICAL WORK was to discount idealism and to de-mystify the origins of culture.[1] He was aligned with the neoevolutionists who wanted to develop a science of culture. However, the idea of cultural materialism itself is still a somewhat dogmatic belief without connections to other empirical sciences. Harris (1979:26–27) called it a "research strategy" rather than a theory. In other words, we are asked to believe that cultural materialism leads to better theories about the way that things work than alternative modes of explanation that can, at first contact, be equally satisfying. The most significant alternatives, for Harris, were the idealist theories that hold that human ideas, not material circumstances, cause culture change. Harris pre-sents cultural materialism as an anti-idealist perspective, a set of axiomatic statements, that he derives from Marx and states in the following terms:

> The cultural materialist version of Marx's great principle is as follows: The etic[2] be-havioral modes of production and reproduction probabilistically determine the etic behavioral domestic and political economy, which in turn probabilistically determine the behavioral and mental superstructures. For brevity's sake, this principle can be referred to as the principle of infrastructural determinism. (Harris, 1979:55–56)

This argument leads to a system of scientific inquiry in which particular cultural phenomena are derived from general laws. Structure is derived from infrastructure, su-perstructure from structure. Thus, Harris's cultural materialism advocates a nomological model of science in which particular phenomena are interpreted as the special results of general principles or laws. This nomological idea of scientific truth, derived from nineteenth-century physics and early twentieth-century positivism, had a profound effect on the social sciences in the twentieth century in spite of the fact that it was replaced by more sophisticated concepts of scientific truth in the natural sciences (Mjøset, 1999). The deductive-nomological model of science has not been of much use in the nonexperimental sciences, such as biology or meteorology, which are more like cultural anthropology, because they deal with large numbers of variables in complex systems. Harris's proposal of a nomological theory such as infrastructural determinism shows that he was thinking of cultural anthropology as a late twentieth-century science of culture, and that he ran into a typical problem: The paradigm of science set out by physics—for example celestial mechanics—was difficult to apply in the social sciences.

Harris's solution to this problem was to propose that a research strategy should guide actual research in order to give coherence to the results (1979:25). According to Harris, there were many research strategies applicable to cultural phenomena, and therefore there were many types of science possible in cultural anthropology. Cultural materialism was just one of them, but, of course, as Harris contended, the best one. Cultural materialism narrows the scientific vision to an special set of related variables. Unlike some sciences, which subdivide themselves by subdividing the subject under study—medicine into urology, cardiology, etc.—cultural anthropology would divide itself metatheoretically into different strategies focusing on the same subject, and thus maintain a nomological coherence within each strategy.

The social sciences in the later twentieth century were unaware of the inherent noncomputability of axiomatic systems that mathematicians like Gödel and Turing had exposed (Davis, 1958). Random stochastic processes and self-organizing systems were not on the social science horizon, and physics, which many social scientists took as the basic paradigm of science, took off in an opposite direction that did not need statistics or systems theory. For example, in his analysis of Indian beliefs about the sacredness of cows, Harris (1974a) focused on their value as draft animals. However, there is also the value of the dung as fuel, the cleaning up of useless vegetable refuse, the provision of milk, the use of cow urine, the provision of hides, etc., to consider. Some cows may not be good draft animals, others may be better, and so forth, so measuring the total value of Indian cows could be a very complex process. Harris's cultural materialism was a way of weighting interrelationships in a complex system so that only certain ones, mostly those related to infrastructure, were taken seriously. Thus he preserved a nomological science of culture.

Cultural materialism was also an extension of neoevolutionary thinking in cultural anthropology. It contains an undeniable Darwinian precept: that cultures evolve in response to the material conditions that affect human survival and reproduction.[3] Leslie White (1949:364) described a tripartite hierarchy in cultural systems: "technology," "social systems," and "ideology." Harris did not retain these terms, using instead the terms "infrastructure," "structure," and "superstructure" to describe the same thing. However, he clearly was following in the footsteps of White and modeling cultural evolution as driven by material interactions. Harris developed White's evolutionism into a research strategy, as he believed White had also done before him (Harris, 1968b:636). In his last book, *Theories of Culture in Postmodern Times,* Harris referred to cultural materialism as "a processually holistic and globally comparative scientific research strategy" (1999b:141). Because it is a strategy and not a scientific theory, it is exempt from providing direct empirical evidence to support it. Above all, it is a refutation of an idealist research strategy, which holds that cultural change is directed by human ideas rather than the material circumstances in which people live.

It is interesting to note, as one searches for the causes of cultural change, that both the idealist and materialist approaches can still be supported with roughly equal satisfaction. Historical particularistic explanations for human events devolve into unique human stories in which actors are motivated by their ideas and act rationally within these intellectual frameworks. Idealist explanations are easily and naturally accepted by human beings because humans have a capacity for sensing and modeling the thought patterns of others, a sensible survival strategy for a species that preys on its own members.[4] Thus, idealist explanations of human behavior relying on narrative are very satisfying and by no means "wrong," because the survival of individuals has shown them to be "right" in that sense. However, are these idealist explanations scientific? They are not. Science is a different pattern of human cognition whose correctness has also been earned by its success in promoting the survival of the species, but it is more collective, more shared, and more dependent on emerging technologies of communication, such as writing, printing, and computing machines.

Neoevolutionary thinking can get bogged down in an effort to resolve this dichotomy between idealist and scientific/materialist explanations. Barrett (1989) and Hatch (1990) argue that White articulated two incompatible theories of culture change. On one hand, White's materialistic-evolutionary model proposed that most aspects of culture are created by energy and material factors; on the other hand, his culturological model states that culture evolves autonomously without outside influences. This seems self-contradictory because the engine of cultural evolution is external in the first instance and internal in the second. Crowe (1990) sees this as a false dichotomy. Likewise, materialist and idealist theories of cultural change seem to be opposed; however, they are only intellectual perspectives on a single process that could have its own systemic unity. Each perspective leaves out something that the other includes. They are both correct within their own limited scope. The correctness of one perspective does not imply the incorrectness of the other. Thus there is no real paradox that has to be resolved.

The cultural materialist perspective on religion is illustrated by Harris in his book *Cows, Pigs, Wars, and Witches* (1974a). A biological evolutionary viewpoint on religion is illustrated by Atran in his book *In Gods We Trust* (2002), but Atran does not regard cultural materialism highly. About materialism, Atran (2002:202) writes:

> Materialism in anthropology, including versions of Marxism, consist largely of reasons that include no material causes known to the natural sciences (e. g., modes of production that generate ideologies). It relies instead on open-textured metaphors drawn from the natural sciences, such as "power" and "revolution" taken from physics or "reproduction" and "evolution" taken from biology.

However, Harris considered these concepts (modes of production, etc.) to be far more than metaphors, as is apparent from the following passage:

The basic premise of empirical science is that there are things outside of the observer whose nature can be known only by interacting with them through observation, logical manipulation, and experiment. Thus all things in their knowable state are *partially* the creations of observational and logical operations. This includes subatomic particles, biological species, ecosystems, tectonic plates, and weather patterns. ...

As long as the model is constructed on an identifiable physical base and is built up according to explicit logical and empirical steps, it can lay claim to having a physical reality. (Harris, 1999b:52–53)

Thus, Harris seems to say that an abstract entity constructed logically and empirically from the observation of human behavior can lay claim to physical reality. Words deceive. Harris's idea of cultural materialism is not a statement about the impact of physical things on human beings, but a statement about the nature of cultural systems, which can include *emic* human responses to perceived environments that have some measurable *etic* physical attributes. It is really a theory about cultural systems, not about material things. There is no real conflict of ideas here.

Culturological-Biological Materialism

I would like to explore the possibility of a larger, more comprehensive model of cultural change that includes both cultural materialist and idealist processes. With a comprehensive model of cultural change, including both materialist and idealist perspectives, among others, the evolutionary view of cultural change might be reintegrated with the natural sciences and become more practical and verifiable. A cultural materialism that dogmatically rejects the impact of ideas does not present the complete picture. Within Harris's materialist strategy, the impact of religion and new ideas on cultural change are disregarded. On the other hand, within a pure idealist strategy the material conditions that stimulate ideas are ignored. Idealist and materialist perspectives need to be united and not left to compete fruitlessly with each other. Harris (1999b:31–48) felt that the ideas of people, their emic world, should be included in an understanding of their culture, but he stopped short of giving these ideas causal influence on evolutionary change.

It is important to note that each strategy, materialist and idealist, has a different time perspective. The material causes of cultural change operate over longer evolutionary time spans and concern the ultimate causes of behavior, whereas the ideational causes of cultural change operate over shorter evolutionary time spans and concern the proximal causes of behavior. Again, one wonders why Harris fought against the idealist perspective when it seems to have a place in an overall science of culture. Perhaps, as Sandstrom notes (Chapter 4, this volume), it was a reaction to an antiscience movement in cultural anthropology.

Harris (1999b) also ruled out genetic influences. I suppose that a "research strategy" can ignore whatever it chooses, but this is done at a price. To embrace evolution and then to ignore the genetic processes in evolution is a bit dogmatic. The commonly accepted idea to which Harris subscribed, that culture changes infinitely more rapidly than genes, which are virtually fixed, may need some rethinking. The human brain, a product of genetic evolution, has obviously provided the means for culture to evolve (Donald, 1991:95–123). It sets the stage for cultural evolution and is active during cultural evolution. Being active, it establishes parameters for cultural evolution at all times. The brain itself could have changed rapidly in the past, when modern *Homo sapiens* were appearing and dominating other hominids with their culture carrying capacity (Eswaran, 2002). Also, cultural evolution may not be as rapid as some culturologists believe. For example, the evolution of the state seems to be locked into long-term equilibria (Flinn, 1997). The speed of genetic evolution and the speed of cultural evolution are not fixed.

At the biological pole of these arguments, Lumsden and Wilson (1981) have challenged culturologists like Harris with an epigenetic theory proposing that all so-called cultural change is just random noise obscuring the basic engine of real cultural change, which is genetic. Along with most cultural anthropologists, Harris defended the traditional culturological view that genetic changes are irrelevant to understanding the evolution of culture. However, the biological basis for culture is simply obvious, and cultural evolution is affected by the genetically carried mental capacity of humans (Tomasello, 1999), which itself is not a fixed capacity.

As Harris presents it, cultural materialism is a research strategy that leads people to look in the "right" direction for causal explanations of cultural things. It is not a scientific theory but a means for restricting thought to focus on the long-term ultimate causes of the evolution of human behavior. For cultural materialism to be extended as a scientific theory, it has to shed some of its simplicity, face up to the true complexity of cultural phenomena, and lean on empirical validations rather than on the wisdom of Marx and the anthropological neoevolutionists. It needs to integrate measurable ideational phenomena. It can do this by considering the biological bases of culture. This overturns Harris's (1999b:99–109) idea that biology should be left out of cultural theory. That particular bit of dogma should be rejected. However, the rest of cultural materialism has great value. It fits many real data. The evolution of culture is profoundly affected by the material conditions of human life. Harris's and White's insight—that the material conditions of life explain much of culture—is certainly worth keeping.

Figure 9.1 presents a model of cultural change that brings biology back into the process. Let us call it *cultural-biological materialism*. It is a coevolutionary model that unifies cultural materialism with Darwinian genetic evolution. The ideational elements enter the picture as cultural representations of the environment. These are included in the box "Cultural Knowledge," which represents the stored and shared symbolic representations belonging to a culture. The material consequences of human action drive cultural change in two ways: by cultural learning, using the ability to encode and culturally interpret the consequences of those actions; and by genetic evolution, using natural selection that alters the gene frequencies and directs the evolution of the brain.[5] The brain interprets reality and affects human action. As Rappaport (1979:97) has expressed it: "Nature is seen by humans through a screen of beliefs, knowledge, and purposes, and it is in terms of their images of nature, rather than of the actual structure of nature, that they act. Yet, it is upon nature itself that they do act, and it is nature itself that acts upon them, nurturing or destroying them."[6]

In Figure 9.1, biological systems and their effects are shown with dashed lines. Cultural learning systems and their effects are shown with dotted lines. A culture trait has material consequences that influence reproductive fitness. It also affects cultural adaptation because people perceive these effects and communicate them. Humans make decisions on the basis of their interpretations. Thus, the material consequences of a culture trait control the cultural system through two feedback loops:

1. The biological feedback loop that leads to a genetic change in the ability to encode and to interpret cultural knowledge (the dashed line in Figure 9.1).
2. The cultural learning feedback loop that leads people to perceive and interpret the material effects of their actions (the dotted line in Figure 9.1).

One must keep in mind that perception and interpretation require the ability to encode and interpret cultural knowledge, which means that successful cultural adaptation always selects some genetic traits that create culture as a means of adaptation.

Biology has given humans the ability to react to material effects and to modify a store of cultural knowledge. Biology also gives them the ability to take a store of cultural knowledge

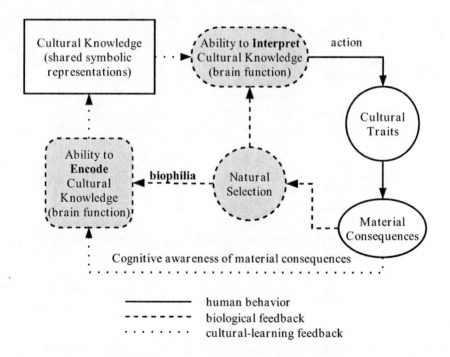

Figure 9.1 Cultural-Biological Materialism

and put it to use in technology or social action, which then leads to modified cultural traits. Both feedback loops, the cultural learning and the biological, lead to cultural evolution, and they interact. Because maladaptive paleolithic human behavior shows up in modern societies, it is often assumed that the biological feedback is much slower than the cultural learning feedback, but biological feedback is not completely absent and could determine the long-term development of a cultural system. Possibly, culturological evolution proceeds rapidly at times and biological evolution proceeds rapidly at other times. For example, biological evolution seems to have moved fast at the time that modern *Homo sapiens* confronted the Neanderthals (Tomasello, 1999; Eswaran, 2002). Now that the species has spread throughout the globe and the human genome is statistically stable, group behavioral differences are due primarily to the cultural differences that have evolved recently. The emphasis on cultural learning as the driving force of human evolution needs to be tempered with an awareness that we are only looking at a small time period in human history.

Harris's cultural materialism was biased against considering the biological evolution of the human brain. James Lett (1987:96–98) notes that, "In short, cultural materialism's list of biopsychological universals omits the one universal predisposition that is quint-essentially human, namely the fact that human beings are meaning-seeking, symbol-using animals." Harris took the ability of humans to encode cultural knowledge out of evolution. By putting this capacity into the superstructure and denying superstructural determinism he denied that symbol-making played a role in cultural evolution. However, it did make his model simpler. Perhaps this was a wise move by Harris, because cultural anthropology's ability to deal systematically with symbolic determinism is poor, but this does not mean that symbolic determinism is completely absent. According to Rappaport (1999), cultural symbols are very important in determining how people respond to the natural environment. Harris simply regarded the symbols as superficial add-ons that tended to mystify rather than illuminate the hidden materialistic process.

It is also unfortunate that Harris rejected "sociobiology," which was the term once used for evolutionary psychology. Harris (1979:56–58) tended to see cultural evolution as driven by the infrastructure, which made technology a prime mover. Technology varies so much from culture to culture that he concluded that the variations in cultural adaptation were too great to be explained by genetic causes (Harris, 1979:124). He failed to integrate cultural materialism with biological evolution, although he was very much on an evolutionary track.

The model of cultural-biological materialism presented here unifies these perspectives by adding the effects of natural selection to a cultural materialist model of cultural change. The cultural system evolves both through a culturally mediated response to material conditions and through the natural selection of the capacity to create and interpret the cultural symbols involved in this learning process.[7]

The Gods of Agriculture

I became aware of the usefulness of cultural-biological materialism while studying the culture of native people in Mexico, the Sierra Ñähñu, often referred to in the anthropological literature as the Sierra Otomí (Dow, 1994, 2002). The Sierra Ñähñu are a population of about 49,000 people who live in and around an eastern arm of the state of Hidalgo. Figure 9.2 shows the state and the Sierra Ñähñu area to the east. They are agriculturalists living in a mountainous tropical forest environment. Much of the original forest has been cut down to make room for their agriculture, which now includes some livestock. Their language and culture has a rich sensitivity to the biological world. There is only one word in their language for a machine, and that word covers everything from guns to airplanes. Yet they have dozens of words for corn and other cultivated and gathered plants.

E. O. Wilson argues in his book *Biophilia* (1986) that the human species has evolved a love of nature because it depends so much on the biological world. Any representation of the natural environment can lead to increased biological feedback, putting the natural environment into an important place in cultural knowledge. This seems to have occurred in Sierra Ñähñu religion.

Figure 9.3 is a modification of Figure 9.1, and shows how biophilia arises from genetic evolution and then affects cultural evolution. Love, being an emotion, is under the control of the human brain, most of whose emotional parameters are set by genes. Cultural knowledge receives this extra dimension of love because of the biological

Figure 9.2 The Sierra Ñähñu Homeland Shown
on an Outline of the State of Hidalgo

he symbolism in which the concepts of nature are encoded also comes
e with nature, in this case primarily from a dependency on agriculture.
So both genes and culture contribute to cultural behavior. Figure 9.3 shows the links
to cultural knowledge. Harris's infrastructural determinism is shown by the line from
"Material Consequences," but Harris had no concept to describe the love (biophilia)
line that also sets the nature of culture.[8]

The Sierra Ñähñu were part of an agricultural civilization for thousands of years.
They cultivate corn (maize), beans (*frijoles*), chilies, tomatillos (*tomates*), green squash
(*calabacitas*), large squash (*chilacayotes*), pumpkins, onions, peanuts, and other veg-
etables. They tend fruit trees, such as small grapefruit (*limón*), banana, small avocado
(*aguacate*), large avocado (*pahua*), orange, peach, fig, and lime. *Chayotes* are cultivated
around the home. They also eat certain semicultigens, such as the various amaranths
(*quelites*) that grow naturally with the corn and the flowers of the *quemite* tree, a thorn
tree that is often planted as a natural fence.

The Sierra Ñähñu experience with agriculture has been incorporated into their
traditional religion. I propose that it has been incorporated through the mechanism
previously outlined. The continued material success with agriculture working on the
human mind primed by biophilia has led to the incorporation of ideas related to
agriculture into Sierra Ñähñu religion.

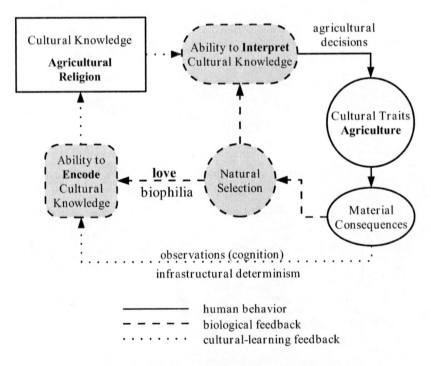

Figure 9.3 Biophilia Feedback in a Cultural System

Like many religions, the traditional Sierra Ñähñu religion incorporates a reverence for life, which it does by postulating a basic animating force in all living beings. The Sierra Ñähñu call this force *zaki*. It is their way of symbolizing a concern for life, reproduction, and survival. Many religions have such life-force concepts, which Tylor (1958[1874]) summarized as *animism*. According to the Sierra Ñähñu, all beings are arranged in a hierarchy depending on the power of their *zaki*. At the top are their nature gods: God Sun, Goddess Lady Water, God Earth, and God Grandfather Fire. Lesser superhuman beings called lords (*zidähmü*) also exist for them, and below these beings in the power hierarchy come humans, animals, and plants in that order.

The plants have their life forces. The Sierra Ñähñu believe that humans should care for the life forces of plants. One of the most important rituals involves taking actual seeds, along with images of their life forces (which shamans cut out of paper), up to the top of a sacred mountain where they are presented to the God Sun to be imbued with greater vitality. Figure 9.4 shows a gathering on the top of a sacred mountain.

Along the way, offerings are left to Goddess Lady Water. There is an uncanny parallel between these rituals and a scientific understanding of energy in ecosystems. The Ñähñu worship the sun, the primary energy source for all living ecosystems. Scientifically speaking, the sun provides the primary energy that creates practically all life on earth. How did these Indians embed such ideas so deeply in their religion, ideas that modern science has just brought to the awareness of the Western public? The answer is through the kind of cultural evolution that has been described. The

Figure 9.4 Gathering atop the Sacred Mountain

infrastructure of agriculture, stated in Harris's terms, gave rise to the superstructure of this religion. The process was a feedback process of the type illustrated earlier. But this could not have taken place without the evolution of the biophilic brain. Thus, cultural materialism can be seen in the wider evolutionary context of gene-culture coevolution, or culturological-biological materialism.

The Gods of Capitalism

A second situation where cultural-biological materialism lent a helping hand to my analysis of Sierra Ñähñu religion came while I was looking at how the people were abandoning their traditional religion and replacing it with Evangelical Christianity. As one might imagine, their traditional religion, no matter how ecologically sane it was, did not fit into the capitalist mode of production sweeping across the world. Many, but not all, of the Sierra Ñähñu people felt that it was wasteful to spend good money on offerings to agricultural gods. It might be better to spend it on a new house or some furniture. This was especially true when they began to earn money by working outside their home villages in more prosperous communities in Mexico and the United States. Eventually, many of them unseated the old gods and put an Evangelical Jesus in their place. The new Protestant god favored individual enterprise and fewer public expenditures. Always ready to make new converts, Evangelical Christian sects moved into the Indian communities to provide them with a legitimate argument against the redistribution of wealth that the old religion favored.

While trying to understand how this religious change was taking place, I noticed a correlation between demographic changes and religious changes. The two villages that adopted Evangelical Protestantism, San Nicolas and Santa Monica, adopted it about twenty years apart (Dow, 2001). A third village, San Pablo, was a more complex case, with two changes from decrease to increase. Figure 9.5 shows the populations of San Nicolas and Santa Monica. Something more than the working of the Holy Spirit was going on. The pueblos were quite close together and there were only minor cultural and historical differences between them. One had to search hard for an historical explanation for why the two pueblos adopted Evangelical Protestantism twenty years apart.

One can always construct an historical explanation of cultural change. There are always differences between situation A and situation B. Historical narrative does not repeat itself. Every case has a different story behind it. In a book I recently edited on conversions to Protestantism in Mesoamerica (Dow and Sandstrom, 2001), every author had a different explanation of why their group converted, yet the phenomenon was widespread throughout the entire region. Harris's genius was to see that there were common material conditions and experiences that drove cultural change.

To understand what was happening in the two pueblos, I looked at the ratio of young men to old men. This required a computer simulation to fill in the gaps in the census data on age-specific male populations (Dow, 2001). The material explanation when it was sketched out was fairly simple. The demographic decline and growth patterns produced a very low ratio of young men to older men about twenty years

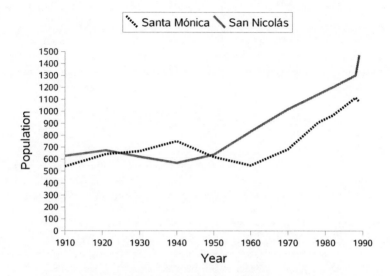

Figure 9.5 Population Growth in Two Mexican Villages

after the population dip. San Nicolas converted to Protestantism around the time of their low ratio, and, twenty years later, Santa Monica converted around the time of their low ratio.

The *cargo* systems maintaining the traditional public religion relied on younger men paying their way into a prestige system dominated by older men. When the ratio of younger men to older men had reached an extreme low, the younger men rebelled against the greater burden of an expense that they could not bear. They changed their religion to one that did not demand such sacrifices. Their ideas about the supernatural world changed because they had a bad experience with their consequences.

The interesting feature of this system from a theoretical viewpoint was that demographic changes caused religious changes. In other words, religion responded to material conditions. Harris was quite convinced that there were material roots to religion, and here I saw one of them in action. However, Harris's infrastructural determinism failed to capture the complete picture. A change in demographic ratios was the trigger for religious change, but not its complete cause. The human capacity for organizing group actions in terms of religion had to be there. Cultural change would not have taken place without a religious movement.

Conclusion

In summary, I would say that Harris opened the door to further theorizing about cultural evolution. He was defending his ideas with "theoretical" arguments. But this is not as good as empirical verification. He added to the work of the neoevolutionists and pointed cultural anthropology toward evolutionary models that can illuminate the evolved structure of cultural systems. Harris saw cultural materialism as a final solution to a complex theoretical issue in cultural anthropology. However, it also can be seen as the beginning of a gene-culture coevolutionary theory that does not have to restrict its variables to the ones dictated by a cultural materialist research strategy.

Notes

1. Harris (1974a:4) says the following about mystification: "Another reason why many customs and institutions seem so mysterious is that we have been taught to value elaborate 'spiritualized' explanations of cultural phenomena more than down-to-earth material ones." Here he blames political propaganda for mystifying the "real" reasons for adopting cultural institutions. However, I would note that these religious spiritualized explanations are so widespread in cultures of all types that they must have a biological basis (Atran, 2002).

2. An important feature of Harris's work is the distinction between *emic* and *etic*. Originally proposed by Pike (1954), this distinction involves the conceptual framework of the describer. Emic descriptions use the framework of the actors and describe the behavior in terms that they would use (Harris, 1968b:571). Etic descriptions, by contrast, "depend on the phenomenal distinctions judged appropriate by the community of scientific observers" (Harris, 1968b:575). These descriptions use scientific terms and do not depend on the subjective meanings and purposes of the actors. All human descriptive and explanatory systems are culturally constructed and encoded in symbols created by the cultural group. The distinction between the emic and the etic system resides in the group that constructs the system, not in some absolute truth. Harris felt that "the concepts of emics and etics provide an epistemological and operational basis for distinguishing between cultural idealism and cultural materialism" (1968b:569). He felt that etic descriptions could illuminate aspects of human behavior that could not be captured by emic descriptions.

3. I use the word neoevolutionary *thinking* here instead of neoevolutionary *theory*, because many sociologists use the word *theory* to describe any way of conceptualizing social behavior or cognition, whereas, in the sciences, theory refers to a set of propositions that requires empirical testing. Therefore, in much of sociology, theory implies an *a priori* validity not implied by the use of the word in the natural sciences.

4. Whereas most mammalian species fear predation by other species, humans focus on the predators within their own species and have developed acute capacities for distinguishing potential human predators from possible allies (Atran, 2002).

5. Note that in this model of cultural change, individual responses to the material consequences are omitted in the interest of explaining cultural evolution. I am only considering cultural things, symbols and behaviors belonging to a group. Certainly individual behavioral capacities that are not cultural are also evolving. For example, an individual fear of snakes would evolve if the genes of people who got too close to snakes were removed from the gene pool by lethal bites.

6. Postmodernists might object to the phrase "actual structure of nature" in Rappaport's statement, because it assumes that there is some sort of scientific absolute view of reality. I believe that Rappaport presents a false view of science here. Science is very humble and will change its views of reality as evidence accumulates. There is no "actual" structure of nature, only different cultural constructions of it. Science is a method of acquiring knowledge. It depends on external

memory (writing, publication, and record keeping), it avoids narrative explanations and other forms of subjectivity, it requires empirical validation, and it has proven to be very useful.

7. Note that I include technology in the category of cultural symbols. A tool carries with it a nonverbal symbolic message that teaches the user how to use the tool.

8. Note that in modern culture, "love" in some sense can develop around technology inasmuch as it contributes successfully to survival. People love their cars and computers. (Some would say it is more of a love-hate feeling toward their computers.) At least there is some sort of emotional reaction to technology.

Chapter Ten

Marvin Harris, Meet Charles Darwin

A Critical Evaluation and Theoretical Extension of Cultural Materialism

Stephen K. Sanderson

THE DEATH OF MARVIN HARRIS in the autumn of 2001 was a huge loss for anthropology and the social sciences in general. Harris was a theoretical genius who not only made a profound contribution to anthropology and related disciplines, but who also had a wonderfully accessible writing style that allowed him to write marvelous books for the general educated public. These books have sold several hundred thousand copies, and many are still in print and continue to sell well. (Harris wrote 18 books, both academic and popular, in all, and they appeared in over a dozen different languages [Margolis and Kottak, 2003].) Harris understood far better than most sociological and anthropological theorists the real function of theories: to explain concrete social phenomena. At least in sociology, most theorists think that their job is to develop extremely abstract conceptual and theoretical schemes that are designed to explain everything but nothing in particular. Harris developed an abstract conceptual and theoretical scheme, of course, but he applied this again and again to concrete social and cultural phenomena: sacred cows and abominable pigs, the potlatch, the origins of agriculture, Aztec cannibalism, social change in America since 1945, the collapse of Soviet Communism, and many others. Harris was an elegant model of what a social scientist should be. It is unfortunate that he was underappreciated by much of anthropology and little known in sociology—despite my best efforts to draw the attention of sociologists to his work.

I first encountered Harris's work in the early 1970s. In 1973 I was in my final year as a sociology graduate student and had just accepted my first teaching position, which I would start in a few months. In the university bookstore one day I noticed a copy of Harris's *The Rise of Anthropological Theory* (1968b). I had never heard of Harris or this book but I thumbed through it and it seemed very interesting. I was going to be teaching social theory in my new position and thought this book might prove useful as a sourcebook for lectures, and therefore bought a copy. Since I was heavily involved in finishing my dissertation, I put the book aside and forgot about it until the next fall. I then pulled it off the shelf but ended up making no use of it for lectures and still had not really read any of it. One thing that struck me about the book was the chapter entitled "Dialectical Materialism." I was surprised that an anthropologist would be writing on Marx.

Then in 1975 I read an article on Harris published in *Psychology Today* and discovered that he was a famous anthropologist and an original theorist. As a result, I bought a copy of his *Cows, Pigs, Wars, and Witches* (1974a) and read it with great interest. However, it was not until 1977 that I finally pulled *Rise of Anthropological Theory* off the shelf and read it. This was a transforming experience of grand proportions. I was immensely taken with Harris's adumbration of his own distinctive theoretical perspective, cultural materialism, and was delighted by his elegant skewering of his main theoretical adversaries (both of these achievements were carried to an even higher level in his later book, *Cultural Materialism* [Harris, 1979], as Harris's position became more thoroughly worked out and polished). I rapidly became converted to cultural materialism. My whole career was reoriented and I began to focus primarily on the study of long-term social evolution from a materialist perspective. This led to several books: *Macrosociology: An Introduction to Human Societies,* originally published in 1988 and revised several times (Sanderson, 1991, 1995a, 1999a; see also Sanderson and Alderson, 2005); *Social Transformations: A General Theory of Historical Development* (1995b, 1999b); and, most recently, *The Evolution of Human Sociality: A Darwinian Conflict Perspective* (2001a). This book contains a more detailed critical assessment of cultural materialism than is possible in this essay.

As a sociologist, I have long tried to interest the members of my own discipline in cultural materialism and to show them that a sharp distinction between sociology and anthropology is not only unnecessary but actually pernicious. I have had little success. I know of two sociologists who have been significantly influenced by cultural materialism (Christopher Chase-Dunn of the University of California at Riverside and Thomas D. Hall of DePauw University), for the most part indirectly through me, but there are probably not many others. Sociologists think that sociology and anthropology are—and, apparently, should be—hermetically sealed off from each other, and thus they seldom read any literature on preindustrial and preliterate societies. Even so-called comparative-historical sociologists seldom venture beyond the historical agrarian empires, some even failing to get beyond other industrial societies. Significantly, the only sociologists who seem to be familiar with cultural materialism and to take it seriously are those few who think comparative sociology should include the whole range of preliterate societies.

Cultural Materialism: A Critical Assessment

The reaction to cultural materialism in general and to Harris in particular has long been polarized. During my ventures to the annual meetings of the American Anthropological Association, especially during the 1980s, I was often shocked and dismayed at the hostility to both such a sensible theoretical approach and, it would seem, to Harris personally. Much of this hostility was based on misunderstanding and oversimplification of cultural materialism, but it was also rooted in the deep entrenchment of idealist and historical particularist ideas in anthropology, thus confirming one of Harris's major arguments.[1] My view has long been that cultural materialism is one of the best theoretical approaches we have in the social sciences. In *Social Transformations* (1995b, 1999b) I developed a comprehensive materialist theory of social evolution that I called *evolutionary materialism*. When I sent Harris a reprint of an article summarizing this theoretical strategy (Sanderson, 1994a), he reacted much more critically than I had expected. His criticisms are stated in the following letter to me dated May 14, 1994:

> Thanks for the reprints—but there are several points that need to be cleared up. First, there is the "significant flaw" you attribute to CM [cultural materialism] on the first page of the Evolutionary Materialism article (EM, p. 47). CM according to you doesn't do well when it comes to explaining the evolution of divergent and convergent forms of the state: the rise of capitalism and industrialism, the rise and fall of dynasties, the commercialization of agrarian states, the rise of Europe to world dominance, or the evolution of the contemporary economic system (EM, p. 48). If this were true, you would have to explain why it is true. Why does this flaw exist? Surely a paradigm that can't deal with the last 5,000 years of human history must have a very significant flaw indeed. Yet there is nothing in the EM paper that remotely resembles a critique of CM's basic theoretical principles with respect to their limited applicability; nor do you advance any new set of theoretical *principles* from which the asserted advantages of EM follow. To add to the confusion, the second half of the paper, which is intended to test EM, doesn't test substantive theories, but continues to list general theoretical *principles* that can be matched almost without exception with the basic theoretical principles of CM.
>
> The Transition from Feudalism to Capitalism paper does not solve the problem. This paper attempts to show that EM leads to a better theory of the origin of capitalism than CM (and other) paradigms. Two problems arise: First, no sustained CM theories of the origin of capitalism have been offered (although sketchy treatments and suggestions can be found in *Cannibals and Kings* and in Johnson and Earle 1987). Ironically, yours is actually the only sustained attempt to present such a theory.
>
> Second, there is nothing included in your theory which in any way contradicts CM's theoretical principles. For example, the inclusion of a long term trend toward global trade certainly does not contradict the principle of the primacy of the infrastructure. I don't happen to think that world system theory is as strategically important or illuminating as a theory that invokes demographic crises in feudal Japan and Europe; nor do I think that you should ignore Wittfogel's theories regarding why China followed a different path than Europe and Japan. (I also think that feudalism was an extremely common form of archaic state and that it is Japan and Europe that are exceptions produced by

the influence of Rome and China.) But these are differences of theory that point to the need for more data; they are not differences of principle.

Perhaps I am missing something. Enlighten me.

I replied to Harris's letter on May 19, 1994, saying the following:

Well, to tell you the truth most of what you say is correct. There is little if anything in my EM that contradicts, at the abstract level of a theoretical (research) strategy, your CM. As I see it, EM is to a considerable extent an elaboration and formalization of CM principles applied to the phenomenon of social evolution. However, I have added quite a few notions of my own, and addressed issues that you either do not address, or do so only implicitly. For example, there is my discussion of the pace of social evolution, of the role of increasing complexity, of the contrasts between social and biological evolution, of different "evolutionary logics" at different world historical periods, of endogenous vs. exogenous causes, and of the role of the "drive for mastery." Most, perhaps even all, of what I have to say about these issues is compatible with CM, but I think I have made some contribution by formalizing and systematizing things to a higher degree. And my point about different "evolutionary logics" at different historical periods, to the best of my knowledge, is not only not found in your work, but might actually contradict it. At the very least it shows CM's incompleteness. I argue explicitly that demography and ecology decrease in importance as societies evolve, and that political economy increases in importance.

When I said that CM hasn't done well in explaining such things as the commercialization of agrarian states, the rise of European capitalism in the sixteenth century, and the evolution of the modern world economic system I didn't mean that CM is incapable of addressing such issues, or that you yourself have not addressed them to some extent. What I meant was that CM has been applied much more extensively to more traditional anthropological concerns and has done *better* in explaining these things. My EM incorporates things like world-system theory into its basic structure, something I think is crucial to understanding the modern world. Whereas demographic and ecological factors are of tremendous importance in the precapitalist, and particularly in the pre-agrarian, world, they seem to me to be of considerably less significance in the modern world of the last 500 years. Here's where the world-economic system becomes crucial, something that CM does not pay all that much attention to (although, of course, *in principle* it can do so).

In sum, EM is basically an extension of CM. It is certainly not in any sense intended as a refutation of CM or anything remotely of the sort. The reason I don't have any systematic critique of CM is that, at the abstract level of theoretical or research strategy, there really isn't any. There is a lot less difference between EM and CM than there is between CM and Marxian historical materialism. You've broadened HM [historical materialism] by adding demography and ecology, but of course you've also explicitly rejected some elements of HM, such as the role of dialectics. I don't explicitly reject any significant part of CM, but I do move it in directions not particularly chosen by you. When I said that a significant flaw in CM was a failure to apply adequately to the full range of social and cultural phenomena, I was in my mind giving emphasis to the word *adequately*. I didn't mean that CM didn't apply at all.

To address your point about my paper on the transition to capitalism: I think what you say here is precisely what I am getting at. The theory of the transition that I offer in the paper is certainly different from and a lot more elaborate than your discussion in *Cannibals and Kings.* I do not accept demography as a major cause of the transition to capitalism, whereas this is your major causal variable. You're right, my theory does not contradict CM; yet it gives emphasis to phenomena—most particularly, world trade networks—not usually stressed by CM.

In my recent book *The Evolution of Human Sociality* (2001a), I developed a more general theory of human society that resembles cultural materialism, and that incorporates evolutionary materialism, but that pushes their principles to a deeper level. (I do not know whether Harris ever saw or read this book, which was published only a few months before he died. He certainly would have disapproved of its basic argument.) Although in the letter I sent to Harris in 1994 I said I did not have any systematic critique of cultural materialism, I later came to develop one and laid it out in this book. Three main problems stand out in my mind: first, difficulties with Harris's conceptualization of "economy"; second, difficulties involving Harris's mixing of the emic-etic and mental-behavioral distinctions with his infrastructure-structure-superstructure distinction; and finally, Harris's rejection of sociobiology. Let me briefly look at each of these.

One of the things that distinguishes Harris's notion of economy from Marx's is his relocation of the "relations of production" from infrastructure to structure, specifically to "political economy." Brian Ferguson (1995) argues that Harris thus distinguishes two types of economy, "infrastructural economy," which involves mostly technological applications to economy, and "structural economy," which involves economic ownership, distribution, and exchange. Harris believed this distinction is crucial because it is largely infrastructural economy that determines structural economy. I think this may often be true in preindustrial and precapitalist societies, but it is often the other way around in modern capitalism, where it is the search for profits that largely determines technology and other aspects of infrastructural economy. And even in precapitalist systems, the search for wealth by ruling classes is often critical to shaping technological applications.

In addition, I am not sure that Ferguson's view that Harris has two conceptually distinct types of economy completely captures how Harris has modified the Marxian notion of economy. In fact, I have trouble getting rid of the idea that Harris ended up with a very messy, inconsistent, and even incoherent notion of economy. Consider his analysis of the collapse of Communism in the Soviet Union, where great emphasis is placed on deteriorating economic conditions since the 1970s (Harris, 1992). If economy is this important, then why is it not formally retained within the infrastructure? After all, Harris's great theoretical principle is the Principle of *Infrastructural* Determinism. There is no corresponding Principle of *Structural* Determinism. I see it as a serious mistake to put so much of economy in the structure, because then we lose most of the explanatory power of capitalism, which Harris obviously wants to retain. And it is even worse to have "technology" in the infrastructure at the same time, because then we have our causation backward—in capitalist societies the production relations, which are part of the structure for Harris, would be determining part of the infrastructure. Again, there is no Principle of Structural Determinism.

To complicate the issue further, there is one very odd aspect of Harris's conceptualization of modern economies, capitalism in particular: his argument that capital and profits are essentially emic and mental categories. This is nothing short of a shocking statement. Capital and profits are not emic and mental phenomena, but rather the most crucial behavioral characteristics of the capitalist system! The search for profits and the ceaseless accumulation of capital are the driving engine of capitalism, the whole material logic of the system. Harris's classification of capital and profits as emic point to a faulty understanding on his part of the emic-etic distinction.

Harris's attempt to incorporate this distinction into the tripartite universal pattern seems to me to have been a serious mistake (Sanderson, 2001a:117–118). As Harris (1968b, 1979) himself has stressed and as others have emphasized (e.g., Lett, 1990), emics and etics are *epistemological* concepts with important methodological implications. What sense does it make, then, to try to integrate them with the concepts of infrastructure, structure, and superstructure, which are *ontological* categories—parts of sociocultural systems? I have reluctantly concluded that the emic-etic distinction is so complicated and so confusing that perhaps the best course of action is to drop it, at least for theoretical purposes (it should probably be retained as a methodological device). Not much is lost, and a great deal of clarity is gained, and besides it has been pointed out that Harris consistently violates his own pronouncements anyway—for example, constantly producing emic explanations while claiming to generate etic ones (Oakes, 1981). If we drop emics and etics out of the universal pattern, then infrastructure, structure, and superstructure can be reformulated rather simply approximately as follows:

Infrastructure consists of those natural phenomena and social forms essential to economic production and biological reproduction, and especially including the technology of subsistence, ecosystems, "economy," knowledge, and ideas concerning the subsistence quest and economic production, and demographic patterns.

Structure consists of those organized patterns of social behavior common to the members of a society, excluding those relating directly to production and reproduction; it includes especially family and kinship patterns, gender roles, politics and war, social stratification, educational systems, and organized patterns of sport, games, and leisure.

Superstructure consists of beliefs, norms, values, and symbols, especially in the areas of religion, taboos, myth, art, music, and literature.

My final criticism of Harris concerns his stance on sociobiology. Harris has been a strong and persistent critic of this approach, although it needs to be acknowledged that his criticisms have been made from a conceptual and scientific standpoint rather than from the political perspective of most of the critics. As a strong defender of sociobiology, I argue that Harris's argument is unnecessary and that he has missed the boat badly because cultural materialism and sociobiology are in some respects compatible and can be synthesized. In fact, I have performed such a synthesis myself under the name of *Darwinian conflict theory* (Sanderson, 2001a). I discuss this synthetic theory and provide an application of it in the final sections of this paper. This will show how I try to reformulate and extend cultural materialism even beyond my earlier evolutionary materialism and, more importantly, how I deepen cultural materialism.

Before explicating and illustrating Darwinian conflict theory, however, let me first address several important questions: Which of Harris's substantive theories have stood the test of time, and which must be judged wanting? Where does Harris get it right, and where does he get it wrong? And where is he somewhere in between, or the data inconclusive?

Harris's Substantive Theories: The Good, the Bad, and the So-So

Despite his strong epistemological commitment to science, Harris advocated it much more strongly than he practiced it himself. Virtually all of the hypotheses he formulated were testable, and he carried out empirical tests of most of them, either by drawing on evidence collected by others, or by producing new evidence himself. However, these tests were often distinctly lacking in rigor. He employed no formal methodologies or rigorous statistical testing of hypotheses (Daniel Gross, personal communication). (A good example of a failure to use a rigorous statistical procedure, when one was clearly required, was the article on tribal warfare that Harris wrote with William Divale [Divale and Harris, 1976]. The analyses of this article were totally inadequate to test Harris's theory.) Often Harris simply collected just enough evidence to satisfy himself that the hypothesis was confirmed, and then stopped. In some cases, his hypotheses seem well corroborated by the evidence, whereas in other cases Harris either ignored or was unaware of disconfirming evidence, and these hypotheses have not survived rigorous testing. Let us see which hypotheses fall into which categories.

The Good

I would say that the very best theorizing Harris has done is with respect to the following six phenomena: food taboos and food preferences; why we eat too much, feast, and get fat; the origins of early Christianity; long-term social evolution; the women's movement; and the collapse of Communism.

1. *Food taboos and food preferences.* Harris's approach to food habits is conceived in direct opposition to cultural idealist approaches, especially the structuralism of Lévi-Strauss and Mary Douglas—the notion that food is "good to think" or represents cryptic messages (Harris, 1987b). Harris's most basic theoretical premise is that people select and avoid potential food sources on the basis of the material costs and benefits that the foods provide in particular environments at particular times. What is chosen provides more benefits than costs, and what is avoided provides more costs than benefits. Foodways are, in short, materially adaptive in most instances, anything but culturally arbitrary or irrational. Harris even makes explicit use of optimal foraging theory, a theory that stems from evolutionary biology and sociobiology (demonstrating, in spite of himself, that cultural materialism and sociobiology can be friends rather than enemies).

Harris's (1966, 1974a) most famous theories of foodways concern the Hindu sacred cow and the Jewish-Muslim abominable pig. Cattle were and still are worshiped in

India because they are much more valuable alive than dead. They are essential traction animals and provide several other important benefits, and the temptation to kill and eat them during times of drought and famine could best be curtailed by a strong religious taboo. The pig in the ancient Middle East became more costly than beneficial when forests were cut down and the pig no longer had enough shade to cool itself. Providing artificial moisture and shade, and feeding pigs that no longer had forests to forage in, overtaxed the resources of the peoples who became Jews and Muslims.

Harris (1985) has insisted that humans have a special kind of hunger that he calls "meat hunger." Meat has special nutritional significance and eating it is an extremely efficient way of getting amino acids and various nutrients; the only way to get all of the essential amino acids is through meat eating. Harris's argument seems well supported by the universality of meat eating in human societies, as well as by the great significance that people give to meat: It is the most highly desired and esteemed food in all societies. Another innate taste emphasized by Harris (1987b) is the taste for sweet substances. This seems to stem from the nutritional importance of fruits in the ancestral environment and in many hunter-gatherer populations. Harris (1985) has also developed a very convincing theory of milk drinking and milk avoidance in human populations. Until a few thousand years ago the vast majority of adults could not digest the lactose in milk, and thus did not drink it. A selective advantage was given to milk drinking, however, in northern European populations. In the cloudy, wet environments of northern Europe, people had difficulty getting enough calcium and Vitamin D for strong bones and teeth, but milk could provide this. As a result, milk drinking and the ability to absorb lactose coevolved. African populations depending on animal herds for their subsistence also evolved the capacity to digest lactose, whereas those with hunter-gatherer or horticultural modes of subsistence did not.

Harris also shows that insect eating is common in societies that have limited supplies of game animals but large supplies of big, swarming insects. And dogs and cats are not eaten in societies with enough animal protein because these animals, being carnivores, have to be fed meat in order to make meat. Dogs and cats are often eaten when animal protein is scarce. Horsemeat is avoided in societies in which the horse is ridden for military or other reasons, but may be eaten in societies in which the horse may otherwise have limited value. Capitalism can also contribute to the costs and benefits of certain potential foods. For example, the shift from pigs to cattle as the high-status meat in American society coincided with the opening of the grasslands of the American Midwest to grazing cattle, the invention of the railroad for transporting cattle to more distant markets, and the invention of the refrigerated boxcar. Cattle became extremely profitable for capitalist ranchers (Ross, 1980b; Harris, 1985).

2. *Why we eat too much, feast, and get fat.* Obesity, sometimes of morbid proportions, has become a major social problem in the contemporary United States, with a very large segment of the population now overweight. And the problem is growing continually. It is hard to ignore the fact that this obesity is largely the result of overeating on the part of Americans, along with the more sedentary lifestyle imposed by modern work habits. Harris points out that humans not only have an innate tendency to eat, but to overeat; we have been built this way by natural selection because such

traits were highly adaptive in the environments that humans lived in throughout 99 percent of their existence. In these environments, during which of course people subsisted entirely by hunting and gathering, there were always periods of time during which people went hungry for weeks or months. They ate, but they did not get enough to eat to provide proper nourishment or maintain their body weights. When these periods ended, people often gorged themselves and held elaborate feasts, and as a result they put on weight and stored fat that could help them through the periods of scarcity that they would invariably encounter again. These periods of scarcity helped to ensure that people would not get fat.

But today we live at a level of affluence unimaginable in the past. We love to eat, and to overeat, but the consequences today are different. There is so much food available all of the time that people now *do* get fat—many of them at least, and many of those to an extremely unhealthy extent. This, at least, is Harris's explanation, and it seems to me eminently sensible. However, there is one point with which I would take issue. Harris correctly says that contemporary overeating "is not a character defect, a longing to return to the womb, a substitute for sex, or a compensation for poverty. Rather, it is a hereditary defect in the design of the human body, a weakness that natural selection was unable to get rid of" (1989:150). However, not everyone overeats and not everyone gets fat. Many people do neither. Harris correctly points out that it tends to be the poor who are most overweight and the rich who are slimmest, pointing out that the poor are less educated and thus have much less knowledge of good nutrition and diet. This is right as far as it goes, but it seems to stop short. It is true that overeating is not a "defect of character," but it would seem to have a lot to do with self-discipline. Not to overeat when food is delicious and highly abundant requires a lot of self-discipline, and this trait is not randomly distributed throughout society. The upper-middle-class and the wealthy seem to have it to a much greater extent than the rest of society. Harris seems too quick to let individuals off the hook for their problems, too quick to cling to an ideology of victimization that is so common in today's society. After all, he does say, "Too long have the victims of obesity been blamed for their affliction" (1989:150). Harris seems to need a more psychological perspective here. Individuals differ in a variety of traits, and the ability to exercise self-discipline is certainly one of these.[2]

3. *The origins of early Christianity.* In *Cows, Pigs, Wars, and Witches* (1974a), Harris laid out a provocative theory of early Christianity. In ancient Palestine there was a long tradition of Jewish military messianism as the result of colonial exploitation, oppression, and misrule. Most of the population consisted of landless peasants, poorly paid artisans, servants, and slaves. The Galilean peasants hated the Jerusalem aristocrats, and the messiahs claimed to be able to deliver their people from oppression and establish the Kingdom of God on earth. These messiahs fused religious and political messages, and often organized armies to fight against their oppressors. Harris viewed Jesus as merely the most important of these military messiahs and stressed that Jesus's actions were highly consistent with the whole tradition of Jewish military messianism. Jesus was a protorevolutionary whose message involved political action and the use of violence; he was not simply the "Prince of Peace." The belief that he was resulted from a reinterpretation of Jesus's teachings after the Jewish forces were defeated in the

messianic war of CE 68–73, and this reinterpretation was a necessary response to the military defeat. According to Harris, it became a practical necessity for Christians to stress that their messiah was different from the zealot-bandit messiahs who had provoked the war and who were a serious political threat. In Harris's words (1974a:195), "A purely peaceful messiah became a practical necessity when the generals who had just defeated the Jewish messianic revolutionaries—Vespasian and Titus—became the rulers of the Roman Empire."

Harris's argument shows how his cultural materialism sometimes converges closely with Marxism, for here he was pushing an "opium of the people" type of argument, and he situated early Christianity in the larger context of millenarian and revitalization movements more generally. Harris's analysis is undoubtedly very incomplete, and there is much more to be learned about early Christianity than we learn from Harris (cf. Stark, 1996). But it seems to have been a good start in a useful direction.

4. *Long-term social evolution.* In *Cannibals and Kings* (1977), Harris laid out an especially impressive theory of long-term social evolution, accounting with considerable success for the origins of agriculture; the rise of social stratification, chiefdoms, and states; and the origins of the modern world. Moreover, he dealt not only with general social evolution, but with specific evolution as well. Harris's theory rested on an individualistic foundation in which people are attempting to make rational decisions about the costs and benefits of a given course of action, and it was highly notable for its antiprogressivist nature (Sanderson, 1990, 2007). The key evolutionary process is one in which environmental depletion, usually as the result of population growth and the intensification of production, has continually led to new forms of technological intensification, which in turn lead to new forms of environmental depletion, and so on. This process occurring within the infrastructure has led to the continual reorganization of structures and superstructures.

Harris's theory was a great achievement and substantially reoriented the study of social evolution. As already noted, my evolutionary materialism (Sanderson, 1994a, 1995b, 1999b, 2007) was an attempt to codify and extend this line of argument about the great social transformations of human history. However, as pointed out earlier, Harris's theory of social evolution suffered from an overemphasis on ecological factors and an underappreciation of economic and political factors. Ecological factors seem to matter most in the earlier stages of social evolution, but diminish in importance and come to be exceeded by the importance of economic and political factors in the later stages, particularly in the last 500 to 1,000 years.

5. *The women's movement.* Harris (1981) made a notable attempt to explain the origins of the women's movement and feminist ideology in Western societies since the end of World War II. He rejected the notion that it was feminist ideology that arose first. Rather, feminism as a set of ideas emerged from preceding structural changes in the position of women. Harris's starting point was the capitalist economy and the changes it began to undergo in the 1940s. The most important change relevant to the position of women was the shift toward a more service- and information-oriented economy. Once this shift got underway, capitalists sought a new type of worker, particularly one that would be highly subordinate and who could be paid a relatively low wage. Women

fit best because they were used to being in a subordinate position to men and because they were seeking work primarily to supplement their husbands' incomes rather than to be the sole breadwinner. Women were thus gradually drawn into the labor force. However, because of inflation and the greater difficulty of families in maintaining their standard of living, women also sought work themselves, and so this was another force bringing women back into the sphere of economic production, a sphere from which they had been largely removed with the emergence of intensive agricultural societies. As women entered the labor force in greater and greater numbers, at least two changes in their consciousness began to occur. First, they began to realize that there was an entire sphere of existence beyond the home that offered opportunities for achievement and self-realization beyond being a housewife and mother. In addition, women also began to realize how little they were paid vis-à-vis men, that is, they came to be aware of the forces of gender discrimination. Thus was the ideology of feminism born.

Harris's analysis rings true to me because the evidence seems to fit it very well. In the late 1940s only about one woman in nine who was married and who had small children was in the labor force, but by the early 1980s this had increased to one woman in two and by the late 1990s had increased to almost two women in three. Moreover, these changes were occurring not only in American society, but throughout Western Europe as well, and women's movements and feminist ideologies also arose in those countries. The progress of the women's movement and feminism seemed to parallel in almost step-by-step fashion the changing sexual composition of the labor force. The causal sequence specified by Harris—that feminist ideology followed rather than preceded the changing sexual composition of the labor force—seems to be correct as well, since feminism was rather tepid at the beginning and has grown increasingly intense and powerful as labor force changes have occurred.

6. *The collapse of Communism.* Harris's (1992) analysis of the collapse of Communism in the Soviet Union was originally presented as the Distinguished Lecture at the annual meetings of the American Anthropological Association in 1991. At this time the collapse had just occurred. Harris wished to emphasize, in typical fashion, the causal priority of infrastructure in the collapse. He argued that "the political-economic (i.e., structural) and symbolic-ideational innovations introduced in the name of Marxian materialism were selected against because they resulted in a stagnant, declining, or increasingly inefficient infrastructure. State communism failed because it decreased the efficiency of its smokestack-type infrastructure and inhibited the application of high-tech innovations to the solution of a deepening technological, demographic, environmental, and economic crisis." Harris emphasized, in the manner of the Hungarian economist János Kornai (1992), the built-in limitations of an economy dependent on centralized planning and lacking any market mechanisms. The costs of such an economic system involved such things as persistent shortages, inhibition of technological innovation, and the lack of sufficient incentives for maximizing productivity. This analysis seems just about right to me, and corresponds to evidence produced by many analysts of the collapse (cf. Sanderson and Alderson, 2005). Although Harris noted that the Soviet collapse was just one more nail in the coffin of Marx's specific historical predictions,

he was also quick to reject Francis Fukuyama's (1992) argument that liberal capitalism represents some sort of "end of history."

The Bad

Where, then, did Harris get things wrong? Here I would point to his theorizing in the following seven areas: war; male domination; the potlatch; the incest taboo; family size; homosexuality; and why we seek status.

1. *War.* Harris (1974a, 1977; Divale and Harris, 1976) viewed war in bands and tribes largely as a population-regulating mechanism. It is population pressure and resource scarcity, especially scarcity in the availability of animal protein, that are the principal causes of warfare. Warfare leads to a male supremacist complex, which in turn helps to provide a justification for female infanticide. This, combined with male deaths from combat, helps to regulate population growth. Warfare also creates "no-man's lands" that help to regulate population against the available supply of animal protein. Harris has used the Yanomamö as an illustration of his theory, but that tribe's principal ethnographer, Napoleon Chagnon (1983), has shown with detailed analyses that the Yanomamö are in fact eating well more than the necessary daily supply of animal protein. Keeley (1996) tested Harris's theory and failed to find any correlation between population density and the frequency of warfare for 87 societies. I conducted my own test using the Standard Cross-Cultural Sample of 186 societies (Murdock and White, 1969). The correlation between warfare and population pressure was not only very low ($r = -.109$), but was actually pointing in the wrong direction.

Brian Ferguson (1984, 1990) has formulated an alternative cultural materialist theory that rejects the protein scarcity hypothesis and that specifies a much broader range of material benefits that can motivate war, such as increasing access to fixed resources, capturing movable goods, or enhancing the power and status of those individuals who make the decisions about going to war. Ferguson nominates Western contact as the most important cause of warfare among the Yanomamö and other Amazonian groups.

Ferguson's theory is a major improvement on Harris's, but his view of Western contact as a critical cause is dubious. It could well intensify warfare, but it is not likely one of its major causes. The major alternative to both Harris and Ferguson's theories is a sociobiological theory. In this way of thinking, warfare is mainly about gaining access to women as sexual partners in order to maximize one's reproductive success. The scarcity of women—which, according to Donald Symons (1979), is always present to at least some extent in all societies—leads to severe male competition for them; when this scarcity is severe enough warfare is the result (Chagnon, 1988; Low, 1993; van der Dennen, 1995:317–331). The most reproductively successful men will usually be the most successful warriors, and men will therefore be strongly motivated to form themselves into bands and go to war (cf. Tooby and Cosmides, 1988). Although this theory requires much more careful study and empirical testing, there is a great deal of evidence from other bands and tribes that conflict over women is a major cause of war (some of this is summarized in Betzig, 1986).

2. *Male domination.* Harris (1974a, 1977, 1989) agreed with the feminists that male domination is not rooted in any basic biological differences between the sexes. Males have no natural tendency to dominate females, he argued, but rather are socially conditioned to do so. Harris singled out militarism and warfare as the primary cause of male domination. The greater the degree to which a society both prepares for and goes to war, the more male dominated it will be. Males will be the warriors in every society, Harris claimed, not because they are naturally more aggressive or warlike, but because in hand-to-hand combat men's greater strength will lead to their cultural selection for war. Any society that made females the warriors would invariably confront societies of male warriors, and the societies with female warriors would have been driven to extinction long ago. Since warfare places a premium on masculine characteristics, the more warlike the society the greater the extent to which males will be induced to exaggerate their masculine qualities and, correspondingly, to denigrate female qualities.

With two colleagues I carried out an empirical test of Harris's argument (Sanderson, Heckert, and Dubrow, 2005). We used the Standard Cross-Cultural Sample and the gender status variables coded for half of these societies by Martin King Whyte (1978). Our findings completely falsified Harris's argument. Depending on which of three measures of male dominance we used, warfare either had no effect on the level of male dominance, or had the opposite effect from that predicted. The variable that contributed the most to the level of male domination was the economic status of women, especially the degree to which women made an important contribution to subsistence. In hunter-gatherer societies where women's gathering provides a great deal of what people eat, their status was relatively high; and in agricultural societies where women provide a great deal of the agricultural labor (as in horticultural as opposed to intensive agricultural societies), their status was also relatively high. Social stratification also made some difference, as women did better in egalitarian than in stratified societies.

One limitation of this study, however, is that it is only able to explain why the level of male domination varies from one society to another. It is unable to explain why male domination is, in fact, a universal feature of human social life. All societies are to at least some extent male dominated in that males are always the primary (and often the only) political leaders and males monopolize every society's high-status social positions. I suggest, contra Harris, that this universality of male domination is a fundamental part of the human biogram. A great deal of evidence has now accumulated to suggest that men are naturally more aggressive and competitive, and that in an open competition with women they will predominate in social positions that require these traits (evidence reviewed in Sanderson, 2001a).

3. *The potlatch.* Early in his career, Harris (1974a) turned his attention to the famous Northwest Coast potlatch, an elaborate giveaway feast in which rival chiefs gave away their property to one another and, in some extreme cases, even burned down their own houses. Harris offered a functionalist theory, contending that the potlatch was one of many mechanisms of economic redistribution found throughout the world's societies. Harris pointed out that the Northwest Coast environment was one that was unusually abundant in resources, but that there was a great deal of variability in productivity from

one microregion to another. Chiefs practiced the potlatch, Harris claimed, as a way of evening out this variability and creating a more egalitarian network of societies.

I had never been completely satisfied with this explanation, and fortunately another much better one has now come along. This is a Darwinian explanation that relies on a special modification of Darwinian natural selection theory known as the *Handicap Principle*. Amotz and Avishag Zahavi (1997) use the Handicap Principle to explain such things as the elaborate plumage of peacocks. For them, the peacock's plumage is an *honest or costly signal* indicating that he is of high quality and thus desirable as a mate. Only healthy peacocks can grow long, beautiful tails because it takes a great deal of energy to do so. The Zahavis also suggest that animals may seek prestige by providing resources to others, thus indicating that they are of high quality. The Handicap Principle would seem to be almost tailor-made to explain the potlatch (Boone, 1998). In terms of this principle, the chief who gave away his property and burned down his house was engaged in a form of *costly signaling* or a *costly display*: He was sending a message to other chiefs that he was so rich that these things didn't matter. He could easily recover from such losses.

Harris's explanation of the potlatch is another example of how he often got caught in functionalist traps. Harris wanted to admit group selection as well as individual selection into his explanatory repertoire, but this seems to me to have been a serious mistake. Harris wanted to see the competition for status in societies without true stratification as driven by egalitarian goals. It is true that people in unstratified societies may demand, and often get, egalitarian economic outcomes—they may prevent, for example, "big men" from becoming too "big"—but this is different from the motivations of the status seekers themselves. Perhaps the bigger problem is that Harris saw status seeking as a cultural phenomenon detached from human nature (see #7 below).

4. *The incest taboo.* In his explanation of the incest taboo Harris showed himself to be a traditional anthropologist and yet again an old-fashioned functionalist. He depended not on cultural materialism at all, but rather on E. B. Tylor's old theory that the incest taboo was motivated by a desire for people to form alliances so they could live in greater peace. Harris even challenged the so-called universality of the incest taboo, pointing to a number of instances of brother-sister marriage in human societies. Harris actually went on to predict, quite startlingly, that the incest taboo may eventually disappear, and claimed that "brother-sister mating is probably on the verge of becoming just another 'kinky' sexual preference of little interest to society" (1989:206).

Harris was quite critical of the major alternative to Tylor's theory, the well-known Darwinian theory of Edward Westermarck. This theory holds that incest is usually avoided because individuals of the opposite sex who are reared together in the same household acquire a sexual indifference or aversion to each other. Although there is now a great deal of research evidence that is highly supportive of Westermarck's theory, Harris questioned the validity of some of it. One line of evidence has involved apparent resistance to consummation of the marriage in Taiwanese *sim-pua* marriages, a type of marriage in which an infant girl is adopted into a family and grows up to marry her adopted brother. Harris argued that the brides and grooms who failed to consummate their marriages were not harboring a sexual indifference, but rather were expressing disappointment and chagrin because the Taiwanese regarded these marriages as distinctly inferior to the more common form of marriage. This criticism seems far-fetched because it is hard to see how being consigned to an inferior form of marriage would produce sexual disinterest rather than some other emotion. Moreover, Harris begged the question by failing to explain why *sim-pua* marriage should be regarded as inferior (it is probably because the Taiwanese know in advance that it often results in sexual disinterest and consequent marital difficulties). A second line of evidence concerns the tendency of Israeli kibbutzim youth to avoid marrying other individuals from the same communal nursery. Referring to Joseph Shepher's (1983) data, Harris argued that out of 2,516 marriages, there were 200 undertaken between kibbutz partners, a number so large that it casts serious doubt on Westermarck's theory. But Harris had his numbers wrong. Shepher studied 2,769 marriages, not 2,516, which is not of dramatic importance, but there were only 13 marriages, not 200, undertaken between members of the same communal nursery. Moreover, those 13 have been carefully studied by Arthur Wolf (1995), who found that in 11 of them the marriage partners did not actually meet until age 4 or older. This has led him to specify that Westermarck's theory depends on a critical period, which is in fact the first three years of life.

There are many other lines of evidence in favor of Westermarck's theory that go unmentioned by Harris (summarized in Sanderson, 2001a; cf. Turner and Maryanski, 2005). Harris's argument in favor of Tylor's theory is weakened by the fact that marriage alliances are only one of several ways to establish solidarity and live in greater peace. Moreover, research has shown that societies that permit cross-cousin marriage, and thus that establish marriage alliances between lineages and clans, do not, in fact, live in any greater harmony than those that have no such alliances (Kang, 1979; M. Ember, 1975). Tylor's theory is a functionalist theory, but the apparent function of the incest taboo and marriage alliances does not exist—surely the test of a functionalist theory if ever there were one.

In short, the evidence for Tylor's theory is nonexistent, whereas the evidence for Westermarck's theory is considerable, Harris's protestations notwithstanding. This is an area of anthropological theory and research where Harris was far off the mark.

5. *Family size.* Harris (1989; Harris and Ross, 1987) devoted considerable attention to explaining why fertility levels are high in agrarian and Third World societies and much lower in modern industrial societies. He related the number of children produced per woman to the economic value of children's labor. In societies where agriculture is still the primary basis for subsistence, the economic value of children's labor is high. Under such conditions, by age 6 children are able to gather firewood, carry water, plant and harvest crops, run errands, sweep floors, take food to adults in the fields, peel and scrape tubers, and grind and pound grains. At a later age they are able to work full time in the fields, cook meals, herd, fish, hunt, and make pots and other containers. Where children can perform so many useful services, couples will be motivated to have many of them. However, as societies industrialize, the economic value of children's labor declines and children's economic value eventually turns negative, and so couples have few of them and family size declines.

Harris used the same type of argument to explain why members of lower-class racial and ethnic minorities in industrial societies such as the United States often have large numbers of children. Here again, Harris argued, children perform economically valuable labor. Having children entitles mothers to welfare support, housing subsidies, educational benefits, and medical care. In their teenage years, children of ghetto families contribute economically through part-time jobs, theft, and drug sales, as well as through protection against thieves and muggers.

Harris was especially critical of the sociobiological argument that humans have an innate procreative imperative. As evidence, he pointed to the frequency of noncoital sex, contraception, and abortion, and especially to the frequency of infanticide throughout the whole range of human societies. Reviewing a wide variety of infanticidal practices, Harris (1989:214) concluded that these practices "would not be possible if the bond between parents and child were a natural outcome of pregnancy and delivery. Whatever the hormonal basis for mother love and father love, there evidently is not sufficient force in human affairs to protect infants from culturally imposed rules and goals that define the conditions under which parents should or should not strive to keep them alive."

Sad to say, but Harris's analysis was very superficial and simplistic—and wrong. It is of course true that humans widely and often frequently practice contraception, abortion, and infanticide, but Harris failed to consider the specific conditions under which these are or are not practiced. Given the strength of the human sex drive, contraception is certainly necessary in order for people to avoid producing far more children than they can possibly care for, and abortion and infanticide become important, and often necessary, when contraception fails, which it frequently does. In particular, Harris seemed unfamiliar with the well-known sociobiological distinction between r-selection and K-selection. r-selection is a reproductive strategy involving having many children but devoting little parental care to each. If enough children are born, the odds are fairly good that some will live to adulthood and go on to have children of their own. This kind of strategy seems to be what is happening where the rate of infant and child survival is relatively low, as in agrarian and Third World societies, or where children's economic prospects are poor, as in lower-class ghettoes. K-selection, by contrast, is a reproductive strategy in which few children are produced but a great deal of parental investment is made in each child. This strategy is what we find among the middle and upper-middle classes of modern industrial societies and seems to be favored when infant and child mortality are very low and children's economic prospects are average or better.[3]

In her excellent book *Mother Nature: A History of Mothers, Infants, and Natural Selection*, Sarah Blaffer Hrdy (1999) makes the extremely important point that maternal care is highly conditional. Mothers are biologically wired to produce children, and to nurture them, but the extent to which they do the latter depends on whether the conditions for rearing are good or poor. Hrdy documents in great detail that in many societies and throughout world history mothers have often practiced infanticide when conditions for rearing are poor, but have avoided it when the conditions for rearing are good. Mothers are naturally predisposed to bond to their infants, but they will avoid doing so when there is not enough food to support an infant, or because the infant will take away food from older children in which a great deal of time and energy has already been invested. A natural predisposition to want children and to bond with them does not mean that the behavior is automatically produced anywhere at anytime.

Recently I engaged in a study of fertility rates in a wide range of contemporary nation-states (Sanderson and Dubrow, 2000). I performed a series of regression analyses designed to determine whether the economic value of children's labor or some other factor was critical in determining fertility rates between 1960 and 1990. The results showed that the economic value of children's labor, as measured primarily by the percentage of the population working in agriculture, mattered very little if at all. The key factor was the infant mortality rate: Where the rate of infant survival was high, fertility was low, and where the rate of infant survival was low, fertility was high. The more likely infants are to die in the first year of life, the more of them people have in order to replace the ones that have been lost. In the same study, analyses were also carried out for the period between 1880 and 1940, the approximate period of the original demographic transition. The results were essentially the same: Infant mortality was the key determinant, and the economic value of children's labor, although somewhat more important for this period, was of fairly minor significance.

Finally, it is worth mentioning that Hillard Kaplan (1994) has carried out research in band and tribal societies designed to see whether children's labor contributes more calories than children actually expend. The answer is a clear no in all of the societies he studied. In fact, children appear to be very economically costly in all societies (we have long known that they are extremely costly to rear in modern industrial societies). Since they do not produce economic benefits that exceed what they themselves cost, why then do people have them? The answer, I believe, is that humans are biologically predisposed to do so because that is how they maximize their reproductive success. It is Darwinian theory, not cultural materialism, that explains reproductive patterns.

6. *Homosexuality.* In his discussion of homosexuality in *Our Kind* (1989), Harris made rather a mess of things. The basic problem is that he treated all homosexual practices as essentially the same. To his credit, at the beginning of his discussion Harris acknowledged that there is now a great deal of evidence that in every society there is a small number of males and females who are genetically predisposed toward homosexual rather than heterosexual sex. He admitted that people do not start out a blank slate in the realm of sex. Harris then went on to say that in many societies institutionalized forms of homosexuality have been found. He discussed homosexual practices among the ancient Greeks, the Etoro and other New Guinea societies, the Azande of Africa, the *berdache* among North American Indian groups, the similar *hijras* of India, and several alleged examples of institutionalized female homosexuality.

Harris was emphatic that in most societies people do not believe that homosexual practices are deviant and bad. They have held such beliefs in the United States and other Western societies with Christian religious traditions, but these societies seem to be in the minority throughout the world. Harris may have overstated the case somewhat, but it is true that homosexuality has been tolerated in many societies. Oddly, for a chapter entitled "Why Homosexuality?" the widespread tolerance of homosexual practices seemed to be Harris's only real concern and he did not actually attempt to explain homosexuality at all. The main difficulty with his analysis, however, was that he failed to make the crucial distinction between *preferential* and *situational* homosexuality. Preferential homosexuality involves same-sex relations between individuals who are not attracted to members of the opposite sex; situational homosexuality, on the other hand, occurs between heterosexuals who are substituting homosexual relations for heterosexual relations when the preferred sexual object, a member of the opposite sex, is unavailable. Homosexual relations among men in prisons is the example of situational homosexuality best known to members of modern industrial societies, but all of the examples of tolerated homosexual practices Harris provides are additional examples of situational homosexuality. There is no single answer to the question, Why Homosexuality? because there is no single type of homosexuality. Situational homosexuality stems from the relative unavailability of heterosexual partners, whereas preferential homosexuality, as Harris suggests, seems to be biologically programmed.

It is also odd that Harris made no attempt to explain situational homosexuality, because explanations are available that seem plausible. One explanation of ancient Greek homosexual practices between male tutors and their boy pupils is that women were secluded, marriage was late, prostitution was disdained, and men therefore had to spend a long period of time without heterosexual relations (Posner, 1992). Since the educational system already brought tutors into contact with boy pupils, the tutors became opportunistic and substituted their pupils for females. Another explanation of the Greek pattern is overpopulation (Percy, 1996), which has also been offered as an explanation of New Guinea man-boy homosexual practices. But why men and young boys? The answer seems to be that boys most closely resemble females, and thus are the best substitute for them.

7. *Why we seek status.* Harris (1989) made the sensible claim that humans have a need for love, approval, and emotional support that is biologically rooted, part of our fundamental human nature. Individuals who have a particularly strong form of this need are the ones who are most likely to become headmen in hunter-gatherer societies and big men in horticultural societies. Individuals who have a strong need for social approval become leaders in band and tribal societies because successful performance of their leadership roles generates a great deal of approval. However, Harris insisted that the innate desire for love and approval stops well short of an innate desire for prestige, wealth, and power. He was highly critical of Thorstein Veblen's famous idea that humans have an innate desire for status that leads them to become conspicuous consumers. The desire for prestige, wealth, and power, which is so characteristic of societies at higher levels of evolutionary development, Harris tells us, is "socially constructed" rather than innate. It is rather astonishing that Harris would use this phrase, since it is normally associated with the idealist and subjectivist theoretical traditions that he found anathema. Be that as it may, Harris went on to say that "the universal drive to emulate the leisure class presupposes that a leisure class exists universally, which is factually untrue" (1989:367). Of course Harris was right that leisure classes are far from being universal, but he was wrong in his claim that they are necessary for individuals to be prestige seekers and conspicuous consumers. All that is required is that individuals have a generalized innate tendency to seek prestige and to turn that

tendency into specific imitation of a leisure class when one comes into existence. But Harris never did explain why ruling classes form in the first place, except to point to certain infrastructural conditions necessary for them to exist, and thus he begged the very question he was trying to answer. It is true that certain minimal infrastructural conditions are required for the existence of ruling classes, but this does not adequately explain why they always arise when those conditions are present. Surely there must be something about the human animal and the way it interacts with those conditions that calls forth ruling classes. In stressing the economically and politically egalitarian nature of band and tribal societies, Harris also failed to point out that these societies are filled with prestige and power seekers whose ambitions must be curtailed by the rest of the society, lest they get out of control. There seems to be more than a desire for love and approval that is motivating leaders in such societies; it is simply that they have to be satisfied with those outcomes because they will not be permitted anything more. (In the last major section of the paper I will discuss the empirical evidence for an innate human desire for status, wealth, and power.)[4]

The So-So

One area where Harris got it partially but not quite right involves the rise of modern capitalism, an issue with which both he and I have had a major concern. He devoted a chapter to this in *Cannibals and Kings,* emphasizing demographic factors and the importance of the feudal mode of production in Europe. When I sent him a copy of my much more detailed and rather different interpretation of the rise of capitalism (Sanderson, 1994a), he objected to much of what I said, commenting that what was right in my article was not original—he had already said it—and that what was original in the article was not right. (Typical Marvin!) He then wrote a paper, "Ecological Factors and the Rise of Capitalism," which he originally presented at a conference in Valencia, Spain. This paper was later published in the language Catalan, and he sent me a reprint. He also said that he hoped to publish an English version and that I would get a chance to write a reply for publication. He published the English version of the essay as Chapter 13 of his book *Theories of Culture in Postmodern Times* (Harris, 1999b), but for whatever reason I never did get a chance to reply. Therefore, I will do it here.

In my analysis of the rise of capitalism (Sanderson, 1994b, 1995b, 1999b), I stressed that capitalism developed not only in Europe after about 1500, but also in Japan at approximately the same time. Previous theorizing has almost totally ignored the Japanese case, but an adequate theory of the emergence of modern capitalism must explain both. My theory consisted of two parts. First, I identified five preconditions that existed in both Western Europe and Japan that gave them a significant head start in capitalist development. These were demography, geography, climate, size, and political structure. Regarding *demography,* I stressed that both regions had experienced substantial population growth during the period in question, but, in contrast to previous theories, I argued that the importance of population growth was its role in increasing the size of markets, not in degrading the environment. Harris said that I made an important contribution in stressing the role of population growth in increasing market size, although this did not commit him to abandoning his ecological degradation argument. He also pointed out that my argument was consistent with cultural materialism in stressing the primacy of the infrastructure.

With respect to *geography,* I stressed the maritime location of the societies in the two regions. England, the Netherlands, and northern France are all located on the North Sea, and Japan is a set of islands off the coast of China. These maritime locations were important because they allowed for the primacy of maritime as opposed to overland trade, with the former being much more efficient than the latter. Harris countered that the maritime location of Japan was not a significant contributing factor because China shared the same sea with Japan and had an enormous coastline. In reply I would say that capitalist and mercantile activity was greatest in China along its southern coastline, which supports my point that maritime location is important. By contrast with China, Japan was *completely surrounded by the sea,* which I think helps to explain the greater significance of mercantile activity there. Much of China was far from the sea, but no part of Japan was, and this helps to explain the developmental potentialities and actualities of the two societies.

I argued that *climate* was another similarity between the two regions: Both had far northerly locations and temperate climates. This was important in the case of Japan because it discouraged attempts at capitalist peripheralization. Harris failed to see this as important, noting that my logic implied that unless a country avoided colonization it could never develop a robust form of capitalism. He then pointed to Hong Kong, Brazil, and Indonesia as former colonies that have experienced significant economic development. But Harris misinterpreted my logic. He was speaking of Hong Kong, Brazil, and Indonesia in the present, and it is true that they are former colonies that have undergone substantial development. However, my point was that peripheralization hindered economic development throughout much of the history of capitalism, and this is precisely true of the three societies Harris mentioned. Again, I was only trying to explain why Japan and Western Europe led in the way in the early development of capitalism, not explain the organization of the world-economy as it looks today. I would add that the absence of peripheralization is not a condition that is itself favorable for the development of capitalism, but instead represents the *absence of a negative condition* that would have prevented significant capitalist development. Harris's rejection of my argument for the importance of the failure of Western Europe to peripheralize Japan is surprising, because he has made the very same point in his general anthropology textbook.

As for the role of *size,* I pointed out that England, the Netherlands, and Japan were very small states and that this was beneficial for them because maintaining a large state is expensive and drains away resources that could be put directly into economic development. Harris challenged this point by arguing that the larger the state the greater the potential volume of trade. My response is that this is certainly true, but this potentially greater trade is only that—potential. The actual volume of trade will likely be restricted in large states that have to divert so many of their resources into the various managerial functions of the state. My point is that the larger the state, the larger its burden of political rule and therefore the weaker its capacity to stimulate commercial activity.

The final precondition shared by Western Europe and Japan was their *feudal politicoeconomic structures*. This was important, I argued, because decentralized feudal states provide much more freedom for commercial activity than large agrobureaucratic states. Big agrarian bureaucracies like China and India stifled the development of capitalism because the economic interests of the nobility conflicted with those of the bourgeoisie, and the nobility controlled the state. In Western Europe and Japan, however, even though the nobility controlled the state, the state was far less effective in curtailing the actions of the bourgeoisie even though it desired to do so. Harris more or less accepted all of this, but took issue with my argument because he believed it stopped short. Feudalism was important, he claimed, but one must also explain why it existed in these regions; since I failed to do so, my explanation was deemed inadequate. In other words, in order to explain the origins of capitalism I also had to explain the origins of feudalism. Harris seemed to be imposing an extremely high standard here that few social scientists could ever meet. If we carry Harris's argument to its logical conclusion, we could never stop until we had explained everything that came before the particular historical phenomenon we were trying to explain. It seems unreasonable to ask scholars to keep explaining the causal factors that lie behind the first set of causal factors, and then explain the causal factors that lie behind the second set, and so on. One has to impose a stopping point somewhere.

The second part of my theory, which I actually regarded as the more important part, focused on the particular timing of capitalist development in the two regions. I argued that it took a very long time for capitalism to develop after the origins of the first cities and states some 5,000 years ago because of what was said earlier: Big agrarian bureaucracies stifle capitalist development. The bourgeoisie struggled for existence within the constraints of these bureaucratic states. Nevertheless, because capitalists provided a wide range of goods that noble classes desired, capitalism could not be dispensed with altogether, and this allowed it not only to gain a foothold, but to expand. Capitalists could be slowed down, but they could not be stopped, and as a result there occurred over time a process of *expanding world commercialization*. The level of world commercialization had reached a critical threshold by about CE 1500, and this is why capitalism began a major developmental spurt at this time, taking off first in those regions that were most hospitable to it. However, capitalism, I argued, would sooner or later have developed anyway because world commercialization would eventually have crashed through the barriers imposed on it by nobilities and their bureaucratic state partners. I estimated that, had there never been regions favorable to capitalism in the ways that Western Europe and Japan were, in another 1,000 or 2,000 years capitalism would have achieved its takeoff point.

Harris seemed to disagree flatly with this analysis, claiming that world trade networks were not an important causal factor and that I selected the figure of another 1,000 or 2,000 years for capitalism to have occurred in the absence of favorable preconditions in an entirely arbitrary manner. But I did not choose these figures arbitrarily. Why not 10,000 years? Because world commercialization had already become very extensive by CE 1000 and, given how much it had developed in the previous 4,000 years, I would not think another 10,000 years would be needed for a capitalist explosion. The figure of 1,000–2,000 years is certainly an estimate, but it is an informed one based on an extrapolation from previous trends. It is not arbitrary.

Now to answer Harris's contention that expanding world trade networks were not important causal factors (and were more *outcomes* rather than causes of capitalism). Harris wanted to emphasize feudalism as the principal causal factor and to link feudalism to ecology (rainfall farming versus irrigation agriculture). Of course I agree that feudalism was important (and Harris may well be correct in his explanation of the origins of feudalism), but my point would be that feudalism by itself was not enough. By the sixteenth century feudalism could interact with extensive world commercialization to produce a capitalist takeoff. *But feudalism in 1000 BCE or even in CE 1 could not have generated a capitalist takeoff.* It could only have made a small difference to the stimulation of mercantile activity. It was the *interaction* of feudalism and world commercialization that made the difference.

As for Harris's point that capitalism created world trade more than world trade created capitalism, I would say it differently: World trade and capitalism created each other in a ratchet-like fashion over several millennia. There was extensive world trade long before there was modern capitalism, but the development of modern capitalism certainly led to a tremendous increase in the volume of world trade. Both created each other in a slow evolutionary fashion over a very long period of time.

In conclusion, Harris's fallback on ecological factors (i.e., in explaining the origins of feudalism) and his resistance to my emphasis on a slow process of expanding world commercialization precisely exemplify my point about the differences between my evolutionary materialism and his cultural materialism. Ecological factors are very important in precapitalist and preindustrial societies, and especially in band and tribal societies, but their causal significance seems to be less important in more complex societies, especially modern ones. In its analysis of more complex societies, evolutionary materialism emphasizes some things that are underplayed in cultural materialism. Expanding world commercialization, derived from world-systems theory, is one such thing.

Conclusion

There are also a number of Harris's theories that I am either unqualified to evaluate, or that cannot be properly evaluated because of a paucity of adequate data. In this regard I would list his arguments on cannibalism, Aztec cannibalism in particular; hydraulic agriculture as the basis for ancient agrobureaucratic states; the rise of the nonkilling religions; the great witch craze; and gay liberation. The jury is still out, I think, on why Africa lags so far behind the rest of the world in economic development.

So cultural materialism in the hands of Harris has made important achievements with respect to many important arenas of human social life, but it has also failed with respect to a variety of other arenas. Looking back over those areas in which Harris's explanations seem to falter, I cannot help but notice that in every single case it is because he failed to take sociobiology seriously. Therefore, we need to push cultural materialism in a sociobiological direction and show how the two perspectives can be synthesized into a more comprehensive perspective whose explanations will be more adequate. This is a step Harris steadfastly refused to take, but it was there for the taking all the time because cultural materialism and sociobiology are, or at least can be made, compatible. They should be friends, not enemies. As noted earlier, I have performed my own synthesis of these two theoretical strategies, which I call Darwinian conflict theory. What does it have to say?

Deepening and Amending Cultural Materialism: Darwinian Conflict Theory

In *The Evolution of Human Sociality* (Sanderson, 2001a), I present the principles of Darwinian conflict theory in full, along with an extensive summary of evidence that I believe supports these principles. Here I will limit myself to an abbreviated version of the theory (more accurately, theoretical strategy).

I. Principles Concerning the Deep Wellsprings of Human Action

1. Like all other species, humans are organisms that have been built by millions of years of biological evolution, both in their anatomy and physiology and in their behavioral predispositions. This means that theories of social life must take into consideration the basic features of human nature that are the products of human evolution.
2. The resources that humans struggle for, which allow them to survive and reproduce, are in short supply. This means that humans are caught up in a struggle for survival and reproduction with their fellow humans. This struggle is inevitable and unceasing.
3. In the struggle for survival and reproduction, humans give overwhelming priority to their self-interests and to those of their kin, especially their close kin.
4. Human social life is the complex product of this ceaseless struggle for survival and reproduction.
5. Humans have evolved strong behavioral predispositions that facilitate their success in the struggle for survival and reproduction. The most important of these predispositions are as follows:

- Humans are highly sexed and are oriented mostly toward heterosexual sex. This predisposition has evolved because it is necessary for the promotion of humans' reproductive interests. Males compete for females and for sex, and females compete for males as resource providers.
- Humans are highly predisposed to perform effective parental behavior, and the female desire to nurture is stronger than the male desire. Effective parental behavior has evolved because it promotes reproductive success in a species like humans. The family as a social institution rests on a natural foundation.

- Humans are naturally competitive and highly predisposed toward status competition. Status competition is ultimately oriented toward the securing of resources, which promotes reproductive success. As the result of sexual selection, the predisposition toward status competition is greater in males than in females.
- Because of the natural competition for resources, humans are economic animals. They are strongly oriented toward achieving economic satisfaction and well-being, an achievement that promotes reproductive success.
- In their pursuit of resources and closely related activities, humans, like other species, have evolved to maximize efficiency. Other things being equal, they prefer to carry out activities by minimizing the amount of time and energy they devote to these activities. A Law of Least Effort governs human behavior, especially those forms of behavior that individuals find burdensome or at least not rewarding in and of themselves. The Law of Least Effort places major limits on the behavior of humans everywhere; much behavior can only be explained satisfactorily by taking it into account.

6. None of the tendencies identified above are rigid. Rather, they are behavioral *predispositions* that move along certain lines rather than others but that interact in various ways with the total physical and sociocultural environment. The behavioral predispositions tend to win out in the long run, but they can be diminished, negated, or amplified by certain environmental arrangements.

7. From the above it follows that humans' most important interests and concerns are reproductive, economic, and political. Political life is primarily a struggle to acquire and defend economic resources, and economic life is primarily a matter of using resources to promote reproductive success.

8. Many, probably most, of the features of human social life are the adaptive consequences of people struggling to satisfy their interests.

II. Principles Concerning Systemic Relations within Societies

1. Human societies consist of four basic subunits:
- Individuals themselves as biological organisms, which we may call the *biostructure*.
- The basic natural phenomena and social forms that are essential to human biological reproduction and economic production, i.e., the ecological, demographic, technological, and economic structures essential for survival and well-being; this we may call the *ecostructure*.
- The institutionalized patterns of behavior shared by individuals, especially the patterns of marriage, kinship, and family life; the egalitarian or inegalitarian structuring of a society along the lines of class, ethnicity, race, or gender; its mode of political life; and its mode or modes of socializing and educating the next generation; these patterns may be identified as the *structure*.
- The primary forms of mental life and feeling shared by the members of a society, i.e., its beliefs, values, preferences, and norms as these are expressed in such

things as religion, art, literature, myth, legend, philosophy, art, and music; these we may refer to as the *superstructure*.

2. These four components of societies are related such that the flow of causation is primarily from the biostructure to the ecostructure, then from the ecostructure to the structure, and finally from the structure to the superstructure; the flow may sometimes occur in the reverse manner, or in some other manner, but these causal dynamics occur much less frequently.

3. According to the logic of II.2, it is clear that the forces within the biostructure and the ecostructure are the principal causal forces in human social life; the biostructure structures social life both indirectly, i.e., through its action on the ecostructure (which then acts on the structure and superstructure), and through its direct effect on some of the elements of the structure and superstructure. It follows, then, that the ideas and feelings within the superstructure have the least causal impact on the patterns of social life.

4. The components of societies are related as they are because such causal dynamics flow from the deep wellsprings of human action. The biostructure and the ecostructure have a logical causal priority because they concern vital human needs and interests relating to production and reproduction.

5. Once structures and superstructures have been built by biostructures and ecostructures, they may come to acquire a certain autonomy. New needs and new interests may arise therefrom, and these new needs and interests, along with reproductive, economic, and political interests, may form part of the human preference and value structure characteristic of the members of a society.

III. Modes of Darwinian Conflict Explanation

1. As is obvious from the principles stated in II, Darwinian conflict explanations are materialist in nature; these explanations may take any or all of three forms: biomaterialist, ecomaterialist, or polimaterialist.

2. *Biomaterialist* explanations explain a social form by direct reference to a basic feature of the biostructure. That is to say, an explanation is biomaterialist if it links a social form to the biostructure without reference to any mediation of the causal relationship by some other social form. *Example*: Polygyny is a widespread feature of human societies because it springs from an innate desire of males for sexual variety and from the tendency of females to be attracted to resource-rich males.

3. *Ecomaterialist* explanations explain a social form by linking it directly to the influence of ecological, technological, demographic, or economic forces, and thus only indirectly to a feature of the biostructure. *Example*: Hunter-gatherer societies frequently display intensive sharing and cooperation because these are behaviors that promote individuals' interests within the configuration of hunter-gatherer technoeconomic systems and natural environments.

4. *Polimaterialist* explanations explain a social form by linking it directly to the political interests or situations of the participants. Political interests or situations

ordinarily spring from the participants' economic interests, which in turn are ultimately derived from the character of the biostructure. *Examples:* Democratic forms of government emerged earliest in those Western societies with the largest and most politically organized working classes. Third World revolutions occur most frequently in societies where the state is highly vulnerable to a revolutionary coalition.

Darwinian Conflict Theory Applied and Illustrated: The Case of Social Hierarchies

Social hierarchies are a universal feature of the human condition, although their nature and extent vary greatly from one society to another. At one end of the continuum, marked by hunter-gatherer and simple horticultural societies, we find few or no differences in wealth or power between individuals and only differences of social esteem or rank. At the other end, marked by agrarian and industrial societies, we find highly stratified societies with major differences in wealth and power between relatively distinct social strata or classes. My argument is that social hierarchies have to be explained by all three modes of Darwinian conflict explanation, that is, bio-, eco-, and polimaterialistically. Social hierarchies are biologically rooted but elaborated by a range of social and cultural conditions, especially those relating to economic and political organization.

A number of social scientists have stressed that hierarchies are biologically rooted. Albert Somit and Steven Peterson (1997) have noted that all human languages contain words referring to distinctions of honor and status. James Woodburn (1982) and Elizabeth Cashdan (1980) point out that, whereas there are a number of societies that have been able to maintain very high levels of social and economic equality, this equality seems to be constantly challenged. In order for it to be maintained, people must be ever vigilant and constantly monitor the tendency of at least some individuals to seek dominance over others. Joseph Lopreato (1984) claims that humans have an innate desire for creature comforts, and Jerome Barkow (1989) argues that there is a natural human hunger for prestige that governs much human behavior. Why should such innate human motivations exist? The answer is that competition for status and resources, not only in the human world but throughout the animal world as well, is essential for mating and thus the promotion of an individual's reproductive success. Hundreds of studies show that social rank and reproductive success are highly correlated among mammals, humans included (Ellis, 1995). However, it should not be assumed in the human case that people seek status and resources only to reproduce. At the proximate level of human experience, humans seek status and privilege for their own sake and find achieving them inherently pleasurable. Nonetheless, the human brain has evolved for status and resource seeking because throughout hominid evolution those individuals who displayed such behavior left more offspring than those who did not.

Alice Rossi (1977, 1984) has argued that a pattern of human behavior can be assumed to have a biological basis if two or more of four conditions are met: the behavior is universal or at least widespread in human societies; the behavior is widely found among other animals, especially nonhuman primates and other mammals; the behavior is found in young children prior to major socialization influences or emerges at puberty; the behavior is closely associated with anatomical or physiological attributes. In the case of hierarchy formation, all four of Rossi's criteria are met. In terms of the second condition, Pierre van den Berghe (1978) is only one of many scholars who have pointed to the virtual universality of hierarchy among primates.[5] Van den Berghe notes that some primate societies display only minimal hierarchies, but among terrestrial primates, from whom humans are descended, strongly hierarchical societies are the rule.

As already noted, hierarchies are universally found in human societies (Rossi's first condition), and, in terms of Rossi's third condition, dominance- and rank-oriented behavior appears to be characteristic of infants and young children, as shown by a variety of ethological studies (e.g., Bakeman and Brownlee, 1982; Missakian, 1980; Strayer and Trudel, 1984; Russon and Waite, 1991). Most of these studies have been of children in American society, but an important cross-cultural study has been carried out by Barbara Hold (1980). She looked at the behavior of German and Japanese kindergarten students as well as that of children of comparable age from the G/wi San, hunter-gatherers from southern Africa. The children established dominance hierarchies in all three societies. In all cases, there were children who sought the limelight. Those children who became the center of attention were much more likely to initiate activities than lower-status children, and the lower-status children frequently imitated the behavior of the dominants.

There are also abundant data to show that Rossi's fourth condition is also well met. Height is a widespread and possibly universal indicator of social status (Freedman, 1979; Brown and Yü, 1993). In a well-known study, ostensible job recruiters were asked to choose between two applicants for a position, one of whom was much shorter than the other. The vast majority of the recruiters chose the taller applicant (Freedman, 1979). In presidential elections throughout the history of the United States, the taller candidate has nearly always won the election. In Africa, shorter tribes have been dominated by taller tribes. In many horticultural societies, the highest-ranking man in a village is often called by a word that literally means "big man." In Russia and England higher-status individuals have tended to be much taller than those of lower status.[6] A common expression of submission throughout the world is bowing or crouching.

If human anatomy is related to status, is physiology as well? The answer appears to be yes. The best candidate for a neurochemical substrate of status-seeking behavior is the neurotransmitter serotonin. Research showing that serotonin and dominance seeking are related in vervet monkeys (McGuire, 1982; McGuire, Raleigh, and Johnson, 1983) has been replicated for humans (Madsen, 1985, 1986, 1994). In one of the most recent studies, Douglas Madsen (1994) examined the relationship between blood serotonin levels, social rank, and aggressiveness in the context of a game-playing situation. He found that the serotonin levels of the participants who played the game nonaggressively declined as their perceived social status rose. By contrast, the serotonin levels of the participants who played the game in an aggressive fashion increased as their perceived social status climbed. Moreover, serotonin is known to play a major role in the regulation of mood, with low brain serotonin levels being associated with depression. Many individuals who have been treated for depression with fluoxetine (trade name = Prozac) have not only seen an improvement in mood, but have also experienced personality changes in the direction of less shyness or reticence and more confidence and boldness (Kramer, 1993). Confidence or boldness are very likely correlated with status-seeking behavior.

How does this natural status- and resource-seeking behavior of humans get translated into the actual systems of inequality and stratification that we observe in human societies? It seems to be the case that where societies are small, simple in scale, technologically rudimentary, and incapable of producing economic surpluses, hierarchies are minimally developed because there is no real wealth that can be contested and thus no basis for the formation of classes (Lenski, 1966). And in these kinds of societies no one is in a position to compel others to work for them and create wealth. Moreover, where people live only or primarily by hunting and gathering, intensive cooperation and sharing are common behaviors. This has been identified as *generalized reciprocity* and explained in terms of a strategy of *variance reduction* (Wiessner, 1982; Cashdan, 1985; Winterhalder, 1986a, 1986b). The argument is that hunting success varies greatly both temporally and spatially, and thus by sharing with others when you have resources others will share their resources with you when you are in need. Sharing is in everyone's long-run self-interest.

In previous publications (e. g., Sanderson, 2001a:269–270) I have been inclined to accept this explanation, but it has had to be completely rethought. In one of the earliest challenges to the variance reduction hypothesis, Kristen Hawkes (1993) showed that it lacked empirical support for three of the most intensively studied hunter-gatherer societies. For the !Kung, in one month one particular hunter provided more than three-fourths of the meat for the entire camp; four men did no hunting at all, but they seemed to acquire sizable portions of meat. Among the Aché, there are very large differences among men in the amount of meat provided, and those who provide little or none still seem to eat about as much meat as others. Among the Hadza, in one sample of 130 observation days over half of the meat provided was procured by only two hunters, and people who provided nothing got substantial shares of meat nonetheless. Hawkes concluded that the main incentive for hunting among these hunter-gatherers is the "social attention" that the most skilled hunters get from displaying their hunting prowess.

Nicholas Blurton Jones (1987) has proposed an alternative argument—that food sharing amounts to "tolerated theft." Because hunter-gatherer societies have no means of individual coercion, individuals who have not killed an animal may demand an equal share of it and the man who killed the animal is unable to prevent him from taking one (this has also been called "demand sharing"). More recently, a number of anthropologists have employed costly signaling theory to argue that meat sharing may result more from status competition than from a strategy of variance reduction. Richard Sosis (2000) found that men on the island of Ifaluk spend a great deal of time torch fishing on atolls for dog-toothed tuna even though the rate of return from this type of fishing is much lower than from trolling for yellow-fin tuna. Sosis found that torch fishing was the type of fishing most widely observed by women, and that through successful torch fishing men seemed to be advertising themselves as high-quality mates. Similarly, Eric Alden Smith and Rebecca Bliege Bird (2000) studied turtle hunting among the Meriam of Torres Strait, Australia. Turtle hunting is energetically very costly, and yet at the feasts at which men distribute turtles, they receive no material compensation, not even getting a portion of their own catch. Only a small number of select men turtle hunt, with just three men accounting for 38 percent of the nominations for good turtle hunters. The authors conclude that demonstrated skill at turtle hunting is the primary means by which men advertise leadership skills, and that the main benefit they receive is high social status. Smith and Bliege Bird regard their results for turtle hunting not only as supporting costly signaling theory, but also as contradicting the expectations of the variance reduction and tolerated theft hypotheses. Spear fishing among the Meriam also seems to contradict these hypotheses, because when men are engaged in spear fishing they ignore the abundant shellfish all around them, which are easy to collect and which would maximize energy returns (Bliege Bird, Smith, and Bird, 2001). It is highly noteworthy that spear fishing confers status but shellfish collecting does not.

In a very compelling study, Bliege Bird, Bird, Smith, and Kushnick (2002) provide a great deal of evidence that is inconsistent with the variance reduction explanation, again using the Meriam as a case study. They found that the size of the harvest predicted sharing better than risk reduction as measured by the hunting failure rate. They also found that households that share more do not receive more in return—that most flows of food were one-way flows—and that there was no bias against free-riders. Individuals who provided nothing over long periods of time still received food from those who had it.

Hawkes, O'Connell, and Blurton Jones (2001a) evaluated the variance reduction hypothesis among the Hadza and found no support for it at all. The most skilled hunters actually spent more time hunting, not less, as the variance reduction hypothesis would suggest. Morever, the authors argue that the style of interaction at kill sites is highly suggestive of tolerated theft as an explanation for much of the sharing of meat. But beyond this, the fact that the most skilled hunters spent so much time hunting seems to support the costly signaling hypothesis.

Polly Wiessner (2002) has attempted to salvage at least part of the reciprocity hypothesis in her study of large game hunting among the Ju/'hoansi (called the !Kung by others). She hypothesized that, even though most Ju/'hoansi hunters do not reciprocate receiving large shares of meat by becoming skilled and generous hunters themselves, it is possible that they may nevertheless be reciprocating in other ways. "Might reciprocity in currency other than meat play a role in the motivation to hunt large game?" she asks (2002:421). And the answer appears to be yes. Her data show that good hunters and their wives had significantly more economic exchange partners than poor hunters and their wives, and that as a result they were able to obtain significantly more household possessions. Good hunters and their families were also able to maintain a core residential group of close kin for almost twice as many years as poor hunters and their families. "In contrast to good hunters," Wiessner (2002:425) says, "poor hunters changed camps frequently and therefore received less sustained support from a steady core of kin." The wives of good hunters had 84 percent of their adult married children coresident with them in the year 1998 compared to only 31 percent for the wives of poor hunters.

Taken as a whole, the research findings discussed above suggest that the variance reduction hypothesis may explain only a small part of hunter-gatherer generosity (cf. Gurven, Allen-Grave, Hill, and Hurtado, 2000). It seems increasingly clear that many forms of hunting and most forms of sharing result from either tolerated theft or costly signaling. When skilled hunters do benefit economically from hunting and generous sharing, the benefits are more likely to come in the form of more indirect and delayed types of reciprocity.

The growing evidence for the role of costly signaling and status competition in hunting success is yet one more strong indicator of a biological basis to status seeking in the human animal. What then happens when societies evolve in size and scale, become more technologically advanced, and become capable of producing large economic surpluses? The answer is that more open forms of status competition become increasingly common because now there are more resources that individuals deem it valuable to compete for (Lenski, 1966). Inequalities of esteem or status not only get magnified, but are accompanied by differences in wealth that develop a rigidly hereditary character. Also critical to this process seem to be changes in political relations that allow some people to be in a position to compel others to produce the economic surpluses that more advanced technology makes possible. As technological, economic, and political evolution continue, stratification systems become more elaborate and extreme.

A close examination of hunter-gatherer societies will show that they seldom extend hierarchies beyond the level of status differences, and often these differences are minimal. Yet we know that the tendency toward stratification is there, not only because of the growing evidence for costly signaling, but also because under certain conditions hunter-gatherers have become stratified, sometimes markedly. One of these conditions is the presence of an environment or economy sufficiently productive to allow people to accumulate and store foodstuffs. Alain Testart (1982) has divided hunter-gatherer societies into two types, those who store food and those who do not. Upon examining 40 contemporary hunter-gatherer societies, he found that the vast majority who stored food had genuine class stratification compared to only a small fraction of the nonstorers. The Kwakiutl of the Northwest Coast of North America, for example, were storing hunter-gatherers *par excellence*, and as a result had developed a highly stratified society led by ruling chiefs who ranted about their own prestige and displayed it by giving away wealth to neighboring chiefs.

In simple horticultural societies the technological and economic base is usually not sufficient to allow for the creation of stratification, but the desire of some individuals for high status and even deference from others is given freer rein than among hunter-gatherers. These societies are often characterized by status-seeking men known in the local language as "big men" (Sahlins, 1963; Harris, 1977). Big men are village leaders and economic organizers. They prod people to work harder and produce more food so they can hold feasts and distribute this food widely, certainly to all of the members of their own village but usually to some of the members of other villages as well. Big men are greatly admired and often given considerable praise and deference. One sees individuals like this among hunter-gatherers only seldom.

Compared to simple horticultural societies, advanced or intensive horticultural societies cultivate the land more intensively and more permanently, squeezing more out of it, and thus are more economically productive. These societies are often divided into social strata or classes that have a highly hereditary or self-perpetuating character. A common pattern is a division into three main social strata, consisting, respectively, of chiefs, subchiefs, and commoners. These strata are distinguished by differences in social status, political power, dress and ornamentation, consumption patterns, the extent of direct involvement in subsistence production, and styles of life. Many African horticultural societies in recent centuries have had stratification systems of this type, as have a number of Polynesian societies. Precontact Hawaii, for example, had a hierarchy consisting of a paramount chief and his family at the top, regional or village subchiefs in the middle, and a large class of commoners at the bottom (Lenski, 1966).

Agrarian societies have been devoted to the cultivation of large fields with the use of the plow and traction animals. As a result, they have been far more economically productive than horticultural societies, which use only hand tools. Agrarian stratification systems have been the most extreme of any found in human history, and they contained numerous social classes (Lenski, 1966). However, the most important of these classes, those that related to the primary axis of economy activity, were the political-economic elite and the peasantry. Lenski has divided the elite class into two segments, the ruler and the governing class. The ruler was the official political leader of society, and he surrounded himself with an administrative apparatus of government. What Lenski calls the governing class might be more accurately called the landlord class, since its members were the major owners of land. The political-economic elite as a whole usually consisted of no more than one or two percent of the population but controlled perhaps as much as half to two-thirds of the total wealth. Wealth was created by imposing rent and taxation on the peasantry, or perhaps by exploiting slave labor, and thus was skimmed off as an economic surplus. It was also created by plundering other societies and incorporating their land, peasants, slaves, and other economic resources, and by receiving economic tribute from them (Snooks, 1996). Elites in most agrarian societies created an elaborate status culture that distinguished them sharply from the rest of society (Annett and Collins, 1975).

As Lenski has noted, in the transition from agrarian to industrial societies after the Industrial Revolution of the last two centuries, there occurred something of a reversal in the relationship between the level of stratification and the degree of technological development. In many respects, modern industrial societies are less stratified than their agrarian predecessors. Agrarian elites controlled much more wealth than do elites in modern industrial societies, and industrial societies have also witnessed a much greater diffusion of income and wealth throughout the large mass of the population. However, industrial societies still exhibit very high levels of stratification.

Another major change in the nature of stratification in the transition to industrial societies is the decline in status and deference cultures and the emergence of a widely accepted ideology of egalitarianism, especially in the United States (Annett and Collins, 1975). This decline, along with the greater economic equality of industrial societies, might be thought to undermine biologically oriented theories of society, such as Darwinian conflict theory. But this is not the case. Once again it is a matter of biological tendencies interacting with a wide array of social conditions. These changes in industrial stratification systems can be linked to the emergence of mass consumer capitalism and the rise of democratic forms of government. Democratic governments—themselves the result largely of the rise of large and powerful working classes and of systems of mass education and widespread literacy—allowed the many to combine against the few in order to restructure society more in their favor. The rise of mass consumer capitalism led to the disintegration of the old patterns of status and deference for several reasons, but especially because increases in the financial resources of the working and middle classes have allowed them to maintain a lifestyle closer to that of the upper classes. In the end, status distinctions have shrunk not because society dominates biology, but because of the very existence of natural status desires on the part of the large mass of the population. It has been through their status-seeking behavior that the status gap between themselves and the old elite has been reduced.

The industrial societies we have been discussing have been industrial *capitalist* societies. So-called state socialist societies emerged earlier in the twentieth century as an alternative form of society that would eventually become highly industrialized and attempt to equal or surpass the capitalist societies in the standard of living and the quality of life. The Soviet Union, of course, was the primary exemplar of this type of society. One of its official aims was to create a "classless" society, and it attempted to accomplish this by means of socializing the means of production. This was rooted in the Marxian assertion that social classes could not exist if there was no private ownership of the means of production. However, despite these changes in the economic system a classless society did not emerge; what developed instead was a new type of class society (Djilas, 1957; Parkin, 1971). Broadly speaking, the most privileged social class was the so-called white-collar intelligentsia, which comprised some twenty percent of the population and consisted primarily of top Communist party bureaucrats, managers of state-owned companies, and learned professionals. This class received higher incomes than the rest of society, but also had access to a range of special privileges unavailable to others. A small segment of this class, consisting of full-time, high-level party bureaucrats and known most often as the *nomenklatura*, constituted a ruling class virtually in the Marxist sense of the term (Parkin, 1971). These developments, occurring as they did in the face of an official policy of classlessness, strongly suggest that the reality of human nature was at work under the surface and behind the scenes, a reality that would make a mockery of public declarations.

It is also highly instructive to see what has happened in Russia since the collapse of Communism in the Soviet Union in 1991. Increasing privatization has created far greater economic inequalities that will probably expand even further in the years to come. The old *nomenklatura* has been broken up, with the careers of many of its members ruined, but other members of this ruling elite have found themselves in a position to benefit from the economic changes. They seem to be forming a new class of private entrepreneurs and have become extremely wealthy, often displaying their wealth in the most garish and ostentatious ways (Zaslavsky, 1995; Kagarlitsky, 2002). These changes of the last decade are also strong evidence for a human primal urge for status-seeking and resource accumulation. Although this urge was always present in the old Soviet Union, privatization of the economy has given it much freer rein, and the results are apparent to all.[7]

Conclusion

Marvin Harris was a great anthropologist who battled vigorously—sometimes a little too vigorously—for a scientific anthropology guided by his cultural materialist theoretical principles. He had a great deal of success, although not as much as he wanted. Many were greatly influenced by his work, but many others demurred. I have been one of the few sociologists to have read and studied Harris's work carefully and to have used it as a basis for my own empirical work and theoretical reformulations. No single scholar has had a greater influence on my thinking and the intellectual trajectory of my career than Marvin Harris. Yet a number of years ago I began to see problems with cultural materialism as a general theoretical strategy as well as with a number of Harris's specific substantive theories. The problem with Harris's thinking was not that it was materialist, but that it was not materialist enough. It needed to move in a more biologically materialist direction by embracing the principles of sociobiology, principles that are needed to take cultural materialism to a deeper level. After all, the infrastructure has priority because it is a response to humans' most basic biological needs and drives. Where cultural materialism works, it is because of the biological needs and drives that give rise to the material interests that are so much a part of Harris's thinking. But where cultural materialism does not work, it is because these biological needs and drives are more fundamental than other material interests. Harris steadfastly refused to take this biological step, but we can take it for him and thus extend the logic of his own paradigm. Harris would not have liked it, but then sometimes people have to be saved from themselves.

Acknowledgments

The first draft of this paper was written by hand while the author was sitting in a wheelchair, hospitalized with a badly broken left leg. It was presented in my absence by Lawrence Kuznar at the annual meetings of the American Anthropological Association in New Orleans in November of 2002. I am grateful to my anthropology colleague Miriam Chaiken for sending the paper to Professor Kuznar in advance of the AAA meetings and for taking 25 hard copies to those meetings. The current paper is a greatly revised and expanded version of the original. I am grateful to the same individuals for comments on the paper, especially to Larry Kuznar for getting me to reconsider the variance reduction argument for hunter-gatherer food sharing and the newer alternatives to it.

Notes

1. In Chapter 4, Alan Sandstrom relates three anecdotes demonstrating that the hostility to Harris and cultural materialism could often reach stratospheric levels. I have an anecdote of my own to relate. At one of the first meetings of the American Anthropological Association I ever attended—I believe it was the 1979 meeting in Cincinnati—there was a major session with a very large audience in which Harris presented his (actually, Michael Harner's) protein deficiency theory of Aztec cannibalism. Once Harris had finished and the question-and-answer period had begun, a man stood up in the row right behind me and, quite literally, started screaming and shrieking in a near hysterical manner. He said something to the effect that "the only protein Marvin Harris has to offer is pure baloney" and some other nasty things that I have now forgotten. I looked at his name tag and saw that he was Paul Diener, a name I immediately recognized from Harris's *Cultural Materialism* (1979:246n) as an anthropologist Harris claimed had severely misrepresented cultural materialism (cf. Diener and Robkin, 1978). Harris remained relatively calm, but said quite forcefully, "Let's all identify ourselves." It is the most extreme instance of hostility that I have ever encountered at a professional meeting in more than three decades of attending such meetings.

It is unfortunately true that some of the hostility to Harris was "self-invited." Harris had a very strong personality and could be dogmatic, intolerant, and sometimes abrasive. Even fellow traveling materialists were sometimes taken aback by Harris's style. Napoleon Chagnon, a vigorous supporter of sociobiology, clashed severely with Harris, often in public, and it was usually a matter of the "irresistible force" meeting the "immovable object." Chagnon's style could be equally dogmatic and intolerant, and when these two exceptionally strong personalities came together it was no-holds-barred intellectual combat. In this regard, I have another anecdote to relate. At another AAA meeting years ago, and again in a major session with an extremely large audience, Harris presented his views on tribal warfare, with the Yanomamö case being particularly emphasized. Of course, Harris contended that the Yanomamö were fighting because of the scarcity of animal protein, whereas Chagnon claimed they were fighting over women. After Harris finished his presentation, Chagnon took the podium to denounce Harris for not only an incorrect theory, but an overall misrepresentation of sociobiology. Chagnon then hurried out of the room without giving Harris a chance to respond. Marvin retook the podium and lamented the fact that Chagnon was not permitting them to have any debate. Unfortunately, it is true that Harris did misrepresent both sociobiology in general and Chagnon's views in particular on numerous occasions.

2. None of this is to deny genetic differences among individuals, and perhaps among populations, in the tendency toward obesity. In any modern industrial population, the most overweight individuals will be those with the greatest genetic tendency toward weight gain and the least self-discipline with respect to overeating, whereas the thinnest will be those with the lowest genetic tendency toward weight gain and the most self-discipline regarding overeating.

3. Some social scientists, and most evolutionary biologists, object to the use of the terms r- and K-selection to refer to differences *within* species rather than to differences *between* species. It is undeniably true that these terms originated to refer only to differences between species. r-selected species tend to be small organisms that leave many offspring and practice low (or no) parental investment (e. g., paramecia, snakes, fish), whereas K-selected species tend to be larger organisms that leave few offspring and practice high parental investment (e. g., birds, mammals). Nevertheless, I still think it is useful to say that, within a species, individuals may use a more "r-like" reproductive strategy in some circumstances and a more "K-like" strategy in other circumstances. We clearly see this in humans, where the more r-like strategy is associated

with higher levels of infant and child death and the more *K*-like strategy with lower levels of infant and child death.

4. It seems highly noteworthy that Harris's explanations of warfare, male domination, the potlatch, the incest taboo, family size, homosexuality, and status seeking all fail for one or both of two reasons: attachment to the notion of group selection (in the form of functionalist reasoning), and failure to take human biology seriously.

5. It might be more appropriate to say "near universality" of hierarchy among primates, given the research findings of recent years on bonobos (*Pan paniscus*). This species of chimpanzee is certainly a lot less hierarchical (and a lot less aggressive) than the common chimpanzee (*Pan troglodytes*), and, perhaps, lacking in hierarchy altogether.

6. This widely observed association between height and social status is by no means being attributed solely to a biological predisposition for individuals to value more positively, and thus to grant higher status to, taller individuals. It is certainly recognized that height is also a function of nutrition, and that the adequacy of nutrition varies among populations and among social classes within populations. The fact that Oxford dons were historically taller, on average, than members of the English working or lower classes, is undoubtedly related to differences in nutrition and dietary intake. I am not trying to explain all of the association between height and social status in terms of a human tendency to elevate taller individuals in status, but simply calling attention to the existence of the phenomenon and its explanatory relevance.

7. It is noteworthy that humans seem to be not only innate prestige seekers, but also innate prestige *conferers*. Humans seek prestige, and its close relatives status and dominance, because these things are the key avenues to productive and reproductive success. But why do humans seem to be so ready to confer prestige and esteem on others? This occurs even in the simplest of hunter-gatherer societies, but of course takes exaggerated form in modern industrial societies, where, for example, people fawn over celebrities, whether rock stars like Mick Jagger, actresses like Jennifer Lopez, or great athletes like Michael Jordan or Tiger Woods. Joseph Henrich and Francisco Gil-White (2001) argue that the tendency to confer prestige on others is an evolved adaptation that, at least in the ancestral environment, allows individuals to get close enough to prestigious individuals to be able to copy their behavior. Imitation of the prestigious, an extremely widespread human trait, is adaptive for the imitators to the extent that the most prestigious individuals also tend to be the most skilled or knowledgeable. This generally holds true in environments approximating the ancestral environment, although will often not be true under modern conditions (and thus no longer adaptive).

Part V

The Legacy of Cultural Materialism: II

Chapter Eleven

What Role Does Population Pressure Play in the Evolutionary Dynamics of Marvin Harris?

Robert L. Carneiro

M ARVIN HARRIS'S CULTURAL MATERIALISM was perhaps the most trenchantly argued and keenly debated approach to the study of culture to emerge during the last decades of the twentieth century. Its basic premise was a simple one. Of the three components into which a sociocultural system could be divided—infrastructure, structure, and superstructure—the infrastructural part was deemed the most important in propelling a society along its evolutionary track.

According to Harris, the infrastructure of a society consists largely of technological and environmental elements. But it is not limited to that. Harris would also include in it demographic elements. According to him, "Cultural materialist principles . . . depart radically from classical Marxism in regarding the production of children as part of the infrastructure" (Harris, 1979:66). And he was convinced that "one can recognize the importance of the mode of reproduction in determining the course of sociocultural evolution" (Harris, 1979:70).

It should be noted that when Harris wrote of demographic factors, he preferred to speak more generally of "the mode of reproduction" rather than more specifically of "population pressure." In the present paper, I propose to look closely at Harris's view of population pressure, in whatever guise he presents it, and to see how he integrated it into his grand evolutionary scheme.

For the most part, Harris avoids speaking of population pressure directly. He seems to be more comfortable talking about population *density*. Thus, referring to societies at the village level, he says: "As population density rises, ... disputes and complaints increase both within the group and between them as well" (Harris, 1971:225). And again, " in the long run, the increment in technoenvironmental efficiency has led to an increment in population density. Denser populations are associated in turn with larger, more populous, and more complex sociocultural systems" (Harris, 1971:217).

In such statements, demography, as a determinant, is poised to act, but is not actually discharged. In Harris's rendering, it constitutes potential energy not yet converted into kinetic energy. At least not expressly so. Yet, only when population *density* reaches the point at which it becomes population *pressure* (one can argue) does it become a motive force in social evolution.

Time and again, where one expects Harris to speak of population *pressure,* he seems to prefer the more neutral, the less committal concept of population *density.* At other times, he speaks instead of population *growth.* It seems to me that he might easily have posited the sequence: population *growth* > population *density* > population *pressure,* a chain of events ultimately leading to fundamental structural developments in societies. Harris, however, appears to truncate this chain by leaving out the middle links, as when he says that "the adoption of maize by the archaic Olmec and Maya laid the basis for rapid population growth and the emergence of complex chiefdoms at an early period" (Harris, 1979:93).

To be sure, Harris does not fail to speak of "pressure" altogether. However, when he does so, it is not entirely clear just what he means. More often than not, he speaks of "reproductive pressure," as if this and population pressure were one and the same. Thus at one point he asserts (somewhat paradoxically), that "even societies with constant or declining populations may be experiencing severe population pressure" (Harris, 1979:69). But then, in another passage, he seems to contradict himself. "'Reproductive pressure'" he tells us, "refers to adverse cost-benefit ratios, as distinct from 'population pressure,' which usually is taken to mean population growth" (Harris and Ross, 1987:33n.).

So, are the two things the same or are they different? And if they differ, what is the essential difference between them? In still another passage, Harris *does* give us a clearer notion of what he means by "population pressure": "Reproduction" he says, "generates *population pressure* (i.e., physiological and psychological costs such as malnutrition and illness) that leads to intensification, diminishing returns, and irreversible environmental depletion" (Harris, 1988:264; see also Harris, 1987c:90).

What Harris means to convey by "population pressure," then, is the physical and psychological damage suffered by individuals in societies practicing such harsh measures as abortion and infanticide. He does *not* appear to mean by population pressure—as we usually take it to be—the pressure a society is under as it competes with its neighbors for diminishing arable land and other natural resources.

As a matter of fact, in much of his writing, Harris seems a good deal more concerned with the factors that *reduce* population pressure than with those that give rise to it. Several passages illustrate this: "Throughout prehistory rates of [population] growth were probably checked well before a population's density reached its habitat's carrying capacity under a particular technoenvironmental regime" (Harris and Ross, 1987:13; see also Harris, 1987c:90).

And again, more explicitly: "Few if any populations have ever risen all the way to the demographic ceiling imposed by energy input and output formula[s]. Before a population approaches the limits of the energy that can be extracted from a habitat under given technoenvironmental conditions, a number of self-regulating processes are activated that prevent further population growth" (Harris, 1971:223).

Harris repeatedly calls attention to effective but violent means (principally abortion and infanticide) that primitive societies employ to restrict their numbers. These, he says, are *internal* methods of population control. But, he adds, *external* ways of doing so come into play as well, and here he singles out warfare as being of most importance.

Time and again, Harris cites warfare as a population-reducing agent. For example, he writes: "We believe that the most parsimonious explanation for the prevalence of warfare in band and village societies is that war was formerly part of a distinctively human system of population control" (Divale and Harris, 1976:527). And again he says: "Warfare also occurs as a systemic means of slowing population growth, conserving resources, and maintaining high per capita levels of subsistence" (Harris, 1979:69).

Indeed, one of the objectives of "Population, warfare, and the male supremacist complex," an article which Harris coauthored with William Divale, was "to explain the perpetuation and propagation of warfare among band and village societies as a response to the need to regulate population growth in the absence of effective and less costly alternatives [to abortion and infanticide]" (Divale and Harris, 1976:521).

Then, applying this general explanation to a particular case, Harris (1988:367–368) says: "The evidence suggests that Yanomamo warfare is best understood as a means of keeping population growth rates down as a precondition for assuring the capture and consumption of high-quality game animals" (see also Harris, 1987c:197).

In fact, Harris consistently views primitive warfare (whatever other functions it might have) as an instrument for keeping population pressure at bay. And it does so in more than one way: "Warfare regulates primitive populations in two principal ways. It reduces total population by combat deaths and, as in the case of the Maori, it distributes population more evenly over inhabitable regions, i.e., it regulates local population density" (Harris, 1971:228–229).

Generalizing this second effect of war more widely, Harris (1977:39) remarks that "the dispersal of populations and the creation of ecologically vital 'no man's lands' ... [confer] very considerable benefits [on band and village societies] ... despite the costs of combat" (see also Harris, 1987c:196).

In treating warfare at the band and village level, then, Harris points not only to its effect in holding down the population of a region through combat deaths, but also to its *dispersive* effects in keeping villages spaced well away from each other. Up to this point, Harris ignores war's *aggregative* effects, namely, the fact that it breaks down village autonomies and forges them into multivillage polities (see Carneiro, 1994:14).

In still other ways, says Harris, population *growth* can head off population *pressure*, thus forestalling the type of warfare that leads to supravillage aggregations. "As population expands," he writes, "production is intensified and new modes of production evolve to satisfy the increased demand for food" (Harris, 1988:264). In this way, "demographic factors help to explain the historic expansion of productive forces"

(Harris, 1979:66). And this economic expansion puts at further remove the onset of warfare of the sort that dissolves local autonomies and puts village societies on the road to chiefdoms.

Still, no matter how often Harris repeats the argument that abortion, infanticide, and war jointly kept primitive populations in check, in this regard they ultimately failed. Beginning with the Neolithic, human numbers underwent a marked increase, as Harris readily agrees. "There is no doubt," he says, "that the spread of agriculture was accompanied by a dramatic rise in the annual rate of population increase " (Harris and Ross, 1987:41). But what, exactly, produced this sharp rise?

As I have noted elsewhere (Carneiro, 1981:78–79), it was Robert Sussman who, in a little-known article published in 1972, presented what I regard as the correct explanation for the post-Neolithic jump in human population. It was not so much that agriculture provided societies with a more reliable subsistence. Rather, it was the fact that it made *sedentism* possible, something that was out of the question with a purely foraging mode of subsistence. Now, with nomadic bands becoming sedentary villages, no longer were women forced to resort to infanticide to keep from having more infants than they could easily rear. By shortening the interval between births, sedentism enabled populations to grow.

We know that Harris was familiar with Sussman's article because he cites it (Harris and Ross, 1987:22). However, he refers only to that part of it that deals with the prevalence of infanticide during the Paleolithic, and its effects of keeping the human population low during this period. But Harris fails to cite the other half of Sussman's argument, namely, that the new sedentism made it possible to ease up on infanticide, thus enabling population to start on its upward climb. From this point on, the harsh measures that Harris frequently alludes to—abortion, infanticide, and war—proved insufficient to keep human numbers in check. And in certain areas of the world, this growth resulted in genuine population pressure.

Let me make it clear that by "genuine population pressure" I do *not* mean the biopsychological stress on individuals that Harris has in mind when he speaks of "population pressure." Rather, I refer to the competitive pressure felt by societies as they increasingly impinge on each other's territory and begin competing over its resources.

In my own attempt to trace the course of political evolution—the historical trajectory from autonomous villages to chiefdoms, and from chiefdoms to states—I make population pressure the major driving force. Does Marvin Harris do the same? Let us see what he had to say on the subject.

Let us look first at the chiefdom, the first multivillage polity, and as such the first big evolutionary step beyond the autonomous village. How does Harris see chiefdoms coming into being? In discussing the factors that lead up to the formation of chiefdoms, Harris finds in the Melanesian "Big Man" the core around which chiefdoms begin to crystallize.

For Harris, the Big Man had two essential functions: an economic one and a military one. On the economic side, the Big Man was at first a more or less evenhanded redistributor, parceling out game and plant food equally to his followers, keeping for himself no more than his fair share. By doing so, he gained prestige, loyalty, and affection, no doubt, but did not gain appreciably in power. Real power accrued to him only when he began to exercise his military functions; when he became, as Harris (1979:101) calls him, an "intensifier-redistributor-warrior." And only at this point—that is, when Harris faces the issue of how village autonomy was transcended and chiefdoms established—does he begin to come to grips with warfare in its *aggregative* phase.

Having examined several Melanesian Big Man societies, Harris became impressed with the importance of war among them. He notes, for example, that the Big Man among the Siuai of Bougainville in the Solomons, while still wielding considerable influence today, had enjoyed greater power in the past, when warfare was frequent and he was the war leader of his village. With this case in mind he comes to the following conclusion: "This ... fits theoretical expectations since the ability to redistribute meat, plant food, and other valuables goes hand in hand with the ability to attract a following of warriors, equip them for combat, and reward them with spoils of battle" (Harris, 1977:73).

Now, given the fact that warfare already existed at this level, what provoked it? On occasion Harris does make statements such as: "In a general sense, we can attribute the underlying causes of primitive warfare to population pressure" (Harris, 1971:227) and again, "population pressure ... played an important role in the development of warfare" (Harris, 1987c:92). But such statements are relatively few and far between. In Harris's writings, population pressure, in any clear and unambiguous sense, is not front and center in his analysis of the causes of war at the level of autonomous villages and early chiefdoms.

Nevertheless, here and there, we find Harris recognizing that warfare, *given an impetus by increasing population pressure,* did play a significant role at these levels. He notes, for example, that "the larger and denser the population, the larger the redistributive network and the more powerful the redistributive *war chief*" (Harris, 1977:76; emphasis added). And speaking of the next higher level of political development, he remarks that "like pristine states, the advanced chiefdoms were thoroughly committed to the relief of reproductive pressure [i.e., population pressure] not through the regulation of fertility but through territorial expansion, military plunder, and the continuous intensification of production" (Harris, 1979:101). Accordingly, he observes that "external warfare," as practiced among Big Man redistributive societies, "would increase and defeated villages would be regularly assimilated [i.e., incorporated] into the tax and tribute network" (Harris, 1977:78).

Once again, speaking of the Trobriand paramount chief, who (it would appear) emerged at a time when warfare was prevalent on that island, Harris (1977:73) says that this fact provides "another illustration of how redistributor war chiefs could have evolved little by little into permanent rulers with coercive control over production and consumption."

To sum up then, Harris believes that "under certain conditions, and in the presence of warfare, these food managers [i.e., Big Man redistributors] could have gradually set themselves above their followers and [as paramount chiefs] become the original nucleus of the ruling classes of the first states" (Harris, 1977:71).

Still, as this passage and other similar ones appear to suggest, when it comes to pinpointing the causes of chiefdom formation, Harris's principal allegiance is not to population pressure, nor to warfare, but to *economic* factors. In this regard, Harris most often points to the chief's role in directing the production and distribution of goods, principally foodstuffs. For example, he argues that "the expansion of the managerial aspects of these functions [i.e., the intensification of production and the furthering of redistribution] rapidly leads to permanent and severe forms of hierarchy, which eventually culminate in there being differential access to strategic resources; this in turn lays the basis for the emergence of classes and of the state" (Harris, 1979:92).

With his power thus increased, the benevolent redistributor of earlier times becomes the demanding expropriator, and rather important results ensue from this change: "Contributions to the redistributive portion of the economy gradually cease to be voluntary; soon they verge on taxation, and at that point, the chiefdoms stand poised at the threshold of becoming states" (Harris, 1979:92).

With the onset of state formation, though, population pressure finally becomes a prominent element in Harris's thinking about political evolution. It does so, however, only under special conditions. "Under what circumstances," he asks, "would the conversion of a redistributive chiefdom to a feudal state be likely to occur?" (Harris, 1977:78). And he replies:

> To intensification, population growth, warfare, and storageable grains, and hereditary redistributors, add one more factor: impaction. Suppose, as Robert Carneiro has suggested, a population being served by redistributors has been expanding inside a region that is circumscribed, or closed off, by environmental barriers. These barriers need not be uncrossable oceans or unclimbable mountains; rather, they might merely consist of ecological transition zones ["ecotones," he later calls them] where peoples who had broken away from overcrowded villages would find that they would have to take a severe cut in their standard of living or change their whole way of life in order to survive. (Harris 1977:78)

In Harris's thinking, "impaction" now becomes a key element in initiating the process of pristine state formation. And "impaction," for him, is a shorthand way of introducing population pressure into the equation. More fully characterized, "impaction" is the condition resulting when a society undergoing a marked increase in population, but finding itself living in a sharply bounded environment, starts pressing hard against the carrying capacity of that environment. Eventually and inevitably, competition with neighboring groups over arable land ensues. And the conquest of the weaker by the stronger takes place, with its predictable consequences. Harris elaborates on this theme:

> With impaction, two types of groups might find that the benefits of a permanently subordinate status exceeded the costs of trying to maintain their independence. First, villages consisting of kinspeople forced to enter the [much less hospitable] transition zones would be tempted to accept a dependent relationship in exchange for continued participation in the redistributions sponsored by their parent settlements. And second, enemy villages defeated in battle might find it less costly to pay taxes and tribute than to flee into these zones. (Harris, 1977:78)

Further characterizing this process, Harris elsewhere declares:

This means the pristine state can be expected to arise only in regions with sharp ecotones. In such regions, the expansionist policies of advanced chiefdoms [fueled by population pressure, I would add] lead sooner or later to the condition [of] ... "impaction": the dissatisfied peasants who cross the ecotone find themselves in a worse situation than those who remain behind—even though those who remain must now pay taxes in labor or kind for the privilege of using their native strategic resources. (Harris, 1979:101–102)

If we examine these words carefully, Harris appears to be reluctant to embrace, fully and wholeheartedly, the theory that, for the most part, he accepts. Thus he turns a fundamentally *coercive* theory into a quasi-*voluntaristic* one. He writes as if those villages subject to impaction undertake a closely reasoned cost-benefit analysis of their plight before deciding whether to take their chances on a hardscrabble terrain, or whether to subordinate themselves to a stronger polity with better land. In this vein he writes: "Villages pressing against the ecotone might accept permanent dependent status in exchange for the privileges of continuing to participate in the redistributions of the more affluent parent villages from which they have fissioned" (Harris, 1979:102). The alternatives are presented almost as if it were a matter of tossing a coin.

Nonetheless, despite his several attempts to paint the decision faced by defeated groups as a calm weighing of alternative disadvantages, Harris, in substance, accepts the basic "scenario" of the circumscription theory. Indeed, he even endeavors to marshal evidence in its favor. "How does the theory of environmental circumscription and impaction accord with the evidence?" he asks. And he answers:

There is a very good fit between this model of pristine state formation and the conditions that existed in the regions most likely on archaeological evidence to have been the centers of formation of pristine states. Egypt, Mesopotamia, northern India, the Yellow River Basin, central highland Mexico south to Tehuantepec, and the Peruvian coastal rivers and Andean highlands are all sharply circumscribed by ecotones that cannot support intensifiable forms of preindustrial agriculture. (Harris, 1979:102)

As a matter of fact, Harris would even submit to careful scrutiny—if not actually challenge—any alternative theory of pristine state formation *not* based on environmental circumscription. Thus he declares that "states found in relatively low-density, unimpacted regions must always be examined with these possibilities in mind [namely, that they could have arisen through gaining control of important trade routes] before concluding that intensification and reproductive pressures [i.e., population pressure] did not cause the evolution of the region's pristine states" (Harris, 1977:81).

Somewhat muted as is Harris's invocation of warfare as a mechanism for the aggregation of villages into chiefdoms, once a certain threshold has been crossed and chiefdoms are firmly in place and on their way to becoming states, Harris is quite amenable to recognizing the role that warfare plays in this process. "The form of political organization which we call the state," he says, "came into existence precisely because ... [chiefdoms were] able to carry out wars of territorial conquest and economic plunder" (Harris, 1977:38).

And once states are fully established, warfare becomes the instrument *par excellence* for their further territorial and political expansion. "Once the state becomes a functional reality," Harris writes, "all neighboring chiefdoms must either rapidly pass across the threshold of state formation, or succumb to the triumphant armies of the new social leviathan" (Harris, 1979:102–103).

The course followed by political evolution, beginning slowly as villages are being gradually fused into chiefdoms, and accelerating as chiefdoms become transformed into states, seems to me to parallel the pace of Marvin Harris's acceptance and application of population pressure as a dynamic element in this process. From a virtual neglect of it initially, to a partial recognition of it under the guise of "reproductive pressure," Harris's appreciation of population pressure as a causal factor in political development grows as societies ascend the evolutionary ladder. Then, when a critical threshold is reached, and Harris encapsulates the process in the term "impaction," he at last assigns to population pressure a critical role in the rise, consolidation, and expansion of the state.

Chapter Twelve

Evolutionary Materialism and Darwinian Conflict Theory

A Critical Analysis of Stephen Sanderson's Extensions of Cultural Materialism

David P. Kennedy

In 1994, Marvin Harris argued that cultural materialism would not go away until something better came along (Harris, 1994). Unfortunately, with the death of Harris in 2001, this claim is being put to the test. Using the Institute for Scientific Information's electronic data base Web of Science, we can trace the influence of cultural materialism on research over the past 25 years. Between 1980 and 2004, there were 371 references to Harris's *Cultural Materialism* (Harris, 1979). There was an average of 23 references to *Cultural Materialism* between 1980 and 1989 and an average of 15.5 between 1990 and 1998. In 1999, the number of references dropped sharply to 3 and between 1999 and 2004 the average was 3.4. Based on this measure alone, cultural materialism seems to be going away. (But see Sandstrom and White, Chapter 1 this volume.) Has something better come along? And is cultural materialism really going away?

In this chapter, I explore these questions by examining the major theoretical works of Stephen K. Sanderson (1995b, 2001a) and compare them with cultural materialism. Sanderson develops two related theoretical perspectives called evolutionary materialism and Darwinian conflict theory. For both of these theoretical perspectives, Sanderson draws on existing theories of human social and cultural change and produces a new theoretical synthesis. Sanderson draws heavily on Harris's cultural materialism for both

238

evolutionary materialism and Darwinian conflict theory. Evolutionary materialism is primarily a synthesis of cultural materialism and world-systems theory, whereas Darwinian conflict theory builds on this synthesis by incorporating a perspective on human behavior informed by Darwinian evolutionary theory.

In this chapter, I argue that Sanderson's attempts at building comprehensive theoretical syntheses have not been sufficiently distant to qualify as being distinct from cultural materialism. Sanderson offers many significant critiques of existing theories of social change, including theories advanced by Harris, that improve our understanding of cultural evolution. However, I argue that Sanderson's critiques are of theories developed using the research strategy of cultural materialism, rather than of the research strategy itself. Also, Sanderson sometimes substitutes a critique of a theory developed by Marvin Harris himself for a critique of the comprehensive and clearly defined research strategy that Harris developed in *Cultural Materialism*. Rather than producing "something better" than cultural materialism, I argue that Sanderson instead strengthens cultural materialism. Sanderson's primary contributions are improving and expanding theories of social change developed using cultural materialism, expanding the range of evolutionary events typically explained by cultural materialism to include modern social change, and overcoming the resistance to incorporating biological variables into the range of explanatory factors of sociocultural evolution.

I first examine Sanderson's *Social Transformations* and critique his treatment of such events as the development of agriculture, state formation, the development of capitalism, and the Industrial Revolution. I argue that while Sanderson has made a valuable contribution toward the development of theories of sociocultural evolution, his theories fit within the paradigm of cultural materialism. I then examine *The Evolution of Human Sociality*, specifically Sanderson's treatment of the question of fertility decline. I argue that, while Harris himself resisted the inclusion of biology into theories of human behavior, Sanderson's incorporation of a biological perspective is not inconsistent with the paradigm of cultural materialism itself. My general conclusion is that Sanderson has done much to advance materialist theories of human sociocultural evolution but that these theories are best characterized as theories within cultural materialism.

Evolutionary Materialism

In Sanderson's first attempt at a comprehensive theoretical synthesis, *Social Transformations: A General Theory of Historical Development,* he indicates that his motivation for the creation of a new "theoretical strategy" is to extend the logic of cultural materialism. He states that "evolutionary materialism is highly compatible with cultural materialism and in no way is intended as any sort of refutation, or even partial rejection of it" (Sanderson, 1994b:2). Although he downplays the three-part division of culture described in Harris's *Cultural Materialism*, Sanderson closely follows the main principles of cultural materialism in describing the origins of some of the major events in world history.

Sanderson's theoretical developments are so consistent with cultural materialism that it is difficult not to consider them as mere theoretical contributions to the cultural materialism paradigm. His particular theories on the origins of agriculture, states, and capitalism do not match up exactly with Harris's, but mere disagreement on the particular mechanisms and causal interactions leading to particular events is not sufficient to support a claim that a new theoretical strategy is being followed. As I will show, the particular theories that Sanderson supports on the evolution of agriculture, the state, and capitalism, meet all of the criteria of a theory that conforms to the paradigm of cultural materialism.

A strategy that Sanderson often employs in developing a theoretical explanation for historical events is to survey the leading explanations that have been developed by other theorists and to choose the elements of those theories he believes to have the most validity in order to create a synthesis of the best ideas. He makes the most use of this strategy in his explanation of the Neolithic Revolution and the origins of the state. In fact, Sanderson offers very little of his own interpretation of these two events and relies mostly on Mark Cohen's population pressure model of the Neolithic Revolution and Robert Carneiro's circumscription model of the origins of the state.

The Neolithic Revolution

Sanderson's view of the Neolithic Revolution conforms to the cultural materialist paradigm because he rejects the idealistic explanation that agriculture originated as an idea that spread around the world because of its self-evident benefits (Sanderson, 1995b:49). He firmly states, in agreement with the theory presented in Cohen's *The Food Crisis in Prehistory* (1977), that the slow and steady buildup of population pressure was the primary influence in the decision of prehistoric people to begin adopting agriculture as the primary mode of subsistence. He also adds that population pressure acted in concert with environmental and technological variables to influence this change (Sanderson, 1995b:42).

Although Sanderson is critical of Harris's theory of the Neolithic Revolution, which focuses on ecological changes resulting from global warming at the end of the ice age, this is not an indication of his rejection of the larger theoretical framework of cultural materialism (Sanderson, 1995b:44). Sanderson does not in fact disagree with the importance of the factors brought to light in Harris's model. His disagreement with Harris lies in the fact that he believes that agriculture was "invented" independently in eight different world regions: southwest Asia, China, southeast Asia, Europe, Africa, Mesoamerica, South America, and North America (Sanderson, 1995b:23). Harris's theory, Sanderson states, does not account for the development of agriculture in southwest Asia, China, or southeast Asia, and does not give enough emphasis to population pressure as an independent force (Sanderson, 1995b:44). Ecological change may have played a significant role in the development of agriculture in the remaining areas of the world, but Sanderson believes that population pressure as defined by Cohen is the ultimate driving force behind the agricultural revolution and is the one common factor in all eight of the original areas.

The two views of Harris and Sanderson regarding the origins of agriculture are not contradictory and only differ on the basis of the relative impact of particular causal agents. This difference is relatively minor compared to the difference between materialist and idealist approaches to the origins of the agriculture. Both Sanderson and Harris emphasize infrastructural variables such as subsistence technology, technoenvironmental relationships, ecosystems, work patterns, and demography.

The Origins of the State

Sanderson's investigation into the origins of the state also relies mainly on elements that are defined as infrastructural determinants in cultural materialism. Sanderson states that Robert Carneiro's theory of circumscription is the best available theory of the origin of the state because of its ability to be applied to every occurrence of worldwide parallel state development (Sanderson, 1995b:79). Carneiro argues that the interaction between geographical obstacles (either in the form of actual physical impediments or concentration of resources) and population pressure are the necessary conditions behind the formation of restrictive social organizations. These conditions lead to groups of people who cannot migrate away from each other to avoid competition for resources, leading to warfare. The increased challenge of war increases the need for a restrictive social organization that exchanges independence of individual members of the society for increased ability to fight and defend. Without the physical impediments limiting the opportunity for migration and without the increased competition spurred by population pressure, individuals would not choose to support a restrictive social organization (Sanderson 1995b:79–82).

Sanderson's selection of Carneiro's theory of circumscription as the best explanation of the origins of the state is consistent with cultural materialism. Harris (1977) himself uses this theory in his explanation of the development of pristine states. Sanderson offers very little direct criticism of Harris's take on state formation and of the theory of circumscription itself. The criticism he does offer—that the theory overemphasizes warfare and political conquest and underemphasizes economic stratification—does not critique the identification of the ultimate causes of state formation (Sanderson, 1995:81). Therefore, there is nothing in his criticism that qualifies as a criticism of a cultural materialist approach to the question of the origins of the first states.

The Origins of Capitalism

Sanderson's approach to understanding the origin of capitalism departs more from cultural materialism than his theories on the origins of agriculture and the first states. Sanderson approaches the question of capitalism by synthesizing cultural materialism and world-systems theory. He summarizes world-systems theory as developed by Immanuel Wallerstein (1974a, 1974b, 1979, 1980, 1989) (Sanderson, 1995b:209–210). A world-system is any relatively large social system exhibiting autonomy, having an extensive division of labor along economic and geographical lines, and containing a plurality of societies and cultures. There have been two types of world-systems: world-empires, which were politically and militarily unified, and world-economies, which were held together only by economic ties and trade. A world-system is broken down into three main parts or zones: the core, the periphery, and the semiperiphery. The core is made up of societies that are economically and politically dominant and that use and produce the most advanced goods and technology. The periphery is made up of societies that use the most outmoded forms of technology and that are economically specialized to produce raw materials for export to the core and semiperiphery. The semiperiphery contains features of both the core and the periphery and it has an intermediate level of economic development. There is another region outside the system called the external arena that has some interaction with the system, but it is not an actual part of it. The core exploits both the semiperiphery and periphery and organizes the economic activities of the other two zones for its own high profit. Just as the core exploits the other two zones, the semiperiphery exploits the periphery. There is a large degree of competition within the core zone, as well as a large amount of cooperation. There is the possibility of movement for a society between zones over time, but this movement is limited and rare. The semiperiphery acts as a buffer between the core and the periphery (Sanderson, 1995b:96–97). These economic zones are paralleled politically by a highly competitive (and sometimes cooperative) interstate system. Sanderson characterizes the relationship between the world-economy and the interstate system as "two sides of the same coin," the coin being the world-system as a whole (Sanderson, 1995b:98).

Certain qualities that Sanderson calls "evolutionary dynamics" are characteristic of the world-system. These qualities include commodification, proletarianization, mechanization, contractualization, and polarization. Commodification indicates that an ever greater part of economic and social life is organized around exchange-values rather than use-values; proletarianization is the transformation of the labor force into wage workers who themselves have exchange-values; mechanization is the continual advancement of technology for production; contractualization is the increasing formalization of economic and other human relationships; and polarization is the increased widening of the economic gap between the core and the periphery (Sanderson, 1995b:97–98). These characteristics of the world-system are the primary forces that contribute to change and these forces exist because of the underlying "evolutionary logic" of the world-system, which is that of "ceaseless capital accumulation" (Sanderson 1995b:99).

Sanderson's explanation of the origins of capitalism relies heavily on this concept of a world-system. Although Wallerstein developed the idea of a world-system with the European-centered, modern world-system in mind and cautions against using this concept in other world-historical contexts (especially the precapitalist world), some world-system theorists have extended the idea of the world-system many thousand years into the past (Frank, 1990, 1991, 1995; Gills and Frank, 1991; Chase-Dunn and Hall, 1997). Although Sanderson acknowledges this criticism, he is sympathetic to the precapitalist world-system theorists. Sanderson puts forth the idea that, although the current world-system is qualitatively different from any previous, precapitalist world-system, there was continual quantitative change between 3000 BCE and CE 1500 in the form of increased reliance on trade between various parts of the world. He argues that increasing world commercialization and the expansion of trade were the overriding conditions that explain the development of capitalism in both Europe and Japan.

Within the context of increasing world commercialization, Japan and the European states that were first in establishing capitalism—England and the Netherlands—had several other characteristics in common: They were small in size, were surrounded or nearly surrounded by large bodies of water, had similarly temperate climates, had similar demographic pressures, and had similar precapitalist political structures (Sanderson, 1995b:169–172). Their small size was an important characteristic because it allowed for easy transportation and communication and it cut down on the amount of resources that were needed for administration. Location near large bodies of water was important because it allowed Japan and the European countries to specialize in maritime trade, which was faster and further reaching than overland trade at the time of capitalism's beginnings. Temperate climates were an important characteristic because Japan and Europe were not areas of the world that were suitable for the production of exotic raw materials; therefore, they had little colonization pressure from the militarily strong precapitalist empires. Although Japan had no equivalent episode of population collapse like that which Europe endured in the fourteenth century, they both had a steady buildup of population pressure and urbanization leading up to the capitalist takeoff. Finally, both Europe and Japan had feudal political systems that allowed more leeway for trade and merchant activities (Sanderson, 1995b:169–172).

Sanderson argues that these characteristics of Europe and Japan created a ripe situation for increasing world commercialization to take hold after a period of quantitative buildup, leading to a qualitative change in economic structure. Although Japan is historically thought of as being completely isolated from the mid-seventeenth century until the mid-nineteenth century, Sanderson supports the claim that Japan was only isolated from the West and in fact continued trade relations with surrounding Asian nations, China in particular (Sanderson, 1994b:17). Sanderson argues that Japan was approaching capitalism for several hundred years before the mid-nineteenth century by noting several tell-tale characteristics, including "large-scale urbanization, commercialization of agriculture, increasing flight of peasants into the towns and cities, the worsening economic condition of the nobility, growth in the wealth and economic importance of the merchant class, increased monetization of the economy, and the beginnings of the factory system" (Sanderson, 1994b:18).

Thus, although Japan is usually thought of as having developed capitalism later than Europe, Sanderson's conclusion is that, while continuing to retain feudal social and political arrangements, its economic system was in fact already capitalist by the middle of the nineteenth century.

Harris (1999b) agrees that Sanderson makes a significant contribution in his comparison of the cases of Japan and Europe, especially in the identification of demographic factors in Japan and Europe that contributed to the rise of capitalism. In *Theories of Culture in Postmodern Times,* Harris compares and contrasts his own approach to the origins of capitalism with that of Sanderson. Harris objects to some of the common characteristics of Europe and Japan that Sanderson argues were important prerequisites for the development of capitalism. Harris disagrees that the climate, the geographic location, and the small size of European states and Japan were important prerequisites of the development of capitalism. Instead of these factors, Harris argues that increasing population pressure caused greater and greater intensification of the manor system until its ecological limits had been reached. This promoted the need to develop a new, more intensifiable mode of production (Harris, 1977). Harris couples this population pressure model with the decentralized political system of feudalism created by the particular climatological conditions of Europe, which allowed Europeans to depend on rainfall for farming as opposed to extensive irrigation. Despite not depending on rainfall for irrigation, Japan was similar to Europe in that it had a geography that led to a decentralized irrigation system, which allowed for a corresponding decentralized political system (Harris, 1999b).

The timing of the start of capitalism is an area of disagreement between Sanderson and Harris. Sanderson argues that increasing world commercialism coupled with feudalism in Europe and Japan led to capitalism in these locations. However, had feudalism never existed, capitalism would still have developed, but more slowly (Sanderson, 1994b:49). Harris (1999b) disagrees with this and argues that feudalism should be an integral part of a theory of the origins of capitalism because in the two instances where capitalism developed, it was preceded by feudalism. Harris also argues that increased trade and world commercialization were consequences rather than causes of capitalism.

Despite these disagreements, the difference between Harris's and Sanderson's approaches to the origins of capitalism is not significant. Sanderson's investigation of the parallels between the European and Japanese cases offers much insight into the development of capitalism. Sanderson and Harris disagree on some aspects of their theories, but they agree on the importance of demographic pressure, feudal political structure, ecological forces, and the increased presence of trading opportunities.

Despite differences in how these variables are hypothesized to have interacted to lead to the parallel formation of capitalism in two different parts of the world, most of what Sanderson believes is responsible for the origins of capitalism fits within a cultural materialist theoretical framework. Throughout his investigation of the origins of capitalism as well as the origins of agriculture and the state, Sanderson accepts the primacy of infrastructural variables when accounting for world-historical change and is often in complete agreement with Harris himself. Sanderson may deviate from theories that were developed using cultural materialism, but for what he considers the most important evolutionary events in human history, his theories are only slight variations on similar theories developed using cultural materialism.

Explanations of Modern Social Change

Sanderson's evolutionary materialism appears most different from cultural materialism when he discusses aspects of the modern world, beginning with the advent of full-fledged worldwide capitalism. Although Sanderson repeatedly asserts the causal primacy of material (infrastructural) variables, his description of evolutionary forces often deviates from cultural materialism when he describes the forces that have shaped sociocultural evolution after the onset of capitalism. The following statements are examples of how his descriptions differ from standard cultural materialist descriptions:

> The expanding level of world commercialization would eventually have gotten its way. It was a force that could be slowed down, but it could not have been stopped. Eventually the level of world commercialization would have become such that the tipover into world-transforming capitalism would have occurred even under generally unfavorable preconditions. Capitalism was a force that could not be denied. Its rise was inevitable at some point or other. (Sanderson, 1995b:175)

> Once in existence, mercantile activity tended to expand of its own accord, and thus the class power of the merchant classes slowly, but surely, increased. And at some point it reached a level beyond which it could not be stopped. (Sanderson, 1995b:177)

Although Sanderson gives importance to infrastructural causes for the development of capitalism, his descriptions of modern events increasingly identify structural forces, such as the increase in world commercialization and the development of the world-system, as causal agents.

This emphasis on structural economic forces as agents of sociocultural change appears to be a sharp departure from cultural materialism and the position of primacy of infrastructural forces. In contrast to Sanderson's description of the emergence of capitalism, Harris stresses the primary causality of the material constraints of population pressure and ecological failure due to greater intensification to meet the demands of the growing population. Harris, like Sanderson, also credits the increase in mercantile activity as having great influence on the choices of individuals to increasingly pursue capitalist activities. But Harris assigns ultimate causality to the infrastructural forces of demography and ecological degradation. The quotes above from Sanderson imply an argument that the activity of mercantilism has a life of its own and expands "of its own accord" once the infrastructural causes put it in place.

This argument at first sounds like a type of developmentalist explanation. Sanderson defines developmentalist explanations as "epistemological conceptions of social evolution that are historicist and that rest on directional or developmental laws or unfolding models" (Sanderson, 1990:34n). I do not believe that Sanderson has any intention of advancing a developmentalist argument. However, his description of systems progressing because of their internal logic without reference to the material forces that create and maintain the system is confusing in light of his obvious materialist intentions. Although Sanderson specifically states that he does not believe that there is an inherent tendency for human beings to participate in capitalism, his characterization of mercantile activity as a force of its own that "at some point ... reached a level beyond which it could not be stopped" seems to contradict the emphasis on ultimate material causes.

When examining his theoretical approach in total, it is clear that Sanderson has no interest in promoting a developmentalist theory of social evolution. When he states that nothing could stop mercantile activity, he is probably arguing that, under the specific material constraints that those particular societies were under at the time of the emergence of capitalism, increased mercantile activity was the most logical way to meet their daily needs. This in turn created a system of feedback in which greater reliance on trade led to a greater need for trade. However, Sanderson's repeated references to systems "expanding of their own accord" confuses the issue and leaves readers wondering if he is disregarding the material forces that are typically identified as causal agents in theories developed within cultural materialism.

Sanderson's seeming departure from cultural materialist approaches to modern sociocultural evolution in *Social Transformations* is clarified in his most recent theoretical work, *The Evolution of Human Sociality* (Sanderson, 2001a). Sanderson argues that a problem with cultural materialism is that for modern societies, structural economic forces are deemed to be more important causal agents than infrastructural factors, such as ecological and demographic factors. Ecology and demography "take a back seat to economics in the modern capitalist world" (Sanderson, 2001a:115). Sanderson argues that, because of the importance of economics, it should be placed in the infrastructure instead of being split between the infrastructure and the structure. Sanderson argues that this makes sense in light of Harris's own inconsistent use of economics as a causal force in modern social evolution. According to Sanderson, Harris sometimes discusses structural relations of production as a causal factor in social change. An example of this is Harris's argument that women increased their representation in the workforce in the United States during the twentieth century because of the spread of capitalism. Sanderson argues that Harris is likely inconsistent in his use of economics as a causal agent because models are sometimes messy, they cannot always explain everything perfectly, and Harris is right in accepting this ambiguity.

I agree that models are not always capable of accounting for each and every detail of reality and theorists must sometimes learn to live with ambiguity. However, I do not agree with Sanderson that Harris is neglecting the infrastructure in the examples he cites. I also do not agree that the economic relations of production that typically are part of the structure should be included within the infrastructure. In the example that Sanderson cites—women entering the workforce—Harris certainly describes the mechanics of the change in economic terms. However, before he describes the structural changes that lead to increased female employment in the United States, he cites the ultimate infrastructural cause: a shift from an agrarian mode of production to an industrial mode (Harris, 1981). In Harris's chapter in *America Now* entitled "Why Women Left Home," he describes a host of economic changes that occurred as a result of the shift from agrarian to industrial production. Among these changes was the entry of women into the workforce.

This analysis is consistent with Harris's description of the primacy of infrastructure in accounting for social change (Harris, 1979). In the three-part system that Harris describes in *Cultural Materialism,* infrastructure, structure, and superstructure are typically in equilibrium in a social system. Any innovation in one part of the system has a ripple effect on the other two parts. Innovations affect the balance of the system and the system responds through either negative feedback, resulting in eventual elimination of the innovation, or adjustments to accommodate the innovation, thus producing a new equilibrium. The principle of the primacy of the infrastructure holds that changes in the infrastructure are more likely to cause changes in the other parts of the system. Innovations in the structure and superstructure will more likely last if they are consistent with the infrastructure and changes in the infrastructure will spread faster if the structure and superstructure are consistent with the changes.

By identifying the ultimate cause of women's increasing representation in the workforce as a shift in the mode of production, Harris is consistent with the primacy of infrastructure. Economics certainly has an important effect on human behavior, but by referencing infrastructural variables, theorists can explain the ultimate causes of economic changes. I believe that many of the arguments that Sanderson makes that seem to contradict his stated commitment to materialism and infrastructural determinism result from this blurring of a distinction between infrastructural and structural economic variables. In the next section, I describe the problems with Sanderson's description of modern evolutionary forces and how they would be improved with an explicit reference to variables that are traditionally included in the infrastructure. In Sanderson's investigation of the evolution of the modern world and world-system, he touches on many facets of the changing world, such as industrialization, hegemonic cycles, underdevelopment, and the collapse of socialism. I will illustrate my argument with reference to his argument about the origins of the Industrial Revolution.

The Industrial Revolution

Sanderson (1995b) does not credit the Industrial Revolution with being the singular event that can be pointed to as the division between the modern and premodern worlds. He describes a continual process of increasing industrialization that has been growing for several hundred years. He considers industrialization as simply "mechanization within capitalism," and argues that capitalism was the primary driving force behind the desire to mechanize (Sanderson, 1995b:257). He points to demographic pressure as an influence in this process, not as a prime mover as it was for the Neolithic Revolution but merely an additional favorable condition. The reason it was favorable was because excess population allowed for a large labor force and for a large supply of consumers for manufactured goods. He believes that demographic variables played a part "only in the context of the rapidly expanding capitalist mode of production" (Sanderson, 1995b:256).

The assertion that the expansion of mechanization was only possible within the context of a particular mode of production in interaction with demographic changes seems, on the surface, to be a reference to the primacy of the infrastructure and highly consistent with cultural materialism. However, Sanderson intentionally does not distinguish between the structural and infrastructural parts of capitalist economies. Instead of describing how the material conditions made mechanization more likely and/or beneficial to societies and how it was highly consistent with the technology of subsistence, Sanderson relies on a description of the system of capitalism as inherently "rapidly expanding."

In emphasizing the essential characteristics of the system as explanations for its expansiveness instead of emphasizing the material forces that created a favorable environment for such an expansive system, Sanderson's argument implies essentialism and teleology. In the context of Sanderson's other writings, it is obvious that he believes material forces are the ultimate causal factors in producing and maintaining this system. However, his decision to combine infrastructural and structural elements of the economy at times makes his arguments sound like he is crediting essential characteristics of economic systems for exhibiting those characteristics.

Harris, on the other hand, explains the same phenomenon in similar terms, but clearly identifies infrastructural factors as having causal priority over structural factors. He agrees that increasing technological advances and increasing mechanization are a result of capitalism, but he does not stop short with a statement that must be taken on faith. He instead points to the fact that technological change is generally a direct response to either "resource shortages or to population growth and relentless reproductive pressures" (Harris, 1977:272). He also adds that "the periods of greatest technological innovation were those of greatest population increase, highest cost of living, and greatest amount of suffering among the poor" (Harris, 1977:272). Thus, his explanation does not credit the world-system made up of incessant accumulation of capital as working behind the scenes to propel societies to create greater and greater technological advances because it is a "rapidly expanding" system. If the system is in fact rapidly expanding, it is due to specific causal forces that are influencing it to be that way.

Sanderson's effort to augment cultural materialism with world-systems theory is a positive step in the interest of producing better explanations of modern social change. However, his decision to lump together structural and infrastructural aspects of the economy is confusing and leads to the appearance of an eclectic selection of different theories to explain different phenomena. Sanderson's argument for putting economy into the infrastructure is because economics has an increased causal role in postcapitalist social evolution. This allows him to assign a greater causal role to the world capitalist economic system than if it were in the structure. However, Sanderson admits that it is not necessary to include economics in the infrastructure when discussing preindustrial societies in which the traditional cultural materialist system categories have a better fit (Sanderson, 1995b:117). I believe that world-systems theory and cultural materialism are compatible theories and can be synthesized into one theoretical perspective, but I believe that maintenance of a distinction between the infrastructural and structural components of economy is important to avoid the appearance of eclecticism.

Sanderson argues that modifications of cultural materialism are necessary because it has difficulty explaining modern social change. It has difficulty explaining "evolutionary events that occur within complex agrarian civilizations and modern world capitalism and industrialism—the rise and fall of dynasties, the commercialization of agrarian states, the rise of Europe to world dominance after the sixteenth century, or the evolution of the contemporary world economic system" (Sanderson, 1994a:48).

Although he offers these criticisms, Sanderson never presents an argument for why cultural materialism is incapable of being used and/or modified to explain the modern world. I do not believe that Sanderson would make such an argument and I believe that his effort to incorporate world-systems theory into his analysis is an effort to modify and expand cultural materialism to explain modern events. I support this effort, but I do not believe that Sanderson has gone far enough to create a synthesis between the two perspectives and leaves himself open to criticisms of eclecticism.

Sanderson himself defines synthesis as an alternative to eclecticism and states that it involves "the selection of elements from different research traditions and their recombination and fusion into a novel research tradition that is similar to its parents, yet notably distinct from them" (Sanderson, 1987:334). Sanderson points out that combining two or more research traditions is extremely difficult and states that there is a "fine line in practice between synthesis and eclecticism" (Sanderson, 1987:338). Eclecticism is different from synthesis in that it does not define something new. Eclecticism is a "mechanical juxtaposition of the elements of different research traditions, a placing of them side by side" (Sanderson, 1987:335).

As I have said, I do not believe that Sanderson's approach to the explanation of precapitalist social evolution is "notably distinct" from cultural materialism. I argue that his combination of world-systems theory and cultural materialism is more mechanical juxtaposition than synthesis because he typically does not use elements of cultural materialism and world-systems theory at the same time. It is true that he employs cultural materialist and world-system causal forces when investigating the rise of capitalism, but his explanation of this specific evolutionary phenomenon is the only one that goes far enough to be called a synthesis. In Sanderson's evolutionary materialist model, the world-system is not credited with having any force in the earliest evolutionary changes, such as the Neolithic Revolution or the origin of the state. Also, as I stated earlier, Sanderson disregards some of the basic tenets of cultural materialism, namely the division between infrastructural and structural economics when he discusses modern social change. This results in the appearance of two distinct theoretical models working separately to explain two different sets of evolutionary phenomena: precapitalist and postcapitalist evolutionary change. Thus, although his explanation of capitalism relies on a true synthesis of cultural materialism and world-systems theory, the majority of the phenomena on which Sanderson focuses are explained by using one model or the other, not a combination of both. Therefore, his theoretical strategy appears more eclectic than synthetic.

However, I do think that combining cultural materialism and world-systems theory into one synthesized theory is entirely possible and easily attained with only slight modifications in Sanderson's approach. The solution is not in the development of a new theoretical approach but to show how world-systems theory as a whole fits into cultural materialism. I do not believe that there is anything inherent in world-systems theory that opposes cultural materialism. The reason that world-systems theory must be included in cultural materialism and not the other way around is that world-systems theory has no ability to explain events in the prehistory of cultures, before there was widespread and intense communication and travel or trade relations. Cultural materialism, on the other hand, makes no explicit assumptions about the historical period in which it is used. It can be used by archaeologists as well as ethnographers (Harris, 1994).

I argue that retaining the division between structural and infrastructural aspects of the economy is essential to finding common ground between world-systems theory and cultural materialism. The phenomena stressed by world-systems theory can easily be placed into the structural level of cultural materialism's three-part cultural model as a form of relations of production. Elements such as hegemonic cycles and shifts in core/periphery relations are merely changes in the political economy, which fall into the structural level of cultural materialism (Harris, 1977). The concept of a world-system is important and is not just another type of political economy. The fact that it is a *world*-system indicates that structural and infrastructural bases must be extended to include a greater variety of cultures and societies. Each society cannot be thought of as having its own structure that is part of an isolated and closed system. The concept of the primacy of the infrastructure must be extended to account for infrastructural innovations in one area of the world that may not have a direct and easily seen relationship with other parts of the world. Because of the world-system, any change in infrastructure in one society is bound to have some ramifications on all other societies connected to the same world-system. Of course these relationships are very complicated and not necessarily transparent, but I believe that this rough outline establishes the possibility of reconciliation between cultural materialism and world-systems theory.

As with precapitalist social evolution, I do not believe that Sanderson's effort to explain modern social change with evolutionary materialism is notably distinct from cultural materialism. Sanderson brings insight to theoretical development and furthers the explanatory power of materialist theories of social change. However, I feel that his theoretical work is so highly compatible with cultural materialism that I find it difficult to understand why Sanderson feels the need to identify his approach with a distinct appellation. Sanderson himself characterizes evolutionary materialism as an extension of cultural materialism (Sanderson, 1995b:1–2). My personal belief is that social science is better served considering work such as Sanderson's as continuations of cultural materialism rather than new theoretical approaches. In the next section, I will make a similar argument with respect to Sanderson's latest theoretical synthesis, Darwinian conflict theory.

Darwinian Conflict Theory

In Sanderson's most recent theoretical work, *The Evolution of Human Sociality*, his most significant contribution is the synthesis of leading sociological theories of human social life with evolutionary theory. He calls this theoretical synthesis *Darwinian conflict theory*. As in *Social Transformations*, Sanderson discusses the positive and negative aspects of cultural materialism and critiques theories developed by Harris. Sanderson also advances his own explanations of significant dimensions of human social behavior using his theoretical synthesis and contrasts his theories with those of other theorists.

Sanderson's incorporation of evolutionary theory allows him to develop improved theories of human behavior that explain more empirical data than theories that make no reference to biological variables. Sanderson's most significant critiques of Harris are those directed at theories developed by Harris in which he resists any reference to human biological predispositions. In this section, I will discuss an example of how

Sanderson's theoretical approach that synthesizes sociological theory with evolutionary theory improves theories that a priori avoid reference to human biology. The example I will discuss is Sanderson's theory of human fertility decline in the modern world. I argue that, while Sanderson's theory of fertility decline is an improvement on Harris's theory, the theory advanced by Sanderson still follows the tenets of cultural materialism. I argue that, ironically, Sanderson's approach is more consistent with cultural materialism than is Harris's own approach. Also, I argue that individual theories developed using cultural materialism, including those developed by Harris himself, can be critiqued without critiquing cultural materialism itself.

Harris (1979) describes cultural materialism as a scientific research strategy or set of guidelines for the selection of variables to be studied, the relationships that these variables exhibit, and the body of theories developed using the strategy. These theories should account for observable phenomena, be parsimonious, and can be corrected, updated, and improved through empirical testing. Harris often resisted the incorporation of biological variables into theories explaining human behavior in the interest of parsimony. In fact, he identifies emphasis on parsimony in the hypothesizing of panhuman psychobiological drives as the primary difference between sociobiologists and cultural materialists: Cultural materialists operate with only a limited number of panhuman psychobiological drives, whereas sociobiologists postulate a significantly larger number of such drives (Harris, 1979). However, despite Harris's reluctance to involve biological variables in theories of sociocultural evolutionary processes, he admitted that there were selective features working at the biopsychological level that were necessary to consider in order to understand the mechanisms through which the infrastructure influences cultural patterns. Harris describes a small set (four items) of biopsychological predispositions in his attempt to develop a comprehensive list of what it is to be human. The predispositions involve food preferences, activity levels, sexuality, and seeking love and affection (Harris, 1979).

Sanderson notes that Harris provides no justification for the selection of these drives over other possible drives and he argues that it is necessary to consider sociobiological theory in order to understand why these drives are essential to human behavior (Sanderson, 2001a). Harris also never justifies why biological variables, as opposed to sociocultural variables, should be chosen for limitation in the interest of parsimony. Harris rightly argues against the proliferation of hypothetical genes to explain all of human behavior with no empirical justification, but the same can be said about sociocultural variables. Harris agrees that human behavior is the result of the interaction between genetic instructions and environmental forces and he admits that in order to understand how infrastructure influences human behavior and sociocultural change an understanding of human biopsychological factors is required (Harris, 1979). However, he opts to focus exclusively on sociocultural variables instead of the interaction between the human genotype and the environment in the interest of parsimony. Harris's effort to maximize parsimony with regard to biological variables sometimes comes at the expense of the development of theories that explain empirical data. I will illustrate this argument with Harris's theory of fertility decline. I will describe and critique Harris's theory and discuss how Sanderson's explanation of fertility decline is more consistent with the principles of cultural materialism than the explanation offered by Harris himself.

Fertility Decline

Harris explains variations in human reproduction with exclusive reference to the economic value of children (Harris, 1989; Harris and Ross, 1987). He argues that people have large families because children are valuable economic resources and that people reduce fertility in response to the increasing ratio of costs to benefits of rearing children. Harris also argues that below replacement fertility is evidence against any biological influence on human fertility rates (Vining, 1986). He contends that there is a biological force operating on reproduction and this force is "exercising a constant pressure for birthing and rearing as many children as human physiology permits" (Harris and Ross, 1987:11). However, he also argues that variation in human fertility proves that this biological force can be completely overwhelmed by cultural forces that limit or suppress fertility altogether.

This theory is parsimonious but does not stand up to empirical test. Hillard Kaplan (1994) tested the theory that high fertility societies had children because of their economic value. Instead of being net economic producers, Kaplan showed that children remained costly even under circumstances seemingly ripe for a net flow of wealth from children to parents. Other studies have also shown that, although children (especially older children) are able to mitigate their costs to parents, they nonetheless remain net drains on resources in circumstances of high fertility (Lee and Kramer, 2002; Turke, 1989). These findings refute the theory that human beings regulate their fertility solely based on the economic value of children.

Harris's characterization of the biological influence on human reproduction is also problematic in that he makes an assumption about a biological drive to maximize reproduction to physiological capacity without empirical evidence or a theoretical perspective to support this assumption. Harris's argument against a biological influence on reproduction and fertility rates based solely on fluctuating fertility rates is only reasonable if one assumes a simplistic, always positive, biological force on reproduction. Sanderson refutes this approach by pointing to theories of fertility decline that explain empirical data more successfully by making reference to biological variables. These theories do not claim that there is a simple, straightforward relationship between biology and fertility rates. On the contrary, these theories show how infrastructural variables interact with human biology to produce lower fertility.

Sanderson reviews alternative theories of fertility decline, including Kaplan's (1996) theory of "embodied capital." Kaplan's explanation for declining fertility rates in modern societies with high standards of living is grounded in life history theory. This theory assumes that human beings, like all organisms, make tradeoffs in energy expenditure at different points in their lives in order to maximize reproductive success (Hill and Kaplan, 1999). One thing they trade off is the energy and time required to produce a large number of offspring against the energy and time required to raise offspring that grow up to be successful reproducers themselves (quantity vs. quality). Depending on the environment, a strategy of low birth rates with high investments in offspring can lead to more successful reproduction in the long run. Human beings evolved physiological and psychological mechanisms to regulate fertility based on varying environmental conditions in order to maximize reproductive success (Kaplan, Lancaster, Tucker, and Anderson, 2002). In environments requiring expensive investments in offspring in order to make them reproductively successful, parents have fewer children.

Kaplan argues that there are novel conditions in the environments of some current human populations that pressure people to have smaller families, even to the point that in some instances they are no longer maximizing reproductive success. This situation is caused by the industrial mode of production, which leads to a system of competitive labor markets requiring the development of skills through years of education. The technology of industrial production allows for the storage of wealth in such things as land, animals, machinery, and money, whereas the ancestral environment only allowed for the storage of wealth as energy in human bodies. The concept of embodied capital includes the physical—organized somatic tissue, such as organ systems, brains, and muscles—and the functional—skills, knowledge, immune systems, etc.—as well as the investments made to develop and maintain embodied capital. Investments in embodied capital aid the pursuit of wealth, which has traditionally been associated with higher fertility and greater reproductive success. The existence of extrasomatic wealth, on the other hand, is often an impediment to fertility. Parents must not only choose between the number of children they have and the amount they will invest in each child's embodied capital; they must also choose between investing in their children's or their own embodied capital. This leads to longer periods of education in order to prepare offspring to compete for income and the accumulation of wealth, with the result that offspring are increasingly expensive to rear (Kaplan, Lancaster, Tucker, and Anderson, 2002). Thus, Kaplan's theory successfully explains empirical data through reference to interacting infrastructural and biological variables.

Sanderson also makes reference to biodemographic theories of fertility decline that describe an interaction between biological and demographic variables using life history theory (Carey and Lopreato, 1995). Sanderson discusses how declining infant mortality is a strong predictor of declining fertility (Sanderson, 2001a, 2001b; Sanderson and Dubrow, 2000). This finding is explained by a reference to an evolved sensitivity to the probability of children surviving to adulthood. Lower infant mortality leads to lower fertility because parents realize that children are likely to survive and there are greater reproductive rewards to spending energy investing in children already born rather than having additional children. Sanderson tested the hypothesis that lower infant mortality leads to lower fertility against alternative hypotheses, including hypotheses invoking the economic value of children and greater female empowerment, and found that infant mortality was the best predictor of fertility decline and female empowerment was a good secondary predictor. However, the economic value of children's labor, as measured by the proportion of the workforce involved in agriculture, generally proved to be unpredictive of fertility levels (Sanderson and Dubrow, 2000; Sanderson, 2001b; Chapter 10 this volume).

These findings successfully counter Harris's argument that changes in the economic value of children is the primary cause of fertility decline and that reference to biology is unnecessary in a theory of fertility decline. The theories derived from Darwinian conflict theory are certainly better able to explain the empirical evidence of fertility decline than the theory advanced by Harris. However, the refutation of Harris's explanation of fertility decline is not necessarily a refutation of cultural materialism. Despite his personal animosity toward theories that incorporated biological variables into explanations of human behavioral similarities and differences, Harris acknowledged that there must be some biological mechanism to explain how infrastructural forces acted on human sociocultural evolution. The theories of fertility decline that incorporate life history theory are simply enhancing our understanding of how infrastructural variables, such as the industrial mode of production and decreased infant mortality, interact with biological mechanisms to produce reproductive outputs. Despite the fact that Harris probably would have resisted the assumptions of these theories, there is nothing about them that contradicts the tenets of cultural materialism. In fact, they reinforce the claim that cultural materialism is a powerful strategy for conducting research and developing theories that explain empirical data on human behavior.

Conclusion

Sanderson makes a strong contribution to the understanding of many important events in the history of human sociocultural evolution. His theories range in their application from the Neolithic Revolution to modern societies. He has made an important contribution in identifying weaknesses in existing theories and in providing alternative theories to overcome these weaknesses. Many times the theories that Sanderson develops are synthesized from multiple existing theories.

I do not believe, however, that the theoretical developments of Sanderson are distinct enough from cultural materialism to merit categorization into a new theoretical paradigm. There are certainly differences with how Sanderson has approached explaining various events in human history. Sanderson has numerous points of disagreement with Harris, but these disagreements do not rise to the level of departure from the cultural materialist research strategy. Sanderson is clear that his theoretical developments are meant to be extensions of cultural materialism rather than refutations. There is probably a fine line between the development of a new research strategy and the modification of an old one. Where to draw that line is likely to be arbitrary in most cases. My personal view is that the burden of proof for claiming a new theoretical paradigm falls on the theorist to show how what is being developed is distinct enough from what has come before to merit classification as something new. Despite the notable differences between prevailing theories under cultural materialism, including those of Marvin Harris, I do not think Sanderson makes a strong enough case.

To answer the questions posed in the beginning of this chapter, I do not believe that cultural materialism has gone away, but I do believe something better has come along. Cultural materialism is alive and well in the theories of the many social scientists, such as Sanderson, who have incorporated it into their approach to understanding human behavior. Despite its current unpopularity in anthropology, I would not be surprised to see a resurgence of references to cultural materialism in the future. The reason I say this is because of the clearly written, powerfully argued, and well organized theoretical work that Harris has left behind. Unlike much of the theoretical work that is currently being produced in anthropology, Harris's work can be understood and appreciated and will stand on its own far into the future. It is my hope that future generations of anthropologists (and other social scientists) will rediscover Harris once the current theoretical trends have run their course.

However, the work of Stephen Sanderson also gives me hope that something better has come along: a new and improved cultural materialism. One of Harris's greatest achievements was the creation of a framework for theoretical development that is based on basic principles that can withstand the modification of theories developed using the framework and that is beyond any one theory or theorist. Sanderson's incorporation of biology into his materialist approach is a perfect example of the flexibility of cultural materialism. Despite Harris's animosity toward the inclusion of biology in theories of human behavior, the research strategy he developed includes an acknowledgement of the importance of understanding human nature. Sanderson's work overcomes some of the theoretical blind spots that Harris the theorist had when approaching issues of biological relevance. However, instead of creating something new, I believe that Sanderson has done much to improve cultural materialism.

Chapter Thirteen

When Is a Theoretical Strategy Not Cultural Materialism?

Comments on Kennedy's Critique of Evolutionary Materialism and Darwinian Conflict Theory

Stephen K. Sanderson

I APPRECIATE KENNEDY'S INTEREST in my work and his thoughtful critique of the two related paradigms that I have developed in the past decade. It is especially gratifying to learn that Kennedy, a former student of Harris, thinks that both my evolutionary materialism and my Darwinian conflict theory are improvements on Harris's cultural materialism and push it in a useful and productive direction.

Regarding his criticisms of my paradigms, Kennedy raises a number of important points that are indeed food for thought. Some of these points I agree with, but I am afraid that with respect to others I must demur. The first major issue raised by Kennedy is whether my evolutionary materialism (EM) is sufficiently distinct from cultural materialism (CM) to constitute a separate paradigm. He argues that it is not, and in fact Harris has made a similar argument (see Chapter 10). I can agree with this, but only up to a point. When I developed EM back in the mid-1990s, I did not claim for it entirely new paradigmatic status. I claimed that it had some novel features not found in EM, but that for the most part it was a formalization and extension of the most basic arguments of CM. And Kennedy is also correct to note that the main differences between EM and CM focus more on theories of specific phenomena than on general principles. The main example he cites, quite appropriately, is Harris's and my

256

explanations of the rise of modern capitalism. Kennedy is right on target to say that our two explanations differ in important ways. Harris emphasizes ecological degradation and downplays the role of most of the factors I emphasize, namely, geography, climate, and societal size in the context of a long-term trend of expanding world commercialization. Indeed, Harris has contended that what is correct in my explanation he had already said, and therefore is not novel, whereas what is novel in my argument is not correct! (See Chapter 10.)

However, there are two critical differences between EM and CM that Kennedy either does not take sufficiently into account, or concerning which he misrepresents my argument. One key difference focuses on how the respective paradigms explain social evolution. Harris thinks that social evolution is a largely unitary process in the sense that the factors that determine major evolutionary transitions are the same for all historical periods. By contrast, I argue quite explicitly that social evolution is not this unitary, and that there are different "evolutionary logics" operating in different historical periods. In precapitalist social evolution, demographic and ecological factors seem to me to loom larger than they do in modern capitalist evolution, whereas in the latter the role of "economic" factors looms larger than it does in precapitalist evolution. This difference is an extremely important one. Whether it is important enough to allow us to regard EM as a separate paradigm from CM is difficult to say. But whether there are two distinct paradigms or simply two different versions of the same paradigm, EM and CM are certainly different.

This difference is closely related to another area of divergence: how to conceptualize "economy" and where to place it within the tripartite compartmentalization of sociocultural systems. Following Brian Ferguson (1995), Kennedy wants to distinguish between "infrastructural economy" (or "subsistence economy") and "structural economy" (or "political economy"), and put them in two separate sociocultural components. Kennedy criticizes me for blurring this important distinction and causing confusion. In this light he goes on to argue that Harris's explanation for the feminist revolution that began in the 1960s emphasizes infrastructural factors. However, I see both of Kennedy's contentions as highly problematic. First, it is much more difficult to distinguish between infrastructural and structural economy than he thinks, and the case of the feminist revolution illustrates this very well. Harris claims that women "left home" for two main reasons: They were pulled into the workforce by the expanding service-and-information sector of the economy, which was looking for cheap and docile labor, and they were pushed into it by inflation and declining living standards. Everyone would undoubtedly agree that these two factors are both "economic." But are they political economy or subsistence economy? In fact, they are both, and almost inseparably so. It could be argued, I suppose, that the economic changes that pulled women out of the home were changes in the sphere of political economy, whereas the changes that pushed them out involved changes in the realm of subsistence economy, meaning economy at the household level. However, this distinction is not as clear as it might appear, since the subsistence (household) economy is an inseparable part of the political economy of capitalism; people are working in the political economy to earn incomes that are part of the household or subsistence economy. This is one of the reasons I am reluctant to embrace the distinction between infrastructural and structural economy.

But there is another reason, which is that if we do so then we end up with the kind of eclecticism that Kennedy does not like and that, in fact, he thinks is characteristic of my own work.[1] Indeed, in formulating the distinction between infrastructural and structural economy, Ferguson contends that Harris was becoming more theoretically flexible as he got older in admitting structural explanations into his explanatory repertoire. Ferguson actually draws a distinction between two versions of cultural materialism, what could be called the broad and narrow versions. The narrow version amounts to explaining all of structure and superstructure by reference to infrastructure, whereas the broad version gives infrastructure the most causal weight while at the same time bringing structure causally into play. It is this broader version that Ferguson believes Harris was using more and more in his later works. But I am skeptical. This would have amounted to eclecticism on Harris's part and a corruption of his own hallowed Principle of Infrastructural Determinism, and it is hard to imagine Harris engaging in such a thing.

Kennedy is also troubled by my contention that capitalism is a system that "expands of its own accord," actually going so far as to claim that this commits me to essentialism and teleology. I don't really know what Kennedy means by the charge of essentialism, but since I do not consider essentialism necessarily to be anything to worry about—indeed, my Darwinian conflict theory is highly essentialist from the point of view of the social constructionists—I will slide over this charge. But teleology? Dr. Kennedy, that is a fighting word! In the book I wrote some sixteen years ago, *Social Evolutionism* (Sanderson, 1990), and that has just appeared in a heavily revised form (Sanderson, 2007), I have taken great pains to separate teleological theories of social evolution from nonteleological ones and to argue that teleological theories are fatally flawed. If anyone would seek to avoid even the slightest whiff of teleology, that person would be I!

In my argument that there is an "inherent tendency" for capitalism to expand, I am simply falling back on one of the most fundamental features of Marxian economics: Marx's argument that the basic principle that drives capitalism is "ceaseless capital accumulation." Capitalism is a system in which the economic producers seek to maximize profits and to accumulate capital over time. Since there are many capitalists rather than just one, they compete with one another. Because they all have the same basic goal, each must behave so as to outcompete the others in terms of maximizing and accumulating profit, and the aggregate effect of this behavior will be continual expansion of the system. This expansion springs entirely from the self-interested economic behavior of individual capitalists. There is nothing mystical about it, and certainly nothing even remotely teleological. When I say that it is the "system" that has an evolutionary logic to expand of its own accord, all that is implied is a process of ratcheting up that is entirely driven by individuals acting in their own interests. There is no transcendent entity that is pulling the system toward some goal or end-state.

Turning now to my Darwinian conflict theory (DCT), I am pleased that Kennedy thinks my biomaterialist theory of fertility decline is better supported by the evidence than Harris's ecomaterialist theory. However, I am astonished to hear Kennedy say that

DCT is not only consistent with CM, but is even more faithful to CM than CM itself! It is probably fortunate for all of us, including Harris himself, that Harris is dead and therefore unable to read Kennedy's remarks, for, knowing Marvin, he would probably be apoplectic if he were to see them. What on earth does Kennedy mean? Kennedy agrees with me and with some of the other contributors to this volume that Harris was wrong to have been so hostile to sociobiological explanations. Kennedy and I also agree that many cultural materialist theories are consistent with sociobiological principles if we regard the materialist theories as proximate explanations that spring from ultimate biological causes. For example, Harris's third biopsychological constant—people are highly sexed and gain pleasure from sexual intercourse, most often heterosexual intercourse—makes perfect sense in terms of a human drive for the maximization of reproductive success (in fact, it makes sense *only* in terms of such a drive).

However, Harris wanted to limit his conception of human nature to just four biopsychological constants. DCT goes much further and identifies well over a dozen. And what is more, many of the features of human nature proposed by DCT are flatly rejected by Harris as being any part of human nature at all. As I showed in Chapter 10 in this volume, whereas DCT holds that humans have innate tendencies to seek prestige, wealth, and power, Harris argues that these are "socially constructed" rather than biologically given human motives. And this is but one example. There are many other instances in which the explanations of DCT are not merely *different from* those of CM, and not merely *inconsistent with* those of CM, but *flatly in direct contradiction to* those of CM. Some of these instances have already been discussed in Chapter 10.

Kennedy says that "the refutation of Harris's explanation of fertility decline is not necessarily a refutation of cultural materialism." Kennedy is correct if by "refutation of cultural materialism" we are talking about a thoroughgoing rejection of its leading principles. Certainly that is true. But, as I have sought to show in Chapter 10, there has now been such an accumulation of Darwinian explanations that are so sharply opposed to Harris's cultural materialist explanations, and that seem to be much better empirically supported, that a substantial part of the cultural materialist apparatus must be called into question. The first part of Kennedy's chapter more or less ends up with the contention that EM is, in fact, just a slightly different version of CM, if not actually CM itself. And while I would not fight to the death to challenge that argument despite my contention that EM has a number of elements that make it distinctive, the claim in the second part of the paper that DCT *is also really CM, just a new and improved version of CM,* compels me to protest, and vigorously. Kennedy says that, although Harris would have resisted them, life history and other evolutionary theories of fertility decline do not contain any elements that contradict the basic tenets of CM. On the contrary, *they most certainly do!* These evolutionary theories propose completely different mechanisms for fertility regulation than Harris has proposed. My own regression analyses (Sanderson and Dubrow, 2000) show that it is not the economic benefits or costs of children that determine fertility levels, as Harris proposes, but rather primarily the rate of infant and child survival (and secondarily the level of female empowerment).

Let me simply conclude with a question for Kennedy. After announcing that EM is in fact mostly CM, and that even DCT is also pretty much CM, when, exactly, is an alternative formulation something other than CM? The reason I raise this question is because I sense in Kennedy's chapter some sort of (perhaps unconscious) inclination to see cultural materialist principles at work no matter what. How else would we interpret Kennedy's utterly baffling statement that my incorporation of biological variables into my materialist approach is "a perfect example of the flexibility of cultural materialism." (As I write this I am trying to imagine the look on the face of Marvin Harris, back from the grave, upon learning of this remarkable flexibility!) Nearly half a century ago, during the time when functionalism dominated American sociology, the well-known sociologist Kingsley Davis (1959) wrote an article in which he claimed that there was nothing special about functionalism and that virtually all sociological approaches were functionalist anyway—an argument a great many sociologists (myself included) have not found persuasive. Kennedy seems on the cusp of being a latter-day anthropological Kingsley Davis.

Note

1. Kennedy thinks that, in relying on world-systems theory, I end up with an eclectic position because he regards the world-system as part of the structure rather than the infrastructure. This is one aspect of the alleged mechanical juxtaposition that he sees as a weakness in EM. The problem is, world-systems theory is not about structure at all, but about infrastructure. It is just as materialist a theory as cultural materialism, and thus all I am doing in borrowing from it is broadening the scope of cultural materialism by bringing it into contact with another materialist theory, one with which it is in principle highly compatible.

Kennedy also sees mechanical juxtaposition in my failure to employ elements of CM and world-systems theory at the same time and for the same phenomena—for example employing CM for precapitalist social evolution and world-systems theory for capitalist evolution. I can only say in response that Kennedy is setting the bar for what should count as a theoretical synthesis unrealistically high. If something is to be counted as a genuine synthesis only if it explains all phenomena at all times in precisely the same way, then I doubt that there have ever been any true syntheses in any of the social sciences, or for that matter even in any of the natural sciences. I cannot meet Kennedy's standards and it is hard to imagine anyone who could.

Moreover, Kennedy's claim that world-systems theory is unable to contribute to the explanation of events in prehistory is highly questionable, and it is untrue that I employ world-systems analysis only for modern times. Andre Gunder Frank and Barry Gills (1993) have applied their own version of world-systems analysis to the past 5,000 years, and Christopher Chase-Dunn and Thomas Hall (1997) have developed a different version of world-systems analysis that is devoted to comparing world-systems and to explaining world-system transformations over an even longer period of time. I was greatly influenced by Frank and Gills's conceptualization of a "5000-year world system" in developing my notion of "expanding world commercialization," a notion that formed a critical part of my explanation of the transition to modern capitalism.

Appendix A: Requiscat in Pace— Obituaries of Marvin Harris

Marvin Harris, 74, Is Dead; Professor Was Iconoclast of Anthropologists

Douglas Martin

MARVIN HARRIS, an anthropologist who spent his career adding fuel to the fires of academic controversy, as when he theorized that the cannibalism of the Aztecs was motivated by protein deprivation, died on Thursday in Gainesville, Florida, where he lived. He was 74.

His daughter, Susan, said the cause was complications after hip surgery.

Dr. Harris, called "one of the most controversial anthropologists alive" by *Smithsonian* magazine in 1986, believed that human social life was shaped in response to the practical problems of human existence. He argued essentially that cultural differences did not matter much, a novel approach in a discipline dedicated to studying cultural differences.

The Washington Post described him in 1983 as "a storm center in his field." And the *Smithsonian* article said he pitted himself "against the mainstream of anthropological thought."

He even took on anthropology's godmother, Margaret Mead, though he was quick to point out that in this he was hardly alone. "There's never been anything other than a good deal of disquiet about her methods," he told *The New York Times* in 1983.

Dr. Harris, who called his approach "cultural materialism," was an anthropology professor at Columbia University from 1953 until 1980, including three years as department chairman. From 1980 until 2000, he held a graduate research professorship at the University of Florida.

But his provocative ideas, and equally provocative presentation, gave him a sphere of influence greatly exceeding that of an ordinary academic. Many of his 17 books were aimed at general audiences.

The Hindu ban on killing cows? Absolutely necessary as a strategy of human existence, Dr. Harris contended: they are much more valuable for plowing fields and providing milk than as a one-time steak dinner.

"Westerners think that Indians would rather starve than eat their cows," he told *Psychology Today.* "What they don't understand is that they will starve if their *do* eat their cows."

In Dr. Harris's view, then, a manufactured "divine intervention" was needed to encourage people simply to do the practical thing.

The Jewish and Muslim bans on eating pork? Pigs eat the same foods as humans, he reasoned, and are expensive to keep.* Sheep, goats and cattle, by contrast, thrive on grass, and provide wool, milk and labor.

Warfare? A way of curbing population when protein gets scarce. Neckties? A badge men wear to indicate they are above physical labor.

Witchcraft? A convenient culprit for the rising protest that church and state faced from the 15th century to the 17th.

Dr. Harris's zest for controversy was suggested by the title of an article he wrote for *The New York Times Magazine* in 1977: "Why Men Dominate Women." So was his contention that Aztec cannibalism sprang from a need for protein sufficiency, a view that drew some strong opposition. "It takes an heroic act of utilitarian faith to conclude that this sacrificial system was a way the Aztecs had for getting more meat," Marshall Sahlins wrote in *The New York Review of Books* in 1978.

Marvin Harris was born in Brooklyn. Growing up in New York City in the 1930s, he wanted to understand the millions of strangers around him. He would stare at the windows of apartment buildings, wondering about the figures behind them. He graduated from Columbia, then earned his doctorate there. As a young professor, he was critical of the university's administration and a strong supporter of student protests of the 1960s. David B. Truman, vice president and provost, accused him of "authoritarian madness."

Though his studies took him throughout the world, from Brazil to Mozambique to India, he kept his own country in his anthropological sights. In *The Anthropology of a Changing Culture* (Simon & Schuster, 1981), he railed against homegrown outrages he perceived, from appliances that did not work to bloated government bureaucracies.

In *The New York Times Book Review,* Robert Lekachman called the book—which was rereleased in 1987 under the author's original title, *Why Nothing Works: The Anthropology of Daily Life*—a "remarkably concise, angry outcry at the current condition of America."

His other books included *Cannibals and Kings* (Random House, 1977) and *Culture, People, Nature,* which became a widely used anthropology textbook.

In addition to his daughter, who lives in the San Francisco area, he is survived by his wife, Madeline.

Reprinted by permission from *The New York Times,* October 28, 2001, p. A36.

*It is important to add that Harris was arguing that pigs are expensive to keep not so much in general, but especially in the hot, dry climate of the Middle East, which is why only the religions that arose in this region banned them. Pigs are eaten widely throughout the rest of the world.—Editors.

Marvin Harris (1927–2001)

Maxine L. Margolis and Conrad Phillip Kottak

Marvin Harris, one of the most prominent contributors to 20th-century anthropological theory, died on October 25, 2001, in Gainesville, Florida. He taught at Columbia University from 1953 until 1980, serving as chair of the Department of Anthropology from 1963 to 1966. From 1980 until his retirement in 2000, he was graduate research professor of anthropology at the University of Florida.

Harris was born on August 18, 1927, in Brooklyn, New York, where he grew up. He attended the Erasmus Hall High School and then entered Columbia College. His first exposure to anthropology came as an undergraduate there, in an introductory course taught by Charles Wagley. The course spanned two semesters—physical anthropology and archaeology the first semester, cultural anthropology and linguistics the second. According to Harris, the basic outline of this course could be traced back to Franz Boas. The essentials of Boas's original course, Harris liked to say, influenced later generations of Columbia anthropologists and the four-field textbooks they eventually wrote (including his own). Although he became a severe critic of Boas's idiographic approach and historical particularism, Harris was a staunch defender of Boas's vision of four-field anthropology, and of the Boasian stance on race, language, and culture,

Harris went on to graduate work in anthropology at Columbia, earning his Ph.D. in 1953. Like others in his cohort, he was trained in four-field anthropology, taking courses and passing graduate-level exams in all the subfields. During his teaching years at Columbia, his colleagues included Harold Conklin, Morton Fried, Joseph Greenberg, Margaret Mead, Harold Shapiro, Ralph Solecki, and Wagley. Throughout his career, Harris addressed large questions in and across the subfields; he admired those, like Greenberg, who did the same.

Harris is best known as the originator of cultural materialism, a theoretical paradigm and research strategy aimed at providing causal explanations for differences and similarities in cultural behavior. Harris introduced the term *cultural materialism* in his magnum opus, *The Rise of Anthropological Theory* (1968b)—"the RAT," as it is known to two generations of students. First published in 1968, the RAT was eventually translated into Italian, Spanish, and Malaysian. In 1991, the Social Science Citation Index and the Arts and Humanities Citation Index named the book a "citation classic."

The RAT was a byproduct of a graduate course Harris gave at Columbia in the 1960s (which both of us took). The course critiqued what he saw as prevailing idealist and idiographic approaches in anthropology. The continued dominance of such paradigms, in what he viewed as their various transformations (ethnoscience, symbolic and interpretive anthropology, structuralism, and postmodernism) would concern Harris until his death. That concern is the theme of his last book, a series of his essays entitled *Theories of Culture in Post-Modern Times* (1999).

Harris organized his course and the RAT to show that earlier social theorists had never developed a totally satisfactory materialist and nomothetic (generalizing) research strategy dedicated to explaining the evolution of sociocultural differences and similarities. The RAT is truly a history of anthropological theory. Through the lens of cultural materialism it analyzes individual theories and schools of thought from the 18th century through the 1960s. It begins with the Enlightenment—the era Harris identifies as the one in which naturalistic causal explanations of cultural phenomena were first established, a modern conception of culture began to evolve, and materialist explanations of cultural similarities and differences first appeared. Harris explores the reaction against naturalism and materialism and their eventual replacement by hardcore biological determinism that, with the notable exception of Marxist materialism, held sway over anthropological theory into the early 20th century. Franz Boas and his followers rescued anthropology from biological reductionism only to replace it with an idiographic strategy that, from Harris's perspective, did little to advance anthropology as a scientific enterprise. This was followed by a return to explanatory models in the form of neoevolutionist and ecological approaches to the study of culture.

The RAT ends with chapters on cultural evolutionism and cultural ecology, which Harris saw as coming closest to the paradigm he was proposing. While admiring a nomothetic cultural evolutionary approach, he faulted Leslie White for his lack of interest in environmental variation and for his emphasis on symboling and culturology. The anthropologist treated most favorably in the RAT was Julian Steward, whose combined interests in cultural evolution and cultural ecology, and whose concept of the culture core, came closest to Harris's own model of techno-environmental determinism.

Although the RAT used cultural materialism as a framework for evaluating previous theories, the full elaboration and defense of Harris's approach was realized in *Cultural Materialism: The Struggle for a Science of Culture* (1979). (Like the RAT, it was reissued in 2001.) The yardstick Harris used in the RAT to evaluate specific theories and schools of thought was the degree to which they aided the understanding of cross-cultural similarities and differences. In his view, cultural materialism is the theoretical paradigm best able to achieve that goal. Cultural materialism evolved from and was influenced by a number of theoretical currents, including evolutionary theory, cultural ecology, and Marxist materialism. Harris acknowledges his debt to all of them, especially the last. But he emphatically separates his own model from dialectical materialism, as well as from the program for political action that is so closely associated with Marxist materialism.

* * *

Harris published 17 books, collectively translated into 14 languages. He applied his theoretical principles in several popular books written in an accessible style (1974, 1977,

1981, 1985, 1989). In all of them Harris attempts to provide scientific explanations for what he calls "the riddles of culture," an approach that made him both highly influential and controversial. He also wrote two widely used introductory textbooks that have gone through several editions each, *Culture, People, Nature* (1997) and *Cultural Anthropology* (2002, with Orna Johnson).

Harris carried out field research in Brazil, Mozambique, India, and the United States. His ethnographic study of Minas Velhas in Bahia state yielded *Town and Country in Brazil* (1956) and a chapter in *Race and Class in Rural Brazil* (Wagley, 1952). Wagley, Harris's dissertation chair and long-time collaborator and associate at Columbia and Florida, was a coauthor of *Minorities in the New World* (1958).

Harris did groundbreaking work on race. *Patterns of Race in the Americas* (1964b) is a systematic comparison, using a cultural materialist framework, of the divergent racial patterns that emerged in Brazil, the United States, the Caribbean, and highland Latin America. Harris took particular issue with "cultural heritage" and national character explanations of racial patterns, particularly those advanced by historian Frank Tannenbaum for the Carribean and by Brazilian social theorist Gilberto Freyre for Brazil. Freyre had stressed the role of Portuguese national character in forming Brazilian race relations, and indeed in creating a "new world in the tropics," based on a penchant for racial tolerance and mixture. Harris argued persuasively for the role of material conditions in forming the patterns of race in different parts of the Americas. He also took issue with Freyre's contention that slaves received more humane treatment in Brazil than in the United States, supposedly because of differences in Portuguese and English national character, religion, and attitudes toward non-Europeans. Harris confronted the harsher dimensions of Brazilian race relations. While providing a vivid description of racial prejudice in Minas Velhas, he also showed that prejudice did not necessarily translate into systematic discrimination. Again, he took issue with the notion that attitudes and temperament are the best predictors of behavior.

Harris is well known for his work on Brazilian racial classification, especially his research on the multiple racial categories in everyday use throughout Brazil and their relation to the categories used in the Brazilian census. The last fieldwork he conducted, in the early 1990s, took him back to Minas Velhas, where he worked with the Brazilian social anthropologist Josildeth Consorte. Their field team conducted an experiment, operating like census takers and using random samples of residents (see Harris et al. 1993). One sample was asked to self identify with reference to the four terms used in the official census; for another sample, the common term *moreno* ("brunet," an intermediate color term) replaced the official term *pardo* ("brown," an intermediate color term). Harris found that when given the opportunity of choosing *moreno* rather than *pardo*, many more Brazilians classified themselves as mixed race, and there were fewer self-identified whites. Harris hoped to convince sociologists and others who routinely make use of Brazilian census data of the serious overestimation of the white, and underestimation of the mixed, segments of the national population.

Writing with Conrad Kottak (1963) Harris coined the term *hypodescent* to contrast U.S. and Brazilian racial classification. With hypodescent, mixed children (e.g., those from a union between an African-American and a Euro-American) are always assigned to the minority category. Hypodescent did not operate in Brazil, where racial classification was based more on phenotype and social perceptions, and where full siblings could be classified as members of different social races (to use a term coined by Wagley 1968).

In 1955–56 Harris traveled to Mozambique to study acculturation among the Ba Thonga. He was critical of Radcliffe-Brown's classic article "The Mother's Brother in South Africa" (1952), questioning its extensionist interpretation and already seeking a materialist alternative. Once in Mozambique Harris became interested in politics and did not complete his planned fieldwork. Nevertheless, he did later offer a convincing materialist alternative to Radcliffe-Brown's extensionist explanation for the South African avunculate (1968b:527–530).

Harris wrote of Mozambican oppression and advocated independence for the country in *Portugal's African "Wards"* (1958), an important but barely known publication. According to Antonio de Figueiredo, who served as his informal assistant in Mozambique, Harris's "one-year field study in Mozambique in 1955–56 and his subsequent denunciations of the plight of Africans under Portuguese rule decisively influenced the abolition of the forced labor system a few years later. He had a close friendship with Eduardo Modlane, who gave up his own academic career in America to lead Frelimo, the Mozambique liberation movement" (2001). Modlane would become the first president of independent Mozambique.

Harris's fieldwork in India was inspired by the reading he did to write "The Cultural Ecology of India's Sacred Cattle" (1966). Again attacking the primacy of the ideological over the material, Harris was concerned with demonstrating the many roles that sacred cattle play in Indian ecosystems. He interpreted the Hindu doctrine of ahimsa as using the full force of religion to conserve a vital resource—the sacred cow. In *Cows, Pigs, Wars, and Witches* (1974), arguably his most influential popular book, Harris turned his materialist gaze on other "riddles of culture," including the Jewish and Muslim taboos against pork.

Cannibals and Kings (1977), another fascinating read, took a historical/diachronic view of some of these cases but extended Harris's analyses to new riddles of culture. The most prominent was Aztec cannibalism, which he interpreted in the context of protein shortages because of the lack of significant animal domestication in Mesoamerica. This position led to an exchange with Marshall Sahlins, whom Harris faulted for what he saw as a conversion from a more materialist evolutionism to Lévi-Straussian structuralism. *Good to Eat* (1985) was an attack on Lévi-Strauss's contention that classificatory systems involving food taboos could be understood mainly because they were "good to think." Harris argued that a better approach is to see animals first as good for the body rather than the mind. Harris's popular books also showed his enduring fascination with the Yanomamö, principally as described by Napoleon Chagnon. He rejected Chagnon's initial sociopolitical explanation for Yanomamö warfare, as well as Chagnon's subsequent use of explanatory models from human evolutionary ecology. Harris insisted that protein shortages provided the best explanation for Yanomamö raiding patterns.

Our Kind (1989) completes a quartet of Harris's books aimed at explaining riddles of culture. His renown spread beyond academic circles through these readable, intriguing, and controversial works. Harris liked to compare the riddles of culture to potato chips—no one can eat just one. Whenever he offered a solution for one riddle, someone would say "yes, but what about X?" Of the books in the quartet, *Our Kind* is most like a bag of potato chips; Harris provides very short explanations for dozens of cultural riddles.

Also popular was Harris's account of the service and information economy in his 1981 book originally entitled *America Now,* later republished as *Why Nothing Works,* Harris's original choice for the title. He sought to highlight and explain the deficiencies of an economy shifting from heavy goods manufacture to services and information. Using his consistent cultural materialist framework, Harris showed how changes in the economy were reflected in U.S. social organization (marriage, the family, gender roles, and sexual relations) and ideology.

Harris was a major force in training students in the science of anthropology. At Columbia and later at Florida, his popular theory courses were filled with hard-driving debates and students who found his critical style invigorating. His concern with the direction the Columbia department was taking during the late 1970s led him to leave that university and his Leonia, New Jersey, home to move to Gainesville. Having earned an early reputation for combativeness in defense of his theoretical principles, Harris mellowed in Florida. There he spent several more productive years teaching, training students, writing books, and practicing his skills in architectural planning and carpentry. For many years Marvin and his wife Madeline summered on the Maine coast on Great Cranberry Island. Guests at their home were treated to memorable dinners, day-long fishing trips, and sunset cocktail cruises aboard the Maddy Sue, Marvin's 36-foot "lobster yacht" built in 1932.

Always a strong proponent of four-field anthropology, Marvin Harris served as President of the General Anthropology Division (GAD) of the American Anthropological Association (1988–90). Concerned about the fragmentation and compartmentalization of anthropology, he and his successors established GAD as the strongest voice of four-field anthropology within the AAA. The AAA recognized his academic achievements by inviting him to give the 1990 Distinguished Lecture.

Harris's influence extended beyond cultural anthropology. As David Hurst Thomas has noted, "roughly half of the practicing American archaeologists consider themselves to be cultural materialists to one degree or another" (1989:120). As a result of the forcefulness of his ideas elaborated in his many publications, Harris's theoretical paradigm has become one of the best known in contemporary social science.

Marvin Harris is survived by Madeline Harris, his wife of almost fifty years, his daughter, Susan Harris, and many students, including the authors of this obituary.

Reprinted by permission from *American Anthropologist,* vol. 105, pp. 685–688, 2003.

Selected Other Obituaries of Marvin Harris

2001

"Marvin Harris, anthropologist: Added fuel to fire of controversy." *Plain Dealer* (Cleveland) (Final ed.), *Metro,* p. B5 (October 29).

"Obituaries, Marvin Harris, 74: Anthropologist, writer." By Myrna Oliver. *Los Angeles Times* (Record ed.), p. B10 (October 30).

"Marvin Harris dies: Anthropologist, educator, writer." *Washington Post* (Final ed.), *Metro,* p. B7 (October 31).

"Expert on human habits: Marvin Harris, anthropologist, born 1927, died October 25, 2001." *Herald Sun* (Melbourne, Australia), *Features,* p. 101 (November 2).

"Marvin Harris." *The Times* (London), *Features, Lives in Brief,* p. 19 (November 12).

"Milestones: Died, Marvin Harris." *Time* 158(21):33 (November 12).

"Obituary of Marvin Harris: Anthropologist who 'explained' taboos." *Daily Telegraph* (London), p. 25 (December 4).

"Obituary: Marvin Harris, making an impact in Mozambique and Brazil." *Guardian* (London) Guardian Leader Pages, p. 24 (December 13).

2002

"Marvin Harris." *Anthropology News* 43(1):31 (January).

"In memory of Marvin Harris 1927–2001." By Patrick Hughes. *CLASnotes* vol. 15–16, no. 12–1 (December 2001–January 2002). Available online at http://clasnews.clas.ufl.edu/news/clasnotes/0112–0201/harris.html.

2004

"Commentary on the obituary for Marvin Harris." By Paula G. Rubel and Abraham Rosman. *American Anthropologist* 106(1):212–213.

Appendix B: Bibliography of Marvin Harris, 1952–2001

Compiled by Pamela Effrein Sandstrom

Sources

This bibliography of writings by Marvin Harris was assembled using documentary sources sent in February 2002 by Harris's colleague at the University of Florida, anthropologist Maxine Margolis. These invaluable sources, presumably created and maintained by Harris during his lifetime, included "Biographical Sketch of Marvin Harris" (eight pages, [1990?]), "Recent Activities Report for Marvin Harris" (four pages, [1997?]), and "Books by Marvin Harris: Editions and Translations" (five pages, revised October 1, 1996). It has not been possible to verify ownership by U.S. or foreign lending libraries for all of the translations identified in the latter source, but the information is included here to alert readers to the existence of these imprints.

The compilation has been augmented to the fullest extent possible to include Harris's published letters, interviews, critical commentaries, book reviews, popular accounts, and reprints of his works in English and other languages. The entries were verified using the following bibliographic resources: the Institute for Scientific Information's Web of Science citation indexes (*Science Citation Index, Social Sciences Citation Index, Arts & Humanities Citation Index*), OCLC's *WorldCat* database, RLG/Eureka's *Research Library Group Union Catalog* and *Anthropology Plus* database (combining *Anthropological Literature* produced by Harvard University, and *Anthropological Index* produced by the Royal Anthropological Institute), *Academic Search Premier* produced by EBSCOhost, H. W. Wilson's *Readers' Guide Retrospective* and *Book Review Index,* the *IngentaConnect* database, ProQuest and LexisNexis Academic newspaper databases, and Web search engines such as Google. Publicly accessible Web sites dedicated to Harris or cultural materialism were consulted as an additional source of bibliographic information but are generally excluded from this compilation. Reviews of Harris's books are excluded.

Note on Arrangement

Works are listed in chronological order and alphabetically by title within years (except for regular columns in popular periodicals, which are chronologically listed). Harris's coauthored works are interfiled, with the order and form of coauthors' names as they appeared on the work.

Note on the CAMEO Analysis

Works marked with an asterisk [*] are source articles in the Institute for Scientific Information's Web of Science citation indexes, and included in the profiles contributing to Harris's publication CAMEO described in Chapter 1.

Acknowledgments

A note of appreciation goes to Maxine Margolis at the University of Florida for providing Harris's baseline bibliographic records, to Christine Smith and colleagues at Walter E. Helmke Library's Document Delivery Services, Indiana University–Purdue University Fort Wayne (IPFW), for their retrieval skills, and to Gail Kieler at IPFW for her typing assistance.

1952

"Race relations in Minas Velhas: A community in the mountain region of central Brazil." Pp. 47–81 in Charles Wagley (ed.). *Race and Class in Rural Brazil*. Paris: UNESCO. 2nd ed., Columbia University Press, 1963. Translations: French, UNESCO, 1952.
Review of Donald Pierson, *Cruz das Almas, a Brazilian Village,* 1948. *Hispanic American Historical Review* 32(2):248–250.

1953

Minas Velhas: A Study of Urbanism in the Mountains of Eastern Brazil. Ph.D. dissertation, Columbia University. UMI Dissertation Abstracts no. 0005191.

1955

Review of Fernando Márquez Miranda, *Región meridional de América del Sur: Periodo indígena,* 1954. *American Anthropologist* 57(4):883–884.

Charles Wagley and Marvin Harris. "A typology of Latin American subcultures." *American Anthropologist* 57(3):428–451. Reprinted as pp. 42–69 in Dwight B. Heath and Richard N. Adams (eds.), *Contemporary Cultures and Societies of Latin America.* New York: Random House, 1965. Spanish translation: Universidad de la Republica, 1963.

1956

Town and Country in Brazil. Columbia University Contributions to Anthropology, no. 37. New York: Columbia University Press. Reprinted by AMS Press, 1969, 1987, Norton, 1969, 1971.

1958

"The a*ssimilado* system in Portuguese Mozambique." *Africa Special Report* 3:7–10.
Charles Wagley and Marvin Harris. *Minorities in the New World: Six Case Studies.* New York: Columbia University Press. Paperback ed., 1959, 1964, 1967, 1970.
"Orellana's discovery of the Amazon." *The Grace Log* 33:12–13.
Portugal's African "Wards": A First-Hand Report on Labor and Education in Moçambique. Africa Today Pamphlets, 2. New York: American Committee on Africa.
Review of Elman R. Service, *A Profile of Primitive Culture,* 1958. *American Anthropologist* 60(6):1213–1214. [*]
Review of Lycurgo de Castro Santos Filho, *Uma comunidade rural do Brasil antigo: Aspectos da vida patriarcal no sertão da Bahai nos séculos XVIII e XIX,* 1956. *Hispanic American Historical Review* 38(3):399–400.

1959

Charles Wagley and Marvin Harris. *A Background Report on Brazil.* New York: Ford Foundation.
"Caste, class, and minority." *Social Forces* 37(3):248–254. [*]
"The economy has no surplus?" *American Anthropologist* 61(2):185–199. [*] Reprinted as pp. 185–189 in Bobbs-Merrill Reprint Series in the Social Sciences, A-107. Indianapolis, IN: Bobbs-Merrill.
"Labor emigration among the Moçambique Thonga: Cultural and political factors." *Africa: Journal of the International African Institute* 29(1):50–66. Reprinted as pp. 91–106 in Immanuel Wallerstein (ed.), *Social Change: The Colonial Situation.* New York: Wiley, 1966.
"Mozambique." In *The World Book Encyclopedia.* Chicago: World Book, Inc.
Review of Leo Kuper, Hilstan Lett Watts, and Ronald Davies, *Durban: A Study in Racial Ecology,* 1958. *American Anthropologist* 61(5):907–908. [*]
"South of Lisbon: See the 10,000,000" [review of James Duffy, *Portuguese Africa,* 1959]. *Saturday Review* 42(30):19–20 (July 25).

1960

"Adaptation in biological and cultural science." *Transactions of the New York Academy of Sciences* 23:32–65.

"Labour emigration among the Moçambique Thonga: A reply to Sr. Rita-Ferreira." *Africa: Journal of the International African Institute* 30(3):243–245 [commentary on A. Rita-Ferreira, "Labour migration among the Moçambique Thonga: Comments on a study by Marvin Harris." *Africa: Journal of the International African Institute* 30(2):141–152].

1961

"Reply to Rotstein's note." *American Anthropologist* 63(3):563 [commentary on Abraham Rotstein, "A note on the surplus discussion"]. *American Anthropologist* 63(3):561–563. [*]

1962

"Race relations in the United States: Research and auspices." *Social Science Information* new series 1:28–51.

"Sun above, mud below" [review of David St. Clair, *Child of the Dark: The Diary of Carolina María de Jesus,* 1962]. *Saturday Review* 45:27,51 (October 6).

1963

"Race." Pp. 36–54 in Joseph Bram et al. (eds.), *The Measure of Mankind.* New York: Dobbs Ferry; National Council of Women of the United States. Reprinted as pp. 123–135 in Lowell D. Holmes (ed.), *Readings in General Anthropology.* New York: Ronald Press, 1971.

Review of Frederick J. Simoons, *Eat Not This Flesh: Food Avoidances in the Old World,* 1961. *American Anthropologist* 65(3):767–768. [*]

Marvin Harris and Conrad Kottak. "The structural significance of Brazilian racial categories." *Sociologia* (Sao Paulo) 25(3):203–208.

1964

"Heritage of blood and dust" [review of Oscar Lewis, *Pedro Martínez: A Mexican Peasant and His Family,* 1964]. *Saturday Review* 47:29–30 (May 2).

The Nature of Cultural Things. New York: Random House. Portuguese translation, Civilização Brasileira, 1968.

Patterns of Race in the Americas. Walker Summit Library, no. 1. New York: Walker and Company. Reprinted by Norton, 1974, Greenwood Press, 1980. Chapters on "Race, culture, and manpower," pp. 11–24, and "The Highland heritage," pp. 25–43, excerpted as pp. 411–429 and pp. 395–409 in Daniel R. Gross (ed.), *Peoples and Cultures of Native South America: An Anthropological Reader.* Garden City, NY: American Museum of Natural History, Natural History Press, 1973. Chapter on "The myth of the friendly master," pp. 65–78, excerpted as pp. 191–209 in Ann J. Lane (ed.), *The Debate Over Slavery: Stanley Elkins and His Critics.* Urbana: University of Illinois Press, 1971. Portuguese translations, Civilização Brasileira, 1967, Ediciones Siglo Veinte, 1973.

"Racial identity in Brazil." *Luso-Brazilian Review* 1:21–28.

1965

"The myth of the sacred cow." Pp. 217–228 in Anthony Leeds and Andrew P. Vayda (eds.), *Man, Culture and Animals: The Role of Animals in Human Ecological Adjustments.* Washington, DC: American Association for the Advancement of Science. Reprinted as pp. 77–79 in Richard A. Gould (ed.), *Man's Many Ways.* New York: Harper & Row, 1977.

Review of Clodomir Vianna Moog, *Bandeirantes and Pioneers,* 1964. *Political Science Quarterly* 80(3):485–488. [*]

1966

"The cultural ecology of India's sacred cattle" [with "Comments" and Author's "Reply"]. *Current Anthropology* 7(1):51–66. Reprinted as pp. 377–384 in Jesse D. Jennings and E. Adamson Hoebel (eds.), *Readings in Anthropology.* 3rd ed. New York: McGraw-Hill, 1972. Reprinted as pp. 204–220 in David W. McCurdy and James P. Spradley (eds.), *Issues in Cultural Anthropology.* Boston: Little, Brown, 1979. Reprinted as pp. 282–296 in R. Jon McGee and Richard L. Warms (eds.), *Anthropological Theory: An Introductory History.* Mountain View, CA: Mayfield Publishing Co., 1996. Reprinted as *Current Anthropology* supplement 33(1):261–276 (1992) in Sydel Silverman (ed.), *Inquiry and Debate in the Human Sciences: Current Anthropology, 1960–1990* [special issue in celebration of the 50th anniversary of The Wenner-Gren Foundation for Anthropological Research]. [*]

Marvin Harris and George E. B. Morren. "The limitations of the principle of limited possibilities." *American Anthropologist* 68(1):122–127. [*]

"Race, conflict and reform in Mozambique." Pp. 157–183 in Stanley Diamond and Fred G. Burke (eds.), *The Transformation of East Africa: Studies in Political Anthropology.* New York: Basic Books.

1967

"The classification of stratified groups." Pp. 298–324 in Anthony Leeds (ed.), *Social Structure, Stratification, and Mobility = Estructura, estratificación y movilidad social.* Estudios y monografías, 20. Seminar on Social Structure, Stratification, and Mobility, Rio de Janeiro, Brazil, June 6–15, 1962. Washington, DC: Pan American Union, General Secretariat, Organization of American States.

"Diary of an anthropologist" [review of Bronislaw Malinowski, *A Diary in the Strict Sense of the Term,* 1967]. *Natural History* 76:72, 74 (August 1967).

"The myth of the sacred cow." *Natural History* 76(3):6–12,12A (March 1967). Reprinted in *Carnegie Magazine* 41(8):279–284 (October 1967). Summarized by John Speicher in "Sacred cow: Food or folly?" *Science World* (October):6–7, with "Teaching Guide" in *Scholastic Teacher* (October 12):5–6.

"Reply." *Current Anthropology* 8(3):252–253 [commentary on John W. Bennett, "On the cultural ecology of Indian cattle." *Current Anthropology* 8(3):251–252]. [*]

Review of Norman E. Whitten, Jr., *Class, Kinship, and Power in an Ecuadorian Town: The Negroes of San Lorenzo,* 1965. *Social Forces* 45(3):471–472. [*]

1968

"Big bust on Morningside Heights." *Nation* 206(24):757–763 (June 10).

"A *CA* book review: *The Rise of Anthropological Theory* by Marvin Harris" [with "Author's précis," sixteen "Reviews," and "Reply by Marvin Harris"]. *Current Anthropology* 9(5):519–533.

"Columbia: Onus of violence" [Cox Commission Report, editorial]. *Nation* 207(14):418–422 (October 28).

"Comment." *Current Anthropology* 9(1):20–21 [commentary on Leo A. Despres, "Anthropological theory, cultural pluralism, and the study of complex societies." *Current Anthropology* 9(1):3–26]. [*]

"Race." Pp. 263–269 in David L. Sills (ed.), *International Encyclopedia of the Social Sciences,* vol. 13. New York: Macmillan Company and The Free Press.

"Reminiscences of Marvin Harris: Oral history, 1968" [interview by John A. Roberts on conduct of the administration and faculty groups, April 23–30, 1968, and background of administration policy on Students for a Democratic Society, 50-page transcript, one audiotape reel]. Columbia University Oral History Project, Columbia Crisis of 1968 Project.

"Reply." *Current Anthropology* 9(2–3):218. [commentary on Walter P. Zenner, "On rationality and India's sacred cattle." *Current Anthropology* 9(2–3):218]. [*]

The Rise of Anthropological Theory: A History of Theories of Culture. New York: Thomas Y. Crowell. Updated ed., AltaMira Press, 2001. Chapter on "'Emics,' 'etics,' and the 'new ethnography,'" pp. 568–604, excerpted as pp. 102–135 in Morton H. Fried (ed.), *Readings in Anthropology.* 2nd ed. New York: Thomas Y. Crowell. British ed., Routledge and Kegan Paul, 1968, 1969. Translations: Italian, Il Molino, 1971; Spanish, Siglo Veintiuno, 1978, 1979, 1991, 1997, Siglo XXI Editores, 1996; Malay, Kementerian Pelejaran, Dewan Bahassa, 1984.

Morton Fried, Marvin Harris, and Robert Murphy (eds.). *War: The Anthropology of Armed Conflict and Aggression.* Garden City, NY: American Museum of Natural History, Natural History Press. Preliminary version published as "War: The anthropology of armed conflict and aggression" [papers from the plenary session of the 66th Annual Meeting of the American Anthropological Association, Washington, DC, November 30, 1967]. Supplement to *Natural History* 76(10):39–70 (December 1967). Translations: Japanese, Perikansha, 1968, 1970, 1977; German, S. Fischer Verlag, 1971.

1969

"Monistic determinism: Anti-Service." *Southwestern Journal of Anthropology* 25(2):198–206 [commentary on Elman Service, "The prime mover of cultural evolution." *Southwestern Journal of Anthropology* 24(4):396–409, 1986]. Reprinted as "Special issue, selected articles, 1945–1985." *Journal of Anthropological Research* 42(3):365–372 (1986). [*]

"Author vs. reviewer" [letter]. *Natural History* 78(1):72 (January) [commentary on Elman R. Service, review of *Rise of Anthropological Theory: A History of Theories of Culture,* 1968]. *Natural History* 77(10):74–75 (December 1968)].

Review of Arthur L. Stinchcombe, *Constructing Social Theories,* 1968. *American Anthropologist* 71(4):788–790.

"Reviews." *Current Anthropology* 10(2–3):203–204 [commentary on Michael Banton, "*CA* book review: *Race Relations.*" *Current Anthropology* 10(2–3):202–210].

1970

"Referential ambiguity in the calculus of Brazilian racial identity." *Southwestern Journal of Anthropology* 26(1):1–14. Published simultaneously as pp. 75–86 in Norman E. Whitten, Jr. and John F. Szwed (eds.), *Afro-American Anthropology: Contemporary Perspectives.* New York: The Free Press, 1970. [*]

"Reply." *Current Anthropology* 11(1):66–67 [commentary by Milton Altschuler, Jesse J. Frankel, and Derek Freeman, "On Harris's *Rise of Anthropological Theory.*" *Current Anthropology* 11(1):65–67, 1970]. [*]

Review of Herbert S. Klein, *Slavery in the Americas: Comparative Study of Virginia and Cuba,* 1978. *Political Science Quarterly* 85(1):146–149. [*]

1971

Culture, Man and Nature: An Introduction to General Anthropology. New York: Thomas Y. Crowell. Reissued as *Culture, People, Nature: An Introduction to General Anthropology,* 2nd ed., 1975. 3rd ed., Harper & Row, 1980. 4th ed., 1985. 5th ed., 1988. 5th ed., Volunteer Services for the Visually Handicapped [sound recording], 1988. 6th ed., HarperCollins, 1993. 7th ed., Addison Wesley Longman, 1997. Translations: Chinese, Gui guan tu shu you xian gong si, 1977, Zhejiang ren min chu ban she, 1992; Spanish, Alianza, 1981, 1987, 1991, 1998, 2002, 2004.

"Comments." *Current Anthropology* 12(2):199–201 [commentary on Alan Heston, "An approach to the sacred cow of India." *Current Anthropology* 12(2):191–209].

Review of Charles A. Valentine, *Culture and Poverty: Critique and Counter-Proposals,* 1968. *American Anthropologist* 73(2):330–331. [*]

1972

"Portugal's contribution to the underdevelopment of Africa and Brazil." Pp. 209–223 in Ronald Chilcote (ed.), *Protest and Resistance in Angola and Brazil.* Berkeley: University of California Press.

"The human strategy: Warfare old and new—Since the original reasons for war are no longer valid, why does it persist?" *Natural History* 81(3):18, 20 (March). [*]

"The human strategy: A trip through Ma Bell's zoo—Where can you find gibbons without fleas, schools of herring but no cod? Why, in your phone book, of course, Mr. Aardvark" [on zoonymy]. *Natural History* 81(4):6, 8, 12 (April). [*]

"The human strategy: Women's fib—Promise men anything but give them peace" [on female subordination]. *Natural History* 81(5):20, 22 (May). [*]

"The human strategy: How green the revolution—In Asia, the seeds of hope may become the seeds of destruction." *Natural History* 81(6):28–30 (June–July). [*]

"The human strategy: You are what they ate—Were our primordial ancestors aggressive meat eaters or supervegetarian freaks?" *Natural History* 81(7):24–25 (August–September). [*]

"The human strategy: Riddle of the pig—There have been many explanations for the dietary laws against pork, but none seemed quite kosher." *Natural History* 81(8):32,

34–36 (October). Reprinted as pp. 339–345 in David H. Spain (ed.), *Human Experience: Readings in Sociocultural Anthropology.* Homewood, IL: Dorsey Press, 1975. [*]

"The human strategy: One man's food is another man's whitewash—Only a peculiar minority of the world's adults drink milk." *Natural History* 81(9):12, 14 (November). [*]

"The human strategy: Bah, humbug!—All the calculators being given this Christmas might well be used to figure out the costs and obligations of gift giving." *Natural History* 81(10):21–25 (December). Reprinted as pp. 138–141 in H. Russell Bernard (ed.), *The Human Way: Readings in Anthropology.* New York: Macmillan, 1975. [*]

1973

"Reply." *Current Anthropology* 14(1–2):170 [commentary on Johannes W. Raum, "On Harris and the German culture-historical school." *Current Anthropology* 14(1–2):169–170].

"The human strategy: What goes up, may stay up—A 300-year-old cycle of ups and downs in Western women's fashions has been shattered, despite the designers." *Natural History* 82(1):18, 20–25 (January). [*]

"The human strategy: Riddle of the pig, II—'Pronouncements about the inexplicability of human events … are themselves often the chief obstacle to the advance of anthropological knowledge.'" *Natural History* 82(2):20, 22–25 (February). [*]

"The human strategy: The withering green revolution—Miracle seeds, like boomerangs, are not something you can cast into the developing countries and turn your back on." *Natural History* 82(3):20–22 (March). [*]

"The human strategy: The rites of summer—The bronzed look of today's sun-worshiping jet set would have been disparaged a century ago." *Natural History* 82(7):20–22 (August–September). [*]

1974

"Comments." *Current Anthropology* 15(3):225–226 [commentary on Derek Freeman, "The evolutionary theories of Charles Darwin and Herbert Spencer." *Current Anthropology* 15(3):211–237]. [*]

Cows, Pigs, Wars, and Witches: The Riddles of Culture. New York: Random House. Vintage Books ed., 1975, 1978, 1989, 1991. Chapter on "Potlatch," pp. 111–130, reprinted in *Annual Editions: Readings in Anthropology 1977–1978.* Guilford, CT: Dushkin Publishing Group. Chapter on "Mother cow," pp. 11–32, reprinted in *Annual Editions: Readings in Anthropology 1981–1982.* Guilford, CT: Dushkin Publishing Group. British ed., Hutchinson, 1975, Fontana, 1977. Translations: Dutch, Wetenshappelijke, 1976; Portuguese, Civilização Brasileira, 1978; Spanish, Alianza, 1980, 1981, 1984, 1986, 1998, 2003; Spanish [excerpts, sound recording], Santiago, Chile [s.n.], 2002; German, Umschau, 1981, Klett-Cotta, 1993; Korean, Han'gilsa, 1982, 2000; Polish, Panstwowy Instytut Wydawniczy, 1985; Japanese, Tokyosogen Sha, 1988; Chinese, Renlei Wenhua Zhimi, 1990, Shanghai wen yi chu ban she, 1990; Turkish, Imge Kitabevi, 1995.

"The emperor's clothing store" [review of John J. Honigmann, ed., *Handbook of Social and Cultural Anthropology,* 1973]. *Reviews in Anthropology* 1(2):170–184.

"The human strategy: Potlatch politics and kings' castles—Hunting and gathering tribes have never made the leap into the struggle for power and prestige." *Natural History* 83(5):10–19 (May). [*]

"Reply." *Current Anthropology* 15(3):323–324 [commentary on Corry Azzi, and Howard Weizmann, "More on India's sacred cattle." *Current Anthropology* 15(3):317–321].

"Why a perfect knowledge of all the rules one must know to act like a native cannot lead to the knowledge of how natives act." *Journal of Anthropological Research* 30(4):242–251. Reprinted as pp. 31–37 in *Annual Editions: Readings in Anthropology 1977–1978.* Guilford, CT: Dushkin Publishing Group. [*]

1975

"Male supremacy is on the way out: It was just a phase in evolution of culture" [interview by Carol Tavris]. *Psychology Today* 8(8):61–69 (January) [with insert by Carol Tavris, "A sketch of Marvin Harris: I don't see how you can write anything of value if you don't offend someone." *Psychology Today* 8(8):64–65]. [*]

"Reply." *Current Anthropology* 16(3):454–456 [commentary on H. Dieter Heinen, "On cultural materialism, Marx, and the 'Hegelian monkey.'" *Current Anthropology* 16(3):450–456]. [*]

1976

"History and significance of the emic/etic distinction." *Annual Review of Anthropology* 5:329–350. [*]

William Tulio Divale and Marvin Harris. "Population, warfare, and the male supremacist complex." *American Anthropologist* 78(3):521–538. [*]

"Lévi-Strauss et la palourde [Lévi-Strauss and the clam]: Réponse à la Conférence Gildersleeve de 1972." *L'Homme: Revue française d'anthropologie* 16(2–3):5–22. [*]

"Reply." *Current Anthropology* 17(2):331 [commentary on Philip Staniford, "On cultural materialism: Which is witch?" *Current Anthropology* 17(2):329–331]. [*]

1977

Cannibals and Kings: The Origins of Cultures. New York: Random House. Vintage Books ed., 1978, 1991. Recording for the Blind & Dyslexic [sound recording], 2005. British ed., Collins, 1977, 1978; Fontana, 1978. Translations: Spanish, Alianza, 1987, 1989, 1997, Argos, 1978, Salvat, 1986; Dutch, Spectrum, 1978; German, Umschau, 1978, Klett-Cotta, 1990; Finnish, Kirjayhtymä, 1979; French, Flammarion, 1979; Italian, Feltrinelli, 1980, 1992, 1996; Japanese, Hayakawa Shobo, 1979, 1990; Swedish, Prisma, 1979; Hebrew, Sifryat Po'alim, 1980; Norwegian, Gyldenda Norsk Forlag, 1980; Chinese, Huaxia chu ban she, 1988; Turkish, Imge Kitabevi, 1994.

"Why men dominate women." *New York Times Magazine,* pp. 46, 115–123 (November 13).

1978

"Celebration of us all" [review of Peter Farb, *Humankind,* 1978]. *New York Times Book Review* 83(11):13 (March 12). [*]

"Comments." *Current Anthropology* 19(3):515–517 [commentary on Paul Diener and Eugene E. Robkin, "Ecology, evolution, and the search for cultural origins: The question of Islamic pig prohibition." *Current Anthropology* 19(3):493–540].

"Dead roots" [letter]. *New York Times*, p. 34 (March 14) [commentary on Orlando Patterson, "Hidden dangers in the ethnic revival." *New York Times*, p. A17 (February 20)].

Marvin Harris and Edward O. Wilson. "Encounter: The envelope and the twig" [Marvin Harris and E. O. Wilson debate the claims of sociobiology]. *The Sciences* (New York) 18:10–15, 27.

Edward O. Wilson and Marvin Harris. "Heredity versus culture: A debate" [a debate on sociobiology moderated by Ann Carroll, excerpted from "Radio Smithsonian," February 15, 1978]. *Society* 15(6):60–63. Portions published as "Nature and nurture come out swinging." *New York Times*, sec. 4, p. 18 (February 26). Reprinted as pp. 459–467 in Jeanne Guillemin (ed.), *Anthropological Realities*. New Brunswick, NJ: Transaction Books, 1981. [*]

Marvin Harris and Eric B. Ross. "How beef became king." *Psychology Today* 12(5):88–94 (October). [*]

"India's sacred cow." *Human Nature* 1(2):28–36 (February) [with "Author's reply." *Human Nature* 1(5):10 (May)]. [*]

William Divale and Marvin Harris. "The male supremacist complex: Discovery of a cultural invention." *American Anthropologist* 80(3):668–671. [*]

"No end of messiahs." *New York Times*, Week in Review, Section 4, p. E21 (November 26).

William Divale, Marvin Harris, and Donald T. Williams. "On the misuse of statistics: A reply to Hirschfeld et al." *American Anthropologist* 80(2):379–386 [commentary on Lawrence A. Hirschfeld, James Howe, and Bruce Levin, "Warfare, infanticide, and statistical inference: A comment on Divale and Harris." *American Anthropologist* 80(1):110–115]. [*]

William Divale and Marvin Harris. "Reply to Lancaster and Lancaster." *American Anthropologist* 80(1):117–118 [commentary on Chet Lancaster and Jane Beckman Lancaster, "On the male supremacist complex: A reply to Divale and Harris." *American Anthropologist* 80(1):115–117]. [*]

Review of Maurice Bloch (ed.), *Marxist Analyses and Social Anthropology*, 1975. *Man* 13(3):483. [*]

1979

"'*Cannibals and Kings*': An exchange." *New York Review of Books* 26(11):51–53 (June 28) [commentary on Marshall Sahlins, "Culture as protein and profit." *New York Review of Books* 25(18):45–53 (November 23, 1978), and William Arens and Marshall Sahlins, "Cannibalism: An exchange." *New York Review of Books* 26(4):45–47 (March 22)]. [*]

"Comments." *Current Anthropology* 20(3):479–482 [commentary on Frederick Simoons, "Questions in the sacred cow controversy." *Current Anthropology* 20(3):467–493].

Cultural Materialism: The Struggle for a Science of Culture. New York: Random House. Vintage Books ed., 1980. Updated ed., AltaMira Press, 2001. New ed., Rowman and Littlefield, 2001. Translations: Spanish, Alianza, 1982, 1985; Italian, Feltrinelli, 1984; Japanese, Hayakawa Shobo, 1987; Chinese, Hua xia chu ban she, 1988, People's Publishing House, 1989; Korean, Minimusa, 1996. Chapter on "The epistemology of cultural materialism," pp. 29–45, excerpted as pp. 408–423 in Paul A. Erickson and Liam D. Murphy (eds.), *Readings for a History of Anthropological Theory*. Peterborough, Ontario: Broadview Press, 2001. Chapter translated as "La epistemología del materialismo" [sound recording]. Santiago, Chile: s.n., 2002.

"The human strategy: Our pound of flesh—Human populations that are conditioned to prefer animal sources of protein are better prepared for the inevitable and unexpected stresses of life." *Natural History* 88(7):30, 32, 34–36 (August–September). [*]

"The human strategy: It's only a cod—As fish stocks are depleted, they are exploited all the more avidly." *Natural History* 88(9):101–103 (November). [*]

"The Yanomamö and the causes of war in band and village societies." Pp. 121–132 in Maxine L. Margolis and William E. Carter (eds.), *Brazil, Anthropological Perspectives: Essays in Honor of Charles Wagley.* New York: Columbia University Press.

1980

"History and ideological significance of the separation of social and cultural anthropology." Pp. 391–407 in Eric B. Ross (ed.), *Beyond the Myths of Culture: Essays in Cultural Materialism.* New York: Academic Press.

Review of Ronald Cohen and Elman R. Service (eds.), *Origins of the State: The Anthropology of Political Evolution,* 1978. *American Anthropologist* 82(2):427–429. [*]

"Sociobiology and biological reductionism." Pp. 311–335 in Ashley Montagu (ed.), *Sociobiology Examined.* New York: Oxford University Press.

1981

America Now: The Anthropology of a Changing Culture. New York: Simon & Schuster. Touchstone ed., 1982. Abridged English ed. published in Japan, Shohakusha, 1985. Updated ed. published as *Why Nothing Works: Anthropology of Daily Life.* Simon & Schuster/Touchstone, 1987. Translations: French-Canadian, Stanké, 1982; Italian, Feltrinelli, 1983; Korean, Han'guk Pangsong Saoptan, 1983, Hwanggum Kaji, 1996; Japanese, Saimaru Shuppankai, 1984; Spanish, Alianza, 1984, 1985, 1994, 2000.

"Foreword." Pp. vii–ix in Leela Gulati, *Profiles in Female Poverty: A Study of Five Poor Working Women in Kerala.* Studies in Sociology and Social Anthropology. Delhi: Hindustan Publishing Corp. Pergamon Press ed., 1982.

"Reply to Freed and Freed." *Current Anthropology* 22:492–494 [commentary on Stanley A. Freed and Ruth S. Freed, "Sacred cows and water buffalo in India: The uses of ethnography." *Current Anthropology* 22(5):483–502].

"Why it's not the same old America" [excerpts from *America Now: The Anthropology of a Changing Culture,* 1981, erroneously titled by editors *Why America Changed: Our Cultural Crisis*]. *Psychology Today* 15(8):23+ (August) [with insert by Howard Muson, "Where Marvin Harris stands." *Psychology Today* 15(8):34–35 (August)]. [*]

1982

A. Vaidyanathan, K. N. Nair, and Marvin Harris. "Bovine sex and species ratios in India" [with "Comments" and "Reply"]. *Current Anthropology* 23(4):365–383. [*]

"Reply to Paul J. Magnarella." *American Anthropologist* 84(1):142–146 [commentary on Paul J. Magnarella, "Cultural materialism and the problem of probabilities." *American Anthropologist* 84(1):138–142, with "Reply to Marvin Harris." *American Anthropologist* 84(1):146]. [*]
Review of Ken Auletta, *The Underclass*, 1982. *Psychology Today* 16(6):81+. [*]

1983

Cultural Anthropology. New York: Harper & Row. 2nd ed., 1987. 3rd ed., HarperCollins, 1991. 4th ed., 1995. Marvin Harris and Orna Johnson, 5th ed., Allyn & Bacon, 2000. 6th ed., 2003. 6th ed., Recording for the Blind and Dyslexic [sound recording], 2002. Translations: Spanish, Alianza, 1986, 1990, 1991, 1998, 2000, 2001; Chinese, Wenhua Renleixue, 1987; German, Campus Verlag, 1988; Italian, Zanichelli, 1990, 1998, 1999; Spanish, Alianza, 1990, 1996, 1998.
"Margaret and the giant-killer: It doesn't matter a whit who's right" [review of Derek Freeman, *Margaret Mead and Samoa: The Making and Unmaking of an Anthropological Myth*, 1983]. *The Sciences* (New York) 23(4):19–21. [*]
"The revolutionary hamburger." *Psychology Today* 17(10):6–8 (October). [*]
"The sleep-crawling question" [review of Derek Freeman, *Margaret Mead and Samoa: The Making and Unmaking of an Anthropological Myth*, 1983]. *Psychology Today* 17(5):24, 26–27 (May). [*]

1984

"Animal capture and Yanomamo warfare: Retrospect and new evidence." *Journal of Anthropological Research* 40(1):183–201. [*]
"Comments." *Current Anthropology* 25(5):648–649 [commentary on Drew Westen, "Cultural materialism: Food for thought or bum steer?" *Current Anthropology* 25(5):639–653].
"A cultural materialist theory of band and village warfare: The Yanomamo test." Pp. 111–140 in R. Brian Ferguson, (ed.), *Warfare, Culture, and Environment*. New York: Academic Press.
"Death by voodoo." *Psychology Today* 18(8):16–17 (August). [*]
"Forbidden flesh" [88-minute videorecording of lecture by Marvin Harris at the University of Utah, October 30, 1984]. Salt Lake City: University of Utah.
"Group and individual effects in selection." *Behavioral and Brain Sciences* 7(4):490–491 [commentary on B. F. Skinner, "Selection by consequences." *Behavioral and Brain Sciences* 7(4):477–481]. [*]
Review of John Van Maanen, James M. Dabbs, Jr., and Robert R. Faulkner, *Varieties of Qualitative Research*, 1982. *Academy of Management Review* 9(1):166–167. [*]

1985

"Comments." *Current Anthropology* 26(2):175–176 [commentary on Mark Kline Taylor, "Symbolic dimensions in cultural anthropology." *Current Anthropology* 26(2):167–185].
Good to Eat: Riddles of Food and Culture. New York: Simon & Schuster. Waveland Press ed., 1985, 1998. Reissued as *The Sacred Cow and the Abominable Pig: Riddles of Food and Culture*, Simon & Schuster/Touchstone, 1987. Excerpted as "The 100,000-year hunt: Man was not made

for a diet of high-fiber, meatless meals." *The Sciences* (New York) 26(1):22–32 [with commentary in "One man's meat" (letters from readers), *The Sciences* 26(4):15–16], and "Marvin Harris replies." *The Sciences* 26(4):16–18]. [*]. British ed., Allen & Unwin, 1986. Translations: Hebrew, Massada, 1987, 1988, Modan, 2001; Japanese, Iwanami Shoten, 1988, 1994, 2001; German, Klett-Cotta, 1991; Spanish, Alianza, 1989, 1991, 1993, 1999; Italian, Einaudi, 1990, 1998; Korean, Han'gilsa, 1992; Chinese, Shangdong hua bao chu ban she, 2001.

James Robertson and Marvin Harris. "Post-industrial futures" [interview with Hazel Henderson]. In *Creating Alternative Futures* [videorecording, cassette 1, segment 2]. Oley, PA: Bullfrog Films.

"Viaggi attraverso il mondo 3: L'antropologia culturale" [Antonio Colajanni intervista Marvin Harris; translated by Mario Baccianini and Margaret Cook]. *MondOperaio* (Rome) 38(7):108–120 (July).

1986

Review of Elman R. Service, *A Century of Controversy: Ethnological Issues from 1860 to 1960*, 1985. *American Ethnologist* 13(2):375–376. [*]

1987

"Bovidicy: Reply to Sebring." *Journal of Anthropological Research* 43(4):320–322 [commentary on James M. Sebring, "Bovidicy." *Journal of Anthropological Research* 43(4):309–319]. [*]

"Comment on Vayda's review of *Good to Eat: Riddles of Food and Culture*." *Human Ecology* 15(4):511–517 [commentary on Andrew P. Vayda, "Explaining what people eat: A review article." *Human Ecology* 15(4):493–510, with "Reply to Harris." *Human Ecology* 15(4):519–521]. [*]

"Comments." *Current Anthropology* 28(2):152–153 [commentary on E. A. Hammel and Nancy Howell, "Research in population and culture: An evolutionary framework." *Current Anthropology* 28(2):141–160].

"Cultural materialism: Alarums and excursions." Pp. 107–126 in Kenneth Moore (ed.), *Waymarks: The Notre Dame Inaugural Lectures in Anthropology.* Notre Dame, IN: University of Notre Dame Press.

Marvin Harris and Eric B. Ross. *Death, Sex, and Fertility: Population Regulation in Preindustrial and Developing Societies.* New York: Columbia University Press. Paperback ed., Columbia University Press, 1990. Translations: Spanish, Alianza, 1991, 1992, 1999.

Marvin Harris and Eric B. Ross. "Foodways: Historical overview and theoretical prolegomenon." Pp. 57–90 in Marvin Harris and Eric B. Ross (eds.), *Food and Evolution: Toward a Theory of Human Food Habits.* Philadelphia: Temple University Press. Paperback ed., Temple University Press, 1990.

1989

Our Kind: Who We Are, Where We Came From, Where We Are Going. New York: Harper & Row. Harper Perennial ed., 1990. Excerpted as "Life Without Chiefs." *New Age Journal* 6(6):42.

Translations: Dutch, De Kern, 1990; Hebrew, Sifriyat Ma'ariv, 1991; Italian, Rizzoli, 1991,
RCS Libri, 2002; Spanish, Alianza, 1991, 1994, 1995, 1997; German, G. C. Cotta'sche,
1992, Klett-Cotta, 1996; Chinese, Shi bao wen hua chu ban qi ye you xian gong si, 1994;
Korean, Minumsa, 1995.
Review of Clarence Maloney, *Behavior and Poverty in Bangladesh,* 2nd ed., 1988. *American
Anthropologist* 91(3):823–824. [*]

1990

"Emics and etics revisited." Pp. 48–61 [with "Harris's reply to Pike," pp. 75–83, and "Harris's
final response," pp. 202–216] in Thomas N. Headland, Kenneth L. Pike, and Marvin
Harris (eds.), *Emics and Etics: The Insider/Outsider Debate.* Newbury Park, CA: Sage
Publications.
Review of Andrew N. Rowan, (ed.), *Animals and People Sharing the World,* 1989. *American
Anthropologist* 92(4):1079–1080. [*]

1991

"Anthropology: Ships that crash in the night." Pp. 70–114 in Richard Jessor (ed.), *Perspectives
on Behavioral Science: The Colorado Lectures.* Boulder, CO: Westview Press.
"The intellectual ancestry of cultural materialism" ["This week's citation classic," a commen-
tary on the *Rise of Anthropological Theory: A History of Theories of Culture,* 1968]. *Current
Contents: Social and Behavioral Sciences* no. 16:8 (April 22) and *Current Contents: Arts and
Humanities* no. 9:18 (April 29). [*]
Review of Thomas M. Stephens, *Dictionary of Latin American Racial and Ethnic Terminology,*
1990. *Ethnohistory* 38(1):86–87. [*]

1992

"Distinguished lecture: Anthropology and the theoretical and paradigmatic significance of the collapse
of Soviet and East European communism." *American Anthropologist* 94(2):295–305. [*]
"Earth odyssey: The rise of Homo sapiens" [review of Richard Leakey and Roger Lewin, *Origins
Reconsidered: In Search of What Makes Us Human,* 1992, and Carl Sagan and Ann Druyan,
Shadows of Forgotten Ancestors: A Search for Who We Are, 1992]. *Washington Post* (Final ed.),
Book World, p. 1 (September 27).

1993

"Evolution of human gender hierarchies: A trial formulation." Pp. 57–79 in Barbara Diane Miller
(ed.), *Sex and Gender Hierarchies.* Cambridge, UK: Cambridge University Press.
Marvin Harris, Josildeth Gomes Consorte, Joseph Lang, and Bryan Byrne. "Who are the

whites? Imposed census categories and the racial demography of Brazil." *Social Forces* 72(2):451–462. [*]

1994

"Comments." *Current Anthropology* 35(3):267–268 [commentary on John F. Martin, "Changing sex ratios: The history of Havasupai fertility and its implications for human sex ratio variation." *Current Anthropology* 35(3):255–280].

"Cultural materialism is alive and well and won't go away until something better comes along." Pp. 62–75 [with "Intellectual Roots," autobiographical-bibliographical essay, pp. 75–76] in Robert Borofsky (ed.), *Assessing Cultural Anthropology.* New York: McGraw-Hill.

"Foreword." P. 9 in Göran Burenhult (gen. ed.), *Traditional Peoples Today: Continuity and Change in the Modern World.* 1st ed. The Illustrated History of Humankind, vol. 5. San Francisco: HarperSanFrancisco. Translation: Spanish, Debate, Círculo de Lectores, 1995–1996.

Review of William S. Abruzzi, *Dam That River: Ecology and Mormon Settlement in the Little-Colorado River Basin,* 1993. *Human Ecology* 22(4):505–507. [*]

1995

"Anthropology and postmodernism." Pp. 62–77 in Martin F. Murphy and Maxine L. Margolis (eds.), *Science, Materialism, and the Study of Culture.* Gainesville: University Press of Florida. Translated and reprinted as "Antropología y postmodernismo." *Catauro: Revista cubana de antropología* (Havana) año 1, no. 0:44–62.

"Comments." *Current Anthropology* 36(3):423–424 [commentary on "Objectivity and militancy: A debate," with Roy D'Andrade, "Moral models in anthropology." *Current Anthropology* 36(3):399–408, and Nancy Scheper-Hughes, "The primacy of the ethical: Propositions for a militant anthropology." *Current Anthropology* 36(3):409–440].

Marvin Harris, Josildeth Gomes Consorte, Joseph Lang, and Bryan Byrne. "A reply to Telles." *Social Forces* 73(4):1613–1614 [commentary on Edward E. Telles, "Who are the morenas?" *Social Forces* 73(4):1609–1611]. [*]

Bryan Byrne, Marvin Harris, Josildeth Gomes Consorte, and Joseph Lang. "What's in a name?: The consequences of violating Brazilian emic color-race categories in estimates of social well-being." *Journal of Anthropological Research* 51(4):389–397. [*]

1996

"Cultural materialism." Pp. 277–281 in David Levinson and Melvin Ember (eds.), *Encyclopedia of Anthropology.* New York: Henry Holt.

"Epilogue: A perilous bridge." Pp. 175–176 in Anna Lou Dehavenon (ed.), *There's No Place Like Home: Anthropological Perspectives on Housing and Homelessness in the United States.* Westport, CT: Bergin & Garvey.

"Ethnomania: Racial and ethnic misadventures in post-modern times." *Teaching Anthropology: SACC Notes* 4, no. 1 (Spring–Summer): 3–4.

"More bones of contention" [review of Milford Wolpoff and Rachel Caspari, *Race and Human Evolution,* 1997]. *Washington Post* (Final ed.), *Book World,* p. 1 (December 29).

Review of R. Brian Ferguson, *Yanomami Warfare: A Political History,* 1995. *Human Ecology* 24(3):413–416. [*]

1997

"Comment." *Current Anthropology* 38(3):410–415 [commentary on Tim O'Meara, "*CA* forum on theory in anthropology: Causation and the struggle for a science of culture." *Current Anthropology* 38(3):399–418].

"Anthropology needs holism; Holism needs anthropology." Pp. 22–28 in Conrad Phillip Kottak, Jane J. White, Richard H. Furlow, and Patricia C. Rice (eds.), *The Teaching of Anthropology: Problems, Issues, and Decisions.* Mountain View, CA: Mayfield Publishing Co.

1999

"Science, objectivity, morality." Pp. 77–83 in E. L. Cerroni-Long (ed.), *Anthropological Theory in North America.* Westport, CT: Bergin & Garvey.

Theories of Culture in Postmodern Times. Walnut Creek, CA: AltaMira Press. Translations: Spanish, Crítica, 2000, 2004.

2001

Cultural Materialism: The Struggle for a Science of Culture. Updated ed. [original 1979], introduction by Allen Johnson and Orna Johnson. Walnut Creek, CA: AltaMira Press. New ed., Lanham, MD: Rowman & Littlefield, 2001.

The Rise of Anthropological Theory: A History of Theories of Culture. Updated ed. [original 1968], introduction by Maxine L. Margolis. Walnut Creek, CA: AltaMira Press.

References

Abrams, Elliot M. 1989. "Architecture and energy." In Michael B. Schiffer (ed.), *Archaeological Method and Theory*. Vol. 1. Tucson: University of Arizona Press.

———. 1994. *How the Maya Built Their World*. Austin: University of Texas Press.

Abu-Lughod, Lila. 1991. "Writing against culture." In Richard Fox (ed.), *Recapturing Anthropology*. Santa Fe, NM: School of American Research Press.

Adams, David. 1983. "Why there are so few women warriors." *Behavior Science Research* 18:196–212.

Adams, Richard N. 1981. "Natural selection, energetics, and 'cultural materialism.'" *Current Anthropology* 22:603–624.

———. 1988. *The Eighth Day*. Austin: University of Texas Press.

———. 1998. "On causation and the struggle for a science of culture." *Current Anthropology* 39:137.

Agar, Michael. 2005. "Agents in living color: Towards emic agent-based models." *Journal of Artificial Societies and Social Simulation* 8:1–19.

Alexander, Richard D. 1974. "The evolution of social behavior." *Annual Review of Anthropology* 5:325–383.

Alkire, William. 1965. *Lamotrek Atoll and Inter-island Socioeconomic Ties*. Illinois Studies in Anthropology No. 5.

———. 1977. *An Introduction to the Peoples and Cultures of Micronesia*. 2nd ed. Menlo Park, CA: Cummings.

———. 1978. *Coral Islanders*. Arlington Heights, IL: AHM Publishing Corporation.

Alkire, William, and Keiko Fujimara. 1990. "Principles of organization in the outer islands of Yap State and their implications for archaeology." *Micronesia Supplement No. 2*:75–88.

Alvard, Michael S., and David Nolin. 2002. "Rousseau's whale hunt? Coordination among big-game hunters." *Current Anthropology* 43:533–559.

Annett, Joan, and Randall Collins. 1975. "A short history of deference and demeanor." In Randall Collins, *Conflict Sociology: Toward an Explanatory Science*. New York: Academic Press.

Appell, G. N. 1989. "Facts, fiction, fads, and follies: But where is the evidence?" *American Anthropologist* 91:195–198.

Athens, J.S. 1990a. "Nan Madol pottery, Pohnpei." *Micronesica Supplement No. 2*:17–32.

———. 1990b. "Kosrae pottery, clay, and early settlement." *Micronesica Supplement No. 2*:171–186.

Atran, Scott. 2002. *In Gods We Trust: The Evolutionary Landscape of Religion*. New York: Oxford University Press.

Axelrod, Robert. 1997. *The Complexity of Cooperation: Agent-based Models of Conflict and Cooperation.* Princeton, NJ: Princeton University Press.

Bakeman, Roger, and John R. Brownlee. 1982. "Social rules governing object conflicts in toddlers and preschoolers." In Kenneth H. Rubin and Hildy S. Ross (eds.), *Peer Relationships and Social Skills in Childhood.* New York: Springer-Verlag.

Bankes, Steven, Robert Lempert, and Steven Popper. 2002. "Making computational social science effective." *Social Science Computer Review* 20:377–388.

Barkow, Jerome H. 1989. *Darwin, Sex, and Status.* Toronto: University of Toronto Press.

Barkow, Jerome H., Leda Cosmides, and John Tooby (eds.). 1992. *The Adapted Mind: Evolutionary Psychology and the Generation of Culture.* New York: Oxford University Press.

Barnes, Barry. 1988. *The Nature of Power.* Urbana: University of Illinois Press.

Barrett, Richard. 1989. "The paradoxical anthropology of Leslie White." *American Anthropologist* 91:986–999.

Barry, Herbert, III, Irvin L. Child, and Margaret K. Bacon. 1959. "Relation of child training to subsistence economy." *American Anthropologist* 61:51–63.

Barth, Fredrik. 1966. *Models of Social Organization. RAI Occasional Paper No. 32.*

Bath, J. E., and J. S. Athens. 1990. "Prehistoric social complexity on Pohnpei: The *Saudeleur* to *Nahnmwarki* transformation." *Micronesica Supplement No. 2*: 275–290.

Battalio, Raymond C., Larry Samuelson, and John van Huyck. 2001. "Optimization incentives and coordination failure in laboratory stag hunt games." *Econometrica* 69:749–764.

Beaton, Ann E., and Paul A. Clement. 1976. "The date of the destruction of the sanctuary of Poseidon on the Isthmus of Corinth." *Hesperia* 45:267–279.

Bender, Byron, Ward Goodenough, Frederick Jackson, et al. 2003. "Proto-Micronesian reconstructions–I." *Oceanic Linguistics* 42(1):1–110.

Bender, Byron, and Judith Wang. 1985. "The status of Proto-Micronesian." In Andrew Pawley and Lois Carrington (eds.), *Austronesian Linguistics and the 15th Pacific Science Congress. Pacific Linguistics* C-88:53–92.

Berger, Allen H. 1976. "Structural and eclectic revisions of Marxist strategy: A cultural materialist critique." *Current Anthropology* 17:290–305.

Berger, Henry G. 1974. "Review of Marvin Harris, *The Rise of Anthropological Theory: A History of Theories of Culture* (Crowell, 1968)." *American Anthropologist* 76:576–578.

Berlin, Isaiah. 1966. *The Hedgehog and the Fox: An Essay on Tolstoy's View of History.* New York: Simon & Schuster.

Bernard, H. Russell. 1995. *Research Methods in Anthropology: Qualitative and Quantitative Approaches.* Walnut Creek, CA: AltaMira Press.

———. 2002. *Research Methods in Anthropology: Qualitative and Quantitative Methods.* Walnut Creek, CA: AltaMira Press.

Berry, Brian J. L., L. Douglas Kiel, and Euel Elliott. 2002. "Adaptive agents, intelligence, and emergent human organization: Capturing complexity through agent-based modeling." *Proceedings of the National Academy of Sciences* 99:7187–7188.

Bettinger, Robert L. 1991. *Hunter-Gatherers: Archaeological and Evolutionary Theory.* New York: Plenum.

Betzig, Laura. 1986. *Despotism and Differential Reproduction: A Darwinian View of History.* New York: Aldine de Gruyter.

Binford, Lewis R. 1987. "The reluctant shift from hunting to horticulture in North America." *Social Science* 72:44–47.

———. 2001. *Constructing Frames of Reference: An Analytical Method for Archaeological Theory Building Using Hunter-Gatherer and Environmental Data Sets.* Berkeley: University of California Press.

Blau, Peter M. 1964. *Exchange and Power in Social Life*. New York: Wiley.

Bliege Bird, Rebecca L., Douglas W. Bird, Eric Alden Smith, and Geoffrey C. Kushnick. 2002. "Risk and reciprocity in Meriam food sharing." *Evolution and Human Behavior* 23:297–321.

Bliege Bird, Rebecca L., Eric Alden Smith, and Douglas W. Bird. 2001. "The hunting handicap: Costly signaling in human foraging strategies." *Behavioral Ecology and Sociobiology* 50:9–19.

Bloch, Maurice (ed.). 1975. *Marxist Analyses and Social Anthropology*. London: Malaby Press.

Bloch, Maurice, and Dan Sperber. 2002. "Kinship and evolved psychological dispositions: The mother's brother controversy reconsidered." *Current Anthropology* 43:723–748.

Blurton Jones, Nicholas G. 1987. "Tolerated theft: Suggestions about the ecology and evolution of sharing, hoarding, and scrounging." *Social Science Information* 26:31–54.

Bolton, Ralph. 1973. "Aggression and hypoglycemia among the Qolla: A study in psychobiological anthropology." *Ethnology* 12:227–257.

Bolton, Ralph, and Constance Vadheim. 1973. "The ecology of East African homicide." *Behavior Science Research* 8:315–342.

Boone, James L. 1998. "The evolution of magnanimity: When is it better to give than to receive?" *Human Nature* 9:1–21.

Borgerhoff Mulder, Monique. 1992. "Reproductive decisions." In Eric Alden Smith and Bruce Winterhalder (eds.), *Evolutionary Ecology and Human Behavior*. New York: Aldine de Gruyter.

Boyd, Robert, Monique Borgerhoff Mulder, William H. Durham, and Peter J. Richerson. 1997. "Are cultural phylogenies possible?" In Peter Weingart, Peter J. Richerson, Sandra D. Mitchell, and Sabine Maasen (eds.), *Human By Nature: Between Biology and the Social Sciences*. Mahwah, NJ: Lawrence Erlbaum.

Boyd, Robert, and Peter J. Richerson. 1985. *Culture and the Evolutionary Process*. Chicago: University of Chicago Press.

———. 2005. *The Origin and Evolution of Cultures*. New York: Oxford University Press.

Boyd, Robert, and Joan B. Silk. 2000. *How Humans Evolved*. 2nd ed. New York: Norton.

Broneer, Oscar. 1953. "Isthmia excavations, 1952." *Hesperia* 22:182–195.

———. 1971. *Isthmia*. Vol. I. *Temple of Poseidon*. Princeton, NJ: American School of Classical Studies at Athens.

———. 1973. *Isthmia*. Vol. II. *Topography and Architecture*. Princeton, NJ: American School of Classical Studies at Athens.

Broude, Gwen J. 1975. "Norms of premarital behavior: A cross-cultural study." *Ethos* 3:381–402.

———. 1976. "Cross-cultural patterning of some sexual attitudes and practices." *Behavior Science Research* 11:227–262.

———. 1983. "Male-female relationships in cross-cultural perspective." *Behavior Science Research* 18:151–181.

Broughton, Jack M., and James F. O'Connell. 1999. "On evolutionary ecology, selectionist archaeology, and behavioral archaeology." *American Antiquity* 64:153–165.

Brown, Donald E. 1991. *Human Universals*. Philadelphia: Temple University Press.

Brown, Donald E., and Yü Chia-yun. 1993. "'Big man' in universalistic perspective." Manuscript, Department of Anthropology, University of California at Santa Barbara.

Brown, James A., and T. Douglas Price. 1985. "Complex hunter-gatherers: Retrospect and prospect." In T. Douglas Price and James A. Brown (eds.), *Prehistoric Hunter-Gatherers: The Emergence of Cultural Complexity*. New York: Academic Press.

Burger, Richard L. 1995. *Chavin and the Origins of Andean Civilization.* London: Thames & Hudson.

Burling, Robbins. 1962. "Maximization theories and the study of economic anthropology." *American Anthropologist* 64:802–821.

Buss, David M. 1999. *Evolutionary Psychology: The New Science of the Mind.* Boston: Allyn & Bacon.

Cancian, Frank. 1972. *Change and Uncertainty in a Peasant Economy.* Stanford, CA: Stanford University Press.

———. 1989. "Economic behavior in peasant communities." In Stuart Plattner (ed.), *Economic Anthropology.* Stanford, CA: Stanford University Press.

Carey, Arlen D., and Joseph Lopreato. 1995. "The evolutionary demography of the fertility-mortality quasi-equilibrium." *Population and Development Review* 21:613–630.

Carley, Kathleen. 2002. "Computational organization science: A new frontier." *Proceedings of the National Academy of Sciences* 99:7257–7262.

Carneiro, Robert. 1970. "A theory of the origin of the state." *Science* 169:733–738.

———. 1981. "The chiefdom: Precursor of the state." In Grant D. Jones and Robert R. Kautz (eds.), *The Transition to Statehood in the New World.* Cambridge, UK: Cambridge University Press.

———. 1991. "The nature of the chiefdom as revealed by evidence from the Cauca Valley of Colombia." In Terry A. Rambo and Kathleen Gillogy (eds.), *Profiles in Cultural Evolution: Papers from a Conference in Honor of Elman R. Service.* Ann Arbor: Anthropological Papers, Museum of Anthropology, University of Michigan No. 85.

———. 1994. "War and peace: Alternating realities in human history." In S. P. Reyna and R. E. Downs (eds.), *Studying War: Anthropological Perspectives.* Langhorne, PA: Gordon and Breach.

———. 1995. "Godzilla meets new age anthropology: Facing the post-modernist challenge to a science of culture." *Europa* 3–21.

———. 1998. "What happened at the flashpoint? Conjectures on chiefdom formation at the very moment of conception." In Elsa M. Redmond (ed.), *Chiefdoms and Chieftaincy in the Americas.* Gainesville: University Press of Florida.

Carucci, Laurence. 1988. "Small fish in a big sea: Geographic dispersion and sociopolitical centralization in the Marshall Islands." In John Gledhill, Barbara Bender, and Mogens Trolle Larsen (eds.), *State and Society: The Emergence and Development of Social Hierarchy and Political Centralization.* London: Unwin Hyman.

Cashdan, Elizabeth A. 1980. "Egalitarianism among hunters and gatherers." *American Anthropologist* 82:116–120.

———. 1985. "Coping with risk: Reciprocity among the Basarwa of northern Botswana." *Man* 20:454–474.

Catling, Hector W. 1988. "Archaeology in Greece: Isthmia." *Archaeological Reports for 1987–88* 34:21–22.

Cerroni-Long, E. L. 1996. "Human science." *Anthropology Newsletter* 37(1):52, 50.

Chagnon, Napoleon A. 1983. *Yanomamö: The Fierce People.* 3rd ed. New York: Holt, Rinehart and Winston.

———. 1988. "Life histories, blood revenge, and warfare in a tribal population." *Science* 239:985–992.

———. 1990. "Reproductive and somatic conflicts of interest in the genesis of violence and warfare among tribesmen." In Jonathan Haas (ed.), *The Anthropology of War.* Cambridge, UK: Cambridge University Press.

Chagnon, Napoleon, and William Irons (eds.). 1979. *Evolutionary Biology and Human Social Behavior.* North Scituate, MA: Duxbury.

Chase-Dunn, Christopher, and Thomas D. Hall. 1997. *Rise and Demise: Comparing World-Systems.* Boulder, CO: Westview Press.

Cheek, Charles. 1986. "Construction activity as a measurement of change at Copan, Honduras." In Patricia A. Urban and Edward M. Schortman (eds.), *The Southeast Maya Periphery.* Austin: University of Texas Press.

Cheetham, Nicolas. 1981. *Mediaeval Greece.* New Haven, CT: Yale University Press.

Childe, V. Gordon. 1951. *Man Makes Himself.* New York: Mentor Books.

Clement, Paul A. 1974. "L. Kornelios Korinthos of Corinth." In Donald W. Bradeen and Malcolm F. McGregor (eds.), *Foros, Tribute to Benjamin Dean Merritt.* Locust Valley, NY: J. J. Augustin.

———. 1975. "The date of the Hexamilion." In Louisa Laourda (ed.), *Essays in Memory of Basil Laourdas.* Thessaloniki, Greece: E. Sfakianakis.

Clifford, James. 1986. "Introduction: Partial truths." In James Clifford and George Marcus (eds.), *Writing Culture: The Poetics and Politics of Ethnography.* Berkeley: University of California Press.

Cohen, Alex. 1990. "A cross-cultural study of the effects of environmental unpredictability on aggression in folktales." *American Anthropologist* 92:474–479.

Cohen, Mark Nathan. 1977. *The Food Crisis in Prehistory.* New Haven, CT: Yale University Press.

Collier, Paul. 2000. *Economic Causes of Civil Conflict and Their Implications for Policy.* New York: World Bank Development Research Group.

Collins, Randall. 1998. *The Sociology of Philosophies: A Global Theory of Intellectual Change.* Cambridge, MA: Harvard University Press (Belknap Press).

Cook, Scott. 1973. "Economic anthropology: Problems in theory, methods, and analysis." In John J. Honigmann (ed.), *Handbook of Social and Cultural Anthropology.* Chicago: Rand McNally.

Cordy, Ross. 1986. "Relationships between the extent of social stratification and population in Micronesian polities at European contact." *American Anthropologist* 88:136–142.

Cosmides, Leda, and John Tooby. 1989. "Evolutionary psychology and the generation of culture, part II: A computational theory of social exchange." *Ethology and Sociobiology* 10:51–97.

Cosmides, Leda, John Tooby, and Jerome H. Barkow. 1992. "Introduction: Evolutionary psychology and conceptual integration." In Jerome H. Barkow, Leda Cosmides, and John Tooby (eds.), *The Adapted Mind: Evolutionary Psychology and the Generation of Culture.* New York: Oxford University Press.

Cowgill, George L. 1975. "On causes and consequences of ancient and modern population change." *American Anthropologist* 77:505–525.

Crane, Diana. 1970. "The nature of scientific communication and influence." *International Social Science Journal* 22:28–41.

———. 1972. *Invisible Colleges: Diffusion of Knowledge in Scientific Communities.* Chicago: University of Chicago Press.

Cronin, Blaise. 1984. *The Citation Process: The Role and Significance of Citation in Scientific Communication.* London: Taylor Graham.

———. 2005. *The Hand of Science: Academic Writing and Its Rewards.* Lanham, MD: Scarecrow Press.

Cronk, Lee. 1991a. "Human behavioral ecology." *Annual Review of Anthropology* 20:25–53.

———. 1991b. "Intention versus behavior in parental sex preferences among the Mukogodo of Kenya." *Journal of Biosocial Science* 23:229–240.

————. 1999. *That Complex Whole: Culture and the Evolution of Human Behavior.* Boulder, CO: Westview Press.

Crowe, Patrick. 1990. "The unity of White's anthropological theory: A response to Barrett." *American Anthropologist* 92:1018–1019.

Currier, Richard L. 1979. "A superman of anthropology? Marvin Harris can leap tall buildings in a single bound." *Chronicle of Books and Arts (Supplement to Chronicle of Higher Education)* 18(20):7, July 23.

Dalton, George. 1969. "Theoretical issues in economic anthropology." *Current Anthropology* 10:63–102.

DaMatta, Roberto. 1994. "Some biased remarks on interpretivism: A view from Brazil." In Robert Borofsky (ed.), *Assessing Cultural Anthropology.* New York: McGraw-Hill.

D'Andrade, Roy. 1995a. "What do you think you're doing?" *Anthropology Newsletter* 36(7):1, 4.

————.1995b. "Moral models in anthropology." *Current Anthropology* 36:399–408.

————.1999. "Culture is not everything." In E. L. Cerroni-Long (ed.), *Anthropological Theory in North America.* Westport, CT: Bergin and Garvey.

Darwin, Charles. 1928 [1859]. *The Origin of Species.* London: J. M. Dent.

Davis, Kingsley. 1959. "The myth of functional analysis as a special method in sociology and anthropology." *American Sociological Review* 24:757–772.

Davis, Martin. 1958. *Computability and Unsolvability.* New York: McGraw-Hill.

Dawes, Robyn. 2001. *Everyday Irrationality: How Pseudo-Scientists, Lunatics, and the Rest of Us Systematically Fail to Think Rationally.* Boulder, CO: Westview.

Dawson, Doyne. 2002. "The marriage of Marx and Darwin?" *History and Theory* 41:44–59.

Diamond, Jared. 1997. *Guns, Germs, and Steel: The Fates of Human Societies.* New York: Norton.

Diener, Paul. 1984. "Comment on Drew Westen, 'Cultural materialism: Food for thought or bum steer?'" *Current Anthropology* 25:646–647.

Diener, Paul, Kurt Moore, and Robert Mutaw. 1980. "Meat, markets, and mechanical materialism: The great protein fiasco in anthropology." *Dialectical Anthropology* 5:171–192.

Diener, Paul, Donald Nonini, and Eugene E. Robkin. 1978. "The dialectics of the sacred cow: Ecological application versus political appropriation in the origins of India's sacred cattle complex." *Dialectical Anthropology* 3:221–238.

Diener, Paul, and Eugene E. Robkin. 1978. "Ecology, evolution, and the search for cultural origins: The question of Islamic pig prohibition." *Current Anthropology* 19:493–540.

Dirks, Robert. 1993. "Starvation and famine." *Cross-Cultural Research* 27:28–69.

Divale, William Tulio. 1974. "Migration, external warfare, and matrilocal residence." *Behavior Science Research* 9:75–133.

Divale, William Tulio, and Marvin Harris. 1976. "Population, warfare, and the male supremacist complex." *American Anthropologist* 78:521–538.

Djilas, Milovan. 1957. *The New Class.* New York: Praeger.

Dole, Gertrude E., and Robert L. Carneiro (eds.). 1960. *Essays in the Science of Culture in Honor of Leslie A. White.* New York: Crowell.

Donald, Merlin. 1991. *Origins of the Modern Mind: Three Stages in the Evolution of Culture and Cognition.* Cambridge, MA: Harvard University Press.

Dow, James W. 1994. "Sierra Otomí: People of the Mexican mountains." In Melvin Ember, Carol Ember, and David Levinson (eds.), *Portraits of Culture: Ethnographic Originals.* New York: Prentice-Hall.

————. 2001. "Demographic factors affecting Protestant conversions in three Mexican villages." In James W. Dow and Alan R. Sandstrom (eds.), *Holy Saints and Fiery Preachers: The Anthropology of Protestantism in Mexico and Central America.* Westport, CT: Praeger.

————. 2002. "Historia y etnografía de los otomíes. Siglos XVI–XX." Colloquium at the Centro de Investigaciones y Estudios Superiores en Antropología Social. Distinguished Visiting Professor Program of the Mexican Academy of Sciences. February 25, 2002. Available on the Internet at http://www.oakland.edu/~dow/personal/papers/ciesaslect/croquis.pdf.

Dow, James W., and Alan R. Sandstrom (eds.). 2001. *Holy Saints and Fiery Preachers: The Anthropology of Protestantism in Mexico and Central America.* Westport, CT: Praeger.

Doxiadis, Constantine A. 1963. *Architecture in Transition.* Oxford, UK: Oxford University Press.

————. 1968. *Ekistics. An Introduction to the Science of Human Settlements.* London: Hutchinson.

Draper, Patricia, and Henry Harpending. 1982. "Father absence and reproductive strategy: An evolutionary perspective." *Journal of Anthropological Research* 38:255–273.

Drees, Ludwig. 1968. *Olympia: Gods, Artists, and Athletes.* New York: Praeger.

Dunnell, Robert C. 1980. "Evolutionary theory and archaeology." In Michael B. Schiffer (ed.), *Advances in Archaeological Method and Theory.* Vol. 3. New York: Academic Press.

————. 1989. "Aspects of the application of evolutionary theory in archaeology." In Carl C. Lamberg-Karlovsky (ed.), *Archaeological Thought in America.* Cambridge, UK: Cambridge University Press.

————. 1992. "Archaeology and evolutionary science." In LuAnn Wandsnider (ed.), *Quandaries and Quests: Visions of Archaeology's Future.* Occasional Paper 20. Center for Archaeological Investigations. Carbondale: Southern Illinois University Press.

Earle, Timothy. 1997. *How Chiefs Come to Power.* Stanford, CA: Stanford University Press.

Edge, David. 1979. "Quantitative measures of communication in science: A critical review." *History of Science* 17:102–134.

Eggan, Fred. 1954. "Social anthropology and the Method of Controlled Comparison." *American Anthropologist* 56:743–763.

Ehrenreich, Jeffrey. 1981. "Comment on Richard N. Adams, 'Natural selection, energetics, and cultural materialism.'" *Current Anthropology* 22:603–624.

————. 1984. "Comment on Drew Western, 'Cultural materialism: Food for thought or bum steer?'" *Current Anthropology* 25:647–648.

Ellis, G. J., G. R. Lee, and L. R. Petersen. 1978. "Supervision and conformity: A cross-cultural analysis of parental socialization values." *American Journal of Sociology* 84:386–403.

Ellis, Lee. 1995. "Dominance and reproductive success among nonhuman animals: A cross-species comparison." *Ethology and Sociobiology* 16:257–333.

Ember, Carol R. 1974. "An evaluation of alternative theories of matrilocal versus patrilocal residence." *Behavior Science Research* 9:135–149.

————. 1975. "Residential variation among hunter-gatherers." *Behavior Science Research* 10:199–227.

————. 1978. "Men's fear of sex with women: A cross-cultural study." *Sex Roles* 5:657–678.

————. 1983. "The relative decline in women's contribution to agriculture with intensification." *American Anthropologist* 85:285–304.

Ember, Carol R., and Melvin Ember. 1972. "The conditions favoring multilocal residence." *Southwestern Journal of Anthropology* 28:382–400.

————. 1992a. "Resource unpredictability, mistrust, and war: A cross-cultural study." *Journal of Conflict Resolution* 36:242–262.

————. 1992b. "Warfare, aggression, and resource problems: Cross-cultural codes." *Behavior Science Research* 26:169–226.

————. 2000. "High CV score: Regular rhythm or sonority?" *American Anthropologist* 102:848–851.

————. 2001. *Cross-Cultural Research Methods.* Walnut Creek, CA: AltaMira Press.

————. 2002. "Father absence and male aggression: A re-examination of the comparative evidence." *Ethos* 29:296–314.

————. 2005a. *Anthropology.* 11th ed. Upper Saddle River, NJ: Prentice-Hall.

————. 2005b. "Explaining corporal punishment of children: A cross-cultural study." *American Anthropologist* 107:609–619.

Ember, Carol R., Melvin Ember, Andrey Korotayev, and Victor de Munck. 2005. "Valuing thinness or fatness in women: Reevaluating the effect of resource scarcity." *Evolution and Human Behavior* 26:257–270.

Ember, Carol R., Melvin Ember, and Burton Pasternak. 1974. "On the development of unilineal descent." *Journal of Anthropological Research* 30:69–94.

Ember, Carol R., Melvin Ember, and Bruce Russett. 1992. "Peace between participatory polities: A cross-cultural test of the 'democracies rarely fight each other' hypothesis." *World Politics* 44:573–599.

Ember, Carol R., and David Levinson. 1991. "The substantive contributions of worldwide cross-cultural studies using secondary data." *Behavior Science Research* 25:79–140.

Ember, Melvin. 1967. "The emergence of neolocal residence." *Transactions of the New York Academy of Sciences* 30:291–302.

————. 1973. "An archaeological indicator of matrilocal versus patrilocal residence." *American Antiquity* 38:177–182.

————. 1974a. "Warfare, sex ratio, and polygyny." *Ethnology* 13:197–206.

————. 1974b. "The conditions that may favor avunculocal residence." *Behavior Science Research* 8:203–209.

————. 1975. "On the origin and extension of the incest taboo." *Behavior Science Research* 10:249–281.

————. 1991. "The logic of comparative research." *Behavior Science Research* 25:143–153.

Ember, Melvin, and Carol R. Ember. 1971. "The conditions favoring matrilocal versus patrilocal residence." *American Anthropologist* 73:571–594.

————. 2000. "Testing theory and why the 'units of analysis' problem is not a problem." *Ethnology* 39:349–363.

Engels, Frederick. 1972[1891]. *Origin of the Family, Private Property, and the State.* New York: International Publishers.

Epstein, Joshua M., and Robert L. Axtell. 1996. *Growing Artificial Societies: Social Science from the Bottom Up.* Cambridge, MA: MIT Press.

Erasmus, Charles J. 1965. "Monument building: Some field experiments." *Southwestern Journal of Anthropology* 21:277–301.

Eswaran, Vinayak. 2002. "A diffusion wave out of Africa: The mechanism of the modern human revolution?" *Current Anthropology* 43:749–764.

Ferguson, R. Brian. 1984. "Introduction: Studying war." In R. Brian Ferguson (ed.), *Warfare, Culture, and Environment.* New York: Academic Press.

————. 1990. "Explaining war." In Jonathan Haas (ed.), *The Anthropology of War.* New York: Cambridge University Press.

————. 1995. "Infrastructural determinism." In Martin F. Murphy and Maxine L. Margolis (eds.), *Science, Materialism, and the Study of Culture.* Gainesville: University Press of Florida.

Figueiredo, Antonio de, with Allan Burns. 2001. "Marvin Harris: Making an impact in Brazil and Mozambique." *The Guardian,* December 13. Electronic document, http://education.guardian.co.uk/obituary/story/

Fisher, Lawrence E., and Oswald Werner. 1978. "Explaining explanation: Tension in American anthropology." *Journal of Anthropological Research* 34:194–218.

Flinn, Mark V. 1997. "Culture and the evolution of social learning." *Evolution and Human Behavior* 18:23–67.

Foss, Clive. 1975. "The Persians in Asia Minor and the end of antiquity." *The English Historical Review* 90:721–747.

———. 1976. *Byzantine and Turkish Sardis.* Archaeological Exploration of Sardis, Monograph 4. Cambridge, MA: Harvard University Press.

Foucault, Michel. 1984. *The Foucault Reader.* Ed. Paul Rabinow. New York: Pantheon.

Fought, John G., Robert L. Munroe, Carmen R. Fought, and Erin M. Good. 2004. "Sonority and climate in a world sample of languages." *Cross-Cultural Research* 38:27–51.

Fox, Robin. 1992. "Anthropology and the 'teddy bear' picnic." *Society* 30 (Nov.–Dec.):47–55.

———.1997. "State of the art/science in anthropology." In Paul Gross, Norman Levitt, and M. Lewis (eds.), *The Flight from Science and Reason.* New York: New York Academy of Sciences.

Frank, Andre Gunder. 1990. "A theoretical introduction to 5,000 years of world system history." *Review (Fernand Braudel Center)* 13:155–248.

———. 1991. "A plea for world system history." *Journal of World History* 2:1–28.

———. 1995. "The modern world system revisited: Rereading Braudel and Wallerstein." In Stephen K. Sanderson (ed.), *Civilizations and World Systems: Studying World-Historical Change.* Walnut Creek, CA: AltaMira.

Frank, Andre Gunder, and Barry K. Gills (eds.). 1993. *The World System: Five Hundred Years or Five Thousand?* London: Routledge.

Frank, Robert H. 1988. *Passions within Reason. The Strategic Role of the Emotions.* New York: W. W. Norton.

Frantz, Alison. 1988. *The Athenian Agora.* Vol. XXIV. *Late Antiquity: AD 267–700.* Princeton, NJ: American School of Classical Studies at Athens.

Freedman, Daniel G. 1979. *Human Sociobiology.* New York: Free Press.

Freedman, Jonathan L. 1975. *Crowding and Behavior.* San Francisco: Freeman.

Friedman, Jonathan. 1974. "Marxism, structuralism, and vulgar materialism." *Man* 9:444–469.

Friedman, Milton, and Leonard J. Savage. 1948. "The utility analysis of choices involving risk." *Journal of Political Economy* 4:279–304.

Fukuyama, Francis. 1992. *The End of History and the Last Man.* New York: Free Press.

Futuyma, Douglas J. 1982. *Science on Trial: The Case for Evolution.* New York: Pantheon Books.

Gangestad, Steven W., and Jeffrey A. Simpson. 2000. "The evolution of human mating: Trade-offs and strategic pluralism." *Behavioral and Brain Sciences* 23:573–644.

Gat, Azar. 2000a. "The human motivational complex: Evolutionary theory and the causes of hunter-gatherer fighting. Part I. Primary somatic and reproductive causes." *Anthropological Quarterly* 73:20–34.

———. 2000b. "The human motivational complex: Evolutionary theory and the causes of hunter-gatherer fighting. Part II. Proximate, subordinate, and derivative causes." *Anthropological Quarterly* 73:74–88.

Gellner, Ernest. 1988. "The stakes in anthropology." *The American Scholar* 57:17–30.

———. 1992. *Postmodernism, Reason, and Religion.* London: Routledge.

Gigerenzer, Gerd. 2001. "The adaptive toolbox." In Gerd Gigerenzer and Reinhard Selten (eds.), *Bounded Rationality: The Adaptive Toolbox.* Cambridge, MA: MIT Press.

Gigerenzer, Gerd, and Reinhard Selten. 2001. "Rethinking rationality." In Gerd Gigerenzer and Reinhard Selten (eds.), *Bounded Rationality: The Adaptive Toolbox.* Cambridge, MA: MIT Press.

Gilbert, G. Nigel. 1977. "Referencing as persuasion." *Social Studies of Science* 7:113–122.

Gills, Barry K., and Andre Gunder Frank. 1991. "5,000 years of world system history: The cumulation of accumulation." In Christopher Chase-Dunn and Thomas D. Hall (eds.), *Core/Periphery Relations in Precapitalist Worlds*. Boulder, CO: Westview Press.

Gilovich, Thomas. 1991. *How We Know What Isn't So: The Fallibility of Human Reason in Everyday Life*. New York: Free Press.

Goodenough, Ward H. 1986. "Sky world and this world: The place of Kachaw in Micronesian cosmology." *American Anthropologist* 88:551–568.

Goodwin, Charles, and John Heritage. 1990. "Conversation analysis." *Annual Review of Anthropology* 19:283–307.

Gregory, Timothy E. 1992. "Kastro and diateichisma as responses to early Byzantine frontier collapse." *Byzantion* 62:235–253.

———. 1993a. *Isthmia*. Vol. V. *The Hexamilion and the Byzantine Fortress*. Princeton, NJ: American School of Classical Studies at Athens.

———. 1993b. "An early Byzantine (Dark Age) settlement at Isthmia: Preliminary report." In Timothy E. Gregory (ed.), *The Corinthia in the Roman Period*. JAR Supplementary Series Number 8. Ann Arbor, MI: Journal of Roman Archaeology.

———. 1995. "The Roman bath at Isthmia: Preliminary report 1972–1992." *Hesperia* 64:279–313.

Gregory, Timothy E., and P. Nick Kardulias. 1989. "The 1989 season at Isthmia." *Old World Archaeology Newsletter* 13(3):14–17.

———. 1990. "Geophysical and surface surveys in the Byzantine fortress at Isthmia, 1985–1986." *Hesperia* 59:467–511.

Gregory, Timothy E., and Harrianne Mills. 1984. "The Roman arch at Isthmia." *Hesperia* 53:407–445.

Gross, Daniel. 1975. "Protein capture and cultural development in the Amazon Basin." *American Anthropologist* 77:526–549.

Gross, Daniel, and Stuart Plattner. 2002. "Anthropology as social work: Collaborative models of anthropological research." *Anthropology News*, November.

Gross, Paul. 1997. "Introduction." In Paul Gross, Norman Levitt, and M. Lewis (eds.), *The Flight From Science and Reason*. New York: New York Academy of Sciences.

Gross, Paul, and Norman Levitt. 1994. *Higher Superstition: The Academic Left and Its Quarrels with Science*. Baltimore, MD: Johns Hopkins University Press.

Gudeman, Stephen. 1978. "Anthropological economics: A question of distribution." *Annual Review of Anthropology* 7:347–377.

Gurven, Michael, Wesley Allen-Grave, Kim Hill, and Magdalena Hurtado. 2000. "'It's a wonderful life': Signaling generosity among the Ache of Paraguay." *Evolution and Human Behavior* 21:263–282.

Gurven, Michael, Kim Hill, Hillard Kaplan, Ana Magdalena Hurtado, and Richard Lyles. 2000. "Food transfers among Hiwi foragers of Venezuela: Tests of reciprocity." *Human Ecology* 28:171–218.

Haaland, Randi. 1995. "Sedentism, cultivation, and plant domestication in the Holocene Middle Nile region." *Journal of Field Archaeology* 22:157–174.

Haas, Jonathan. 1982. *The Evolution of the Prehistoric State*. New York: Columbia University Press.

Hage, Per. 1999. "Linguistic evidence for primogeniture and ranking in proto-Oceanic society." *Oceanic Linguistics* 38:366–375.

Hage, Per, and Jeff Marck. 2002. "Proto-Micronesian kin terms, descent groups, and interisland voyaging." *Oceanic Linguistics* 41:159–170.

Haldon, John F. 1990. *Byzantium in the Seventh Century: The Transformation of a Culture.* Cambridge, UK: Cambridge University Press.

Handwerker, W. Penn. 1989. *Women's Power and Social Revolution.* Newbury Park, CA: Sage.

Hardman, M. J. 1985. "On cultural materialism." *Current Anthropology* 26:288.

Harner, Michael. 1977. "The ecological basis for Aztec sacrifice." *American Ethnologist* 4:114–135.

Harris, Marvin. 1952. "Race relations in Minas Velhas." In Charles W. Wagley (ed.), *Race and Class in Rural Brazil.* Paris: UNESCO.

———. 1956. *Town and Country in Brazil.* New York: Columbia University Press.

———. 1958. *Portugal's African "Wards": A First-Hand Report on Labor and Education in Moçambique.* New York. American Committee on Africa.

———. 1959. "The economy has no surplus?" *American Anthropologist* 61:185–199.

———. 1964a. *The Nature of Cultural Things.* New York: Random House.

———. 1964b. *Patterns of Race in the Americas.* New York: Walker and Co.

———. 1966. "The cultural ecology of India's sacred cattle." *Current Anthropology* 7:51–66.

———. 1968a. "A *CA* book review: *The Rise of Anthropological Theory,* by Marvin Harris" (with Author's précis, 16 reviews, and replies by Marvin Harris). *Current Anthropology* 9:519–533.

———. 1968b. *The Rise of Anthropological Theory: A History of Theories of Culture.* New York: Crowell. (Reprinted in 2000 by AltaMira Press.)

———. 1971. *Culture, Man, and Nature: An Introduction to General Anthropology.* New York: Crowell.

———. 1974a. *Cows, Pigs, Wars, and Witches: The Riddles of Culture.* New York: Random House (Vintage Books).

———. 1974b. "The emperor's clothing store." *Reviews in Anthropology* 1:170–184.

———. 1975. "Why a perfect knowledge of all the rules one must know in order to act like a native cannot lead to a knowledge of how natives act." *Journal of Anthropological Research* 30:242–251.

———. 1976a. "History and significance of the emic/etic distinction." *Annual Review of Anthropology* 5:329–350.

———. 1976b. "Lévi-Strauss et la palourde." *L'Homme* 16(2–3):5–22.

———. 1977. *Cannibals and Kings: The Origins of Cultures.* New York: Random House (Vintage Books).

———. 1979. *Cultural Materialism: The Struggle for a Science of Culture.* New York: Random House. (Reprinted in 2001 by AltaMira Press.)

———. 1981. *America Now: The Anthropology of a Changing Culture.* New York: Simon & Schuster. (Reprinted in 1987 under the title *Why Nothing Works.*)

———. 1985. *Good to Eat: Riddles of Food and Culture.* New York: Simon & Schuster.

———. 1987a. *Why Nothing Works: The Anthropology of Daily Life.* New York: Simon & Schuster (Touchstone). (Originally published in 1981 as *America Now.*)

———. 1987b. "Foodways: Historical overview and theoretical prolegomenon." In Marvin Harris and Eric B. Ross (eds.), *Food and Evolution: Toward a Theory of Human Food Habits.* Philadelphia: Temple University Press.

———. 1987c. *Cultural Anthropology.* 2nd ed. New York: Harper & Row.

———. 1987d. "Comment on Vayda's review of *Good to Eat: Riddles of Food and Culture.*" *Human Ecology* 15:511–517.

————. 1988. *Culture, People, Nature: An Introduction to General Anthropology.* 5th ed. New York: Harper & Row.

————. 1989. *Our Kind: Who We Are, Where We Came From, Where We Are Going.* New York: Harper & Row.

————. 1991a. "Anthropology: Ships that crash in the night." In Richard Jessor (ed.), *Perspectives on Behavioral Science: The Colorado Lectures.* Boulder, CO: Westview Press.

————. 1991b. "The intellectual ancestry of cultural materialism." (This Week's Citation Classic, a commentary on *The Rise of Anthropological Theory: A History of Theories of Culture.*) *Current Contents: Social and Behavioral Sciences* no. 16 (April 22):8.

————. 1992. "Distinguished lecture: Anthropology and the theoretical and paradigmatic significance of the collapse of Soviet and East European communism." *American Anthropologist* 94:295–305.

————. 1994. "Cultural materialism is alive and well and won't go away until something better comes along." In Robert Borofsky (ed.), *Assessing Cultural Anthropology.* New York: McGraw-Hill.

————. 1995a. "Comment on Roy D'Andrade and Nancy Scheper-Hughes, 'Objectivity and militancy: A debate.'" *Current Anthropology* 36:423–424.

————. 1995b. "Anthropology and postmodernism." In Martin F. Murphy and Maxine L. Margolis (eds.), *Science, Materialism, and the Study of Culture.* Gainesville: University Press of Florida.

————. 1996. "Cultural materialism." In David Levinson and Melvin Ember (eds.), *Encyclopedia of Cultural Anthropology.* 4 vols. New York: Henry Holt.

————. 1997a. "Anthropology needs holism; holism needs anthropology." In Conrad Philip Kottak, Jane J. White, Richard H. Furlow, and Patricia C. Rice (eds.), *The Teaching of Anthropology: Problems, Issues, and Decisions.* Mountain View, CA: Mayfield.

————. 1997b. *Culture, People, Nature: An Introduction to General Anthropology.* 7th ed. Boston: Allyn & Bacon.

————. 1997c. "Comment on Tim O'Meara, 'Causation and the struggle for a science of culture.'" *Current Anthropology* 38:410–418.

————. 1999a. "Science, objectivity, morality." In E. L. Cerroni-Long (ed.), *Anthropological Theory in North America.* Westport, CT: Bergin & Garvey.

————. 1999b. *Theories of Culture in Postmodern Times.* Walnut Creek, CA: AltaMira Press.

Harris, Marvin, Josildeth G. Consorte, Joseph Lang, and Bryan Byrne. 1993. "Who are the whites? Emics and etics of the racial demography of Brazil." *Social Forces* 72:451–462.

Harris, Marvin, and Orna Johnson. 2002. *Cultural Anthropology.* 5th ed. Boston: Allyn & Bacon.

Harris, Marvin, and Conrad P. Kottak. 1962. "The structural significance of Brazilian racial categories." *Sociologia* 25:203–209.

Harris, Marvin, and Charles W. Wagley. 1958. *Minorities in the New World.* New York: Columbia University Press.

Harris, Marvin, and Eric B. Ross (eds.). 1987. *Death, Sex, and Fertility: Population Regulation in Preindustrial and Developing Societies.* New York: Columbia University Press.

Hatch, Elvin. 1990. "Leslie White's materialism: A comment on Barrett." *American Anthropologist* 92:1018.

Hawkes, Kristen. 1993. "Why hunter-gatherers work: An ancient version of the problem of public goods." *Current Anthropology* 34:341–361.

Hawkes, Kristen, and Rebecca Bliege Bird. 2002. "Showing off, handicap signaling, and the evolution of men's work." *Evolutionary Anthropology* 11:58–67.

Hawkes, Kristen, J. F. O'Connell, and Nicholas G. Blurton Jones. 2001a. "Hadza meat sharing." *Evolution and Human Behavior* 22:113–142.

———. 2001b. "Hunting and nuclear families: Some lessons from the Hadza about men's work." *Current Anthropology* 42:681–709.

Hayward, Christopher L. 1996. "High-resolution provenience determination of construction stone: A preliminary study of Corinthian oolitic limestone quarries at Examilia." *Geoarchaeology* 11:215–234.

Headland, Thomas N. 1990. "Introduction: A dialogue between Kenneth Pike and Marvin Harris on emics and etics." In Thomas N. Headland, Kenneth L. Pike, and Marvin Harris (eds.), *Emics and Etics: The Insider/Outsider Debate*. Newbury Park, CA: Sage.

Headland, Thomas N., Kenneth L. Pike, and Marvin Harris (eds.). 1990. *Emics and Etics: The Insider/Outsider Debate*. Newbury Park, CA: Sage.

Heinen, H. Dieter. 1975. "On cultural materialism, Marx, and the 'Hegelian monkey.'" *Current Anthropology* 16:450–456.

Hendrix, Lewellyn. 1985. "Economy and child training reexamined." *Ethos* 13:246–261.

Henrich, Joseph. 2001. "Cultural transmission and the diffusion of innovations: Adoption dynamics indicate that biased cultural transmission is the predominate force in behavioral change." *American Anthropologist* 103:992–1013.

Henrich, Joseph (rapporteur), Wulf Albers, Robert Boyd, Gerd Gigerenzer, Kevan A. McCabe, Axel Ockenfels, and H. Peyton Young. 2001. "Group report: What is the role of culture in bounded rationality?" In Gerd Gigerenzer and Reinhard Selten (eds.), *Bounded Rationality: The Adaptive Toolbox*. Cambridge, MA: MIT Press.

Henrich, Joseph, and Francisco J. Gil-White. 2001. "The evolution of prestige: Freely conferred deference as a mechanism for enhancing the benefits of cultural transmission." *Evolution and Human Behavior* 22:165–196.

Herzfeld, Michael. 2001. *Anthropology: Theoretical Practice in Culture and Society.* Oxford: Blackwell.

Hider, Philip M. 1996. "Three bibliometric analyses of anthropology literature." *Behavioral and Social Sciences Librarian* 15:1–17.

Hill, Kim, and Hillard Kaplan. 1999. "Life history traits in humans: Theory and empirical studies. *Annual Review of Anthropology* 28:397–430.

Hold, Barbara C. L. 1980. "Attention structure and behavior in G/wi San children." *Ethology and Sociobiology* 1:275–290.

Homans, George. 1968. "Social behavior as exchange." In Edward E. LeClair, Jr., and Harold K. Schneider (eds.), *Economic Anthropology: Readings in Theory and Analysis*. New York: Holt, Rinehart and Winston.

Hrdy, Sarah Blaffer. 1999. *Mother Nature: A History of Mothers, Infants, and Natural Selection.* New York: Pantheon.

Hunter-Anderson, Rosalind L. (ed.). 1990. "Recent advances in Micronesian archaeology." *Micronesica, Supplement No. 2.*

Huntington, Ellsworth. 1919. *Civilization and Climate.* New Haven, CT: Yale University Press.

Irons, William. 1979. "Cultural and biological success." In Napoleon Chagnon and William Irons (eds.), *Evolutionary Biology and Human Social Behavior.* North Scituate, MA: Duxbury.

Isaac, Barry. L. 2005. "Karl Polanyi." In James G. Carier (ed.), *Handbook of Economic Anthropology.* Cheltenham, UK: Edward Elgar.

Jackson, Frederick. 1983. "The Internal and External Relationships of the Trukic Languages of Micronesia." Ph.D. diss., University of Hawaii.

Jackson, William A. 1996. "Cultural materialism and institutional economics." *Review of Social Economy* LIV:221–244.

Jardine, Nick. 2004. "Emics and etics (not to mention anemics and emetics) in the history of the sciences." *History of Science* 42:261–278.

Johnson, Allen. 1984. "Comment on Drew Westen, 'Cultural materialism: Food for thought or bum steer?'" *Current Anthropology* 25:649–650.

Johnson, Allen, and Timothy Earle. 1987. *The Evolution of Human Societies: From Foraging Group to Agrarian State.* Stanford, CA: Stanford University Press.

Kaegi, Walter E. 1989. "Variable rates of seventh-century change." In Frank M. Clover and R. Stephen Humphreys (eds.), *Tradition and Innovation in Late Antiquity.* Madison: University of Wisconsin Press.

Kagarlitsky, Boris. 2002. *Russia Under Yeltsin and Putin.* London: Pluto Press.

Kang, Gay Elizabeth. 1979. "The nature of exogamy in relation to cross-allegiance/alliance of social units." *Behavior Science Research* 4:255–276.

Kaplan, Hillard S. 1994. "Evolutionary and wealth flows theories of fertility: Empirical tests and new models." *Population and Development Review* 20:753–791.

———. 1996. "A theory of fertility and parental investment in traditional and modern human societies." *Yearbook of Physical Anthropology* 39:1–45.

Kaplan, Hillard S., and Kim Hill. 1985. "Hunting ability and reproductive success among male Ache foragers: Preliminary results." *Current Anthropology* 26:131–133.

Kaplan, Hillard S., Kim Hill, Jane Lancaster, and Ana Magdalena Hurtado. 2000. "A theory of life history evolution: Diet, intelligence, and longevity." *Evolutionary Anthropology* 9:156–185.

Kaplan, Hillard S., Jane B. Lancaster, W. Troy Tucker, and K. G. Anderson. 2002. "Evolutionary approach to below replacement fertility." *American Journal of Human Biology* 14:233–256.

Kardara, Chrysoula. 1961. "Dyeing and weaving works at Isthmia." *American Journal of Archaeology* 65:261–266.

Kardulias, P. Nick. 1992. "Population estimates at ancient military sites: The use of historical and contemporary analogy." *American Antiquity* 57:276–287.

———. 2005. *From Classical to Byzantine: Social Evolution in Late Antiquity and the Fortress at Isthmia, Greece.* Oxford, UK: British Archaeological Reports.

Kazhdan, Alexander, and Anthony Cutler. 1982. "Continuity and discontinuity in Byzantine history." *Byzantion* 52:429–478.

Keeley, Lawrence H. 1996. *War Before Civilization: The Myth of the Peaceful Savage.* New York: Oxford University Press.

Kent, Susan. 1996. "Hunting variability at a recently sedentary Kalahari village." In Susan Kent (ed.), *Cultural Diversity among Twentieth-Century Foragers.* Cambridge, UK: Cambridge University Press.

King, Thomas F., and Patricia L. Parker. 1984. *Pisekin Noomw Noon Tonaachaw: Archaeology in the Tonaachaw Historic District, Moen Island.* Carbondale: Southern Illinois Center for Archaeology Investigations Occasional Paper No. 3.

Kirch, Patrick. 1997. *The Lapita Peoples.* Oxford: Blackwell.

———. 2000. *On the Road of the Winds.* Berkeley: University of California Press.

Kirch, Patrick, and Roger Green. 2001. *Hawaiki: Ancestral Polynesia.* Cambridge, UK: Cambridge University Press.

Klein, Gary. 2001. "The fiction of optimization." In Gerd Gigerenzer and Reinhard Selten (eds.), *Bounded Rationality: The Adaptive Toolbox.* Cambridge, MA: MIT Press.

Knudson, Kenneth. 1970. "Resource Fluctuation, Productivity, and Social Organization on Micronesian Coral Islands." Ph.D. diss., University of Oregon.

Köchly, Hermann, and Wilhelm Rustow (eds.). 1885. *De Re Strategica.* In *Griechische Kriegschriftsteller*, II, 2. Leipzig: W. Engelmann.

Kohler, Timothy A. 2000. "Putting social sciences together again." In Timothy A. Kohler and

George J. Gumerman (eds.), *Dynamics in Human and Primate Societies: Agent-Based Modeling of Social and Spatial Processes*. New York: Oxford University Press.

Kohonen, Teuvo. 1989. *Self-Organization and Associative Memory*. 3rd ed. New York: Springer-Verlag.

Kornai, János. 1992. *The Socialist System: The Political Economy of Communism*. Princeton, NJ: Princeton University Press.

Kottak, Conrad. 1999. "The new ecological anthropology." *American Anthropologist* 101:23–35.

Kramer, Peter D. 1993. *Listening to Prozac*. New York: Penguin.

Kuhn, Thomas S. 1970. *The Structure of Scientific Revolutions*. 2nd ed. Chicago: University of Chicago Press.

Kuznar, Lawrence A. 1989. "The domestication of South American camelids: Models and evidence." In Don S. Rice, Charles Stanish, and Phillip Scarr (eds.), *Ecology, Settlement, and History in the Osmore Basin, Peru*. Vol. 545. Oxford, UK: British Archaeological Reports International.

———. 1997. *Reclaiming a Scientific Anthropology*. Walnut Creek, CA: AltaMira.

———. 2001. "Risk sensitivity and value among Andean pastoralists: Measures, models, and empirical tests." *Current Anthropology* 42:432–440.

———. 2002a. "Evolutionary applications of risk sensitivity models to socially stratified species: Comparison of sigmoid, concave, and linear functions." *Evolution and Human Behavior* 23:265–280.

———. 2002b. "Risk prone peasants: Cultural transmission, or sigmoid utility maximization?" *Current Anthropology* 43:787–789.

———. In press. "High fidelity computational social science in anthropology: Prospects for developing a comparative framework." *Social Science Computer Review*.

Kuznar, Lawrence A., and William G. Frederick. 2003. "Environmental constraints and sigmoid utility: Implications for value, risk sensitivity, and social status." *Ecological Economics* 46:293–306.

———. 2005a. "The effect of nepotism on political risk taking and social unrest." Paper presented at the annual meeting of the North American Association for Computational Social and Organizational Science, June.

———. 2005b. "The effect of global wealth distribution on utility, risk sensitivity, and politics: A preliminary analysis." Unpublished manuscript.

Kuznar, Lawrence A., and Ted L. Gragson. 2005. "The distribution of hunting skill and its implication for male status in hunter-gatherer societies." Unpublished manuscript.

Kuznar, Lawrence A., and Robert L. Sedlmeyer. 2005. "Collective violence in Darfur: An agent-based model of pastoral nomad/sedentary peasant interaction." *Mathematical Anthropology and Cultural Theory* 1(4):1–22. Available on the Internet at www.mathematicalanthropology.org.

Kuznar, Lawrence A., Robert L. Sedlmeyer, and William G. Frederick. 2005. "Agent-based models of risk sensitivity: Applications to social unrest, collective violence, and terrorism." Paper presented at the Third Lake Arrowhead Conference on Human Complex Systems, Lake Arrowhead, CA, May.

Kuznar, Lawrence A., Robert L. Sedlmeyer, and Allyson Kreft. In press. "NOMAD: An agent-based model (ABM) of nomadic pastoralist/sedentary peasant interaction." In Hans Barnard (ed.), *Nomadic Cultures*. Los Angeles: Cotsen Institute, University of California at Los Angeles.

Leake, William M. 1968 [1830]. *Travels in the Morea*. London. Reprinted by Adolf Hakkert, Amsterdam.

LeClair, Edward E., Jr., and Harold K. Schneider (eds.). 1968. *Economic Anthropology: Readings in Theory and Analysis.* New York: Holt, Rinehart and Winston.

Lee, Richard B. 1979. *The !Kung San: Men, Women, and Work in a Foraging Society.* New York: Cambridge University Press.

Lee, Ronald D., and Karen L. Kramer. 2002. "Children's economic roles in the Maya family life cycle: Cain, Caldwell, and Chayanov revisited." *Population and Development Review* 28:475–499.

Leeds, Anthony. 1978. "Comment on Paul Diener and Eugene E. Robkin, 'Ecology, evolution, and the search for cultural origins: The question of Islamic pig prohibition.'" *Current Anthropology* 19:517–518.

Lenski, Gerhard E. 1966. *Power and Privilege: A Theory of Social Stratification.* New York: McGraw-Hill.

———. 1970. *Human Societies: A Macro-Level Introduction to Sociology.* New York: McGraw-Hill.

Lett, James.1987. *The Human Enterprise: A Critical Introduction to Anthropological Theory.* Boulder, CO: Westview.

———. 1990. "Emics and etics: Notes on the epistemology of anthropology." In Thomas N. Headland, Kenneth L. Pike, and Marvin Harris (eds.), *Emics and Etics: The Insider/Outsider Debate.* Newbury Park, CA: Sage.

———. 1991. "Interpretive anthropology, metaphysics, and the paranormal." *Journal of Anthropological Research* 47:305–329.

———. 1996. "Scientific anthropology." In David Levinson and Melvin Ember (eds.), *Encyclopedia of Cultural Anthropology.* New York: Henry Holt.

———. 1997. *Science, Reason, and Anthropology: The Principles of Rational Inquiry.* Lanham, MD: Rowman & Littlefield.

Levin, Michael. 1976. "Eauripik Population Structure." Ph.D. diss., University of Michigan.

Levinson, David. 1979. "Population density in cross-cultural perspective." *American Ethnologist* 6:742–751.

Lévi-Strauss, Claude. 1969. *The Elementary Structures of Kinship.* Trans. J. H. Bell, J. R. von Sturmer, and R. Needham. Boston: Beacon Press.

Lewis, William W. 2004. *The Power of Productivity: Wealth, Poverty, and the Threat to Global Stability.* Chicago: University of Chicago Press.

Lichtenberk, Frantisek. 1986. "Leadership in proto-Oceanic society: Linguistic evidence." *Journal of the Polynesian Society* 95:341–356.

Lindenbaum, Shirley. 1972. "Sorcerers, ghosts, and polluting women: An analysis of religious belief and population control." *Ethnology* 11:241–253.

Lloyd, Kenneth E. 1985. "Behavioral anthropology: A review of Marvin Harris's *Cultural Materialism.*" *Journal of the Experimental Analysis of Behavior* 43:279–287.

Lopreato, Joseph. 1984. *Human Nature and Biocultural Evolution.* Winchester, MA: Allen & Unwin.

Low, Bobbi S. 1990. "Marriage systems and pathogen stress in human societies." *American Zoologist* 30:325–339.

———. 1993. "An evolutionary perspective on war." In William Zimmerman and Harold K. Jacobsen (eds.), *Behavior, Culture, and Conflict in World Politics.* Ann Arbor: University of Michigan Press.

Lumsden, Charles J., and Edward O. Wilson. 1981. *Genes, Mind, and Culture.* Cambridge, MA: Harvard University Press.

Luttwak, Edward N. 1976. *The Grand Strategy of the Roman Empire*. Baltimore: Johns Hopkins University Press.

Mace, Ruth. 2000. "An adaptive model of human reproductive rate where wealth is inherited: Why some people have small families." In Lee Cronk, Napoleon Chagnon, and William Irons (eds.), *Adaptation and Human Behavior: An Anthropological Perspective*. New York: Aldine de Gruyter.

Madsen, Douglas. 1985. "A biochemical property relating to power seeking in humans." *American Political Science Review* 79:448–457.

———. 1986. "Power seekers are different: Further biochemical evidence." *American Political Science Review* 80:261–269.

———. 1994. "Serotonin and social rank among human males." In Roger D. Masters and Michael T. McGuire (eds.), *The Neurotransmitter Revolution*. Carbondale: Southern Illinois University Press.

Magnarella, Paul J. 1982. 'Cultural materialism and the problem of probabilities." *American Anthropologist* 84:138–142.

———. 1984. "Comment on Drew Westen, 'Cultural materialism: Food for thought or bum steer?'" *Current Anthropology* 25:650–651.

———. 1993. *Human Materialism: A Model of Sociocultural Systems and a Strategy for Analysis*. Gainesville: University Press of Florida.

Magubane, Bernard. 1981. "In search of an ideological alternative to Marxism." (Review essay on Marvin Harris, *Cultural Materialism: The Struggle for a Science of Culture*. New York: Random House, 1979.) *Contemporary Sociology* 10:69–73.

Manczak, Witold. 1991. "Nouvelle classification des langues romanes." *Revue Romane* 26:14–24.

Marck, Jeff. 1994. "Proto-Micronesian terms for the physical environment." *Austronesian Terminologies: Continuity and Change, Pacific Linguistics* C-127:3–1–328.

Marcus, George. 1986. "Afterword: Ethnographic writing and anthropological careers." In James Clifford and George Marcus (eds.), *Writing Culture: The Poetics and Politics of Ethnography*. Berkeley: University of California Press.

———. 1992. "Introduction." In George Marcus (ed.), *Rereading Cultural Anthropology*. Durham, NC: Duke University Press.

Margolis, Maxine, and Conrad Kottak. 2003. "Marvin Harris (1927–2001)." *American Anthropologist* 105:685–688.

Marling, William. 1992. "The parable of the prodigal son: An economic reading." *Style* 26:419–436.

Mason, Leonard. 1968. "Suprafamilial authority and economic process in Micronesian atolls." In Andrew P. Vayda (ed.), *Peoples and Cultures of the Pacific*. New York: Natural History Press.

McGowan, Andrew. 1994. "Eating people: Accusations of cannibalism against Christians in the 2nd Century." *Journal of Early Christian Studies* 2:413–442.

McGuire, Michael T. 1982. "Social dominance relationships in male vervet monkeys." *International Political Science Review* 3:11–32.

McGuire, Michael T., M. Raleigh, and C. Johnson. 1983. "Social dominance in adult male vervet monkeys II: Behavior-biochemical relationships." *Social Science Information* 22:311–328.

Meggitt, Mervyn. 1964. "Male-female relationships in the highlands of Australian New Guinea." *American Anthropologist* 66:204–224.

———. 1977. *Blood Is Their Argument: Warfare among the Mae Enga Tribesmen of the New Guinea Highlands*. Palo Alto, CA: Mayfield.

Melchert, Charles F. 1992. "Wisdom is vindicated by her deeds." *Religious Education* 87:127–151.

Merton, Robert K. 1968. "The Matthew Effect in science: The reward and communication systems of science are considered." *Science* 159:56–63.

———. 1976. "The normative structure of science." In Norman K. Storer (ed.), *The Sociology of Science: Theoretical and Empirical Investigations.* Chicago: University of Chicago Press.

Miller, Stephen G. 1990. *Nemea: A Guide to the Site and Museum.* Berkeley: University of California Press.

Minturn, Leigh, and William Lambert. 1964. "The antecedents of child training: A cross-cultural test of some hypotheses." In Leigh Minturn and William Lambert (eds.), *Mothers of Six Cultures: Antecedents of Child Rearing.* New York: Wiley.

Missakian, Elizabeth A. 1980. "Gender differences in agonistic behavior and dominance relations of Synanon communally reared children." In Donald R. Omark, Fred F. Strayer, and Daniel G. Freedman (eds.), *Dominance Relations: An Ethological View of Human Conflict and Social Interaction.* New York: Garland.

Mjøset, Lars. 1999. "Understanding theory in the social sciences." ARENA Working Papers, WP99/33. Available on the Internet at http://www.arena.uio.no/publications/wp9933.htm.

Monceaux, Paul. 1884. "Fouilles et récherches archéologiques au sanctuaire des jeux isthmiques." *Gazette Archéologique* 9:273–285, 354–363.

———. 1885. "Fouilles et récherches archéologiques au sanctuaire des jeux isthmiques." *Gazette Archéologique* 10:205–214, 402–412.

Moran, Emilio. 1982. *Human Adaptability.* Boulder, CO: Westview Press.

Morgan, Lewis Henry. 1974[1877]. *Ancient Society.* Gloucester, MA: Peter Smith.

Munroe, Robert L., Carmen R. Fought, and John G. Fought. 2000. "Rhythmicity or sonority: Response to Ember and Ember's 'Cross-language predictors of consonant-vowel syllables.'" *American Anthropologist* 102:844–848.

Munroe, Robert L., Ruth H. Munroe, and John W. M. Whiting. 1981. "Male sex-role resolutions." In Ruth H. Munroe, Robert L. Munroe, and Beatrice B. Whiting (eds.), *Handbook of Cross-Cultural Human Development.* New York: Garland.

Munroe, Robert L., Ruth H. Munroe, and Stephen Winters. 1996. "Cross-cultural correlates of the consonant-vowel (CV) syllable." *Cross-Cultural Research* 30:60–83.

Munroe, Robert L., and Megan Silander. 1999. "Climate and the consonant-vowel (CV) syllable: A replication within language families." *Cross-Cultural Research* 33:43–62.

Murdock, George P., and Douglas R. White. 1969. "Standard Cross-Cultural Sample." *Ethnology* 8:329–369.

Murphy, Martin F., and Maxine L. Margolis (eds.). 1995. *Science, Materialism, and the Study of Culture.* Gainesville: University Press of Florida.

Murphy, Robert F. 1990. "The dialectics of deeds and words: Or anti-the-antis (and the anti-antis)." *Cultural Anthropology* 5:331–337.

Neff, Hector. 1992. "Ceramics and evolution." In Michael B. Schiffer (ed.), *Archaeological Method and Theory.* Tucson: University of Arizona Press.

Netting, Robert McC. 1974. "Agrarian ecology." *Annual Review of Anthropology* 3:21–56.

———. 1977. *Cultural Ecology.* Menlo Park, CA: Cummings.

Norris, Christopher. 1997. *Against Relativism: Philosophy of Science, Deconstruction, and Critical Theory.* Oxford: Blackwell.

Nuñez, Lautaro. 1983. "Paleoindian and Archaic cultural periods in the arid and semiarid regions of northern Chile." *Advances in World Archaeology* 2:161–203.

Nyce, James M., and Nancy P. Thomas. 1999. "Can a 'hard' science answer 'hard' questions? A response to Sandstrom and Sandstrom." *Library Quarterly* 69:295–298.

Oakes, Guy. 1981. "The epistemological foundations of cultural materialism." *Dialectical Anthropology* 6:1–21.

O'Brien, Michael J. (ed.). 1996. *Evolutionary Archaeology: Theory and Application.* Salt Lake City: University of Utah Press.

O'Brien, Michael J., and Thomas D. Holland. 1992. "The role of adaptation in archaeological explanation." *American Antiquity* 57:36–59.

———. 1995. "The nature and remise of a selection-based archaeology." In Patrice A. Teltser (ed.), *Evolutionary Archaeology: Methodological Issues.* Tucson: University of Arizona Press.

O'Meara, Tim. 1989. "Anthropology as empirical science." *American Anthropologist* 91:354–369.

———. 1995. "Comment on Roy D'Andrade and Nancy Schepher-Hughes, 'Objectivity and militancy: A debate.'" *Current Anthropology* 36:427–428.

———. 1997. "Causation and the struggle for a science of culture." *Current Anthropology* 38:399–418.

———. 2001. "Causation and the postmodern critique of objectivity." *Anthropological Theory* 1(1):31–56.

Orans, Martin. 1996. *Not Even Wrong: Margaret Mead, Derek Freeman, and the Samoans.* Novato, CA: Chandler and Sharp.

O'Sullivan, David. 2004. "Complexity science and human geography." *Transactions of the Institute of British Geographers* 29:282–295.

Otterbein, Keith F. 1968. "Internal war: A cross-cultural study." *American Anthropologist* 70:277–289.

———. 1979. "A cross-cultural study of rape." *Aggressive Behavior* 5:425–435.

Parkin, Frank. 1971. *Class Inequality and Political Order: Social Stratification in Capitalist and Communist Societies.* New York: Holt, Rinehart and Winston.

Pausanias. 1964. *Description of Greece.* With an English Translation by W. H. S. Jones. 4 vols. Cambridge, MA: Harvard University Press.

Pawley, Andrew. 1982. "Rubbish-man, commoner, big man, chief? Linguistic evidence for hereditary chieftainship in proto-Oceania society." In Jukka Siikala (ed.), *Oceanic Studies: Essays in Honour of Aarne A. Koskinen.* Helsinki: Finnish Anthropological Society.

Pawley, Andrew, and Malcolm Ross. 1993. "Austronesian historical linguistics and culture history." *Annual Review of Anthropology* 22:425–459.

———. 1995. "The prehistory of the Oceanic languages: A current view." In Peter Bellwood, James J. Fox, and Darrell Tryon (eds.), *The Austronesians: Historical and Comparative Perspectives.* Canberra: Australian National University Press.

Pearson, Harry W. 1957. "The economy has no surplus: Critique of a theory of development." In Karl Polanyi, Conrad M. Arensberg, and Harry W. Pearson (eds.), *Trade and Market in the Early Empires: Economies in History and Theory.* Glencoe, IL: Free Press.

Pellicani, Luciano. 1995. "Methodological individualism." *Telos* 104:159–175.

Peoples, James. 1985. *Island in Trust.* Boulder, CO: Westview Press.

———. 1990. "The evolution of complex stratification in eastern Micronesia." *Micronesica* Supplement No. 2:291–301.

———. 1992. "Power and material forces in Micronesia." Paper presented at the annual meetings of the American Anthropological Association, San Francisco.

———. 1993. "Political evolution in Micronesia." *Ethnology* 32:1–17.

Percy, William Armstrong, III. 1996. *Pederasty and Pedagogy in Archaic Greece.* Urbana: University of Illinois Press.

Petersen, Glenn. 1982. *One Man Cannot Rule a Thousand.* Ann Arbor: University of Michigan Press.

————. 1993. "*Kanengamah* and Pohnpei's politics of concealment." *American Anthropologist* 95:334–352.

Petersen, Larry R., Gary R. Lee, and Godfrey J. Ellis. 1982. "Social structure, socialization values, and disciplinary techniques: A cross-cultural analysis." *Journal of Marriage and the Family* 44:131–142.

Pike, Kenneth. 1954. *Language in Relation to a Unified Theory of the Structure of Human Behavior.* Vol. 1. Glendale, CA: Summer Institute of Linguistics.

Polanyi, Karl. 1947. "Our obsolete market mentality." *Commentary* 3:109–117.

Polanyi, Karl, Conrad M. Arensberg, and Harry W. Pearson (eds.). 1957. *Trade and Market in the Early Empires: Economies in History and Theory.* Glencoe, IL: Free Press.

Posner, Richard A. 1992. *Sex and Reason.* Cambridge, MA: Harvard University Press.

Pospisil, Leopold. 1963. *The Kapauku Papuans of West New Guinea.* New York: Holt, Rinehart and Winston.

————. 1972. *Kapauku Papuan Economy.* New Haven, CT: Human Relations Area Files.

Price, Barbara J. 1982. "Cultural materialism: A theoretical review." *American Antiquity* 47:709–741.

Price, T. Douglas, and James A. Brown (eds.). 1985. *Prehistoric Hunter-Gatherers: The Emergence of Cultural Complexity.* Orlando, FL: Academic Press.

Pryor, Frederic L. 1986. "The adoption of agriculture: Some theoretical and empirical evidence." *American Anthropologist* 88:879–897.

Quilter, Jeffrey. 1991. "Late preceramic Peru." *Journal of World Prehistory* 5:387–438.

Radcliffe-Brown, A. R. 1952 [1924]. "The mother's brother in South Africa." In A. R. Radcliffe-Brown (ed.), *Structure and Function in Primitive Society.* Glencoe, IL: Free Press.

————. 1965 [1939]. "Taboo." In A. R. Radcliffe-Brown (ed.), *Structure and Function in Primitive Society.* Glencoe, IL: Free Press.

Rainbird, Paul. 1994. "Prehistory in the northwest tropical Pacific: The Caroline, Mariana, and Marshall Islands." *Journal of World Prehistory* 8:293–349.

————. 2004. *The Archaeology of Micronesia.* Cambridge, UK: Cambridge University Press.

Randsborg, Klavs. 1990. "Between classical antiquity and the Middle Ages: New evidence of economic change." *Antiquity* 64:122–127.

————. 1991. *The First Millennium AD in Europe and the Mediterranean.* Cambridge, UK: Cambridge University Press.

Rappaport, Roy A. 1967. *Pigs for the Ancestors.* New Haven, CT: Yale University Press.

————. 1979. *Ecology, Meaning, and Religion.* Richmond, CA: North Atlantic Books.

————. 1999. *Ritual and Religion in the Making of Humanity.* New York: Cambridge University Press.

Rautman, Marcus L. 1990. "Archaeology and Byzantine studies." *Byzantinische Forschungen* 15:137–165.

Read, Dwight W. 2002. "A multitrajectory, competition model of emergent complexity in human social organization." *Proceedings of the National Academy of Sciences* 99:7251–7256.

Rehg, Kenneth. 1995. "The significance of linguistic interaction spheres in reconstructing Micronesian prehistory." *Oceanic Linguistics* 34:305–326.

Reyna, S. P. 1994. "Literary anthropology and the case against science." *Man* 29:555–581.

Richerson, Peter J., and Robert Boyd. 1992. "Cultural inheritance and evolutionary theory." In Eric Alden Smith and Bruce Winterhalder (eds.), *Evolutionary Ecology and Human Behavior.* New York: Aldine de Gruyter.

————. 2005. *Not By Genes Alone: How Culture Transformed Human Evolution.* Chicago: University of Chicago Press.

Riesenberg, Saul H. 1968. *The Native Polity of Ponape.* Smithsonian Contributions to Anthropology, Vol. 10. Washington, DC: Smithsonian Institution Press.

Rindos, David. 1984. *The Origins of Agriculture: An Evolutionary Perspective.* New York: Academic Press.

Ritter, Madeline L. 1980. "The conditions favoring age-set organization." *Journal of Anthropological Research* 36:87–104.

Robarchek, Clayton A. 1989. "Primitive warfare and the ratomorphic image of mankind." *American Anthropologist* 91:903–920.

Robbins, Lionel. 1972 [1932]. *An Essay on the Nature and Significance of Economic Science.* London: Macmillan.

Rohner, Ronald P. 1975. *They Love Me, They Love Me Not: A Worldwide Study of the Effects of Parental Acceptance and Rejection.* New Haven, CT: HRAF Press.

Rosenberg, Michael. 1994. "Pattern, process, and hierarchy in the evolution of culture." *Journal of Anthropological Archaeology* 13:307–340.

Ross, Eric B. 1978. "Food taboos, diet, and hunting strategy: Adaptations to animals in Amazonian cultural ecology." *Current Anthropology* 19:1–36.

———. 1980a. "Preface." In Eric B. Ross (ed.), *Beyond the Myths of Culture: Essays in Cultural Materialism.* New York: Academic Press.

———. 1980b. "Patterns of diet and forces of production: An economic and ecological history of the ascendancy of beef in the United States diet." In Eric B. Ross (ed.), *Beyond the Myths of Culture: Essays in Cultural Materialism.* New York: Academic Press.

Ross, Eric B. (ed.). 1980c. *Beyond the Myths of Culture: Essays in Cultural Materialism.* New York: Academic Press.

Rossi, Alice S. 1977. "A biosocial perspective on parenting." *Daedalus* 106:1–31.

———. 1984. "Gender and parenthood." *American Sociological Review* 49:1–19.

Rostoker, William, and Elizabeth R. Gebhard. 1980. "The sanctuary of Poseidon at Isthmia: Techniques of metal manufacture." *Hesperia* 49:347–363.

Rothaus, Richard M. 1993. "Pagan Cult and Late Antique Society in the Corinthia." Ph.D. diss., Ohio State University.

Russell, Bertrand. 1961. *History of Western Philosophy.* London: George Allen & Unwin.

Russell, James. 1986. "Transformations in Early Byzantine urban life: The contribution and limitations of archaeological evidence." In *The 17th International Byzantine Congress Major Papers.* New Rochelle, NY: Aristides D. Caratzas.

———. 2001. "The Persian invasions of Syria/Palestine and Asia Minor in the reign of Heraclitus: Archaeological, numismatic, and epigraphic evidence." In Eleonora Kountoura-Galake (ed.), *The Dark Centuries of Byzantium (7th–9th c.).* The National Hellenic Research Foundation Institute for Byzantine Research International Symposium 9. Athens: The National Hellenic Research Foundation.

Russon, A. E., and B. E. Waite. 1991. "Patterns of dominance and imitation in an infant peer group." *Ethology and Sociobiology* 12:55–73.

Ruttan, Vernon W. 2001. "Imperialism and competition in anthropology, sociology, political science, and economics: A perspective from development economics." *Journal of Socio-Economics* 30:15–29.

Sagan, Carl. 1993. *Broca's Brain: Reflections on the Romance of Science.* New York: Ballantine Books.

Sahlins, Marshall. 1958. *Social Stratification in Polynesia.* Seattle: University of Washington Press.

———. 1963. "Poor man, rich man, big man, chief: Political types in Melanesia and Polynesia." *Comparative Studies in Society and History* 5:285–303.

———. 1976. *Culture and Practical Reason.* Chicago: University of Chicago Press.

———. 1999. "What is anthropological enlightenment?" *Annual Review of Anthropology* 28: i–xxiii.

Sallach, David L. 2003. "Social theory and agent architectures: Prospective issues in rapid-discovery social science." *Social Science Computer Review* 21:179–195.

Sallach, David L., and Charles M. Macal. 2001. "Introduction: The simulation of social agents." *Social Science Computer Review* 19:245–248.

Salmon, John B. 1984. *Wealthy Corinth.* New York: Oxford University Press.

Salmon, Wesley. 1984. *Scientific Explanation and the Causal Structure of the World.* Princeton, NJ: Princeton University Press.

Salzman, Philip Carl. 1999. "Is inequality universal?" *Current Anthropology* 40:31–61.

———. 2001. *Understanding Culture: An Introduction to Anthropological Theory.* Prospects Heights, IL: Waveland.

Sanday, Peggy R. 1981a. *Female Power and Male Dominance: On the Origins of Sexual Inequality.* New York: Cambridge University Press.

———. 1981b. "The sociocultural context of rape: A cross-cultural study." *Journal of Social Issues* 37:5–27.

Sanderson, Stephen K. 1987. "Eclecticism and its alternatives." *Current Perspectives in Social Theory* 8:313–345.

———. 1988. *Macrosociology: An Introduction to Human Societies.* New York: Harper & Row.

———. 1990. *Social Evolutionism: A Critical History.* Oxford: Basil Blackwell.

———. 1991. *Macrosociology: An Introduction to Human Societies.* 2nd ed. New York: Harper Collins.

———. 1994a. "Evolutionary materialism: A theoretical strategy for the study of social evolution." *Sociological Perspectives* 37:47–73.

———. 1994b. "The transition from feudalism to capitalism: The theoretical significance of the Japanese case." *Sociological Review* 17:15–55.

———. 1995a. *Macrosociology: An Introduction to Human Societies.* 3rd ed. New York: Harper Collins.

———. 1995b. *Social Transformations: A General Theory of Historical Development.* Oxford: Blackwell.

———. 1999a. *Macrosociology: An Introduction to Human Societies.* 4th ed. New York: Addison Wesley Longman.

———. 1999b. *Social Transformations: A General Theory of Historical Development.* Expanded ed. Lanham, MD: Rowman & Littlefield.

———. 2001a. *The Evolution of Human Sociality: A Darwinian Conflict Perspective.* Lanham, MD: Rowman & Littlefield.

———. 2001b. "An evolutionary interpretation of fertility decline: New evidence." *Population and Environment* 22:555–563.

———. 2007. *Evolutionism and Its Critics: Deconstructing and Reconstructing an Evolutionary Interpretation of Human Society.* Boulder, CO: Paradigm Publishers.

Sanderson, Stephen K., and Arthur S. Alderson. 2005. *World Societies: The Evolution of Human Social Life.* Boston: Allyn & Bacon.

Sanderson, Stephen K., and Joshua Dubrow. 2000. "Fertility decline in the modern world and in the original demographic transition: Testing three theories with cross-national data." *Population and Environment* 21:511–537.

Sanderson, Stephen K., D. Alex Heckert, and Joshua Dubrow. 2005. "Militarist, Marxian, and non-Marxian materialist theories of gender inequality: A cross-cultural test." *Social Forces* 83:1445–1462.

Sandstrom, Alan R. 2000. "Contemporary cultures of the Gulf Coast." In John Monaghan (ed.), *Ethnology. Supplement to the Handbook of Middle American Indians.* Vol. 6. Victoria R. Bricker, gen. ed. Austin: University of Texas Press.

———. In press. "Blood sacrifice, curing, and ethnic identity among contemporary Nahua of Mexico." In Frances Berdan, John Chance, Alan R. Sandstrom, Barbara Stark, James Taggart, and Emily Umberger (eds.), *Ethnic Identity in Indigenous Mesoamerica: Views from Archaeology, Ethnohistory, and Contemporary Ethnography.* Salt Lake City: University of Utah Press.

Sandstrom, Alan R., and Pamela Effrein Sandstrom. 1995. "The use and misuse of anthropological methods in library and information science research." *Library Quarterly* 65:161–199.

———. 1998. "Science and nonscience in qualitative research: A response to Thomas and Nyce." *Library Quarterly* 68:249–254.

———. 1999. "Antiscientific approaches to the study of social life: A rejoinder to Nyce and Thomas." *Library Quarterly* 69:299–303.

Sandstrom, Pamela Effrein. 1994. "An optimal foraging approach to information seeking and use." *Library Quarterly* 64:414–449.

———. 1998. "Information foraging among anthropologists in the invisible college of human behavioral ecology: An author co-citation analysis." Ph.D. diss., Indiana University, Bloomington.

———. 1999. "Scholars as subsistence foragers." *Bulletin of the American Society for Information Science* 25(3):17–20. Available on the Internet at http://www.asis.org/Bulletin/Feb-99/sandstrom.html.

———. 2001. "Scholarly communication as a socioecological system." *Scientometrics* 51:573–605.

Sangren, Steven P. 1988. "Rhetoric and the authority of ethnography: 'Postmodernism' and the social reproduction of texts." *Current Anthropology* 29:405–435.

Sanjek, Roger. 1995. "Politics, theory, and the nature of cultural things." In Martin F. Murphy and Maxine L. Margolis (eds.), *Science, Materialism, and the Study of Culture.* Gainesville: University of Florida Press.

Sapire, David. 1989. "Comment on Paul Roth, 'Ethnography without tears.'" *Current Anthropology* 30:564–565.

Saradi-Mendelovici, Helen. 1990. "Christian attitudes toward pagan monuments in Late Antiquity and their legacy in later Byzantine centuries." *Dumbarton Oaks Papers* 44:47–61.

Scheper-Hughes, Nancy. 1995. "The primacy of the ethical: Propositions for a militant anthropology." *Current Anthropology* 36:409–420.

Schiffer, Michael B. 1983. "Review of Marvin Harris, *Cultural Materialism: The Struggle for a Science of Culture* (Random House, 1979)." *American Antiquity* 48:190–194.

Schneider, Harold K. 1971. "Comment on Alan Heston, 'An approach to the sacred cow of India.'" *Current Anthropology* 12:191–209.

———. 1974. *Economic Man: The Anthropology of Economics.* New York: Free Press.

Schvaneveldt, Roger W. (ed.). 1990. *Pathfinder Associative Networks: Studies in Knowledge Organization.* Norwood, NJ: Ablex.

Scranton, Robert L. 1969. "Greek building." In Carl Roebuck (ed.), *The Muses at Work: Arts, Crafts, and Professions in Ancient Greece and Rome.* Cambridge, MA: MIT Press.

Sellen, Daniel W., Monique Borgerhoff Mulder, and Daniela F. Sieff. 2000. "Fertility, offspring quality, and wealth in Datoga pastoralists: Testing evolutionary models of intersexual selection." In Lee Cronk, Napoleon Chagnon, and William Irons (eds.), *Adaptation and Human Behavior*. New York: Aldine de Gruyter.

Selten, Reinhard. 2001. "What is bounded rationality?" In Gerd Gigerenzer and Reinhard Selten (eds.), *Bounded Rationality: The Adaptive Toolbox*. Cambridge, MA: MIT Press.

Service, Elman R. 1962. *Primitive Social Organization: An Evolutionary Perspective*. New York: Random House.

———. 1968. "The prime-mover of cultural evolution." *Southwestern Journal of Anthropology* 24:396–409.

Shennan, Stephen. 2002. *Genes, Memes, and Human History*. London: Thames & Hudson.

Shepher, Joseph. 1983. *Incest: A Biosocial View*. New York: Academic Press.

Shweder, Richard. 1991. *Thinking Through Cultures*. Cambridge, MA: Harvard University Press.

Sidky, H. 2003. *A Critique of Postmodern Anthropology: In Defense of Disciplinary Origins and Traditions*. Lewiston, NY: Edwin Mellen Press.

———. 2004. *Perspectives on Culture: A Critical Introduction to Theory in Cultural Anthropology*. Upper Saddle River, NJ: Prentice-Hall.

Simon, Herbert. 1957. "A behavioral model of rational choice." In Herbert Simon (ed.), *Models of Man: Rational and Social*. New York: Wiley.

Simpson, David. 2000. "Review of John Higgins, *Raymond Williams: Literature, Marxism, and Cultural Materialism*." *Modern Language Quarterly* 61:559–561.

Simpson, Jeffrey A., Steven W. Gangestad, P. Nels Christensen, and K. Leck. 1999. "Fluctuating asymmetry, sociosexuality, and intrasexual competitive tactics." *Journal of Personality and Social Psychology* 76:154–172.

Smith, Eric Alden, and Rebecca L. Bliege Bird. 2000. "Turtle hunting and tombstone opening: Public generosity as costly signaling." *Evolution and Human Behavior* 21:245–261.

Smith, Eric Alden, and Mark Wishnie. 2000. "Conservation and subsistence in small-scale societies." *Annual Review of Anthropology* 29:493–524.

Snooks, Graeme Donald. 1996. *The Dynamic Society: Exploring the Sources of Global Change*. London: Routledge.

Snow, Charles Percy. 1959. *The Two Cultures and the Scientific Revolution*. Cambridge, UK: Cambridge University Press.

Sokal, Alan, and Jean Bricmont. 1998. *Fashionable Nonsense: Postmodern Intellectuals' Abuse of Science*. New York: Picador USA.

Somit, Albert, and Steven A. Peterson. 1997. *Darwinism, Dominance, and Democracy: The Biological Bases of Authoritarianism*. Westport, CT: Praeger.

Sosis, Richard. 2000. "Costly signaling and torch fishing on Ifaluk atoll." *Evolution and Human Behavior* 21:223–244.

Sperber, Dan. 1996. *Explaining Culture: A Naturalistic Approach*. Oxford: Blackwell.

Spiro, Melford E. 1986. "Cultural relativism and the future of anthropology." *Current Anthropology* 27:259–286.

———. 1996. "Postmodernist anthropology, subjectivity, and science: A modernist critique." *Comparative Studies in Society and History* 38:759–780.

Staniford, Philip. 1976. "On cultural materialism: Which is witch?" *Current Anthropology* 17:329–331.

Stark, Rodney. 1996. *The Rise of Christianity*. Princeton, NJ: Princeton University Press.

Steward, Julian H. 1955. *Theory of Culture Change: The Methodology of Multilinear Evolution*. Urbana: University of Illinois Press.

Stocking, George W. 1968. "A historical brief for cultural materialism." *Science* 162:108–110.

Strayer, F. F., and M. Trudel. 1984. "Developmental changes in the nature and function of social dominance among young children." *Ethology and Sociobiology* 5:279–295.

Sturgeon, Mary C. 1987. *Isthmia*. Vol. IV. *Sculpture I: 1952–1967*. Princeton, NJ: American School of Classical Studies at Athens.

Sussman, Robert W. 1972. "Child transport, family size, and increase in human population during the Neolithic." *Current Anthropology* 13:258–259.

Swanson, Donald R. 1987. "Two medical literatures that are logically but not bibliographically connected." *Journal of the American Society for Information Science* 38(4):228–233.

Symons, Donald. 1979. *The Evolution of Human Sexuality*. New York: Oxford University Press.

Tainter, Joseph A. 1988. *The Collapse of Complex Societies*. Cambridge, UK: Cambridge University Press.

Tavris, Carol. 1975. "A sketch of Marvin Harris: I don't see how you can write anything of value if you don't offend someone." *Psychology Today* 8(8):64–65.

Teltser, Patrice A. (ed.). 1995. *Evolutionary Archaeology: Methodological Issues*. Tucson: University of Arizona Press.

Testart, Alain. 1982. "The significance of food storage among hunter-gatherers: Residence patterns, population densities, and social inequalities." *Current Anthropology* 23:523–537.

Thomas, David Hurst. 1979. *Archaeology*. Fort Worth, TX: Holt, Rinehart and Winston.

———. 1989. *Archaeology*. 2nd ed. Fort Worth, TX: Holt, Rinehart and Winston.

Thomas, Nancy P., and James M. Nyce. 1998. "Qualitative research in LIS—Redux: A response to a [re]turn to positivistic ethnography." *Library Quarterly* 68:108–113.

Thompson, Homer A., and Richard E. Wycherley. 1972. *The Athenian Agora*. Vol. XIV. *The Agora of Athens: The History, Shape, and Uses of an Ancient City Center*. Princeton, NJ: American School of Classical Studies at Athens.

Tobin, Jack. 1958. "Land tenure in the Marshall Islands." *Land Tenure Patterns, Trust Territory of the Pacific Islands* 1:1–76.

Tomasello, Michael. 1999. "The human adaptation for culture." *Annual Review of Anthropology* 28:509–529.

Tooby, John, and Leda Cosmides. 1988. "The evolution of war and its cognitive foundations." Institute for Evolutionary Studies, Technical Report No. 88–1.

———. 1992. "The psychological foundations of culture." In Jerome H. Barkow, Leda Cosmides, and John Tooby (eds.), *The Adapted Mind: Evolutionary Psychology and the Generation of Culture*. New York: Oxford University Press.

Trigger, Bruce G. 1984. "Archaeology at the crossroads: What's new." *Annual Review of Anthropology* 13:275–300.

———. 1990. "Monumental architecture: A thermodynamic explanation of symbolic behavior." *World Archaeology* 22:119–132.

———. 1998. *Sociocultural Evolution: Calculation and Contingency*. Oxford: Blackwell.

Trombley, Frank. 1985. "The decline of the seventh-century town: The exception of Euchaita." In Speros Vryonis (ed.), *Byzantine Studies in Honor of Milton V. Anastos*. Malibu, CA: Undena Publications.

Turke, Paul W. 1989. "Evolution and the demand for children." *Population and Development Review* 15:61–90.

Turner, Jonathan H., and Alexandra Maryanski. 2005. *Incest: Origins of the Taboo*. Boulder, CO: Paradigm Publishers.

Tyler, Stephen. 1986. "Post-modern ethnography: From document of the occult to occult document." In James Clifford and George E. Marcus (eds.), *Writing Culture: The Poetics and Politics of Ethnography*. Berkeley: University of California Press.

Tylor, Edward Burnett. 1958 [1874]. *Primitive Culture.* New York: Harper.

Ueki, T. 1990. "Formation of a complex society in an island situation." *Micronesica Supplement* No. 2:303–316.

van den Berghe, Pierre L. 1978. *Man in Society: A Biosocial View.* 2nd ed. New York: Elsevier.

van der Dennen, Johan M. G. 1995. *The Origin of War: The Evolution of a Male-Coalitional Reproductive Strategy.* Groningen, Netherlands: Origin Press.

van Huyck, John, Raymond C. Battalio, and Richard O. Beil. 1990. "Tacit coordination games, strategic uncertainty, and coordination failure." *American Economic Review* 80:234–248.

Vining, Daniel R. J. 1986. "Social versus reproductive success: The central theoretical problem of human sociobiology." *Behavioral and Brain Sciences* 9:187–216.

Vitruvius. 1926. *The Ten Books on Architecture.* Trans. M. H. Morgan. Cambridge, MA: Harvard University Press.

Wagley, Charles W. 1968 [1959]. "The concept of social race in the Americas." In Charles W. Wagley (ed.), *The Latin American Tradition.* New York: Columbia University Press.

Wallerstein, Immanuel. 1974a. "The rise and future demise of the world capitalist system: Concepts for comparative analysis." *Comparative Studies in Society and History* 16:387–415.

———. 1974b. *The Modern World-System: Capitalist Agriculture and the Origins of the European World-Economy in the Sixteenth Century.* New York: Academic Press.

———. 1979. *The Capitalist World-Economy.* New York: Cambridge University Press.

———. 1980. *The Modern World-System II: Mercantilism and the Consolidation of the European World-Economy, 1600–1750.* New York: Academic Press.

———. 1989. *The Modern World-System III: The Second Era of Great Expansion of the Capitalist World-Economy, 1730–1840s.* San Diego: Academic Press.

Werner, Dennis. 1975. "On the societal acceptance or rejection of male homosexuality." M.A. Thesis, Hunter College of the City University of New York.

———. 1979. "A cross-cultural perspective on theory and research on male homosexuality." *Journal of Homosexuality* 4:345–362.

Westen, Drew. 1984. "Cultural materialism: Food for thought or bum steer?" *Current Anthropology* 25:639–653.

Wheler, Sir George. 1682. *A Journey into Greece.* London: W. Cademan.

White, Howard D. 1992. "External memory." In Howard D. White, Marcia J. Bates, and Patrick Wilson, *For Information Specialists: Interpretations of Reference and Bibliographic Work.* Norwood, NJ: Ablex.

———. 1996. "Literature retrieval for interdisciplinary syntheses." *Library Trends* 45(2):239–264.

———. 2000. "Toward ego-centered citation analysis." In Blaise Cronin and Helen Barsky Atkins (eds.), *The Web of Knowledge: A Festschrift in Honor of Eugene Garfield.* ASIS Monograph Series. Medford, NJ: Information Today.

———. 2001. "Author-centered bibliometrics through CAMEOs: Characterizations Automatically Made and Edited Online." *Scientometrics* 51:607–637.

———. 2004. "Reward, persuasion, and the Sokal Hoax: a study in citation identities." *Scientometrics* 60(1):93–120.

White, Howard D., Jan Buzydlowski, and Xia Lin. 2000. "Co-cited author maps as interfaces to digital libraries: Designing pathfinder networks in the humanities." *Information Visualization 2000.* Proceedings of the IEEE International Conference on Information Visualization, July 19–21, 2000, London. Los Alamitos, CA: IEEE Computer Society.

White, Howard D., and Belver C. Griffith. 1981. "Author co-citation: A literature measure of intellectual structure." *Journal of the American Society for Information Science* 32(3):163–171.

White, Howard D., Xia Lin, and Katherine W. McCain. 1998. "Two modes of automated domain analysis: Multidimensional Scaling vs. Kohonen Feature Mapping of information science authors." In Widad Mustafa el Hadi, Jacques Maniez, and Steven A. Pollitt (eds.), *Structures and Relations in Knowledge Organization.* Wurzburg, Germany: Ergon Verlag.

White, Howard D., and Katherine W. McCain. 1989. "Bibliometrics." *Annual Review of Information Science and Technology* 24:119–186.

———. 1997. "Visualization of literatures." *Annual Review of Information Science and Technology* 32:99–168.

White, Leslie A. 1949. *The Science of Culture: A Study of Man and Civilization.* New York: Grove Press.

Whiting, John W. M. 1960. "Resource mediation and learning by identification." In Ira Iscoe and Harold Stevenson (eds.), *Personality Development in Children.* Austin: University of Texas Press.

———. 1964. "Effects of climate on certain cultural practices." In Ward H. Goodenough (ed.), *Explorations in Cultural Anthropology: Essays in Honor of George Peter Murdock.* New York: McGraw-Hill.

———. 1981. "Environmental constraints on infant care practices." In Ruth H. Munroe, Robert L. Munroe, and Beatrice B. Whiting (eds.), *Handbook of Cross-Cultural Human Development.* New York: Garland.

Whiting, John W. M., John A. Sodergren, and Stephen M. Stigler. 1982. "Winter temperature as a constraint on the migration of preindustrial peoples." *American Anthropologist* 84:279–298.

Whiting, John W. M., and Beatrice Blyth Whiting. 1975. "Aloofness and intimacy of husbands and wives: A cross-cultural study." *Ethos* 3:183–207.

———. 1978. "A strategy for psychocultural research." In George D. Spindler (ed.), *The Making of Psychological Anthropology.* Berkeley: University of California Press.

Whyte, Martin King. 1978. *The Status of Women in Preindustrial Societies.* Princeton, NJ: Princeton University Press.

Wiessner, Polly. 1982. "Risk, reciprocity, and social influence on !Kung San economies." In Eleanor Burke Leacock and Richard B. Lee (eds.), *Politics and History in Band Societies.* New York: Cambridge University Press.

———. 2002. "Hunting, healing, and hxaro exchange: A long-term perspective on !Kung (Ju/'hoansi) large-game hunting." *Evolution and Human Behavior* 23:407–436.

Wilk, Richard R. 1996. *Economies and Cultures: Foundations of Economic Anthropology.* Boulder, CO: Westview Press.

Williams, Michael. 2001. *Problems of Knowledge: A Critical Introduction to Epistemology.* New York: Oxford University Press.

Wilson, David J. 1999. *Indigenous South Americans of the Past and Present: An Ecological Perspective.* Boulder, CO: Westview Press.

Wilson, Edward O. 1975. *Sociobiology: The New Synthesis.* Cambridge, MA: Harvard University Press.

———. 1978. *On Human Nature.* Cambridge, MA: Harvard University Press.

———. 1986. *Biophilia.* Cambridge, MA: Harvard University Press.

———. 1998. *Consilience: The Unity of Knowledge.* New York: Random House (Vintage Books).

Wilson, Patrick. 1977. *Private Knowledge, Public Ignorance: Toward a Library and Information Policy.* Westport, CT: Greenwood Press.

Wilson, Scott. 2002. "Revisiting keywords of cultural materialism." *European Journal of English Studies* 6(3):307–325.

Winterhalder, Bruce. 1986a. "Diet choice, risk, and food sharing in a stochastic environment." *Journal of Anthropological Archaeology* 5:369–392.

———. 1986b. "Optimal foraging: Simulation studies of diet choice in a stochastic environment." *Journal of Ethnobiology* 6:205–223.

Winterhalder, Bruce, Flora Lu, and Bram Tucker. 1999. "Risk-sensitive adaptive tactics: Models and evidence from subsistence studies in biology and anthropology." *Journal of Archaeological Research* 7:301–348.

Wiseman, James R. 1978. *The Land of the Ancient Corinthians*. Studies in Mediterranean Archaeology, Vol. 50. Göteborg, Sweden: Paul Åströms Förlag.

Wolf, Arthur P. 1995. *Sexual Attraction and Childhood Association: A Chinese Brief for Edward Westermarck*. Stanford, CA: Stanford University Press.

Wolf, Eric R. 1982. "Materialists vs. mentalists: A review article." *Comparative Studies in Society and History* 24:148–152.

Woodburn, James. 1982. "Egalitarian societies." *Man* 27:431–451.

Zahavi, Amotz, and Avishag Zahavi. 1997. *The Handicap Principle: A Missing Piece of Darwin's Puzzle*. New York: Oxford University Press.

Zaslavsky, Victor. 1995. "From redistribution to marketization: Social and attitudinal change in post-Soviet Russia." In Gail W. Lapidus (ed.), *The New Russia: Troubled Transformation*. Boulder, CO: Westview Press.

Index